CONTENTS

THE TEMPUS

HISTORY OF WALES

25,000 B.C. – A.D. 2000

PRYS MORGAN (EDITOR)

TEMPUS

In association with THE NATIONAL LIBRARY OF WALES

First published 2001

PUBLISHED IN THE UNITED KINGDOM BY:

Tempus Publishing Ltd
The Mill, Brimscombe Port
Stroud, Gloucestershire GL5 2QG
Tel: 01453 883300
www.tempus-publishing.com

PUBLISHED IN THE UNITED STATES OF AMERICA BY:

Tempus Publishing Inc.
2 Cumberland Street
Charleston, SC 29401
Tel: 1-888-313-2665
www.arcadiapublishing.com

Tempus books are available in France and Germany from the following addresses:

Tempus Publishing Group   Tempus Publishing Group
21 Avenue de la République   Gustav-Adolf-Straße 3
37300 Joué-lès-Tours   99084 Erfurt
FRANCE   GERMANY

British Library Cataloguing in Publication Data.
A catalogue record for this book is available from the British Library.

ISBN 0 7524 1983 8

Typesetting and origination by Tempus Publishing.

CONTRIBUTORS

THE EDITOR

Prys Morgan is Reader in History at the University of Wales, Swansea and has been teaching the history of Wales for over thirty years. His other books include *Wales: the Shaping of a Nation* (with David Thomas), *Welsh Surnames* (with T.J. Morgan) and *The University of Wales, 1939-1993*.

CONTRIBUTORS

Stephen Aldhouse-Green is Professor of Human Origins and Head of Archaeology at University of Wales College, Newport. His other books include *Prehistoric Wales* (with F. Lynch and J.L. Davies), the edited volume *Paviland Cave and the 'Red Lady'*, *Pontnewydd Cave* and (with E. Walker) *Ice Age Hunters*.

Miranda Green is Professor of Archaeology and Director of the SCARAB Research Centre at University of Wales College, Newport. Her numerous books include *Dying for the Gods, Exploring the World of the Druids, Symbol and Image in Celtic Religious Art* and *The Gods of the Celts*.

Ralph Griffiths is Professor of Medieval History and Pro Vice-Chancellor of the University of Wales, Swansea. *Conquerors and Conquered in Medieval Wales, The Oxford Illustrated History of the British Monarchy* ('A valuable and most readable work of scholarship' *The Times;* 'a sumptuously illustrated volume' *The Sunday Telegraph;* 'a monumental work' *The Independent on Sunday)* and *The Reign of King Henry VI* are among his numerous books.

Michael Hamilton is Lecturer in Archaeology at University of Wales College, Newport. He has published extensively in the field of British Neolithic and Bronze Age ceramics, such as *Exploratory Excavations and Survey of Mesolithic, Bronze Age and Iron Age sites at Golden Ball Hill, near Alton Barnes, Wiltshire* (with I. Dennis).

Ray Howell is Lecturer in History and Medieval Archaeology at University of Wales College, Newport. His other books include *A History of Gwent* and (with M. Green) *Celtic Wales*.

Geraint H. Jenkins is Professor and Director of the Centre for Advanced Welsh and Celtic Studies at the National Library of Wales, Aberystwyth. His other books include *The Foundations of Modern Wales, 1642-1780*, and *The University of Wales 1893-1993, an illustrated history* and he has edited the many recent volumes of the series *The Social History of The Welsh Language*.

John Graham Jones is the assistant archivist of the Welsh Political Archive at the National Library of Wales, Aberystwyth. His other books include *A Pocket Guide: The History of Wales,* and *Lloyd George Papers at the National Library of Wales and other repositories.*

Kari L. Maund is Lecturer in Medieval Welsh History at Cardiff University. Her other books include *The Welsh Kings* ('revealing' *The Western Mail;* 'Will be interesting to both medievalists and those interested in their own local history' *The Cambrian News)* also published by Tempus.

Joshua Pollard is Lecturer in Archaeology at University of Wales College, Newport. His other books include *Neolithic Britain,* and (with A. Whittle and C. Grigson) *The Harmony of Symbols: The Windmill Hill causewayed enclosure.*

A. Huw Pryce is Senior Lecturer in History at University of Wales, Bangor. His other books include *Native Law and Custom in Medieval Wales* and he is completing *The Acts of The Welsh Rulers, 1120-1283.*

ACKNOWLEDGEMENTS

I am very grateful to Nancy Edwards for her helpful comments on my chapter and for providing some of the illustrations.

A. Huw Pryce.

Editor's Foreword

I had dreamed for many years of producing an illustrated history of Wales, but it had seemed unthinkable because it was so difficult to know what visual resources might be available. During the last twenty years it has become possible to think the unthinkable because so many books have appeared which set forth the richness of Welsh visual material. To name but a few, we have had the series on the *Buildings of Wales* (the 'Welsh Pevsner'), the surveys of buildings from the Royal Commission on Ancient and Historic Monuments in Wales, such as Peter Smith's *Houses of the Welsh Countryside,* Paul Joyner's survey of artists of the eighteenth and nineteenth centuries, and Peter Lord's three-volume series on *The Visual Culture of Wales.* These, and many others, have changed our views of the material available, and pointed out to historians how they should use this valuable resource. I hope that a start has been made with this present book.

I am most grateful to Jonathan Reeve of Tempus for pursuing this book so eagerly and for making available the visual materials in Tempus' own collections; also to one of the contributors to this book, Professor Geraint H. Jenkins, as Director of the Centre for Advanced Welsh and Celtic Studies at Aberystwyth and to Ms. Lindsay Clements, for making available the reproductions of the illustrations collected for Peter Lord's *Visual Culture of Wales* series; and also to the staff of the National Library of Wales, Aberystwyth, especially to Dr. Gwyn Jenkins, Keeper of Manuscripts, Mr. D.M. Francis, Dr. Paul Joyner and Ms. Lona Mason of the department of pictures and maps for making available the incomparable collections of prints, pictures and photographs at the National Library of Wales. This book would not have been possible without their kind co-operation.

Prys Morgan
Swansea
Summer, 2001

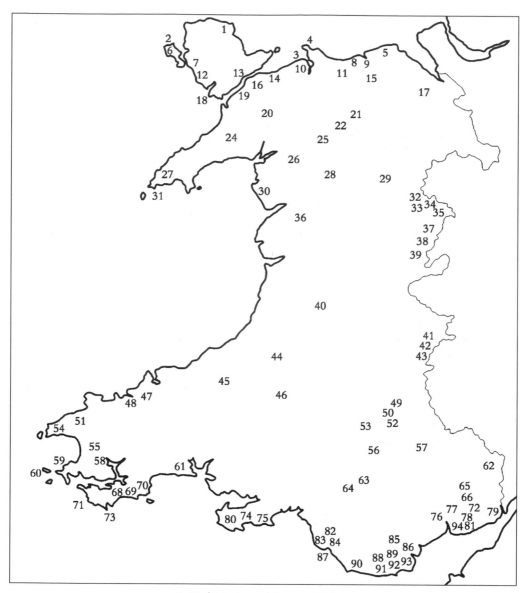

1. Prehistoric and Roman Wales.

1

WALES' HIDDEN HISTORY
c.25,000 BC – c.AD 383

Edited by S. Aldhouse-Green, with contributions by S. Aldhouse-Green, M.J. Green, M. Hamilton, R. Howell & J. Pollard

HUNTER-GATHERER COMMUNITIES IN WALES
Stephen Aldhouse-Green

Wales is first known to have been peopled a quarter of a million years ago. From then, until as recently as 9200 years ago, Wales was only inhabited episodically because of dramatic shifts both in climate and sea level. Even then, during what is usually termed the Postglacial period, the land continued to be peopled by hunters, gatherers and fishers until the arrival of the first farming communities some 6000 years ago. This period of 250,000 years can be divided up in several different ways, whether by types of human being, archaeological period, or climatic phase. My approach here will be to take a few important sites and use these as a snapshot of life in prehistoric Wales.

The Paleolithic

Pontnewydd Cave was first recorded in the 1870s by McKenny Hughes and Boyd Dawkins. By this time a length of 25m of deposit had been excavated or quarried away and archaeologists generally believed that the cave had been cleared of all archaeological evidence. A few stone tools had been found along with bones of Ice Age animals and a human tooth believed to have been ancient and, presumptively, Neanderthal. A programme of excavation, initiated in 1978 and continuing until 1995, revealed a remarkable fact: that the cave had been infilled by a series of mud-slides or debris-flows. This meant that evidence of human settlement, in the form of stone tools and actual human remains, was preserved deep within the cave system.

The archaeological evidence from Pontnewydd shows that the main occupation took place around 225,000 years ago, possibly just after a temporary period of severe cold. The bones of many species of animal were found mixed with artefacts, including numerous stone handaxes, sharp flakes and points, and hide-scrapers. The animals included rhinoceros, leopard, hyena, bear and horse. Only the last two can definitely be associated with the human presence at the site, for some of their bones had been cut-marked with stone tools. It evokes an image of Neanderthals, armed with thrusting spears and javelins, hunting horse in the open ground of the Elwy Valley or venturing into the dark recesses of the cave at times when it was used by hibernating bears and killing and dissecting a bear for the skin and meat.

The occupants of the site were not modern humans but Neanderthals. These latter had evolved in Europe where they can be recognised with confidence from c.300,000 years ago or earlier. However, our best evidence for Neanderthals comes from the last cold period (broadly the last 100,000 years) during which not only are remains more abundant, but actual burials occur in which the skeletal remains are, in consequence, complete. From these a detailed picture of Neanderthal physique and physiology may be built up. The body from the neck down was similar to our own but was very much more robust, a reflection of constant activity. The lower arms and legs were relatively short in relation to the thighs and upper arms, an adaptation seen among circumpolar peoples which is designed to conserve body heat. In just the same way, the large nose may also be a cold climate adaptation, enabling the warming of air before it entered the lungs. Other features of the face were a low forehead with the eyes consequentially placed high on the face. These eyes, large in size, looked out from beneath generous brow ridges. Finally the middle of the face was 'pulled forward' and the chin was missing. DNA has been found preserved in the bones of Neanderthal skeletons and shows that this is indeed a separate species which died out without significant evidence of having interbred with modern humans. These latter had evolved in Africa and colonised Europe from about 40,000 years ago, reaching Wales 10,000 years later.

Paviland Cave is a site with at least half a dozen separate phases of human presence. Although the site was once deeply stratified, the poorly recorded activities of excavators, combined with the action of the sea, have destroyed much of the evidence of their original sedimentary contexts.

Neanderthals were almost certainly present at Paviland. It seems likely that they visited Coygan Cave near Laugharne, across the then dry Carmarthen Bay, some 50,000 years ago. There seem to have been two points in time when Neanderthals were present in western Britain. First, it may be that a colonising group of Neanderthals arrived around 50,000 years ago or a little earlier when the climate, ameliorating after the extremely cold conditions of the period between 75-60,000 years ago, had opened up the northern lands of the British peninsula to settlement. These settlers are associated with distinctive hand axes. They take a subtriangular form whose affinities lie with a French industry made by Neanderthals and sometimes known as the hand axe Mousterian. Artefacts probably of this age at Paviland are likely to belong to this industry, which would appear to be virtually the only Mousterian cultural assemblage represented in Britain. It may of course be the case that the distinctiveness, and therefore the archaeological visibility, of the hand axe forms is a factor in their preferential recognition. However, it now seems clear that the known Mousterian facies on the Continent represent a chronological succession. The hand axe Mousterian is the last of the succession of Mousterian assemblages and it is probably the case that humans were simply not present in Britain during the last cold stage until after its appearance on the Continent after 60,000 years ago.

Second, the later Neanderthals are probably to be associated with the industry typified by leaf-shaped spearpoints, sometimes known in Britain as the Lincombian. As originally set out, this term defined a mixed industry in which Aurignacian artefacts – that is to say the tools of the earliest modern humans in Europe – and leaf-points were associated. Increasingly the term is used to refer to British leaf-point industries regardless of whether or not other elements were mixed in.

These two Neanderthal phases are to some extent notional. It is not clear whether there was continuous settlement of the British peninsula nor whether Neanderthals were still present in Britain when anatomically modern humans – probably to be identified with

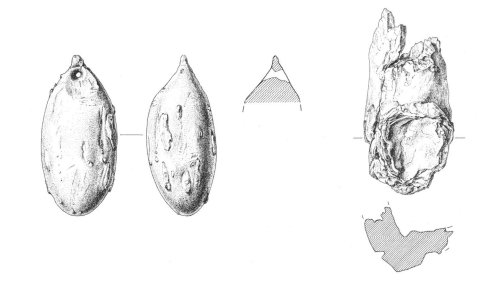

2. Pontnewydd Cave. Excavations here yielded remains of six Neanderthals dated to around 225,000 years ago.

3. Paviland. Goat's Hole controlled a possible animal migration route to the Gower plateau and overlooked an area of plain. It was well positioned as a hunting intercept site. It was also the site of the ceremonial burial of the so-called 'Red Lady' interred 26,000 years ago.

4. Paviland Cave. Ivory Pendant and fragment of mammoth tusk. This artefact was shaped around 24,000 years ago from a natural growth in the tusk of a mammoth. The fragment of diseased tusk illustrated here was excavated by Buckland in 1823. The pendant was found by Sollas in 1912.

people of Aurignacian material culture – first arrived. It seems likely, however, that Neanderthal presence was confined to a number of discrete episodes in keeping with broader evidence for episodic human peopling of the more northerly parts of Europe. It is a reasonable expectation, moreover, given the complexity of the climatic history of the last glacial period, that such presences may have coincided with the milder, so-called 'interstadial' periods which are known to have occurred as episodes within the cold glacial stages.

The richest of the archaeological assemblages at Paviland is the Aurignacian. This is represented artefactually by a series of distinctive stone tools including specialised forms of engraving tools and scrapers. These cannot be directly dated but they are likely to be of the same age as large quantities of bone charcoal dated to *c*.29-28,000 years ago. This dating is not only supported by the appearance of burnt Aurignacian artefacts at Paviland, but also from the dating of an Aurignacian bone spearhead found at Uphill to around 28,000 years ago. However, the most important phase in the history of the site dates to 26,000 years and concerns a burial known as the 'Red Lady'. Only the left side of the skeleton survived to be recovered by Dean Buckland in AD 1823, who described the skeleton as:

> *…enveloped by a coating of a kind of ruddle… which stained the earth, and in some parts extended itself to the distance of about half an inch* [12 mm] *around the surface of the bones… Close to that part of the thigh bone where the pocket is usually worn… surrounded also by ruddle* [were] *about two handfulls* [sic] *of small shells of the Nerita littoralis* [common periwinkle]… *At another part of the skeleton, viz in contact with the ribs* [were] *forty or fifty fragments of ivory rods… from one to four inches in length…* [Also]… *some small fragments of rings made of the same ivory and found with the rods… Both rods and rings, as well as the Nerite shells, were stained superficially with red, and lay in the same red substance that enveloped the bones*

Buckland *Reliquiae Diluvianae*

Positioned nearby was the skull of a mammoth which may have played a part in the ritual of the burial and so became part of the grave furniture. It was certainly a commonplace among comparable European burials for remains of mammoth and rhino to be included in the grave or form a part of its structure. Some such burials seem to have been the graves of shamans and it is possible that such animal remains may symbolise the shaman's spirit helper.

The period following the burial was one of extreme cold leading to the peak of the last glaciation at 20,000 years ago when most of Wales disappeared under vast sheets of glacial ice. Even so, visits to Paviland Cave continued. Two represent episodes of ivory-working on the site (at 24,000 and 21,000 years ago). The earlier of these is marked by the manufacture on site of a unique ivory pendant made from a growth in the tusk of a mammoth. A further event 23,000 years ago involved a deposit of three schematic anthropomorphic figurines of a kind undocumented in Western Europe but with parallels on the Russian plains. It is postulated that these were visits by far ranging task groups for whom the site had a sacred as well as a secular importance.

With the coming of the ice sheets, Wales was abandoned. Eight thousand years later, around 13,000 years ago, during a period of mild climate, hunter-gatherers reoccupied Wales. The history of that period can be pieced together from the finds at a number of caves, most notably Hoyle's Mouth near Tenby where the discovery of flints deep in the darkness zone of the cave is suggestive of initiation rites or possibly shamanic rituals. The reoccupation of

Wales was, however, a false dawn. During the eleventh millennium, cold climate returned and, for the most part, people migrated south. Wales was eventually re–populated around 9200 years ago and that date presents a mystery for it falls fully 500 years after the colonisation of England. At this stage it is not clear whether this late *adventus* of the Mesolithic postglacial hunter-gatherers was a genuine historical fact or whether evidence is yet to be found for settlement earlier in the tenth millennium.

The Mesolithic

Mesolithic settlement was focused on the coastal plains and the uplands seem to have been exploited only by specialist hunting groups. Beaches provided the coastal dwellers with easily accessible raw materials in the form of flint, chert and occasional flakeable volcanic rocks. In the midst of the Mesolithic, at *c*.8500 years ago, Britain finally became an island and one time hunter-gatherer territories were progressively submerged. The sites of Frainslake and Lydstep amid the submerged forests of Pembrokeshire bear particular testimony to this process. At Frainslake a probable Late Mesolithic flint scatter was associated with a windbreak of gorse, birch and hazel which 'ran in a gentle curve for 4-5 yards'. Again, at Lydstep a pair of microliths – perhaps components of the armature of a Mesolithic arrow – was found in a context suggestive of the arrow having been embedded in the neck of a pig.

The postglacial rise in sea level, and consequential inundation of the coastal plains, may have had an impact on the diet and social relations of the hunters. The sea now lay in many areas at the foot of high cliffs and it may be that it was there some groups were denied access to the sea. This may explain the evidence of nitrogen and carbon ratios in human bone which suggests that some of the very latest Mesolithic people in Wales had moved to a diet composed of meat or cereals. This is in direct contrast to the evidence of the exploitation of sea-foods seen in the earlier Mesolithic people. In this period raw materials for stone tools were more local in origin, again implying reduced territorial ranges and reduced mobility. Other key changes in the Mesolithic were progressive afforestation, a change at *c*.8700 years ago from broad blade to narrow blade microlith forms used as arrow armatures and finally evidence for the human management of the landscape through the use of fire to create cleared areas in order to foster aggregations of game.

Wales has a multitude of Mesolithic sites but has no certain evidence of houses or long term campsites which may have been used as home bases. The Nab Head, Pembrokeshire, has occupation in both early and late phases of the Mesolithic. The site is located on a promontory high above the sea but would have lain, during its early Mesolithic occupation, on a hill with gently sloping sides easily accessible to the then coastal plain. The Early Mesolithic site on the Nab Head produced no certain structures. It is, however, well known for the large numbers of perforated stone beads it has produced. In all 690 artificially perforated natural mudstone pebbles are known. A type of drill bit made of flint is common on the site and is called a *mèche de foret*; it is likely to have been associated with stone bead production. There has been speculation that the beads once formed sets of jewellery and came from disturbed burials on the site. Modern excavation has found no trace of these. There is evidence for traffic in these perforated stone beads, examples being known from south-west Wales at Palmerston Farm and Freshwater East and, in upland Wales, from Waun Fignen Felen in the Black Mountains of Breconshire. The latter was probably also a production site for it has yielded broken beads and a flint *mèche de foret* suggestive of on-site manufacture. The Waun Fignen Felen beads were made of a very unusual spotted mudstone, possibly selected for its aesthetic properties. The Late Mesolithic site at the Nab Head produced several features. One of these is a possible house-site: here, three concentrations of artefacts defined an 'empty area' around five metres in diameter, an area comparable in size with Mesolithic houses known from elsewhere in the British Isles. The 'concentrations' may represent middens of material discarded from activities associated with the house.

The upland moorland of Waun Fignen Felen preserves a number of lakeside sites and displays both early and Late Mesolithic periods of activity covering several millennia. Its upland setting is very unusual. Human presence there has been interpreted as seasonal hunting forays and certainly not as year-round exploitation. It is noteworthy that the artefacts found there generally reflect hunting rather than processing activities. There are several lithic scatter sites at Waun Fignen Felen which may once have been very short lived locations designed for hunting waterfowl. Some are located upwind of the point where use of the Haffes gorge could allow a hunter to approach the lake unseen. This upland site is one of a number presenting evidence of the use of fire to manage the local environment (here heathland) to create grazing for game. The mobility of Mesolithic hunter-gatherers is reflected by the distances that raw materials travelled to reach Waun Fignen Felen. Thus, during the Early Mesolithic phase there, both beach flint and Greensand chert were exploited. The nearest sources to Waun Fignen Felen would seem to lie at least 80 kilometres distant.

The site of Goldcliff lies on the edge of the Severn Estuary. Like Waun Fignen Felen, there is evidence for the deliberate use of fire with charcoal present in the peat surrounding the site and for hunting and fishing. Actual remains attest the presence of red deer, roe deer, wild pig, wolf and otter; hoof-prints of aurochs and red deer are present. Birds identified include coot and possibly mallard and a number of fish species have been recovered. The settlement areas at Goldcliff lay on the former dryland margins of Goldcliff Island and arose from cyclical reoccupations of the reed swamp-fringed edges of the island. Exploitation of the local environment took place during a phase of marine regression. No house sites were found, nor constructed hearths, and the single posthole found was interpreted as possibly having formed part of a drying frame for smoking fish. Occupation in the winter to spring period has been inferred from a study of mammal and fish remains. Red deer, wild pig, roe deer and otter bones had all been butchered, presumably for human consumption. The occurrence of burnt fish and bird bones is suggestive of Mesolithic barbecues. Indeed, on one occasion two microlithic barbs of an arrow seem to have become embedded within a wild pig carcass and to have been roasted with it.

It is appropriate to leave the Mesolithic literally in the footsteps of its Mesolithic inhabitants. At Uskmouth near Newport, footprint trails preserved in intertidal deposits have been dated to the seventh millenium. Four humans were involved, three adults and a child. A perforated antler mattock found nearby, dated by radiocarbon to be more than 6000 years old, may have been used by one of the walkers. The area, then as now, was one of intertidal mud flats. Prints of animals and wading birds in the estuarine clay attest the richness of the environment of the last Welsh hunter-gatherer communities.

The Neolithic – Joshua Pollard

Defining the 'Neolithic' and understanding of the mechanisms of its introduction are subject to considerable debate. Traditionally, it has been viewed as the period that witnesses a shift from a subsistence base of gathering/hunting/fishing to one of settled farming, but the reality is more complicated. Not all Neolithic communities appear to have been fully fledged mixed farmers, and changes in subsistence regime are, anyway, just one part of a series of sometimes marked transformations in material culture, ideology and technical practices occurring a century or so around 4000 BC. Wales is not distinct in this respect; the appearance of domesticated plants and animals, ceramics, monuments to the dead and new lifestyles occurred with synchronicity across much of north-western Europe. Both colonisation by Neolithic groups from the Continent and indigenous adoption of Neolithic lifestyles by local gatherer-hunters have been put forward as mechanisms for these changes, the latter currently being the favoured scenario. Mixed Late Mesolithic-early Neolithic flint scatters in regions such as Pembrokeshire and Breconshire certainly imply continuity of use of certain locations in the landscape by the same populations, if not continuity of lifestyles. This acknowledged, domesticated animals, cereals and new technologies (such as the production of pottery) lack local antecedents and must have been brought in from outside, either through existing networks of exchange and contact, or through limited population movement.

In contrast to the highly visible and durable monuments built by Neolithic groups to honour the dead, ancestors and a range of other spiritual agencies, evidence for settlement, subsistence and other aspects of routine life is markedly ephemeral. As with much of Britain, sedentary settlement was the exception rather than the norm. Many communities appear still to have led quite mobile lives, some perhaps involved in seasonal transhumance, others engaged in practices of short-term sedentism where areas might be cleared, occupied and cultivated for a few years before moving on. For the earlier part of the period, pollen evidence suggests localised short-term clearances, sometimes linked to limited cereal cultivation, in what was quite extensive deciduous woodland. Affected by both natural processes such as lightning strikes and tree-throw, as well as human interference, limited woodland clearance is known to have occurred during the Mesolithic, though the scale and extent of this increased during the fourth millennium BC.

The most abundant evidence for occupation comes from surface scatters of flint and stone tools (for example, in the Walton basin and Usk valley), the durable component of former middens and spreads of refuse. Pits containing selections of domestic refuse, such as that at Coygan Rock, Carmarthenshire, are also indicative of short-lived settlement. Whilst many occupation sites have suffered through subsequent natural erosion and the effects of agriculture, a number survive reasonably intact by virtue of being sealed under the earthworks of Neolithic and Bronze Age monuments or sand dunes. One such site, dating to the later fourth millennium BC, has recently been excavated at Ogmore-by-Sea on the coast of Glamorgan. Sand dunes here seal an extensive scatter of worked flint, pottery and waste from the manufacture of lignite artefacts, along with hearths and the post settings of temporary shelters. The scale of this site indicates either episodic settlement over a long period of time, or a place of aggregation. Similar evidence has been recovered from the old land surfaces under later cairns at Cefn Bryn, Gower, and Gwernvale, Breconshire.

Structures associated with habitation are few, no more than about twenty being known from Wales. Portable tent or yurt-like dwellings suited to a mobile lifestyle may have been commonplace. From the earlier Neolithic there is a substantial (13 x 6m) rectangular post-built house at Llandegai, Bangor, associated with Grimston pottery, flintwork and an axe polishing stone. This particular building has parallels with contemporary structures in Ireland. Rectangular timber houses of early Neolithic date are also known from Clegyr Boia,

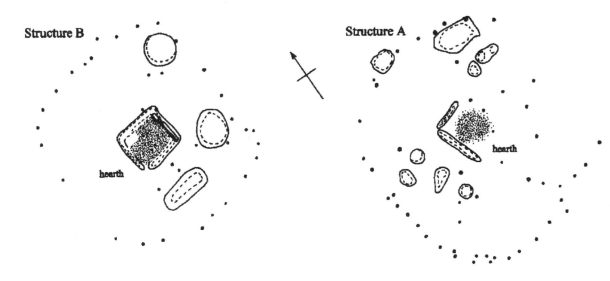

5. Goldcliff Island Mesolithic site lies on the edge of the Severn Estuary.
6. Later Neolithic stake-built dwellings at Trelystan (after Britnell).

St David's, and Gwernvale. Although in each instance associated with hearths and occupation refuse, the rarity and context of these buildings suggests that such houses were not the norm, and might even have been special purpose buildings (e.g. cult houses). The two structures at Clegyr Boia may have existed within an enclosure, and at Gwernvale the building immediately pre-dates the construction of a chambered tomb.

The construction and use of rectangular buildings continued into the later Neolithic (c.3000-2400 BC) – seen at Cefn Glas, Rhondda, and Mount Pleasant, Nottage, both Glamorgan – though stake-built round and oval dwellings now became commonplace. Examples include the two small (under 5m diameter) oval structures sited on a hill crest above the Severn valley at Trelystan, containing hearths and internal pits. Their location strongly suggests they were used for seasonal occupation, maybe upland herding, and occupied by only some members of the community. Two very similar and near contemporary structures have recently been excavated at Upper Ninepence, Walton. This particular site offers our clearest insight into the character and nature of later Neolithic settlement in Wales. Activity here spans the fourth and third millennia BC, with two or more phases of occupation occurring around 3000 and 2700 BC. The first is evidenced by an artefact scatter containing Peterborough pottery, flint tools and pits containing deliberate burials of artefacts and soil; the latter suggested by the excavator to be bound up with ideas of symbolic renewal and regeneration of resources. There is evidence of cereal cultivation (wheat), the consumption of hazelnuts, cooking of meat (probably beef) in pottery vessels, and leather and bone working. The second phase is associated with Grooved Ware ceramics and is somewhat different in kind. Artefact scatters, pits and the two stake-built structures are flanked on one side by a curving ditch. Evidence for the cultivation of cereals is not so strong and pork seems to replace beef as the principal source of meat. The deliberate deposition of objects in pits continues. Indicative of long-distance exchange networks, much of the flint used in the manufacture of stone tools is of a high quality, some deriving from as far afield as Lincolnshire and the Thames Valley.

The settlement at Walton is unusual in providing good evidence of the subsistence base of these Neolithic communities. Due to the presence of acidic soils over much of Wales, bone rarely survives, or survives well. Likewise, plant remains will normally only survive if intensively charred. From scant remains we know that domesticated cattle, pig, sheep and goats were kept, and that red deer and perhaps wild cattle and pig were occasionally hunted. If analogy is drawn with other areas of Britain, cattle dominated the livestock economies of the earlier Neolithic, with pig becoming more important during the later. Cereal cultivation can be inferred through pollen, charred grains and the presence of quern stones. Good plant assemblages are rare, but that from Plas Gogerddan has produced emmer wheat, barley, hazelnut and crab apple; and an impression of Celtic bean occurs on a sherd from Ogmore. Overall, wild plant foods seem more abundant than cereals, and, tentatively, it might be suggested that cereal cultivation was more extensive during the fourth rather than third millennium BC.

Indirect dietary evidence comes from recent work on stable isotopes in human bone. In stark contrast to the situation common to the late Mesolithic, no early Neolithic samples have shown evidence for significant consumption of marine foodstuffs, indicating a rapid and marked shift in diet at, or shortly before, the beginning of the Neolithic. Whether this is due to restricted access to coastal resources, or ideological change forcing new dietary preference, is open to debate. At Parc le Breos on the Gower peninsula, much of the dietary protein seems to have come from animal sources (meat, and perhaps milk or blood), with little input from cereals or other plant foods.

Recent re-analysis of human remains from tombs in the Black Mountains and Gower has shed considerable light on the detail and diversity of lifestyles practised by earlier Neolithic groups. The incidence of decay and periods of arrested development in teeth can tell of the nature of diets and the presence or otherwise of periods of physiological stress caused through food shortage; and musculoskeletal stress markers are an indication of repetitive or extreme activities. Amongst the remains from Ty Isaf in the Black Mountains, the dental profile suggests that cereal products played a very minor role in the diet of this population, and there is little indication of significant nutritional deficiencies. In contrast, the populations buried at the nearby tombs of Penywyrlod and Pipton suffered from a higher incidence of decay, implying a greater input of carbohydrates or softer cooked meat, and incidents of arrested tooth growth may indicate periodic nutritional shortages. Such differences may reflect the relative importance of wild versus domesticated/cultivated food substances, different modes of preparing food, and the relative flexibility of subsistence practices. Periodic food shortages amongst the groups buried at Penywyrlod and Pipton could, for example, relate to a static subsistence base involving the cultivation of cereals and other domesticated foodstuffs, and in which occasional poor harvests were a feature.

Musculoskeletal data suggest gender differences in terms of lifestyles and participation in routine labour tasks. Males were more physically active in the sense of having developed leg muscles created through running, jumping or other strenuous exercise. They may have been more actively involved in hunting, herding and transhumance. This gender-based distinction is particularly marked amongst the population from Parc le Breos, where the male population was particularly robust and the female markedly less so. Perhaps physical prowess in males (in the hunt or through recreational activities) was highly valued. This may not be universal though, as the pattern is not replicated to the same degree amongst the populations of other tombs, such as Tinkinswood in the Vale of Glamorgan.

It is difficult to be dogmatic about the nature of social organisation during the period. Many communities may have been semi-autonomous and largely self-sufficient, though linked through alliances and networks of marriage and exchange. There is no evidence for institutionalised power relations, and position may have varied according to age, gender and achieved rather than inherited status. Friction did exist, either over control of resources or perceived violation of acceptable behaviour, as evidenced by an arrowhead found embedded in a human rib from Penywyrlod.

The material equipment of these communities comprised ceramics, stone and bone tools, and almost certainly a range of items made of wood, leather, basketry and other perishable materials that have not survived. Ceramics make their first appearance during the Neolithic, linked to new ways of preparing and serving food, and show a successive series of style changes throughout the period. The earliest, named after the site of Grimston in East Yorkshire, comprise finely potted carinated bowls, undecorated with rounded bases. Decorated bowl pottery was produced from the first half of the fourth millennium BC, and so-called Peterborough wares towards the end of that millennium. By about 2800 BC we see the appearance of a new style of ceramic known as Grooved Ware; flat based, in a range of sizes and vessel forms, some profusely decorated with grooved, incised, impressed and applied motifs. Distributed widely across Britain and Ireland, Grooved Ware may have had its origins far to the north in the Orkneys, its spread to the south representing an instance of long-distance transmission of new ideas, technologies and practices.

7. *Top* Earlier Neolithic 'Grimston' bowls from Gwernvale (after Britnell and Savory); *Bottom* Grooved Ware from Upper Ninepence, Walton (after Gibson).

In an age before metal, stone provided a valuable medium for making sharp-edged and resilient tools such as knives, scrapers, projectile points, awls and axes. Flint was a preferred material, though only occurring as small pebbles from beach and drift deposits in selected areas of Wales, leading to the occasional importation of prepared cores and even finished implements from regions such as southern and eastern England, and even Antrim. Ground and polished axes of igneous and metamorphic rocks were produced at specialist production sites (erroneously termed 'axe factories') in the north and south-west of Wales. Excavations at two of these, at Mynydd Rhiw, Llŷn Peninsula, and Graig Lwyd, Penmaenmawr, have produced evidence for the extraction of rock from surface outcrops and buried seams, along with flake debris from the manufacture of axes, and other tools such as knives, scrapers and awls. Production at both sites may have begun quite early in the Neolithic, though the products of Graig Lwyd tend to be more widely distributed towards the end of the fourth millennium BC. There is no evidence that axe production was a full-time specialist activity. Instead, it may have been undertaken on a seasonal or episodic basis by a range of groups or individuals claiming generalised rights over raw material sources. Whilst the products of Mynydd Rhiw tend to be concentrated around the Llŷn Peninsula, those of Graig Lwyd and some of the south-west Welsh production sites circulated much further afield, a number turning up in south, central and eastern England. Conversely, Cumbrian axes are known in numbers from mid-Wales and the Marches, flint examples in the south-east (along the Severn valley), and Cornish implements in mid and south Wales. There are even occasional finds of imported Scandinavian axes (e.g. from the Usk valley). Such extensive distributions are not uncommon and illustrate that the value of stone axes sometimes lay far beyond that of their role as clearance and woodworking tools. Made of rock from particular places of special, perhaps even mythical, importance, axes circulated widely as gifts as well as commodities, some perhaps carrying lengthy biographies of previous ownership that enhanced their desirability.

The earlier part of the period is characterised by often complex funerary rituals and, though not universal, the housing of the dead in elaborate stone-built tombs. Bone survival is poor in many regions of Wales and our knowledge of mortuary practices largely derives from deposits encountered in megalithic tombs in the Black Mountains, Vale of Glamorgan and Gower, where conditions of preservation are favourable. Here, tombs contain collective deposits of up to fifty or more individuals. At Parc le Breos, Gower, the remains of at least forty people were encountered, including adults (male and female), adolescents, children and infants. At Penywyrlod and Pipton, both in the Black Mountains, children and infants seem under-represented, implying a degree of selection in burial. Typically, the bones are found in a disarticulated state (i.e. not full skeletons), a result of prior burial or exposure of the corpse. Surviving bones were then gathered up and placed with some care in the chambers of these tombs. Significantly, at Penywyrlod groups of bone contained a fairly balanced range of skeletal elements, though were drawn from two or three individuals in each case, a process of 'making up' skeletons from the bones of disparate individuals. Cremation was occasionally practised during the earlier Neolithic, as evidenced at Ty Isaf and a few chambered tombs in south-west Wales (e.g. Carreg Samson and Carreg Coetan Arthur). The breaking down of the corpse and burial *en masse* are seen as processes that asserted a sense of collectivity in death, and transformed the dead into a community of ancestors.

A more varied range of funerary practices emerged during the late fourth and earlier third millennium BC, after the construction and use of collective tombs largely ceased. A few

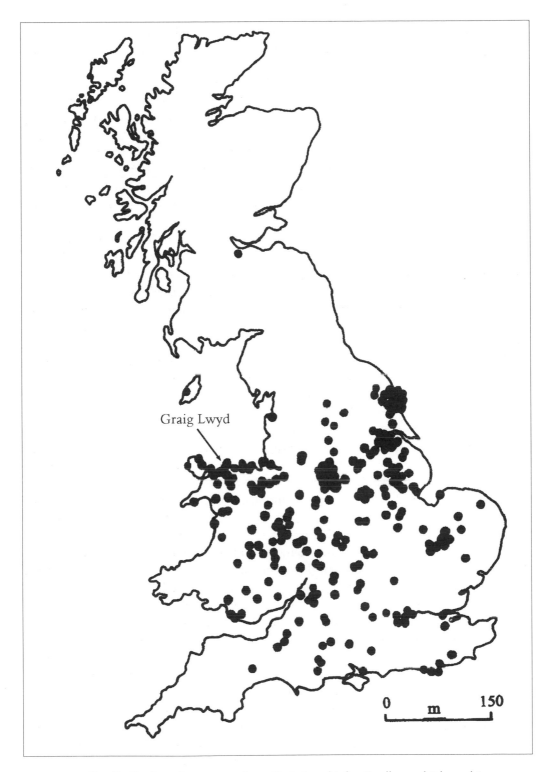

8. The distribution of stone axes from Graig Lwyd (after Bradley and Edmonds).

examples suffice. At Four Crosses, Llandysilio, a late fourth millennium BC round barrow sealed a substantial pit containing the crouched burial of an adult with a pottery bowl and cattle jaw: at either end of this pit, cut into its base, were graves containing two further adult inhumations. Ten kilometres to the south, a simple cairn-marked grave of the same date, containing an inhumation and cremation, was excavated high above the Severn at Trelystan. Natural places also became locales where mortuary rites were enacted. A particularly spectacular burial deposit from Gop Cave, Prestatyn, comprised at least fourteen inhumations, buried successively, and accompanied by Peterborough-ware bowls, a polished flint knife and jet belt sliders. Cremation is known to have been practised on some scale during the later Neolithic. It must be acknowledged that the total burial population for the period is small, and that the majority of people were treated in death in ways that left no archaeological trace.

Monuments dominate the archaeological record for the period. Constructed variously to house the dead, honour ancestors and other spiritual agencies, and to serve as foci for communal ceremonial activity, they also stood as makers of place and emblems of new identity. From the earlier Neolithic there are tombs and associated megalithic structures, enclosures and cursus monuments (considerably elongated rectilinear ditched enclosures); from the later a variety of henge monuments, some stone circles and massive timber palisaded enclosures.

Megalithic tombs are known in numbers from south-east, south-west and north-west Wales. They vary in architectural style: from stone-built chambered long cairns (so-called Cotswold-Severn tombs) that ultimately belong to a tradition of long mound construction stretching back to early fifth millennium BC continental Europe; to simple mounded or free-standing, box-like chambers with sloping capstones (portal dolmens), and later passage-graves, that have affinities with megalithic structures in many regions of the Atlantic façade. These typological categories are not rigid and there is an element of local inventiveness. Distributions are geographically focused, with Cotswold-Severn monuments predominantly in the south-east, portal dolmens in the south- and north-west, and passage-graves in the north-west. Two earthen long mounds, of a type common in southern and eastern England, have recently been recognised near Welshpool.

Available dates and material associations, such as the Grimston bowls from Dyffryn Ardudwy, Merioneth, show early fourth millennium BC beginnings for these structures. Some are multi-phased and potentially long-lived; Dyffryn Ardudwy beginning as a portal dolmen, but later incorporated within a long mound with its own chamber; and Trefignath, Anglesey, being progressively enlarged, eventually comprising a long cairn with three chambers. The latest megalithic tombs are probably the developed passage-graves of north Wales, famously Barclodiad y Gawres and Bryn Celli Ddu on Anglesey. Dating to the latest fourth or early third millennia BC, the former is a cruciform passage-grave similar to examples from County Meath, Ireland, and is decorated with geometric motifs that link it with sites in the Boyne valley. The sequence at Bryn Celli Ddu begins with a ring-ditch or henge monument enclosing a circle of free-standing stones, over which the passage-grave was built. Cremation burial appears as the dominant rite associated with these monuments.

Aerial reconnaissance has led to the recognition of a range of previously unsuspected Neolithic monument types in lowland Wales. Until very recently, no earlier Neolithic enclosures were known from Wales, but two have been recognised as cropmarks within close proximity at Ogmore and Corntown in the Vale of Glamorgan. Known as causewayed enclosures, after the interrupted lengths of ditch that define them, they are of a monumental tradition that extends across much of north-western Europe. Some acted as points of episodic aggregation for dispersed communities, many show evidence for feasting and conspicuous acts of deposition, whilst mortuary rituals may have taken place at others. That at Corntown comprises of up to six concentric circuits of ditch and encloses several hectares. Large quantities of earlier Neolithic worked flint, including thirty leaf arrowheads and fragments of axe, have been collected from the surface of the site, implying episodes of occupation. A single ditch enclosure is claimed on Anglesey; and in the south-west there is an argument for seeing the small stone-walled enclosure of Clegyr Boia as of early Neolithic date, on analogy with securely dated sites such as Carn Brea and Helman Tor in Cornwall.

Most enigmatic of all are the handful of cursus monuments known from Wales. Constructed during the fourth millennium BC, there are three definite examples (Llandegai, Sarn-y-Bryn-Caled and Walton), and five possible. That at Walton is in the order of 500m long. Potentially associated with mortuary or ancestor rituals, they are sited in valley locations, and provided the focus for the development of elaborate 'monumental landscapes' during the later Neolithic. At Llandegai, two large henge monuments (circular embanked earthworks) and a series of 'hengiform' pit circles associated with deposits of cremated bone were constructed adjacent to the cursus during the earlier third millennium BC. A similar sequence is seen at Sarn-y-Bryn-Caled near Welshpool. It begins with the construction of the cursus in cleared woodland around 3800 BC. A double-ditched monument 380m long and only 10m wide, it has multiple causeways along its length, allowing ready access to the interior. The next phase, 3500-2500 BC, sees the construction of large free-standing posts, a penannular ring-ditch associated with cremation deposits, and a possible henge monument. Activity continues into the earlier Bronze Age with the construction of a timber circle and several small ring-ditches. It may have been a desire to emulate and respect the achievement of earlier generations that generated the momentum to construct complexes of monuments within these landscapes.

Though leaving no surface trace in today's landscape, some of the most impressive monuments are the wooden palisades of the later Neolithic. Two are known from the Walton basin, at Walton and Hindwell (the latter being the largest in Britain). The Walton palisade is made up of a circuit of separate post-pits, that at Hindwell by a continuous palisade trench, 2m deep, and containing closely-spaced oak timbers. The latter encloses 35ha, originally with a post wall standing 6m or more above ground, and would have required around 6300 tonnes of fresh oak in its construction. There is no evidence for occupation within its interior, the enclosure seemingly built to define an area of sacred space. Half a kilometre to the north lie the transient remains of the Upper Ninepence settlement. In a world where the dwellings of the living seem so ephemeral, the sheer investment of labour in the construction of monuments is thrown into sharp focus.

Bronze Age – Mike Hamilton

Alongside the first copper tools occurs the distinctive Beaker pottery tradition. These shapely vases are the most obvious manifestation of major changes in British society. Beaker pottery is found across western and central Europe and probably originated in the Lower Rhine area. Until the 1970s migration of a distinctive racial type (the 'Beaker Folk') was the accepted medium for its appearance, but now the pottery is seen as reflecting exchange and transmission of ideas. Other manifestations of changes include more frequent burial under round cairns or barrows, greater emphasis on the individual, at least in burial, marked agricultural intensification and, after the insularity of the Late Neolithic, links with the rest of Europe. The metal tools are simple flat axes, flat tanged and riveted daggers, halberds, and awls. Non-metal objects include jet buttons, archers' wristguards of stone, and flint daggers and barbed and tanged arrowheads. All but the latter are rare in Wales.

The impact of these changes on Welsh Neolithic society is problematical because of the limited knowledge about the preceding Late Neolithic period. Elsewhere in Britain the users of Beaker pottery treated Late Neolithic ritual sites with a mixture of destruction and appropriation; few of the sites show continuity in function and many are abandoned. Three Beakers in pits (possibly graves) from the henge at Llandegai are suggestive of a similar process of appropriation. Something similar may be occurring with the deposit of Beaker pottery in the possible henge at Coed-y-Dinas. The situation is confused because Beaker pottery is usually divided into three styles: Early, Middle and Late, though radiocarbon dating has queried this sequence. Wales has remarkably little Early and Middle style Beakers, the styles most often found on ritual sites in England. The Beakers from Llandegai were Late and this may suggest a longer continuation of Neolithic traditions than elsewhere in Britain. The multiple timber ring at Sarn-y-Bryn-Caled is dated to the Early Bronze Age, but appears more akin to Late Neolithic ritual sites. It has been argued that some of the Early Bronze Age funerary sites echo monument traditions of the Late Neolithic. Possibly resistance to change is an issue at the beginning of the Welsh Bronze Age.

Beaker pottery is associated with an inhumation burial tradition, where the corpse is buried in a crouched position, either in a grave or a stone cist, often covered in a cairn or barrow. These graves are very structured, with the associated Beakers and other grave-goods in particular positions. The orientation and facing of the bodies appears to be significant. Though much of the Welsh evidence has been poorly recorded by antiquaries, and the soils of Wales are often too acidic to preserve bone, it appears that the skeleton was generally orientated north-south and in most cases was facing east, the familiar pattern for southern Britain. Much of the bone analysis is old, but it suggests a high incidence of adult males, more so than elsewhere. There are no indications of a female burial tradition with the heads towards the south as found elsewhere. Many contemporary graves in Britain have 'warrior' symbolism, involving early copper or flint daggers, archer wristguards, stone battle axes and flint arrowheads. This appears to be true also for Wales but the evidence is less secure.

It is worth stressing that many contemporary graves are similar in appearance but lack the distinctive Beakers. Exactly what they represent is uncertain, as it is not clear what the Beaker pot signifies. They could represent symbolism associated with belief or perhaps some broader social category concerned with status or clique.

Food Vessel pottery, mostly squat bowls, replaced Beakers in the funerary role, to be in turn replaced by Food Vessel Urns, Collared Urns and miniature accessory vessels. The metalwork grew more sophisticated as single piece moulds gave way to double piece moulds. Jet and amber was imported into Wales, along with glass 'faience' beads, possibly of continental origin, and this material was also used in burials.

Early Bronze Age burial mounds can be roughly divided into two forms, earthen round barrows and circular stone cairns. This distinction is rather arbitrary and probably simply a product of geology. Many of the round barrows have rings of stake holes, probably reflecting hurdling. This may have defined the areas of the barrow for symbolic purposes and claims have been made linking these circles with Late Neolithic timber circles or the contemporary house form. The stake rings may also have been concerned with the order in which the mound was created, and these hurdles may have retained a bank, which provided an arena for the burial rite. In cairns, kerbs and rings of stones largely duplicate this pattern, and stratigraphy often demonstrates that a stone bank predates the burial rite and the construction of the cairn proper. Again it is claimed that this echoes Late Neolithic monumental practice in stone circles and henges. Some sites combine both stone rings and stake circles. The construction of these burial mounds was a sacred act which explains the order and care taken in their formation. This often included features such as the stripping of topsoil which would be invisible after construction. Many of these sites contain a central primary burial. These sites may be frequently reused, sometimes a simple grave, but sometimes a wholesale remodelling of the site.

The inhumation tradition associated with Beaker seems to have continued with some of the Food Vessels before being replaced by a cremation rite. Elsewhere in Britain this period is notable for its rich grave-goods, but Wales has only one outstanding example. This is the Mold gold cape, of stamped gold sheet, found wrapped around the upper torso of a male skeleton in a cairn at Bryn–yr–Ellyllon. Associated were a large number of amber beads. There is dispute over the dating, but the burial rite seems more appropriate to the Early Bronze Age.

Beyond burial it is difficult to identify much in the way of coherent ritual activity. Sarn–y–Bryn–Caled appears to be a late timber circle. Classic free–standing stone circles elsewhere in Britain generally belong to the Late Neolithic and nothing in Wales has disproved this, though fieldwork has been limited. However, there is considerable ambiguity in Wales between apparent stone circle variants and similar features found under barrows/cairns. Embanked 'stone circles' such as the Druid's Circle, on Cefn Coch, seem to have a regular association with Early Bronze Age burial. It has been claimed that some standing stones belong to the Early Bronze Age, though excavation has also identified sites to the Neolithic and later Bronze Age.

One tenet of Welsh Bronze Age studies is the notion that the Bronze Age (and Late Neolithic) saw an expansion from the fertile lowlands into the uplands. This idea was originally based on the limited lowland distribution of Early Neolithic tombs contrasted with the wide distribution of Early Bronze Age funerary sites throughout Wales. However, the distribution of ritual sites is not necessarily a direct reflection of settlement patterns and it is notable that distribution of Neolithic stone axes is not biased towards tomb concentrations. The rational approach would be directly to identify settlement and compare the chronological patterns, however, there are too few non-funerary sites for meaningful comparison. Environmental archaeology, through the analysis of fossil pollen, offers a solution. Many pollen sequences exist, but many are poorly dated, and most are from the uplands. Generally this work does identify greater upland woodland clearance in the Late Neolithic/Bronze Age, though recent analysis from the Severn Levels suggests this is also true for the lowlands. This recent work also demonstrates that the extent and permanence of Neolithic clearance in the lowlands had been over-stated. It seems more likely that the Bronze Age represents agricultural intensification in upland and lowlands.

One continuity from the Neolithic is the difficulty of identifying settlements; a problem not unique to Wales. There are a small number of suggested houses, though none is entirely clear of ambiguity. All those that form a coherent plan appear to be small (around 5m diameter) and round. The visibility of settlement may simply be poor survival and limited fieldwork. Certainly the known examples are fragile and are all preserved by being sealed under later monuments. An alternative possibility is one of perception. It is possible much occupation was of a less substantial, and therefore less permanent nature and left fewer obvious traces, and small scatters of flint and pottery may be the only physical traces. The failure to conduct systematic fieldwalking in most of Wales has limited this evidence.

The three possible houses found at Stackpole Warren are the clearest example of Early Bronze Age settlement, though suggestions of continuity with the later Middle Bronze Age ritual use of the site casts doubt on their domestic interpretation. Nearby were ploughmarks associated with Early Bronze Age pottery. Gullies suggested a field edge. Many known occupation sites are coastal (e.g. Merthyr Mawr Warren and Newborough Warren) and are close to shell middens which evidence the exploitation of marine foods. At Caldicot, on the Gwent Levels, was a possible fish weir so it is likely they were exploiting marine resources, a similar pattern to that found in Western Scotland.

The most successful modern research conducted in Bronze Age Wales has been copper mining. The most recent summary lists seven confirmed and fifteen possible sites. On the Great Orme, Llandudno, part of an enormous site has been investigated. Alongside extensive underground galleries is large scale open cast working and a number of sites show evidence for ore extraction with bone tools, pebble hammers and fire-setting. Copa Hill even had evidence of elaborate timber drainage. However, there is still absence of evidence for ore processing.

The future challenge for this work is to go beyond the technology and investigate the social aspects of mining. None of the sites has evidence for an associated settlement. The galleries on the Great Orme are sometimes tiny, suggesting child labour. It is not clear if these sites are worked seasonally or all year round. It is not known if the workers are local or outsiders. As these mines were providing much of the copper used in Britain the resulting contacts must have impacted on local society.

The links between Ireland and north-west Wales which are clearly present in the Middle Neolithic seem to be absent by the Early Bronze Age. This is best illustrated by the distribution of Irish metalwork. Though a form of gold neck ornament, known as a lunula, was found at Dolbenmaen ('Llanllyfni') in north-eastern Wales, this has to be compared with eighty-five examples in Ireland. A similar pattern applies to halberds, common in Ireland, but rare in Wales.

Given the apparent richness of central southern Britain (Wessex) in the Early Bronze Age, separated from fertile south-east Wales only by the Cotswolds, it comes as a surprise that it is North Wales which has the greatest concentration of rich grave-goods. As some grave-goods are made of (or imitate) Whitby jet it has been argued that North Wales had contacts with developments and rites practised in northern Britain. This contact with the east coast would also explain the occasional finds of amber in north Wales. It is possible that this reflects contacts brought about by copper mining. By comparison south Wales has very few rich grave assemblages. A fragmentary boat recovered at excavations at Caldicot, on the Gwent Levels, demonstrations that the technology for communication across the Severn Estuary was clearly present.

In the rest of southern Britain the later Bronze Age is characterised by a high visibility for settlements and field systems. This pattern occurs both on the lowlands but also in more marginal areas. While enclosed Middle Bronze Age settlement is easier to recognise, it is clear that open settlement was probably more common.

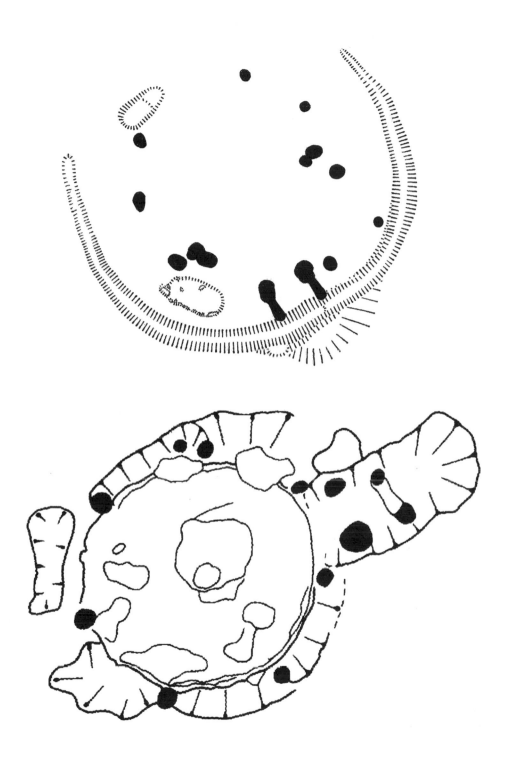

9. Bronze Age houses.

Middle Bronze Age pottery, consisting of large bucket and barrel-shaped pots, occurs rarely in Wales, but is related in broad terms to the pottery traditions of southern and central England, often termed the Deverel-Rimbury tradition. By comparison the Late Bronze Age in Wales largely lacks pottery, which has serious implications for the study of this period. Aerial photography is also a problematic guide to settlement patterns as many small enclosed settlements, which in southern England would be expected to date to the Bronze Age, in Wales actually date to the Iron Age or later.

Later Bronze Age settlement in Wales has proved remarkably elusive, except on the Gwent Levels. A number of circular houses are recorded, ranging in size from 5-10m, but few of the proposed structures are free of ambiguity and some are not convincing as buildings. Conversely, four or five substantial rectangular buildings have also been identified. The largest measured 11.5 x 4.5m. These appear to be unique for Wales at this date. It is striking that the Gwent Levels produce the most concentrated evidence of later Bronze Age settlement in Wales, yet the Levels were probably partly salt marsh and may have functioned as summer pasture. This abundance of settlement evidence in such a marginal part of the landscape may have more to do with the preservative properties of this landscape, together with the crude techniques applied in most terrestrial archaeological assessment.

Elsewhere in Wales the number of excavated settlement sites of this period is tiny. The indications for the Middle Bronze Age are that unenclosed settlement was occurring, whereas no enclosed settlement is known. The evidence includes the discovery of a 7.1m diameter round house at Glanfeinion, as well as numerous finds in Rhuddlan. By comparison the Late Bronze Age appears to be identified with a series of enclosures. Coed y Cymdda appears to be partly enclosed in its Late Bronze Age/Early Iron Age phase. The first hillforts appear towards the end of the Later Bronze Age. Frequently this evidence rests on radiocarbon dates, unfortunate as the dating generally overlaps into the traditional Iron Age. However, sites such as the Breiddin, Dale, and possibly Dinorben and Moel y Gaer, begin in this period. The Breiddin is the most convincing, with defences enclosing an area of 28ha. This scale of occupation marks a major expansion in the sizes of settlement, though it is not clear if they contained permanent inhabitation. The Breiddin also had a timber-framed box-rampart, which not only created an impressive barrier, but was also practical as a defence, indeed it was suggested that its destruction indicated increasing conflict. It is not clear where the impetus for hillfort development arose, since it seems to have no antecedents in Early Bronze Age Wales.

Field systems have proved even more difficult to locate in Wales. In southern England such systems appear to be the norm, for example those found on Dartmoor or in Wessex. Many of these systems seem to reflect a laying-out on a massive scale over a relatively short period and the coherence suggests considerable vision and planning. In Wales small scale work on the Denbigh Moors found small settlements associated with field walls, though rather irregular in layout. The other Welsh evidence is rather scrappy and largely undated. The most coherent series of field systems is that found on Skomer Island. These are prehistoric but otherwise undated, and are integrated with a series of unenclosed settlements. These few examples have to be set alongside fieldwork which has singly failed to find any such land divisions, suggesting their absence from much of Wales may be genuine. Instead there is abundant evidence of clearance cairns, small piles of stone, presumably piled up to clear land for more intensive agricultural use. Though generally accepted as prehistoric there is little firm dating. It is now thought that the visibility of field boundaries in the English Late

Bronze Age is reflecting not an economic imperative but a social one, with a need to demonstrate ownership seen as important. The clearance cairns, which often form linear patterns, or field systems, would equally serve the purpose. Another possibility is that for social or economic reasons there was less need to create rigid and visible boundaries in Wales.

The Middle Bronze Age in Wales continues the Early Bronze Age tradition of burial in urns, though grave-goods are now extremely rare. However, the few if any of the cairns or barrows seem to constructed in this period, and generally older sites are reused. One notable tradition is the use of caves in South Wales.

The visibility of burial declines towards the end of the Bronze Age and after 1000 BC there are few examples. It is unclear what was done with the dead, however, it was notable that during recent work at Goldcliff, on the Gwent Levels, parts of two skulls were found, suggesting a tantalising possibility of dead being deposited in watery places. Human bone has also been found on some later Bronze Age settlement sites suggesting less dichotomy between the living and dead than evident in the Early Bronze Age.

Across Britain there is general assumption that standing stones belong to the Neolithic or the Early Bronze Age. However, south-west Wales has convincing evidence that erection of standing stones, together with elaborate settings, was also occurring in the later Bronze Age. The best evidence comes from Stackpole Warren and consisted of a large standing stone, the 'Devil's Quoit', at the south-western end of a roughly trapezoid setting of small stones. This regional picture is a marked contrast to the rest of Britain.

Deliberate deposition of artefacts either into the ground or into water has a long history in Europe, as demonstrated by the treatment of Neolithic stone axes. At the beginning of the Bronze Age this tradition was continued with simple axes of copper and bronze, then more complex flanged axes and sustained with palstaves and socketed axes to the end of the Bronze Age. In common with the rest of Early Bronze Age Britain, metal axes were a rare grave item, whereas daggers and knife-daggers occurred with some frequency. While most metalwork is found as 'single finds', there is a tendency for collections of metalwork, 'hoards', to become more common by the Late Bronze Age. This is balanced by a decline in metalwork in graves. Whilst axes are clearly the most striking form of deposition, it is clear similar treatment was recorded to other objects. Early Bronze Age perforated stone 'battle-axes' and 'axe-hammers', arrowheads, copper halberds are frequently recorded as single finds. In the later Bronze Age spearheads, copper shields, rapiers, swords, and gold ornaments are also found.

It seems likely that the same philosophy is behind the deposition of single finds and hoards. Whilst suggestions have been made for underlying economic factors, it seems more likely that this activity is essentially one of belief.

THE IRON AGE IN WALES
Miranda Green

The latest phase of British and European prehistory has long been labelled 'Iron Age' because, for the first time in the first millennium BC, the smelting and production of iron for tools and weapons became common. Traditionally, the Welsh Iron Age begins in the seventh century BC and ends with the Roman Conquest which began in the mid-first century AD. It is necessary to remember that important though iron was to communities in late prehistoric Wales, it would be a mistake to read into its advent a cause for cultural dislocation. Indeed, there is plenty of evidence for a degree of continuity, in terms of settlement patterns and traditions. Nevertheless, as the Iron Age advanced, it is clear that some significant changes did take place, not least in the arena of trading contact with the Continent and the development of the Atlantic seaways as agents for close-knit networks between Britain – including Wales – and Europe. It is equally clear that, for many late Iron Age communities, the Roman invasion did not disrupt their way of life to any extent, and many settlements show signs of occupation that continued seamlessly into the Roman period. The discussion that follows is focused on the sites and finds that have made the most significant contribution to our understanding of the period.

A deposit of bronze- and ironwork was discovered in 1911 at Llyn Fawr near Rhigos in Glamorgan. The site was an ancient lake, the focus of apparently ritual activity involving the episodic deposition of prestigious items of metalwork as offerings to the supernatural forces perceived as residing in the water. Llyn Fawr is by no means the only aquatic votive Iron Age site in Wales. However, what makes it particularly special is the nature and chronology of the assemblage, which contained bronzes, including two cauldrons, socketed axes, sickles and horse-gear together with the earliest iron pieces known from Wales: a fragment of a Hallstatt C sword, which dates to around 600 BC, a socketed sickle and a spear-head. All were manufactured of wrought-iron, the first two arguably of a form unsuited to iron technology and perhaps fashioned by a craftsman more familiar with cast bronze-working techniques. It has to be remembered that, in European antiquity, the production of bronze differed considerably from that of iron, in so far as copper-alloy could be melted and cast into complex shapes, using moulds, whereas iron had to be wrought from a solid, spongy bloom.

The iron objects from Llyn Fawr were in association with material belonging to a Late Bronze Age horizon: the axes and the cauldrons probably date to the eighth century. The discrepant dates of the assemblage suggest that the hoard came about as the result of periodic deposition over two centuries or more; the alternative model of interpretation is that the first use of iron in Wales was as early as the eighth century, at least a hundred years earlier than is generally accepted for the adoption of iron technology in this region.

The inhabitants of Wales during the Iron Age lived in a variety of dwellings ranging from single-family farms to large, communal settlements, known as hillforts; some were enclosed, either for defence or to contain stock, others were open dwellings. The archaeological evidence demonstrates that many sites were occupied for several centuries, some being modified considerably over time. Interestingly enough, there seems to have been substantial continuity of settlement not only between the latest phase of the Bronze and the Iron Age and throughout the period of the Iron Age but also into the Roman period suggesting that, for many communities, the Roman occupation had little, if any, serious impact.

The most highly visible settlement sites in Wales are the defended upland enclosures, the hillforts. Some of them were clearly permanent proto-urban centres of population; others may have been used seasonally or only at times of danger. One of the best-recorded hillforts (more properly a promontory fort) was at Castell Henllys in North Pembrokeshire, a small defended settlement which has been reconstructed as an educational enterprise, to show visitors what life in the Iron Age might have been like. Excavation of the interior revealed signs of dense occupation, with circular houses, granaries and external hearths, perhaps for feasting; it had strong defences, in the form of banks and ditches, and included a splendid example of *chevaux de fries*, a series of small upright stones that acted as a form of 'tank-trap'. This is thought to have been designed as a symbol of ostentatious prestige: some of the stones were of quartz and would have been dazzlingly bright in sunshine. There were elaborate gateways with timber towers and heavy wooden doors. A large hoard of slingstones, brought from the nearest stream, is testimony to the need for defence. One of the problems of sites like Castell Henllys is the dearth of material culture: the cultural tradition of the region lacked pottery, and the acid soil is inimical to the survival of animal bones. But some evidence for the economy of the site is present: there were signs of blacksmithing, and a few iron tools have been excavated; bronze was also worked here; spindle-whorls testify to the production of wool; carbonised seeds represent the consumption of cereals that appear to have been grown locally and stored in the stronghold.

The pattern of enclosing settlements, like Castell Henllys, is repeated all over Wales; the tradition appears to have begun during the later Bronze Age, and presumably reflects a growing need for physical security among many communities and, perhaps, an increasing sense of territoriality. This trend for fortifying settlements is seen during the earliest Iron Age, a phenomenon echoed elsewhere in Britain, particularly in the south. In Wales, these hillforts invariably began life with single ramparts, consisting of a surrounding bank and ditch; many were quite small: Moel-y-Gaer, for example, at 2.7 hectares, is one of the larger ones. During the middle Iron Age (between about 400 and 200 BC), again following the pattern in southern Britain, there was a tendency to rationalise hillfort-occupation: some sites were abandoned, whilst others were re-fortified and sometimes greatly enlarged. The Breiddin, in Montgomeryshire, occupied 28 hectares and Llanymynech a huge 57 hectares. As part of the enlargement programme, many of these communal settlements had extra ramparts and outworks added to their defensive systems.

It is debatable as to whether the majority of hillforts were designed to be occupied permanently, though some most certainly seem to have been well-organised internally, being densely occupied with round houses, roadways and storage buildings. In common with hillforts elsewhere in Britain, it is likely that, alongside the function of ramparts as protective barriers, there was an element of showy prestige in their construction. Such ostentation is reflected in other parts of western Europe, notably in Celtiberia, where the defences of some hillforts, such as Contrebia and Ocenilla (Castilla-León), were far too elaborate for a purely functional interpretation to make sense.

A number of small farms or hamlets have been the subject of recent investigation which has thrown new light on a range of settlements occupied in Iron Age Wales. Most non-hillfort sites seem to have been supported by a broadly subsistence, mixed economy, and to have been based upon the almost universal template of the round house. Bryn Eryr (Anglesey) was occupied in the fifth century BC, when a single house was erected within a wooden palisade; about a century later, a second house was added, the dwelling protected by a bank and ditch enclosure. During the early Roman period, the two houses were replaced by a single, more substantial house with stone footings.

The tradition of circularity was present also in south-west Wales where enclosed sites, called raths, were constructed at, for instance, Walesland in west Pembrokeshire. Here there were at least three houses, as well as outbuildings, perhaps designed to support an extended family. Archaeologists have, for some time, explored the possible cosmological implications of living in round houses, arguing that these may mirror the world and the movement of the sun around the space inside the house; many British round houses (together with hillforts, shrines and some tombs) are orientated east or south-east, and this appears to be associated with alignment on the rising sun. It is of considerable interest that the south-eastern Welsh site of Thornwell Farm, near Chepstow, appears to show definite signs of similar cosmological perceptions. Thornwell consisted of a large round house which excavators identified as having two distinct and discrepantly-treated halves: the builders had constructed the two segments of the enclosing wall differently from one another and, what is more, a differential patterning of finds within the house seemed to reflect divergent usage, with discernment of possible 'public' and 'private', light and dark, or living and sleeping areas.

Very different from other settlements in Wales is Goldcliff on the Severn Levels, in the intertidal zone of the Severn Estuary. The excavation of this site presented both difficulties and opportunities: the site is flooded with seawater at high tide which leaves behind a challenging layer of mud as the tide ebbs. But this wetland environment makes for incredible levels of preservation, including the survival of organic material which, on a dry site, would never have survived. Goldcliff was investigated during the early 1990s, revealing trackways made of brushwood and a remarkable series of rectangular structures of a form whose construction and use in the Estuary spans a thousand years of the later Bronze Age and early Iron Age. It may be that the site was occupied only seasonally, to exploit the rich resources of the estuarine zone, but the site is exceptional in its contravention of the almost universal British round house tradition, its buildings appearing, instead, to conform to architectural forms that were common on the Continent during the Iron Age.

The later Bronze and Iron Ages in parts of Britain and continental Europe are characterised by a range of ritual activities that display a blend of commonality and idiosyncrasy over space and time. A distinctive form of arguably religious behaviour consisted of the deposition of high-status metalwork in watery places, presumably as offerings to the spirit world. A variety of objects were treated in this manner, the emphasis being on military and feasting equipment. Iron Age Wales was no exception; pools and marshes were the repository for many finely crafted votive gifts. One of the earliest deposits was the assemblage from Llyn Fawr in South Wales, mentioned earlier in this chapter in connection with the first evidence for the use of iron. Much later in date is the hoard of metalwork from Llyn Cerrig Bach, at the other end of Wales, on Anglesey, which may have been the focus of such activity from the second century BC to the first century AD. The material at Llyn Cerrig was discovered during the construction of the RAF Valley airfield in 1943, a project requiring the extraction of peat from the nearby marsh. The deposit comprised, in the main, martial objects, including iron swords, spears, chariot-fittings and horsegear, together with a highly ornate bronze shield-boss, a crescentric plaque decorated with a bird-headed triskele, part of a trumpet and, as at Llyn Fawr, a pair of cauldrons. A number of animal bones were also found but, sadly, the majority of these were not kept. However, a recent radiocarbon dating programme on the few that survive (those of cattle, sheep, dog and pony-sized horse) has revealed evidence that they belong to a horizon at least 200 years earlier than the deposition of the metalwork. If these animals were part of the ritual activity at the site, their presence may reflect an early tradition involving the sacrifice of animals, a custom later replaced by the offering of prestigious objects.

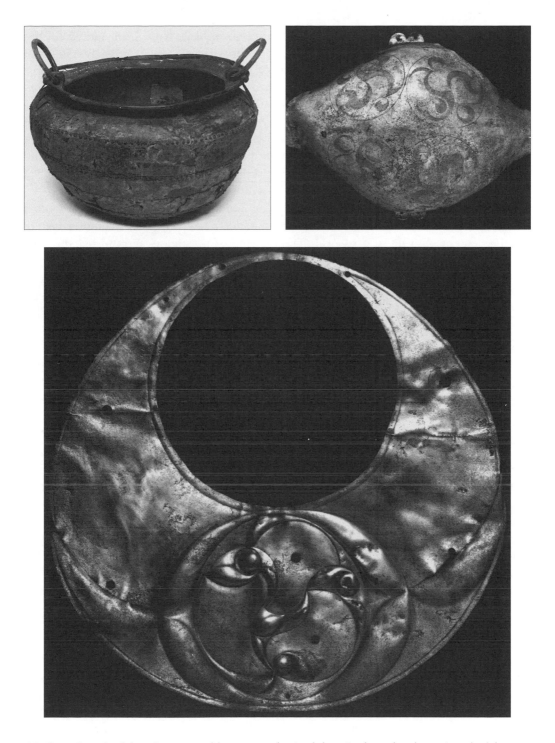

10. One of a pair of sheet-bronze cauldrons, part of a ritual deposit of metalwork cast into the lake as a ritual act in about 600 BC; Llyn Fawr, Rhigos, Glamorgan.

11. Detail of a shield-boss, showing its curvilinear designs, from the late Iron Age hoard of votive objects found at Llyn Cerrig Bach, Anglesey.

12. Sheet-bronze plaque decorated with bird-headed triskele motif, from Llyn Cerrig Bach, Anglesey.

Llyn Cerrig Bach represents the largest votive assemblage from Iron Age Wales, but other precious objects also found their way to watery places as votive gifts. Two items of high-status feasting equipment from north Wales, of first century AD date, deserve special mention. The first is the great tankard from Trawsfynydd, made of yew and covered in sheet-bronze, with a decorative handle, its size suggesting that it was used as a communal drinking vessel, perhaps for beer or fermented berry juice. The second is the iron fire-dog from Capel Garmon, which was found deliberately placed in a watery context beneath two large stones. This surely highly-valued piece of hearth-furniture represents the apogee of the blacksmith's skill: its terminals are in the form of elaborately-wrought yet delicate cattle heads, with fine horns and horse-like manes.

Watery deposits in Iron Age Wales need to be understood within the broader context of ritual behaviour in Britain and Europe that seems to have involved a complex system of engagement with the spirit world. The offering of prestigious gifts in marshes and pools may be concerned with the perceived need for the symbolic renewal of allegiance to that otherworld beyond the human dimension, at locations acknowledged as liminal or threshold spaces, interstices between the realms of people and the supernatural forces. At the same time, such episodic ritual behaviour may have provided mechanisms for bonding between groups of people, action perhaps symbolised by the presence of feasting equipment as well as weapons.

It is possible that many of the fine pieces of Iron Age art on metalwork possessed a primary symbolic function. Local artists copied and adapted the European tradition of La Tène art, named after the Swiss 'type-site' on the shores of Lake Neuchâtel, to produce superbly crafted ornament that has survived principally on high-status metal objects. Most of this art in Wales belongs late in the Iron Age, to the first centuries BC and AD. In addition to the pieces mentioned above (in the context of watery deposition), reference should be made to objects like the bronze collar fragment from Llandysul in West Wales, the lid – or helmet – fragment from a burial-cist at Cerrig-y-Drudion in Denbighshire (perhaps produced in Brittany, according to metallurgical analysis) and the plaques decorated with conjoined human heads, from Tal-y-Llyn in Meirioneth. Also the beautiful little enamelled cat's face which once decorated a bowl, found in the vicinity of Snowdon. Notable, too, is the series of bronze cattle heads once attached to bucket handles as decorative escutcheons.

Very few, if any, buildings in Iron Age Wales can be identified as formal shrines. Indeed, it is likely that – in common with many non-western religious traditions – ritual took place in domestic contexts as well as in natural places, such as bogs and lakes. Indeed, the Roman writer and historian Tacitus alludes to sacred druidic groves on the island of Anglesey, the focus of the Roman governor, Suetonius Paulinus's attack in AD 60-61. Certain archaeological sites have been identified as Romano-British temples: a putative shrine at Gwehelog in south-east Wales has shown up in the course of aerial reconnaissance; a hoard of Roman bronze votive objects found by metal detector at Llys Awel, Abergele in north-east Wales suggests the presence of a temple. It is possible that, in common with many religious structures of Roman date in Britain and Gaul, both these sanctuaries were first used during the Iron Age.

In his description of the Roman destruction of the sacred groves on Anglesey, Tacitus specifically mentions the human sacrifice of war captives in the context of druidic ritual. There is a mass of both archaeological and literary evidence for the practice of ritual murder in Iron Age Britain and Europe, although the data are seldom unambiguous. Although it took place just outside Wales, Britain's best evidence for human sacrifice comes from a peat bog at Lindow Moss in Cheshire, where more than one body has been found to have been killed violently. In the mid first century AD, just prior to the Roman conquest of the region, a young man met a 'triple-fold' death: he was dealt two savage blows to his head, fracturing his skull, was strangled and his throat cut before being cast naked and face down in the marsh. About a hundred years later, a second man was placed there after being decapitated. Although both men might have been executed malefactors, it is at least highly possible that they were sacrificial victims.

At the time of the early Roman campaigns in Wales, Roman writers, such as Tacitus, were able to identify named native polities or tribes, notably the Demetae in the south-west, the Deceangli in the northern marches, and two especially belligerent groups, the Ordovices in the north and the Silures in the south-east: the pacification of this latter tribe was to cause Rome particular and persistent problems. It is likely that this political organisation of Wales originated much earlier and may, indeed, have come about as early as the Late Bronze Age.

Contact with the Gaulish mainland and, further east, with the Classical world, was probably maintained – in however sporadic a form – throughout the Iron Age, as would have also obtained with Ireland in the west. The Atlantic seaways would have been the major agent for such contact, and there is archaeological evidence for such linkages. It is known that the south Breton tribe of the Veneti was crucial to such networks, and we can envisage complex and dynamic systems of trade and exchange – both material and ideological – taking place in western Europe, in which Wales would have played its part: the Breton origins of the Cerrig-y-Drudion bronze are testimony to such relationships. A voluble piece of evidence consists of a lead anchor stock, found off the Llŷn Peninsula at Porth Felen, thought to be of Mediterranean origin and to have come from a merchant ship plying between Britain and the Continent during the early first century BC. The Greek geographer Strabo, writing in the later first century BC, makes specific mention of sea-trading between Britain and Gaul. He refers to exports from Britain at this time, including hunting dogs, metal, hides and slaves. In the context of this last reference, it is interesting to note the presence of two iron slave-gang chains in the votive hoard found at Llyn Cerrig Bach.

The European Iron Age – including Wales – belongs to the last phase of prehistory and, that being so, we would not expect to find much evidence for written languages. Indeed, Wales has produced no linguistic material certainly relating to pre-Roman communities. Continental Europe is slightly better in this regard, in so far as there is some scattered evidence for language from both inscribed objects and certain place names (whose identity is preserved in later Roman documents). A small number of inscriptions, in 'Celtic' languages is recorded, some dating as early as the fourth century BC, from Gaul, North Italy and Iberia. They range from informative documents, such as the 'curse-tablet' from Larzac in southern France, to simple names, like that of Korisios, an armourer who stamped his Gaulish name on a sword at Port in Switzerland. Celtic place names, recorded in Roman imperial texts, such as the *Antonine Itinerary* and Ptolemy's *Geography*, suggest that topographical words, like *nemeton* (sacred place) and *dunum* (fortified place) were common to large areas of Iron Age temperate Europe, including Britain, yet it is not until the Roman period that the textual 'voice' of Wales can be heard.

13. Iron slave gang chain from Llyn Cerrig Bach, Anglesey.
14. Late Iron Age bronze bucket-escutcheon in the form of a bull's head, from Welshpool, Mid-Wales.
15. A view of the south wall at Venta Silurum shows one of six towers which were built onto the wall to strengthen the defences of the town in the fourth century. In places the south wall still stands to a height of five metres.

ROMAN WALES
Ray Howell

Late Iron Age Britain had well-established trade links and other contacts with the Continent and sufficient wealth to make it appealing to an expanding Roman empire. Perhaps not surprisingly, it was Julius Caesar himself who mounted the first invasions in 55 and 54 BC. The actual conquest, however, occurred nearly a century later with the Claudian invasion of AD 43. Command of the successful invading forces was entrusted to Aulus Plautius who was governor of Pannonia on the Danube. When he took up his new command, he brought a legion, IX Hispana from Pannonia, and drew three additional legions from the Rhine frontier including II Augusta from Strasbourg, XIV Gemina from Mainz and XX Valeria Victrix from Cologne. The legions were joined by auxiliary troops to form an invading army of over 40,000 men.

In spite of the scale of the Roman military intervention, there was initially strong resistance. Notable among the native leaders were the Catuvellaunian brothers Caratacus and Togodumnus who led initial skirmishes before massing their forces for a two-day battle on the River Medway. The Romans eventually triumphed, in part through the aggressive intervention of legionary soldiers commanded by the future emperor Vespasian. The Britons, however, continued to skirmish as they fell back toward the Thames and in these later exchanges Togodumnus was killed. Despite continuing sporadic fighting, it was not long before the large and well-disciplined Roman army established control in the south-east of what is now England and Claudius himself arrived to revel in an imperial victory sealed by his triumphal entry into the Catuvellaunian capital, Camulodunum, modern Colchester. The victory procession included elephants for special impact. In the aftermath, some tribes like the Dobunni sought peace with the Romans. Others, like the Durotriges of Dorset resisted and archaeology confirms heavy fighting at hillforts in their territory including Maiden Castle. Nevertheless, within about five years of the initial invasion, southern England was firmly under Roman military control. The situation in what is today Wales, however, was very different. Caratacus fled west to continue resistance and he was naturally drawn to the warlike Silures of south-east Wales. Soon the Silures emerged as the focus of resistance and the might of the Roman military machine was directed toward Wales.

Aulus Plautius became the first governor in Britain and he spent the following four years consolidating control while creating a new province in the south and east. The tribes in the north and west, however, remained hostile and when a new governor, Publius Ostorius Scapula, arrived in AD 47, they attacked. Ostorius responded immediately sweeping from Severn to Trent and then launched the first large-scale attack into Wales, striking into the territory of the Deceangli in the north-eastern marches. The Roman historian Tacitus, who chronicled the fighting in Wales, reported that Ostorius 'ravaged their territory and collected extensive booty'. It seems likely that the campaign against the Deceangli was based on a strategic decision to try to drive a wedge between the Brigantes in the north of England and the powerful Welsh tribes, notably the southern Silures and the Ordovices of north Wales.

The Silures, noted for aggressiveness, were particularly resistant to Roman domination. Tacitus reported that 'neither sternness nor leniency' tempered their opposition to Rome, an opposition made even more intractable by the influence of Caratacus. In AD 49, Ostorius attacked the Silures and it seems clear that the

16. An artist's impression shows the *palaestra*, open-air swimming pool and fortress baths at the
Roman fortress of Isca, modern Caerleon.

17. The *basilica* and forum at Venta Silurum, modern Caerwent, are shown in this artist's
impression. The *basilica* functioned as an 'assembly hall' for the tribal capital of the Silures.

Catuvellaunian war leader helped to organise the tribal resistance. While the line of the Roman advance is uncertain, archaeology is clarifying the picture. The fortress built at Usk was eventually important and excavations have confirmed an early military presence at Monmouth; it is probable that the Usk and Wye river valleys provided access for the Roman invaders. It also seems likely, although it is difficult to demonstrate archaeologically, that naval activity in the Bristol Channel supported the overland advance.

It may be that growing military pressure in south Wales caused Caratacus to attempt to establish a link with the Ordovices. He moved north with an army only to be drawn into a set piece battle somewhere overlooking the Severn. The site of the battle is uncertain, but we do know that Caratacus held the high ground overlooking the river. Fighting was intense as the Romans crossed the river under a shower of missiles. In their *testudo* (tortoise) formations, with walls and roof of locked shields, the Romans advanced and eventually defeated the native forces. Among the prisoners taken were the wife and daughter of Caratacus. Caratacus himself escaped and fled to the Brigantes, only to be surrendered to the Romans by the Brigantian queen Cartimandua. He and his family were taken to Rome as prisoners where, after a triumphal procession, their fate might have seemed sealed. Tacitus explains, however, that Caratacus made a defiant speech before the emperor saying:

> *I had horses, men, arms and wealth. Are you surprised that I am sorry to lose them? If you want to rule the world, does it follow that everyone else welcomes enslavement? If I had surrendered without a blow before being brought before you, neither my loss nor your victory would have become famous.*

The Romans were sufficiently impressed to spare Caratacus and his family. Meanwhile in Wales, despite the loss of an important war leader, the Silures remained hostile. Indeed, they seem to have been even more ferocious and anti-Roman in the aftermath of the capture of Caratacus.

Ostorius had certainly not helped the situation by announcing that the only way to deal with the tribe was through their extermination or transplantation to Gaul. The threat must have seemed a real one as the Romans embarked on a programme of fort building within the tribe's territory. The Silures responded by attacking selected Roman targets; Tacitus reports that a large group of Roman troops was surrounded and, before they could be rescued, they suffered heavy casualties reflected in the loss of the camp commandant (*praefectus castrorum*), eight centurions and a large number of men. Shortly after this success, the Silures attacked a foraging party and then routed the cavalry force sent to rescue them. Fighting became the order of the day as, in the words of Tacitus, 'battle followed battle'. The 'exceptionally stubborn' Silures mounted a series of lightning strikes in their wooded hillsides during a highly effective guerrilla war. As this Silurian War dragged on, Ostorius died, worn out by the strain of the conflict. As Tacitus explained, the Silures 'exulted that so great a general, even if not defeated in battle, had at least been eliminated by warfare'.

Aulus Didius Gallus was named the new governor but before he arrived an even larger military disaster befell the Romans at the hands of the Silures. The general Manlius Valens attempted to defeat the tribe before the governor's arrival and committed a legion,

18. An *intaglio* is one of eighty-eight engraved gem stones excavated from the drain of the fortress baths at Isca, Caerleon.

19. A coin shows the image of Magnus Maximus, Macsen Wledig in Welsh tradition. Maximus, a general commanding troops in Britain, proclaimed himself emperor in AD 383.

20. A fragment of a wooden waterwheel from the Roman gold mine site at Dolaucothi provides the basis for this National Museum of Wales reconstruction. Waterwheels draining the mine were part of one of several sophisticated hydraulic systems at Dolaucothi.

probably the XX, to the campaign. Remarkably, the Silures defeated the legion and by the time Didius arrived in Britain they were reported to be ranging 'far and wide'. The new governor could only try to maintain order in the province and accept the *status quo* with the Welsh tribes. Hostilities were not resumed until AD 57 and the arrival of a new governor with a considerable military reputation, Quintus Veranius. He mounted limited probing attacks against the Silures but, as these proceeded, he too died.

The next governor was Gaius Suetonius Paulinus who probably arrived in AD 58. A well-established general, he resumed the fighting in Wales but shifted the attack to the north. His objective was Anglesey, an important centre of the Druids. The Romans built flat-bottomed boats to cross the Menai Straits and many of the cavalrymen swam across with their horses. They were initially taken aback by what confronted them. Tacitus describes the island defenders as a terrifying dense, armed mass of people including the Druids 'raising their hands to heaven and shouting dreadful curses' and 'black-robed women with dishevelled hair like Furies, brandishing torches'. Initially the Romans were 'paralysed with fear' but Suetonius forced the attack taunting his men not to fear a 'horde of fanatical women'. The close quarter fighting which followed resulted in a massacre as the Romans killed indiscriminately with many of the islanders being 'enveloped in the flames of their own torches'. Suetonius ordered the destruction of Anglesey's sacred groves and would probably have consolidated control in north Wales had he not been forced to respond to the revolt of Boudica, a revolt which nearly forced the Romans from Britain altogether.

In the aftermath of the Boudican revolt, the legions in Britain were re-deployed and it is likely that responsibility for Wales passed from the XX legion to the II Augustan which was moved to Gloucester. There it was well placed to resume the offensive on orders from Vespasian who took the throne in AD 69. The new emperor, founder of the Flavian dynasty, had campaigned in Britain and he ordered a forward policy with respect to Wales. Central to implementing that policy was Sextus Julius Frontinus who became governor in AD 73 or 74; unfortunately, we have few details of his campaigns either from Tacitus or the archaeological record. Tacitus simply informs us that 'after a hard struggle, he conquered the powerful and warlike nation of the Silures, overcoming both the valour of his enemies and the difficulty of the terrain'. By AD 74 or 75, the Romans were sufficiently secure in Silurian territory to begin construction of a new legionary fortress at Caerleon.

Frontinus also began construction of the legionary fortress at Chester although it was his successor, Agricola, who led the final campaign into north Wales. The Ordovices defeated a Roman cavalry unit and Agricola responded with a campaign of genocide in which many members of the tribe were killed and Anglesey was annexed. The conquest of Wales, however, had been achieved at a high cost to the Romans. With the hostility of the Ordovices and the protracted Silurian War, it is not surprising that in AD 78 there were some 30,000 Roman troops in Wales.

Excavation of a number of sites helps us to understand the scale and nature of the military occupation. Particularly important was Caerleon in the heartland of the Silures. Initially consisting in large part of timber-frame buildings, within a decade or two the fortress was rebuilt in stone, including a 1.5m thick wall with turrets and gateways enclosing the site. Buildings included large and elaborate fortress baths, an amphitheatre with sufficient seating to accommodate the 5000-6000 troops of the legion, and a central tetrapylon which may have served as a triumphal arch as well as a central focus for the fortress. A network of permanent forts for auxiliary troops, providing for units of between 500 and 1000 men, was also established. These sites provide particular insights. Tombstone and other evidence suggests that Spanish auxiliaries occupied forts such as Brecon Gaer and Llanio. Inscriptions indicate that the Belgic Nervians occupied Caergai. By about AD 80, Wales was dominated by this network of forts which was maintained for half a century. While there was then a period of consolidation, the most strategically important forts were maintained.

As Roman military control was consolidated, new structures of society were put in place. The introduction of a cash economy was a case in point. New towns emerged such as Cowbridge (Bovium) which became the market centre for the Vale of Glamorgan where a villa economy was developing with important type sites including Ely, Llandough, Llantwit Major and Whitton. Whitton is particularly interesting as there appears to have been continuous occupation from *c.*AD 30 until the mid-fourth century; early phase occupation was in round houses but these gave way to Roman-inspired rectilinear structures. The courtyard villa at Llantwit with baths, hypocausts and mosaics suggests both comfort and prosperity. Industrial activity also contributed to economic development. In the early post conquest period, the extractive industries were important in Wales; copper and zinc were extracted at sites like Parys Mountain on Anglesey, the Great Orme in Gwynedd and Llanymynech Hill in Powys. Lead and silver were also mined in Wales and iron production was widespread. A particularly important site was the gold mine at Dolaucothi where hand cut adits, an aqueduct system and surviving fragments of a timber Roman waterwheel indicate operations on a large scale. In time, textile production and ceramic manufacture also became important, as did brewing. In the late third century price edict of Diocletian the price of British beer was fixed at twice that of beer from Egypt!

One of the key elements in the imposition of *romanitas* was the creation of *civitas* administration. *Civitates* were units of administration based on the tribe and two were created in Wales. Each of the *civitates* had a capital and Carmarthen (Moridunum Demetarum) filled that role for the Demetae. A larger capital was Caerwent (Venta Silurum) in the territory of the Silures. This 44-acre town was divided in half by a 'high-street' running east-west, flanked by two parallel streets. Four streets ran north-south, dividing the town into twenty *insulae* or blocks. The whole of the town was enclosed by earthen banks and ditches which were eventually replaced by large stone walls and gates. The high street was lined with shops and the central *insulae* were given over to public buildings such as the forum and basilica. The basilica contained the chamber where the tribal senate, the *ordo*, met and recent excavations suggest a Hadrianic date for its construction. It seems likely that after the long and bitter Silurian War, it was not until the 120s and withdrawal of significant numbers of troops for construction duty on Hadrian's Wall that *civitas* administration was extended to the Silures.

Foundations like Caerwent provided an impetus for the adoption of *romanitas*. Significantly, however, there is good evidence for native continuity in the *civitas* capital. There is, for example, clear indication of conflation in religious practice with physical fusion of native and Roman deities. A stone altar from Caerwent was dedicated to Mars Ocelus and a statue base was inscribed to Mars Lenus or Ocelus Vellaunus. Moreover, some objects from the town seem to be purely native in their inspiration including a stone head from an apparent shrine chamber in a late Roman house and a seated mother goddess found near the temple adjacent to the forum-basilica. A particularly revealing site is Thornwell Farm near Chepstow where excavation confirms occupation from the late Bronze Age/early Iron Age to the fourth century AD. Throughout that long period, occupation was in round houses at a site only some 6km from Caerwent. If we accept round house occupation as an indication of native survival, the implication is that traditional lifestyles persisted, almost in the shadow of the *civitas* capital, throughout the Romano-British period. It would follow that *romanitas* in upland Wales may have been a very thin veneer, indeed.

Whatever the balance between native and Roman tradition in later Romano-British society, new influences clearly brought significant changes. Among the most important of these was Christianity. Two of the three British Christian martyrs known by name, Julius and Aaron, died in Wales. Moreover, there is every reason to believe that at the time of Constantine's 'Peace of the Church' in AD 313, Christianity was already well established in Britain. In AD 314, three British bishops and the representative of a fourth attended the Council at Arles, confirming the existence of an early episcopal structure which would undoubtedly have included Wales. A pewter bowl with a *chi-rho* symbol, probably part of an *agapé* service, helps confirm Christianity in late Roman Caerwent.

While increasing Christian influence and apparent economic prosperity were features of fourth century Romano-British society, so too was increasing political instability. External threats and internal discord caused political upheaval and a reorientation of troops. In Wales, northern coastal defences were concentrated at Caergybi and Caernarfon while in the south, the fort at Cardiff was rebuilt, eventually replacing Caerleon as the main military centre. Coups and counter-coups became frequent occurrences with troops from Britain sometimes playing an important role. Particularly significant in this respect was the attempt of Magnus Maximus, Macsen Wledig in Welsh tradition, to claim the throne in AD 383. Attacking with troops from Britain, Maximus was able, for a time, to establish himself as senior Augustus in the west. Eventually, however, he was killed in a lightning strike by Theodosius I in 388. While these events did not mark the end of Roman influence, it is unlikely that large numbers of Roman troops were permanently garrisoned in Britain again. By 410, the conventional date for the end of Roman Britain, responsibility for matters such as local self defence was probably already in British hands.

It is important to recognise that the end of Roman Britain was a process rather than an event, and as new social and political systems developed, Wales itself emerged as a recognisable entity. The new society was one heavily influenced by the long period of Roman control but, as has been seen, it was also one in which earlier native traditions survived. It may be significant that some hilltop sites again became attractive with early medieval occupation at places like Dinas Emrys, Degannwy, Dinas Powys and Lodge Hill. It is remarkable the extent to which early medieval Welsh kingdoms have apparent geographical affinities with Iron Age tribal regions. In some cases, continuity may have been through the *civitates* but the parallels are striking and probably significant. An interesting and perhaps particularly telling piece of evidence is a land grant for a monastery in post-Roman Caerwent. The land was given by a king of Gwent named Caradog, the Welsh form of Caratacus. This grant seems to provide an insight into the balance of the Romano-British inheritance in Wales. In the aftermath of an extended period first of conflict and then of conflation lasting well over 300 years, while the name of the emerging kingdom of Gwent was derived from the *civitas* capital, the name of the king was that of an Iron Age resistance leader!

2

'DARK AGE' WALES
c.383 – c.1063

Kari L. Maund

The period between the end of Roman rule in Britain and the coming of the Normans was one of the most dramatic and important in the history of Wales. The earliest centuries are only thinly documented in our extant sources and the origins of the Welsh kingdoms are shrouded in later legend and political propaganda. However, between the early age of hilltop chiefdoms and legendary heroes, and the arrival of the Normans in the 1060s, Wales saw the construction and expansion of what became its main political units, the slow decline of the early royal houses and the rise during the ninth century of an aggressive new royal line which would dominate Welsh political life down to 1283. This period also witnessed the development of native church organisation and a series of invasions, raids and attempts at settlement by outside peoples, including the Irish, the Anglo-Saxons and the Vikings. This chapter will present an introduction to the early medieval period, with discussion of its major themes, issues and developments.

THE EARLIEST KINGDOMS

Throughout the period of Welsh independence, Wales was a land of multiple kingdoms, each with its own ruling house and, in the early period at least, with its own traditions and origin legends. The exact number of kingdoms in Wales at the beginning of the early medieval period is unknown, and their history is often obscure. Roman rule in Britain had left its traces on what became Wales, and kings and historians in medieval Wales were to look back to the Roman period as one means of establishing the legitimacy and antiquity of Welsh kingdoms. Historical figures of the Roman period – some with little or no connection to Britain – were assimilated into Welsh genealogical tradition, and when the Welsh kingdoms began to enter the written historical record, the pedigrees of many Welsh kings included Roman emperors as ancestors, alongside native British heroes and Biblical figures.

However, the written sources for the sub-Roman period are thin, and mainly retrospective. Wales itself was yet to form, but with the withdrawal of Rome, the native Britons faced new problems of self-government and foreign invasion. From the late fourth century, Roman control had been weakening, and a series of 'emperors' had been proclaimed from within the army stationed in Britain. Two of these, Magnus Maximus and Constantine, would be remembered in later Welsh tradition, although neither seems to have had any demonstrable connection to Wales, and Maximus was not of British origin. After the final withdrawal of Rome, no single political authority emerged in Britain. Wales – still at this point not yet defined as a separate place – seems to have passed into the control of a number of regionally-based leaders, arising from the local populations, but possibly drawing on Roman administrative divisions. It is probably at this point that the ancestors of the medieval kingdoms emerged, some based around the remains of Roman settlements, as occurred in the south east, around Caerleon (Roman *Venta Silurum*), or in western Shropshire, around the old city of Wroxeter, and perhaps laying claim to quasi-Roman power; others forming around hill-fort sites, as at Coygan Camps in south west Wales.

It is difficult to gain any clear idea of the range and nature of the political powers exercised by sub-Roman British leaders. In the sixth century, a British monk, Gildas, wrote a polemic on the state of Britain. Gildas did not set out to write a formal history, and his account is highly coloured, heavily influenced by Old Testament models, and intended more to provide moral examples than an accurate record. He viewed the period of Roman rule as a lost Golden Age, and was highly critical of his contemporary rulers, whom he saw as inadequate, weak and sinful. According to Gildas, however, some of the British leaders of the fifth and sixth centuries represented themselves as the heirs to Roman authority, and may have been descended from Roman officials who had settled and intermarried in Britain.

The late Roman period had seen the beginning of a new era of migrations throughout much of Europe, and both the eastern and western coasts of Britain had experienced raids and attempts at colonisation from peoples from Ireland, northern Scotland, and continental Europe. West Wales – and particularly south-west Wales – experienced settlements by the Irish. Germanic tribes had been settled in parts of Britain, particularly in the north, under Roman direction, perhaps as early as the third century, but during the fifth century, invasions from Northern Europe increased, and the newly emerging British polities faced an ever-increasing threat from these new neighbours. Reactions to this varied. Some British leaders put up determined resistance, others made alliances with the incomers, employing bands of federated Germans as defenders and buffers against other invading groups. Gildas depicted this period – the Anglo-Saxon settlement era – as one of conflict and violence. He approved those British leaders, such as the shadowy Ambrosius Aurelianus, who put up resistance, and criticised those who made alliances, whom he blamed for encouraging further Germanic settlement and reducing British power. The details of the fifth century are vague, and Gildas' account often obscures as much as it illuminates. He presents the fifth century as a period of cataclysm, by the end of which much of Britain was overrun by foreign invaders. It seems, however, that alongside the invasions, the early kingdoms of Britain and Wales were emerging.

Gildas gives few details, and no dates, but he does refer to a small number of rulers who had been early contemporaries of his own. These – Maglocunus, Constantine, Aurelius Caninus, Vortepor, and Cuneglasus – include two (Maglocunus and Vortepor) who can be located with reasonable certainty within Wales, and who left traces in later historical sources relating to known early Welsh kingdoms. We do not know the exact boundaries of the lands controlled by either, but Gildas tells us that Vortepor was ruler of the *Demetae*. This had been the name of one of the British tribes in Wales, and gave rise to the medieval kingdom name of Dyfed.

In Gildas' eyes, at least, Maelgwn seems to have been the most important king within native Britain in his own time, the 'dragon of the island' and 'higher than almost all the leaders of Britain'. He would come to occupy a significant place in the later historiography of Gwynedd, and to be regarded as a key ancestor of its first medieval royal dynasty, yet the nature and scope of his power, and the details of his career, are unknown. Gildas' accounts of him, and of the other kings, are designed not to inform but to teach, and the kings are described mainly to be used as illustrations of negative royal power – they are tyrants who oppress the church, abuse Christian notions of kingship, mistreat their people, and reject Christian models of marriage and behaviour. They are also forceful military figures who place a high premium on wealth and status. It is difficult, given the lack of other evidence, to judge the accuracy of Gildas' descriptions, but it appears from this that there was some tension between the monastic ideal of a king promulgated in educated circles, and the reality of leadership in a period of political and social upheaval. The early Welsh kingdoms formed from the remains of Roman overlordship and against a background of foreign invasion; their earliest leaders are likely to have been pragmatic, forceful, and practical men.

The Anglo-Saxons were not the sole immigrants into Britain. Gildas writes also of invasions by Picts (from Northern Scotland and the Isles) and Irish. Migration across the Irish Sea had begun long before the end of Roman rule, and archaeological and written evidence demonstrates that there was a marked Irish element in early medieval Wales. Vortepor, Gildas' 'tyrant of the Demetae', probably had Irish blood. His kingdom of Dyfed, in the south-west, contains the richest evidence for an Irish presence in Wales. Wales possesses a fair number of early medieval inscribed stones, dating to the fifth century onwards, commemorating high status individuals. These are inscribed in Latin, using the Latin alphabet, but a certain number of them are also inscribed in Ogom, a writing system developed and used in Ireland for writing Irish. The majority of the surviving ogom-inscribed stones come from Dyfed, suggesting the presence there in the fifth to seventh centuries of an élite social group with Irish or Irish-influenced names, and using an Irish script alongside the Latin one inherited from the Romans. The stones thus represent a fusion of Irish culture with the memory of Roman: the erection of such stones imitated Roman practice, suggesting that those who commissioned them were aware of – and perhaps deliberately referring to – the Roman past of Britain. It appears from the inscriptions that in the fifth and sixth centuries, native rulers in parts of Wales still sought to identify themselves at least to a degree with the governmental model of Rome. This may support the representation of Roman rule as a source of legitimate power and social order found in Gildas' writing, and in some later Welsh historiography. However, the use on the stones of titles such as 'protector', while echoing Roman models, does not necessarily demonstrate that in life any native leader consciously imitated Roman practice. It may be that such titles were considered appropriate to memorials, and have little bearing on daily behaviour and practice.

Vortepor himself features on a memorial stone, from Castelldwyran, Dyfed, with an inscription both in Latin and in ogom. The ogom simply gives his name, 'Votecorigas', but the Latin reads 'Memoria Voteporigis protictoris', the Memorial of Vortepor the Protector. The inscription is more than just confirmation for the existence of Vortepor. It serves to tie him to the Irish element settled in Dyfed, and is a strong indication that these incomers occupied high social status. Further confirmation of this can be found in the extant genealogies for the first royal house of Dyfed. An Irish text, *The Expulsion of the Deisi*, composed by the ninth century, contains the origin legend of the Demetian kings. It relates how, under their leader Eochaid mac Artchorp, the Deisi, an Irish people from the Waterford area, were expelled from their Irish lands. They went across the sea 'to the land of *Demed*' and there made themselves kings. The text supplies a pedigree of the descendants in Dyfed of Artchorp, ending in a Welsh name, *Tualador* (Tewdwr or Tewdos) who may represent a historical figure from eighth century Dyfed. The text also includes amongst the descendants of Eochaid one *Gartbuir*, an Irish rendering of Vortepor. Welsh pedigrees for Dyfed, which seem to have been compiled independently of this Irish text, also suggest an Irish element in the first royal line. Further evidence comes from place names, supporting this Irish presence in Dyfed at an early period. The element *cnwc*, perhaps from Irish *cnoc*, hillock, is found in place names from an area broadly reflecting what is known of the old boundaries of Dyfed, for example at Cnwc-Eithinos, near Llanddewibrefi, and in Pen-y-Cnwc, a name found in several parts of Dyfed. *Loch*, the Irish word for lake, occurs in place names from the Dyfed heartland, including Lochdwrffin, Lochmeilir and Lochdyn. There are problems of interpretation with this material – inscriptions are hard to date, place names are subject to later reworking and to problems of transmission, pedigrees can be subjected to manipulation and rewriting to suit politically successful groups of a later period, but the combination is strong evidence for a politically important, and perhaps dominant, Irish presence in early Dyfed.

What were the causes of this migration? It used to be thought that the settlement was in some way official, with the Irish migrants being deliberately introduced (or at least granted official recognition) into western Britain by either the Roman authorities or by a sub-Roman British leader, to act as a buffer zone between the native inhabitants and raiders active in the Irish sea. However, this view raises more problems than it solves. The nature of authority in early Dyfed, and the degree to which is was Romanised, is unclear; nor is it possible to date the settlement with certainty. Gildas suggests that Irish raids and attempts at settlement belong to the late Roman and sub-Roman period, by which time Roman control over the remoter parts of Britain may have been less than total. An invitation to an alien, non-Christian group to settle in a distant area as a defence against more raiders of the same people in a period of political disturbance and disruption seems rather unlikely. Moreover, it should be borne in mind that the fourth and fifth centuries saw migrations and population movements throughout much of Europe; the Irish movement into Wales can be more straight-forwardly explained as part of this trend. Political changes within Ireland, leading to the exclusion from power of certain groups probably also contributed to the migration, and the story told in *The Expulsion of the Deisi* goes some way to support this.

Dyfed was not the only part of Wales to receive Irish settlers. Later tradition identifies an Irish element in two other kingdoms, Brycheiniog and Gwynedd. Brycheiniog, like Dyfed, had a royal line who by the tenth century at the latest claimed Irish ancestry, and possesses a corpus of memorial stones inscribed with ogom as well as Latin, arguing for the presence of at least some Irish speakers at élite level. The Irish presence in Gwynedd seems to have been smaller, or less influential over time, although one part of that kingdom, the Llŷn peninsula, may owe its name to an Irish tribal name, Ui Liathain.

There is also a scattering of inscribed stones of an early date which contain Irish names (*Cunogosos*, on a stone from Llanfaelog, *Maccvdecceti*, on one from Penrhos Llugwy) or which have ogom inscriptions. The foundation legend of Gwynedd, preserved in the ninth century *History of the Britons*, compiled in Gwynedd, also refers to the Irish. The legend describes how the founder of the first royal line of Gwynedd, Cunedda, came to north Wales with his sons, and drove out the Irish who were settled there, before imposing themselves as the new kings.

The historicity of Cunedda is debatable. He is said to have come from *Manau Gododdin*, a British kingdom in the area of Edinburgh. A number of British kingdoms persisted in what is now southern Scotland and the northernmost part of England through the sixth to around the ninth centuries, and these were to feature in a substantial body of later Welsh tradition and poetry. North British heroes and kings also became seen as desirable, legitimating ancestors for later kings within Wales. The Cunedda legend forms part of this, and as such

21. Early medieval Welsh inscribed stone, commemorating *Iaconus*.
22. The Vortepor stone, from Castelldwyran, near Carmarthen.
23. Early medieval Welsh inscribed stone, commemorating *Similius*, from Clocaenog, Dyffryn Clwyd.
24. The *Maccvdecceti* stone, from Penrhos Llugwy.

25 The Pillar of Elise.

its authenticity is dubious. Certain elements within the legend are particularly suspicious. A tenth-century pedigree describes how Gwynedd was divided amongst his sons; the names of the latter are closely related to the names of later known territorial divisions of Gwynedd. It is likely that the names of the supposed sons were drawn from the region names, and that some or all of them may originally have been wholly unconnected to the main dynasty of Gwynedd (which claimed Cunedda as founding ancestor). The eponyms of these regions may have become attached to the genealogy of the first dynasty of Gwynedd as the latter rose in power to become dominant over the whole region. This served to explain the control over these areas by the kings of Gwynedd and to justify their ambitions to expand and dominate areas outside their own boundaries. There is no extant evidence for the early expansion of Gwynedd, but by the ninth century, its kings were trying to annex their southern neighbour, Ceredigion, which possessed its own, separate, royal line. By the tenth century, Ceredigion had been overrun, and its eponym, Ceredig, had been attached to the line of Cunedda as a grandson, this allowing the later kings of Gwynedd to legitimise their conquest.

This exploitation of genealogy to justify annexation, expropriation and expansion was a common practice in early medieval Wales, and most of our surviving pedigrees have been manipulated to explain or excuse the political ambitions of later kings and their families. The history of Wales in the early period is thus viewed through a lens of later legend and propaganda. In particular, successful dynasties affiliated themselves to the lines of those they had expropriated or displaced, as was to occur with the highly successful and aggressive Venedotian House of Merfyn from the ninth century. Legend and pedigree were also manipulated to the detriment of rival lines, as was to occur in the case of the first royal line of Powys. Almost all the extant sources for early medieval Wales were produced under the influence, direct or indirect, of the House of Merfyn, and this has had important consequences for our knowledge and interpretation of Wales in the early medieval period. The House of Merfyn displaced the line of Cunedda (of which Maelgwn Gwynedd was a member), but took over at least some aspects of its traditions, not least the Cunedda legend. The founder of this dynasty, Merfyn Frych, was himself an outsider, coming probably from the Isle of Man. In the early ninth century, perhaps in Merfyn's reign, perhaps in that of his son, Rhodri Mawr, the Cunedda legend seems to have been pressed into service to provide a model for the legitimacy and, more to the point, the suitability, as king of a militarily gifted, aggressive and ambitious immigrant.

The impact of this dominance is nowhere more clear than in the surviving versions of the origin legend of the early kings of Powys. The process of the formation of Powys is obscure to us, but there are indications in our records that, like Gwynedd, it may have grown out of two or more earlier, smaller kingdoms, one perhaps based in central mid–Wales north of Builth, one including land now in Shropshire (together with the territory around Welshpool and Llangollen), and perhaps another between these two.

Medieval poetry and tradition reveal traces of at least two, and perhaps three royal houses in the early period: the Cadelling house, the line of Cynddylan, (which may have been related to the former), and a line claiming descent from Vortigern. The latter seems to have become politically dominant by the ninth century, and was seeking to affiliate itself with the memory of Rome. A king descended from this line, Cyngen ap Cadell, erected a stone pillar in honour of his grandfather, Elise. The Pillar still survives, near Llangollen, but its inscription is long lost; fortunately, it was recorded by the antiquary Edward Lhuyd in the seventeenth century. It described Elise's achievements as a successful campaigner against the Anglo-Saxons, together with a statement of the family's ancestors, culminating in a claim of descent from both Vortigern and Magnus Maximus. Both are presented in a wholly heroic light, Maximus as a victorious general, Vortigern as a man blessed by St Germanus, or Garmon, an important saint within Powys: the effect is both to legitimate and praise their descendants, and to justify their power in terms of inherited right and martial skill. The Pillar is the sole statement of the origins of the line of Powys to have been certainly created within that kingdom. Other statements derive from the *Historia Britonnum*, composed in the early ninth century in the sphere of influence of the kings of Gwynedd, long enemies and rivals to Powys. This latter account is clearly aware of the native Powysian tradition, and seeks to erode it. Vortigern is depicted not as a hero but as a weak, treacherous, incestuous and ultimately culpable king at whose door is laid the responsibility of the Anglo-Saxon invasions – he is said to have invited them to settle but then been unable to check their ambitions. The connection with Garmon/Germanus is denied; far from blessing Vortigern, Garmon is said to have rejected him and replaced him with another king, Cadell Ddrynllug (the linear ancestor of the Cadellings, from whom Cyngen may also have claimed descent), who is said to be of base origins. The effect is to belittle the ninth century ruling house of Powys, representing it as treacherous and base-born. The accounts of both the Pillar and *Historia Britonnum*, like the Cunedda legend, probably tell us more about later rivalries, claims and counter-claims, than about early conditions, but provides us with a clear illustration of how traditions could be recast, reworked, and used in the promotion of the political ambitions of later groups and individuals.

The Nature of Early Medieval Society

Little evidence survives to give us a picture of this early Welsh culture. Economically, Wales was poor. The economic basis of society was pastoral farming, with cows being the primary livestock. Settlements were probably small and dispersed, and there may have been seasonal shifts, with at least some people moving into upland pastures for parts of the year, following their herds. Kings and nobles received renders in food and other goods from the farmers (often of unfree status) who worked the land. To collect these renders, kings moved around their domains with their households, and consumed what was due to them in or near the place where it was produced.

Across Wales the same language was spoken and there was an awareness that the ethnic origins of the Welsh – who throughout the early medieval period seem at least partly to have continued to characterise themselves as 'Britons' – were different to that of their neighbours in the English kingdoms and in Ireland. Despite this, the idea of Wales as a single unit may have been less well formed – there would be only one period, and that lasting only nine years, when all Wales would be politically united, and political identity was a potent force. Early medieval Welsh political identity centred more on region than on common language and origins. Groups and individuals identified themselves with their home territory – Gwynedd, Ceredigion, Gwynllŵg – and rivalries between territories were intense, important and often violent. Alongside identity defined by the home kingdom or chiefdom was a powerful sense of identity defined in terms of kinship, and this latter may well have been the dominant form of identity for most people. Direct early evidence is sparse, and much must be inferred from later medieval sources, in particular law codes. Kinship – and in particular details of descent – were a key way in which the individual was defined and located within society.

It has been mentioned how genealogies were manipulated and rewritten to justify annexations, legitimacy and claims to power, and the insistence in these texts on the importance of royal ancestors vividly illustrates the importance of kinship. Ancestry in particular defined the individual's right to inherit property, land and status. Land was owned by extended family groups, and not by individuals, and individuals' right to exploit it depended on their ability to prove their connection by blood. Land was the basis of wealth and also of status. Kin-groups which owned land were the highest ranks of society, and their leaders its most influential men. It is likely that some kings were drawn originally from these groups. Men were only considered fully adult when they came into possession of their father's land, so that the sons of landowners remained subordinate even in adulthood, so long as their fathers lived. Many people did not belong to land owning families, and were dependent on the landowners whose lands they worked: some of these may have been bound directly to the land, and effectively the property of their lords.

Popular mythology insists that women in Wales (and indeed in the other Celtic countries) enjoyed unusual social and sexual freedom, but this was, in fact, not the case. Women were denied access to own land, and had little or no control over the bulk of property. Their social position was defined in terms of the status of their nearest male relative – father, husband, brother, son – and not in terms of themselves. At no point did women enjoy full control over their lives: marriages were arranged through kin-groups, and women used to cement alliances formed between factions, neighbours and rivals. Even virginity and sexual chastity were in many respects the possessions not of the woman, but of her male kin and her overlord (the landowner, or the local king), and they received compensation from her husband's family on her marriage, as her virginity was a valuable commodity. Rape was a crime against property, not just an assault on the woman, and her male kin were thus owed compensation.

With the social emphasis placed on rank and position in the hierarchy, many people enjoyed less than full rights (in modern terms). Adulthood seems in some ways to have been defined in terms of a particular, male, model. The only people who enjoyed full participatory rights were men of free birth and high rank, and who were senior in their kin-groups. Women, younger men whose fathers were still living, and men from lower social classes lacked the ability to participate fully in the regulation of society and had restricted rights in law. The fully adult individual seems to have been conceived of in terms of warrior-hood. Society was dependent on the agricultural base (and thus on those who worked in it), but such people enjoyed less respect than those who were free to cultivate martial skills and participate in public warfare on a non-mandatory basis. Participation in raids and wars was a duty of the male nobility and it is their exploits and abilities which are most highly praised in extant poetry.

Political action too seems to have been restricted to a warrior élite, and their support was vital to every king. In order to maintain power, a king needed the approval and backing of the major nobility of his lands, and to keep this, he had to woo them with regular gifts, rewards and honours. A king who lost the support of his nobility was liable to be overthrown, expelled, replaced with a rival, or even murdered. The importance of noble support was all the greater because kingship in early medieval Wales was not inherited on a simple father – eldest son basis (male primogeniture). Rather, as with land, any male descendant had at least a theoretical right to become the next king – this included illegitimate sons alongside those born from formal marriages, as well as nephews, brothers, and cousins over several degrees.

Clockwise from top left:
26. Early medieval decorated slab from Llangammarch church, Powys.
27. Early medieval pillar cross from Llandough, Glamorgan.
28. Early medieval decorated slab from Llangyfelach, Glamorgan.

Where land was concerned, it might be divided amongst heirs, or exploited communally, but this was much less practical where kingship was concerned. It was not impossible – there are instances in early medieval Wales of groups of brothers ruling together, as, for instance, occurred in Gwynedd in the mid-tenth century under the sons of Idwal Foel. However, shared kingship often led to rivalries, factionalism, and open conflict, and the deaths of kings could often be followed by bloodshed as the various eligible parties manoeuvred for position and power. As a result, the warrior nobility played a vital part in the maintenance of kingdoms and the ordering of society, and indeed some members of the nobility even rose so high as to displace the old royal house with their own.

The Churches In Early Medieval Wales

Christianity had come to Wales during the Roman period. No details survive as to its conversion, including how long it took for the kingdoms of what became Wales to be fully Christianised, but by the time they emerge into the historic record in the sixth and seventh centuries, it seems that Christianity was widely and well established.

The nature of the early church (or perhaps more correctly churches) in Wales cannot be determined very precisely. Gildas depicts a sub-Roman British church organised on semi-familiar lines. He describes bishops ruling over what seem to be territorially defined dioceses, drawn from the upper echelons of society and involving themselves in the conduct of secular political life. He also wrote of monasteries, which formed centres of education and scholarship. The Anglo-Saxon monk Bede, writing in the early eighth century, knew of British bishops living at the time of St Augustine, the leader of the Roman mission to the Anglo-Saxons which traditionally began in 597 AD. He also wrote of British monks, but gave few details. He knew of no traditions of any involvement of British Christians in the conversion of the Anglo-Saxons (who were pagan when they first settled in Britain) and considered this as a critical flaw in the nature of British Christianity. The Anglo-Saxon invasions had to some degree served to isolate the churches in Britain from the rest of Western Christendom, and, as a result of this isolation, by the time Bede was writing, the Welsh churches had some differences to mainstream, Roman-centred Christianity.

An important issue for the early church everywhere was when to celebrate the moveable feasts of the Christian year, especially Easter. The date of Easter had to be calculated in advance, to ensure that it was celebrated uniformly on the same day. Sets of computational aids – Easter tables – had been created for this purpose and disseminated from Rome and other centres, but early versions of these were unsatisfactory, and there were a number of revisions. By the sixth century, Rome and the churches subject to and in regular contact with it, were using the Dionysian tables, but the churches in Wales (and also in Ireland and what became Scotland) were still using earlier tables which gave different dates. Thus, in any given year, the Anglo-Saxon churches and the Welsh churches would be celebrating not only Easter but also its associated events, including Lent, at different times. This variation in practice created problems between representatives of the different methods, and was considered negative and divisive by Bede, who felt that all churches should be in line with Rome. The discrepancy was not resolved easily or swiftly, and the churches in Wales continued to operate their own system of calculating Easter some time after Bede's lifetime (the traditional date for the adoption of Roman Easter in Wales is 768). This probably contributed to the largely negative picture he gave of them.

Evidence for the Welsh churches between the early eighth and the eleventh centuries is thin. The Welsh chronicles, known as the *Annales Cambriae* (written in Latin, and extant in three different but related versions known as A, B and C) and the *Brutiau* (written in Welsh, and extant in three different but related versions known as Pen. 20, RB and BS) give a few brief glimpses of the early Welsh churches. They note the deaths of a handful of bishops along with a few other items of church interest (such as the construction in *c.*645 of the monastery of St David's). It is by no means clear that these entries were made contemporaneously with the events they record; indeed, episcopal deaths and monastic foundations are the types of information which tend to be preserved in local tradition, to be inserted into historical texts and to have dates back-calculated. However, from these scattered references we can identify a number of ecclesiastical centres which existed in Wales by the ninth or tenth centuries at the latest, including a see at St David's, another perhaps at Bangor, and monastic foundations at Llancarfan, Llanilltud Fawr, Llanbadarn, Llandudoch, Llandeilo, and Clynnog Fawr. Most of these centres were associated with particular saints – Dewi (David), Padarn, Cadog, Illtud, Deiniol, Teilo and others, and the monasteries may have had loose networks of dependent churches or centres dedicated to the same saint as the patron of the main house.

The nature of ecclesiastical life in Wales in this period is obscure. From the chronicles, and from the evidence of the late ninth century *Life of King Alfred*, written by a Welsh churchman from St David's, Asser, it appears that at ninth-century St David's, at least, the community was considered a monastery, but its head was a bishop, not an abbot. St David's possessed various dependencies, from which it derived revenue, probably mainly in kind, and it was a centre of scholarship, at which churchmen were educated and worked. Llandeilo Fawr seems similarly to have possessed lands and influence over an extensive hinterland. Some of these churches were closely linked to particular families, who held offices within them and passed these offices on to their children as both bishops and abbots could be married. It may be that some of the monks also belonged to hereditary monastic clans who worked church lands and had an interest in the activities and welfare of their monastery or church. This is not to say that the churches were entirely secular. It is clear from extant evidence that there was a fair amount of literary and scholarly activity at churches in Wales. The Lichfield Gospels, a fine illuminated manuscript dated to the eighth century, may have been produced in Wales, and certainly were kept at Llandeilo Fawr in the ninth century. Also in the ninth century, Asser was summoned to the court of the Anglo-Saxon king, Alfred the Great to assist him in his programme to increase the level of scholarship and learning in his kingdom of Wessex. Welsh scholars seem to have travelled to Ireland, and there were teachers of Welsh origin in Anglo-Saxon England in the tenth century (and probably earlier). Welsh monks composed and compiled chronicles (and perhaps genealogies) at St David's in the mid-ninth century, and at the end of the eleventh century the churches of St David's, Llanbadarn, Llandaff and Llancarfan all possessed communities of talented, and well-trained men who composed Saints' Lives, wrote poetry in Latin, and defended traditional Welsh ecclesiastical life against the reforming tendencies of the incoming Normans.

THE RISE OF THE HOUSE OF MERFYN

At the beginning of the early medieval period, Wales was a land of many small kingdoms and many competing royal dynasties. Over time, a number of the smaller ones were absorbed by larger or more expansionist neighbours. Others transferred backwards and forwards between the spheres of influence of larger kingdoms, or were intermittently part of larger blocks, but returned to smaller bounds from time to time. The history of these changes and developments is complex, and much of it remains obscure, not least because historical records have not survived uniformly across Wales. We are far better informed about kingdoms of the west – Dyfed, Ceredigion and Gwynedd, than about, for example, Gwent and Glywysing in the south-east. While part of this may be due to simple accidents of survival, much of it is due to the domination of Welsh medieval historiography by one particular royal family. This was the House of Merfyn Frych (also known as the House of Rhodri Mawr and the Second Dynasty of Gwynedd), which dominated Welsh political life from the early ninth century down throughout much of the early middle ages and on to the Edwardian Conquest in 1283.

Merfyn Frych ap Gwriad does not seem to have been a member of any of the old royal dynasties of Wales, and there is some evidence to suggest his family may have come from the Isle of Man. During the early part of the ninth century, down to about 825, there was a faction fight going on in Gwynedd. The combatants were brothers, Hywel and Cynan sons of Rhodri, and they claimed their descent from Cunedda and Maelgwn Gwynedd. By 816, Hywel emerged triumphant over his brother, but when he died in 825, he was not replaced from within his dynasty. Instead, the new king of Gwynedd was Merfyn Frych. It may be that Merfyn belonged to, or had become part of, the higher nobility of Gwynedd; he might even have served in the military household of Hywel. No reliable details of his rise survive, but he must have been able to gather sufficient resources and support to make himself king, and to maintain that position. A pedigree, surviving in a manuscript of c.1100 AD, and composed perhaps in the middle of the tenth century, claims that his mother was Essyllt, a daughter of Hywel's brother, Cynan. However, other pedigrees claim that Essyllt was his wife: the tradition is unstable, and owes more to a later desire to legitimate Merfyn's rise to power than to ninth-century reality. However he gained control of Gwynedd, he seems to have held it securely, and his position was accepted by the leaders of society. In was in his reign in Gwynedd that the *Historia Britonnum*, with its attacks on the legitimacy of the royal line of Powys, was composed. We do not know if Merfyn played any part in the creation of this text, and it may well have been written without his knowledge, but its author does not question Merfyn's legitimacy as king, and to a degree validates him.

Merfyn died around 844 as king of Gwynedd, and was succeeded by his son, Rhodri. The heirs to the old royal house of Gwynedd – if there were any – apparently lacked the support or power to threaten him. Rhodri – known to history as Rhodri Mawr, the Great – is often regarded as the true architect of his family's success. He seems to have been aggressive and ambitious, and, moreover, able to benefit from political upheavals in Anglo-Saxon England. This was the era of the First Viking Age, and the Anglo-Saxon kingdoms were under increasing threat from land-hungry Viking invaders and settlers. Beleaguered Anglo-Saxon kings had no time to raid Wales or depress the ambitions of a Welsh king. Additionally, Mercia, the kingdom bordering Wales, had been in decline since the early ninth century and its leaders pressured by the expansionist plans of their southern neighbour, Wessex. In this atmosphere, Rhodri was able to consolidate his power over Gwynedd, and probably to look to expand his control beyond it. Certain later genealogies linked him to the royal line of Powys, by claiming that his mother was Nest, sister of Cyngen, king of Powys. As with the pedigrees for Merfyn the tradition is unstable – another text states Nest was Rhodri's grandmother – but as with Merfyn there are indications of an attempt to justify later political reality through manipulation of the kinship records. Powys had had its own separate royal line, but in *c.*856 its last representative, Cyngen, died at Rome. When Powys reappears in the historical record, it is subject to the overlordship of Gwynedd, and it may be that Rhodri was the instigator of this conquest. He also seems to have pushed south at the expense of the coastal kingdom of Ceredigion. As with Powys, the last representative of the old royal house of Ceredigion, Gwgan ap Meurig, died (by drowning) during the reign of Rhodri. Again, later pedigrees affiliate Rhodri to the displaced house, stating that he married Gwgan's sister, Angharad. For much of his long reign, he seems to have dominated Welsh political life. Only late in his life is he known to have faced serious danger, and that from the Vikings. He died in battle in 878, still fighting to defend and expand Gwynedd.

By the time of his death, he may have dominated much of northern and central Wales. He was succeeded by his three sons, Anarawd, Cadell and Merfyn, who may have held their lands in common, ruling as co-kings, although Anarawd, the eldest, was senior among them. Under these three, the expansion of the dynasty was consolidated, and conquests which may have been tentative or partial under Rhodri became definite, and, in at least one case, permanent. By around 904, the House of Merfyn had annexed south west Wales, ending its old, Irish-descended royal line.

The details of the rise of the House of Merfyn remain obscure, and it is debated to what extent the expansion was engineered by Rhodri, or by Rhodri's sons, but by 904, this incoming dynasty had changed the face of Welsh political life forever. The line divided into two, the northern and southern branches. The northern branch, the descendants of Anarawd, were kings of Gwynedd, the southern branch, kings of Deheubarth (Dyfed and Ystrad Tywi together). Up until the second decade of the tenth century, the House of Merfyn enjoyed unusual unity amongst its members, but this was to change under the generation after Anarawd (died *c.*916): thereafter conflict and rivalry between the northern and southern branches became a major theme in Welsh political life. There are several reasons for this. In the first place, as the dynasty's lands expanded, they also became harder to control, and degrees of regional difference increased. To maintain domination over lands once independent a local presence was needed and ties to local leading men had to be formed. It is likely, therefore, that certain members of the dynasty developed closer links to particular areas. This in turn would tend to foster regional loyalties and perhaps lead to rivalry. Moreover, while groups of brothers may well be able to sustain unity while acting in a common interest, trans-generational groups (uncles and nephews, say) or groups of cousins, enjoy looser bonds of affection and loyalty and have less incentive to foster shared, as opposed to individual, interest.

The dynasty reached its early medieval peak in the tenth century, in particular under two kings, both from the southern branch – Hywel Dda ap Cadell and Maredudd ab Owain ap Hywel Dda. Hywel was a grandson of Rhodri Mawr; his father, Cadell, had played a part in the annexation of Deheubarth from its old royal line, along with his brothers Anarawd and Merfyn. According to later tradition, the three brothers had divided their lands between them, Anarawd taking Gwynedd, Merfyn Powys and Cadell Deheubarth. This cannot be proved, however, and should be regarded as unreliable at best: the order of expansion of the dynasty is not certain, and in its earlier generations it is likely its members operated as a group, rather than taking separate territories. However, it is the case that the grandsons of Rhodri are found at least initially restricting themselves to specific areas of Wales. This is not

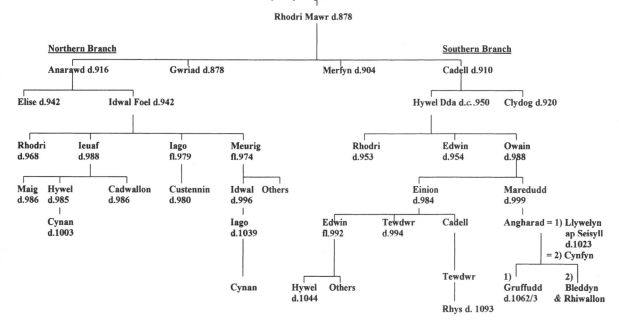

29. The House of Merfyn, ninth to mid-eleventh centuries.
30. The Hywel Dda coin, the only known coin to bear the name of a medieval Welsh ruler.

to say that they considered themselves to have a right only to those territories in which they are first found ruling, as will be seen. Hywel at first ruled Deheubarth jointly with a brother, Clydog, but when Clydog died in 920, Hywel was left as sole king.

The political landscape of Wales in Hywel's lifetime was considerably different to what it had been a hundred or a hundred and fifty years earlier. Much of this change was down to the rise of the House of Merfyn, which had ended the independence of a number of other kingdoms. However, external factors had also played a part. The Viking invasions of the ninth century had resulted in considerable changes in neighbouring England. Some of these changes had already been underway at the dawn of the Viking age – the central midland kingdom of Mercia, which was the closest to Wales and had probably had the most regular relations with Welsh kings and kingdoms, had declined in influence from the beginning of the ninth century, and had faced increased aggression from its south-western neighbour, Wessex. Viking invasions and settlements had put an end to the Anglo-Saxon kingdoms of Northumbria, East Anglia and, eventually, Mercia, leaving only Wessex independent. New Viking dynasties had imposed themselves and created new kingdoms from the old Anglo-Saxon ones. The most influential of these was one stretching across the Irish Sea, uniting the cities of York and Dublin. New political groups had been created and the political geography of the British Isles had been redrawn. Inevitably, this affected Wales. Rhodri Mawr and his sons had benefited from Anglo-Saxon distraction, and especially the eclipse of Mercia, in their expansion of the lands held by their line. However, the destruction of most of the former Anglo-Saxon kingdoms would in the long run lead to the dominance over all England by the kings of Wessex, and this process was already considerably advanced when Hywel became king. Hywel had to deal with a more centralising English neighbour, and as a result was to operate on a wider political stage than many of his predecessors.

From the time of Alfred the Great, Welsh kings had been drawn into at least nominal submission to the kings of Wessex. This reached its peak in the time of Hywel, who paid a number of visits to the court of the kings of Wessex. He was joined in this by other kings from Wales, in particular from south-east Wales (the last area to retain its old dynasties), but Hywel seems to have been treated as the foremost amongst them, and to have been regarded with respect. The early years of Hywel's reign are relatively obscure, and it is difficult to know what factors influenced this high status. In North Wales, rule had passed to Anarawd's son Idwal Foel, who was largely hostile to the kings of Wessex: on at least one occasion, he was temporarily expelled from his lands by the English king Athelstan (924-939). Athelstan was a forceful and effective king, and a dangerous potential enemy. Hywel seems to have chosen to avoid confrontation with him, and to accept his overlordship to preserve the peace and stability of his own lands. It has been argued that Hywel may have admired Athelstan or his grandfather, Alfred the Great, and to have adopted a pro-English stance as a result. In the context of the early tenth century, there is some logic to this. Wales had suffered largely only indirectly from the Vikings, but their impact throughout the British Isles had been extensive, and ties of trade and communication across the Irish Sea had been disrupted or even, perhaps, severed. The kings of Wessex had proved the most successful force resisting further Viking expansion, and Anarawd had been able to benefit from an alliance with Alfred the Great to expand his power southwards against the old royal line of Dyfed. Hywel may well have become king in a time when alliance with the most powerful English king was a sensible and pragmatic political act. It is certainly likely that he recognised the military and political talents of Athelstan, and the relatively small resources of a Welsh kingdom by comparison with those available to the king of Wessex. War with, or resistance to Athelstan, may well have appeared dangerous or even impossible.

This is not to say, however, that Hywel was not himself ambitious. There is some, admittedly late, evidence to suggest that he may have taken steps to strengthen and expand the nature of his personal kingship by associating himself with the operation of law in Wales. Welsh law was customary – it had come into being through use and practice, rather than through the decrees of kings, and kings had little or no direct control over its operation. The prefaces attached to some Welsh legal manuscripts ascribe to Hywel a deliberate codification and revision of law throughout Wales. It is not possible to demonstrate that this tradition is reliable, but what does emerge from it is that Hywel was remembered within Welsh history as a ruler with the necessary status and authority potentially to have done such a thing.

He clearly possessed considerable political insight. For the first part of his reign, while Athelstan dominated political life within much of Britain, Hywel seems to have restricted himself to his lands in south west Wales, avoiding negative attention. In this, he contrasted with his cousin, Idwal of Gwynedd, who seems to have resented Athelstan's dominance. Hywel had not forgotten that his father and uncles had held sway over most of Wales. In c.942, Idwal met his death, fighting the Anglo-Saxons. By this time, Anglo-Saxon overlordship over the Welsh kings seems to have weakened, and Hywel moved swiftly to capitalise on this opening. He drove Idwal's sons from Gwynedd and took it for his own, recreating the hegemony of Anarawd and his brothers. Before 944, he had also moved west, seizing the small kingdom of Brycheiniog and extinguishing its old royal line. Only the south east (Morgannwg) lay outside his control, and he would retain his dominant position for the rest of his life. He would also be remembered as one of the most widely influential of the early rulers in Wales. When he died in 949 or 950, his sons were unable to retain Gwynedd, which was regained by the sons of Idwal, but they did not lose their interest in the south east, and would put consistent pressure on Gower and Morgannwg.

It may be to Hywel's son Owain that we owe the origins of what has been characterised as the 'cult' of Hywel. Owain enjoyed a long and secure reign in Deheubarth, and, like Merfyn Frych, may have been a patron of historical writing. During Owain's reign, the earliest extant version of the native Welsh chronicles, the A-Text of the *Annales Cambriae*, was compiled, using a mixture of local tradition, older Welsh records and chronicles from Ireland. Alongside this chronicle, a series of pedigrees were recorded, giving many of the old, defunct lines of Wales, plus that of the House of Merfyn. At the time these were being written down, Gwynedd was in the hands of the sons of Idwal, but the pedigrees omitted all of the House of Merfyn descended from Anarawd ap Rhodri Mawr. This gave the impression both that the sole legitimate representative of the line in the mid-tenth century was Owain ap Hywel Dda, leader of the southern branch of the dynasty, and that Owain and his sons were the rightful rulers of Gwynedd as well as Deheubarth. The claim of the southern branch to North Wales was to be resurrected more directly by Owain's son, Maredudd, king of Deheubarth c.984-999. Maredudd exploited internal feuding within the northern branch in the 980s to intrude himself into at least intermittent control over Gwynedd. Like his grandfather, Hywel Dda, Maredudd would be remembered in the Welsh chronicles as 'king of the Britons', a title reserved only for kings with powers extending beyond the boundaries of their original lands.

Maredudd's career has been overshadowed by Hywel's and he lived in a more difficult age. English intervention in Wales began to increase again from around the 970s, and the same period saw a new wave of Viking raids on Welsh coastal lands. With his elder brother, Einion, Maredudd had put considerable pressure on the south-eastern Welsh kingdoms, and may have achieved at least a loose overlordship over parts of them. Einion seems to have had an eye to the north, but was thwarted by its most effective late tenth-century king, Hywel ab Ieuaf ab Idwal. The death of Hywel, however, which occurred c.985, provided Maredudd with an opportunity to strike north at the expense of Hywel's brother Cadwallon. Viking attacks troubled Maredudd's hold on the north, particularly in Anglesey, and his core territories remained those of the south, but it is clear that his influence was wide reaching, and he probably excluded the northern branch from Gwynedd for much of the last fifteen years of the tenth century.

His importance to the medieval Welsh state was greater in his own lifetime and in the subsequent century or so than is now remembered, for descent from him was to be recalled or claimed as a legitimising factor by a number of eleventh century kings. He would be the last member of the House of Merfyn in the direct male line to enjoy wide power or lasting and significant political influence in Wales in the pre-Norman period, however. After his death, the House of Merfyn went into eclipse, and its importance only really re-emerged in the twelfth century, under Owain Gwynedd, a great, great, great, great grandson of Idwal Foel.

RELATIONS WITH ANGLO-SAXON ENGLAND

Anglo-Saxon England was a major influence on the development of early medieval Wales. Even the word 'Wales' is Anglo-Saxon in origin, reflecting their word for foreigner, and the shape of the eastern borders of Wales were shaped in part by the process of annexation and colonisation of British lands by the Anglo-Saxons. The activities of Anglo-Saxon kings and settlers would play a significant role in the development of Welsh political life. The record of contacts is incomplete, and piecemeal over both time and geographically, but it is still possible to draw at least an outline of this long and complex process.

The very earliest contacts were probably violent, although it is likely that once settlement was underway, there was also more peaceful contact, trade and intermarriage, and some Anglo-Saxon kingdoms, such as *Magonsaete* (in the border between England and Wales) had ruling lines with British blood. It is in the seventh century, however, that the record begins to be fuller. The exact shape of the Anglo-Welsh border at this period is not certain, but it is known that kings from the northern English kingdom of Northumbria had been expanding over the Pennines and threatening lands subject to kings from Powys and Gwynedd. This movement not only affected the extent of native rule, it also impacted on relations between the various northern Welsh kingdoms. At least one royal house, which may have been a sub-division or cadet branch of the first dynasty of Powys, had once held lands in what is now Shropshire, from which they were expelled in the sixth and seventh centuries. The displacement of rulers and their followers would have led to increased pressure on the resources of their neighbours, and might have altered the balance of Welsh native politics through the removal of an ally or a rival. Around 615, the Northumbrians won a battle against the Welsh of Powys, and perhaps also Gwynedd. This conflict may have destabilised the balance of power in north-east Wales, and probably served to weaken the kings of Powys. It also left the Northumbrian kings with a lasting interest in the lands around Chester and to the west.

Early Anglo-Saxon England was not a single or united polity, however, and it was not only the North Welsh who were threatened by Northumbrian ambitions. Northumbria's neighbour, the midland kingdom of Mercia, also stood to suffer. Mercia had borders with Wales, and it is very likely that there had already been considerable contacts – both violent and peaceful – between Welsh and Mercians at all social levels. The expansion of Northumbria created an environment which was to produce the first certain recorded alliance between Welsh and English kings. The Welsh king was Cadwallon ap Cadfan of Gwynedd, whose lands had been under pressure from the Northumbrian king Edwin; the English king was Penda of Mercia, whose independence was also under threat. The two formed an alliance in or before c.633, and took the offensive against Edwin. Invading his lands, they killed him in battle. However, the removal of their common enemy seems to have been only one stage in their plan: after Edwin's death, Penda and Cadwallon continued to harass and attack Northumbria, killing two potential successors to Edwin. Their aim was probably to destabilise the kingdom, perhaps to reduce it to its original, rival, components (Bernicia and Deira) and to put an end to the threat it represented to their own lands and ambitions. Cadwallon pushed as far east as York, and, according to Bede, arrogated to himself some aspects of the Northumbrian kingship. From this, it appears likely that Cadwallon was the senior partner in the alliance, and it may even be the case that he was its instigator, yet his eminence was short-lived. By 635, Cadwallon too had been killed in battle by a new Northumbrian king, Oswald. Penda survived him, and in c.642, killed Oswald in battle near Oswestry, in a battle which may have involved Welsh leaders.

Although the evidence for this alliance covers only a short period, it is of great importance. It represents a new stage in Anglo-Welsh relations, with a Welsh king electing to participate actively (and, for a time, successfully) in Anglo-Saxon political life, exploiting rivalries and tensions within an English kingdom to his own advantage. The alliance may have survived Cadwallon's death; Mercia is only thinly recorded for this period, but there is some reason to believe that Cadwallon's successor, Cadfael ap Cynfyn, also had an alliance with Penda, and Penda is said to have recovered and restored Welsh treasures from Oswald's successor, Oswiu. Cadfael may have been involved in Penda's wars against Oswiu. The alliance with Cadwallon had proved useful and valuable to Penda, and it seems that he chose to maintain good relations with Wales – or parts thereof – after Cadwallon's death. His relations with Powys are less clear than those with Gwynedd, and there are hints in place-name evidence that he (or his heirs) may have made some inroads into Powysian lands. This suggests that at this period Gwynedd may have been the stronger of the North Welsh kingdoms, and another aspect of the Mercian-Venedotian alliance may have been mutual expansion at the expense of Powys. It should be remembered, however, that our knowledge of the extent of early Welsh kingdoms is limited, and it is also possible that, in order to secure his border, Penda may have had friendly relations with some Powysian leaders but not others.

Mercia was to prove one of the most significant forces in Anglo-Welsh relations, and its importance was probably greater than is apparent from the surviving records. Both Mercia, and its western neighbour Powys were, in the long-term, to be losers in the battle for dominance over England and Wales, and much of their history is lost to us. It is likely that, as in the earliest period, contacts were a mixture of raids, warfare, territorial aggression, trade, intermarriage, and cultural exchange.

The zenith of Mercian power occurred during the eighth century, under kings Aethelbald and Offa, and the Welsh chronicles record expeditions by Offa into Wales. The Pillar of Elise refers to English aggression, particularly against Powys, and implies that there may well have been attempts at settlement of Powysian lands, again in the eighth century. To Offa's reign, also, is ascribed the construction of Offa's dyke. The interpretation of the dyke is controversial, and parts of it were probably constructed before Offa: it may have represented a buffer zone, an agreed frontier, a defence against raiders, or even a final line of defence for English settlers in Wales. However, the presence of the dyke suggests that whoever organised its building was in some respects more interested in establishing an agreed *status quo* than in conquering Wales in totality. Offa, whose name was attached to the dyke from a fairly early period, had wide-ranging influence and territorial interests across much of Anglo-Saxon England. Like Penda before him, the stability of his lands was aided by peaceful or controlled relations with Wales. His policy, insofar as it may be recovered, appears to have been a combination of selective aggression, and negotiated or imposed assignation of borders.

The earlier stages of Anglo-Welsh relations were characterised by a process of cultural negotiation, as each side sought both to adjust to their neighbours and to establish their own separateness. The arrival in the late eighth and especially the ninth century of the Vikings would alter this for good. As has been mentioned, the creation of new, Scandinavian-controlled states in England and Ireland, the disappearance of many of the old Anglo-Saxon kingdoms, and most of all the rise to supremacy of Wessex led to a new political order. Against the background of change – and in the era of the rise and expansion of the House of Merfyn – a number of kings from South Wales entered into a new alliance with Alfred the Great, king of Wessex, who had made himself the focus of English resistance to the Vikings, and who represented a strong, organised political force.

Welsh kings sought Alfred's aid for a number of reasons. Two, Hyfaidd of Dyfed and Tewdwr of Brycheiniog, wanted protection against the sons of Rhodri Mawr. However, the king of Glywysing, Hywel ap Rhys, and the joint-kings of Gwent, Ffernfael and Brochfael sons of Meurig, whose lands lay in the south east, asked for help against the Mercians. Much of northern and eastern Mercia – the parts furthest from south Wales – was by now subject to the Vikings, but southern and western Mercia had remained in English hands, under the dominance of Alfred. It may be that in the wake of Viking settlements, people from Mercia sought to move south, and attempted to seize new lands, or to replace lost resources by plundering Wales. South-east Wales was possessed of good agricultural land, but its borders were difficult to defend and its kings in this period seem to have been relatively weak. An appeal to Alfred, who as overlord of English Mercia had authority over the Mercians, was a pragmatic move on the part of the native Welsh rulers. Similarly, Alfred may have presented a usefully powerful – but conveniently distant – ally against Anarawd ap Rhodri and his brothers. In the 880s, Alfred may have been encouraging contacts with Wales; he was also attempting to rebuild learning and scholarship within England, and had summoned scholars from throughout Europe, including St David's, to assist him. The presence at Alfred's court of the senior Welsh cleric, Asser, may have raised the profile of Alfred in Wales, and of Wales in Alfredian circles.

However, regardless of the immediate causes, the alliance of the Welsh rulers with Alfred had long-reaching effects. For one, Alfred seems to have been the senior partner in the relationship, and to have regarded the Welsh kings as his inferiors and subordinates, a distinct difference from the relations of Cadwallon and Penda. For another, Alfred may have decided to intervene in internal Welsh affairs to his own advantage. Anarawd and his brothers were the most powerful and politically effective group in Wales and at first had remained aloof from Alfred. More, they had formed an alliance with the Viking king of York, which could

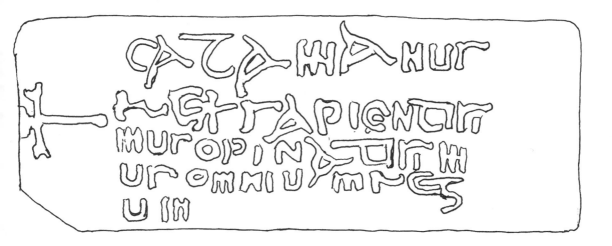

31. Inscribed stone from Llangadwaladr, Anglesey, commemorating Cadfan,
father of Cadwallon.
32. Offa's Dyke, near Knighton, Powys.

potentially pose a threat to Alfred's hegemony. They seem to have considered they had nothing to gain from allying with Alfred.

However, by 893, an alliance had been brokered between Alfred and Anarawd. How this arose is not known. It may be that Anarawd had become disenchanted with his Scandinavian ally and looked for an alternative. It may be that Alfred had sought for and found ways to attract Anarawd into his own sphere of influence. Anarawd was received at court and treated with greater respect than any of the other Welsh kings – a situation which should have rung warning bells for those Welsh rulers whose lands were under threat from the House of Merfyn. The southern Welsh kings (and perhaps also Anarawd) had assisted Alfred's army in campaigns against the Vikings in the Severn-Wye area in 893 and 894. However, the sequel to this was by no means beneficial to all the allies. The Anglo-Saxon force, or part thereof, seems to have remained in the area, and in c.895 assisted Anarawd in an attack on Dyfed. Hyfaidd, the Demetian king who had entered into alliance with Alfred, had died in 893, but he had left heirs. It seems that Alfred chose not to extend the alliance to include these, perhaps recognising that to retain the support of the useful and ambitious Anarawd, some concessions were necessary. The House of Merfyn had succeeded in turning English overlordship into a situation beneficial to themselves, and, during the first half of the tenth century, it became clear that submission to the kings of Wessex brought no automatic right of protection by them from the aggressive rulers of Gwynedd.

Alfred's alliances had another consequence. His heirs and successors inherited the idea of promoting overlordship over the Welsh. The first half of the tenth century saw the gradual re-conquest by the West Saxons of the formerly Anglo-Saxon lands occupied by the Vikings, and an accompanying expansion of West-Saxon royal power. Alfred's successor and son, Edward the Elder, built fortified towns – *burhs* – across southern and central England; one was also built at Rhuddlan. The presence of the latter suggests considerable English influence in north Wales (although it does not have to mean domination – it could equally reflect co-operation). Edward was king of Wessex and overlord of Mercia, which was ruled for him by his sister Aethelflaed and her husband. Both Edward and Aethelflaed took an interest in Wales, suppressing activities which threatened the security of the border, and assisting Welsh leaders against the Vikings. It seems they wished to maintain Welsh support, but also to ensure that they kept a visible position of military supremacy. This is not to say that they enjoyed any direct power in Wales: they did not have the right to raise taxes, for example. But a position was being created in which the king of Wessex was promoted as the senior amongst all kings within Britain, and they took similar steps with regard to kings in North Britain and the Viking areas. Under Edward's son, the forceful and effective Athelstan, Welsh kings were encouraged to visit the English court as honoured subordinates. This served to bind them closer to the king of Wessex, to acquaint them with the extent of his wealth and power, and perhaps to reassure them that their support was valued and their own positions regarded with respect. A number of them served as witnesses to charters granted by Athelstan, their names being recorded high in the witness lists, a mark of honour. Athelstan in particular may have served as a brake on the ambitions of the House of Merfyn. Hywel Dda, as has been seen, waited until well after his death to act on his ambitions to hold Gwynedd, while Hywel's cousin, Idwal Foel of Gwynedd, may have offered resistance to Athelstan, and was punished by brief expulsion.

Athelstan's successors proved less effective. In the 940s, during the reign of Athelstan's brother Edmund, Idwal Foel rebelled and attacked the Anglo-Saxons, an act which cost him his life. Hywel, as has been seen, exploited this to take Gwynedd. Hywel had taken care never to show hostility towards the West Saxon king, and this may be one reason why the expansion of his power met with no resistance from England. However, it may also be that the resources of Edmund, and his successor Eadred, were committed to the war against the Vikings of York – Dublin, and Wales had declined in importance. After the death of Athelstan, no Welsh king is known to have visited the English court, and Edmund and Eadred adopted a more distant attitude to them. Later in the tenth century, Eadred's son Edgar may have tried to impose a nominal submission on some Welsh kings, travelling to Chester to meet them (kings from Scotland and North Britain may also have been present). It has been suggested that the main focus of this was to create an alliance of all kings with lands abutting the Irish sea, an area in which the Vikings were still active: certainly, there seem to have been no immediate military or political consequences for the Welsh kings, none of whom visited Edgar's court or witnessed his charters.

The meeting may have provided an opportunity for one Welsh king to make another kind of alliance, however. This was Hywel ab Ieuaf, who in 973 was engaged in a feud with his uncle for control of Gwynedd. In c.978, Hywel launched a raid on his uncle's lands, accompanied by a force of Anglo-Saxons. They came, probably, from Mercia: Hywel is known to have had an alliance with Aelfhere, the earl of Mercia, by 983 at the latest, by which time he had achieved dominance over Gwynedd and was seeking to move south, at the expense of Einion ab Owain. The motivation behind this alliance on Hywel's side is likely to lie in simple pragmatism: in a divided Gwynedd, he was unable to gather sufficient reliable support and resources to achieve his ambitions. A Mercian earl was a logical ally: Aelfhere had no direct interest in Wales, but it was to his advantage to have a secure border, and a friendly neighbour in Wales, who might help to prevent other Welsh rulers from raiding or harassing English lands. Aelfhere may have had other reasons, too: King Edgar had died in 975, and the reign of his elder son, Edward, was brief and troubled, with factions forming at court. Edward was murdered in 978, in favour of his younger brother Aethelred, who was a minor, and under the influence of a faction to which Aelfhere was opposed. Aelfhere may well have wanted an ally outside Anglo-Saxon England to help bolster his own position. This situation would repeat itself in the mid-eleventh century. Ultimately, however, the alliance rebounded on Hywel: Aelfhere died before 985, and in 985 Hywel was attacked and killed by the Anglo-Saxons, perhaps in punishment for his dealings with Aelfhere, perhaps because his growing power threatened the border.

While the picture of Anglo-Welsh relations before the eleventh century remains sketchy, one thing is very clear. Neither side could afford to ignore the other. Political and military contacts have left the clearest marks, but other kinds of interchange must also have happened. In the border zone, trade and intermarriage will have played a part in producing a culturally and linguistically mixed society. Scholars from Wales visited centres of learning in England as teachers, and perhaps also as pupils. Changes in the Anglo-Saxon world had long-lasting effects on Welsh life, and some Welsh kings may have adopted aspects of Anglo-Saxon practice in their own behaviour.

THE VIKINGS

The Vikings are first recorded as active in Wales in the mid-ninth century – considerably later than our earliest records of Viking activity elsewhere in the British Isles. This is not to say that the Vikings came late to Wales: it is likely, given that Viking fleets were active in the Irish sea from the late eighth and early ninth centuries, that there had been earlier attacks on Wales which had gone unrecorded. Indeed, a late Irish text, the *War of the Gael and the Gaill*, may refer to a Viking attack on Anglesey in the late eighth century. As has been argued above, Viking raids on Anglo-Saxon England had a significant impact for Wales, not least in terms of changes in Anglo-Welsh relations. Viking activity within Wales is more difficult to assess, and much of the evidence is slight or hard to interpret. Recent archaeological discoveries, however, are fleshing out our knowledge, and may eventually provide a more secure context for our understanding.

The Welsh chronicles record sporadic raids, mostly on coastal locations, particularly monasteries, from the mid-ninth down to the late eleventh centuries. These may be supplemented by written sources from England and Ireland, which give information on the movements of Viking fleets and armies. There is no reliable early written record of any long-term attempt at settlement within Wales by Vikings, which is in contrast to events in England, Ireland, Scotland and on the Continent. The main evidence for possible settlement comes from place name studies and from archaeology. The place name evidence consists of a number of names, predominantly attached to coastal locations and features, which appear to contain Scandinavian personal names or words of Scandinavian origin: examples include Anglesey, including the Norse name Ongul; Swansea, perhaps incorporating 'Swein'; Fishguard, and Priestholm. Many of these places possess parallel Welsh names which are thought to have been in use over very long periods of time. It has been argued that for the Scandinavian-influenced names to have survived there must have been Scandinavian speakers settled in nearby areas. However, it must also be borne in mind that parts of the Welsh coast, and particularly the Bristol Channel and the north coast, were regularly travelled by ships engaged in trade throughout the Irish Sea (and in particular trade focusing on Bristol, Chester and Dublin). Throughout much of the medieval period many of the ships involved were Scandinavian, or Hiberno-Scandinavian. The coastal names – many of which are attached to features such as rocks which would have been important in navigation – may have arisen as a by-product of this trade and not through Viking settlers within Wales. Moreover, in the early twelfth century, the Norman king of England, Henry I, introduced settlers from Flanders into south-west Wales. The language spoken by these Flemings has also left a mark on place-name evidence, and it can be hard to distinguish between Flemish and Scandinavian influence in some cases. Place names are notoriously difficult to interpret, and can and do change over time: it is very hard indeed to date them, and as a result we cannot always be sure of either their original form or of when they were first applied. It cannot be said with any certainty that any of the place names in Wales which seem to show Scandinavian influence go back in time to the Viking age.

This is not to deny that there may have been a Scandinavian presence, at least intermittently, in Wales. Until the 1990s, archaeological evidence for the Vikings in Wales was thin. A number of coin hoards are known from coastal north Wales, dateable to the Viking period, and perhaps associated with the trade route from Chester, or reflecting raiding activity in that area (known to have occurred in the later ninth and tenth centuries). In the Chester hinterland are several carved stone monuments whose decoration shows Scandinavian influence (again reflecting contact, and perhaps the presence of Scandinavian craftsmen or craftsmen trained to Scandinavian tastes). On Anglesey a single grave has been found showing Scandinavian influence: the burial is of a woman, and the body is accompanied by grave goods of a Scandinavian type (the presence of grave goods may also suggest a pagan, rather than Christian, context, as Christian burials do not usually contain grave goods). Another grave from north east Wales also contains a brooch of a Scandinavian type. In both cases, the individuals buried may have been Scandinavian, and the presence of a Scandinavian woman in particular might well suggest at least a small-scale attempt at settlement. However, goods are not a certain indicator of ethnicity, and individuals could be and were buried with items not native to their culture but acquired through raiding, gift, or trade.

One Irish chronicle (*The Fragmentary Annals of Ireland*) records an attempted settlement in Wales in the early years of the tenth century. It relates how a leader named Ingimund, having been driven out of Dublin, came to north Wales in around 903 and attempted to settle on Anglesey. However, he met with resistance from the local Welsh king and was expelled, eventually finding lands to settle in the Wirral, with the permission of Aethelflaed of Mercia. This text is late and the authority of its details is not unquestionable (notably, it names the north Welsh king as 'the son of Cadell son of Rhodri', presumably intending Hywel Dda, impossible at this date). However, taken with the other material, it contributes to a picture of some small scale attempt at settlement in north Wales, probably during the tenth century. The most convincing evidence to date for this comes from Glyn, Llanbedrgoch, on Anglesey. Excavations at this site have revealed traces of a settlement of Scandinavian type, with evidence of craft-working and trade as well as some agriculture. It is suggested that the site operated as a seasonal market, visited by travelling craftsmen and by ships using the Dublin – Chester route. The settlement's origins seem to predate the Viking period but it seems to have been occupied by Scandinavians during the Viking age, and the occupation seems to have lasted over a fair length of time during the tenth century and perhaps into the eleventh.

The most difficult question to answer is perhaps that of the political context of the Viking presence in north Wales. The politics of north Wales in the tenth century (and especially the second half) are complex, with an ongoing struggle for power between not only members of the northern branch of the House of Merfyn but also involving members of the southern branch. The 970s saw a rise of Viking activity in north Wales, with particular interest coming from the Scandinavian colony on the Isle of Man, led by the sons of Harald, who undertook a series of raids on Welsh lands. It has been argued that Godfrey Haraldsson effected a temporary conquest of some or all of Gwynedd, and certainly of Anglesey at this time. The settlement at Glyn could be interpreted in this context, as a by-product of Viking control. However, it must be pointed out that the evidence for domination by Godfrey – or any other Viking leader – is thin, and much of it is indirect and late. Contemporary Welsh records suggests his presence in Wales was intermittent, and that the succession to power in Gwynedd by members of the House of Merfyn was not interrupted by any outsider (although there was much internal conflict within the family). It is equally possible that the sons of Harald had entered into an alliance with one segment of the northern branch, perhaps because they had an interest in the trade centre on Anglesey, and needed or wanted the compliance of a local leader to help secure it. The kings of Gwynedd could also have derived advantage from this settlement in terms of revenue and access to luxury trade goods. Some of the Viking activity in north Wales in the 970s and 980s also looks opportunistic, with bands taking advantage of local conflicts to make raids and extract danegeld payments. The picture is incomplete, but it is clear that there was at least small-scale Scandinavian settlement in Wales and with it some cultural, economic and perhaps political exchange. During the eleventh century, Welsh kings facing threats from rivals would on several occasions flee to the

33. Arm-rings of Hiberno-Scandinavian type, from Red Wharf Bay, Anglesey.
34. Richard's Castle, Herefordshire. Nest, daughter of Gruffudd ap Llywelyn and Ealdgyth, married its lord, Richard FitzScrob.

Hiberno-Scandinavian settlements in Ireland in search of mercenary fleets to help them regain power. This argues that there was some ongoing contact across the Irish sea (this is also reflected in items of Welsh interest found in Irish chronicles): one king of Gwynedd in the late eleventh and twelfth centuries was to have Hiberno-Scandinavian blood. While the Vikings never played as large a role within Wales as they did elsewhere in the British Isles, and while in the long run their main impact on Wales was indirect, resulting from the political changes they helped produce in England, by the end of the early medieval period, they were a familiar part of the Welsh cultural world.

THE ELEVENTH CENTURY

The rise of the House of Merfyn from the early ninth century, combined with the impact of the Vikings and the changes in Anglo-Saxon England had altered the face of Welsh politics, ending almost all the old royal lines and, probably, making a major contribution to the development of more permanent larger kingdoms. However, as the tenth century ended, the House of Merfyn entered a period of eclipse. In both Gwynedd and Deheubarth, new dynasties would appear, and it was these, not the House of Merfyn, which would shape much of the eleventh century. The House of Merfyn had not disappeared – in the south in particular, certain members continued to operate, and operate successfully, but it would not regain its dominance of Welsh political life fully until the late eleventh and twelfth centuries.

At some point in the first decade of the eleventh century, one Llywelyn ap Seisyll became king of Gwynedd. His origins are obscure – later tradition affiliated him to the southern branch of the House of Merfyn, but this is unlikely to be reliable. Probably he came from amongst the nobility of north Wales (perhaps north east Wales): certainly, he was a gifted and ambitious leader, who was able to assemble sufficient support not only to secure the kingship of Gwynedd but also to threaten the south. Extant records are thin for the early part of the eleventh century, but it appears that by c.1022 he was in a position to be considered at least the overlord of Deheubarth, when he is found defending that kingdom against an attempt at conquest by one Rhain, who is said by the Welsh chronicles to have been an Irishman claiming descent from Maredudd ab Owain. The account of the chronicler – who at this point was very probably based in south Wales – is very favourable to Llywelyn. This is significant in itself, as it shows that while later historians would question the 'legitimacy' of several eleventh-century Welsh kings on the grounds that they were not descended from the House of Merfyn, this view was not shared by the writers contemporary with these rulers. Llywelyn died c.1023, but during his obscure reign it seems he laid important political foundations, upon which his son, Gruffudd ap Llywelyn, would build.

Gruffudd was probably still young when his father died, and he does not enter our records until 1039. Between Llywelyn's death and the emergence of Gruffudd, Gwynedd was ruled by a minor member of the House of Merfyn, Iago ab Idwal. In the south, the second of the new dynasties made its first appearance. This line came not from Deheubarth but from Gwent: the founder was one Rhydderch ab Iestyn. Like Llywelyn, Rhydderch probably came from the ranks of the nobility, and while he and his descendants held power over at least parts of Morgannwg for much of the period between c.1023 and 1081, they coexisted with at least one of the old royal lines of the south east, and focused much of their attention on control of Deheubarth. As with Llywelyn, no details survive of Rhydderch's rise to power, but at his death in 1033, he had intruded himself into rule over Deheubarth, a claim which would be inherited by his sons, who immediately laid claim to the kingdom against representatives of the House of Merfyn. Their initial bid failed, and Deheubarth passed into the hands of a member of the southern branch of the House of Merfyn, Hywel ab Edwin. Hywel, as far as we know, held Deheubarth securely until 1039, but would spend the last five years of his life, down to 1044, fighting to retain it in the face of a determined onslaught from the north, headed by Gruffudd ap Llywelyn.

Gruffudd was to become the single most effective king Wales had ever possessed, with the widest hegemony, covering all four of the major kingdoms. In 1039, he made himself king of Gwynedd, and almost at once made it clear that he would not be satisfied with this alone. He struck south, forcing Hywel into temporary exile, and then turned east, which was to be his second main area of ambition, ravaging the English border. Notice had been served of his intention to dominate as much of Wales as was possible. Like his father Llywelyn, Gruffudd was not a member in the male line of the House of Merfyn. Llywelyn, however, had married Angharad, a daughter of Maredudd ab Owain of Deheubarth. This marriage, and the resulting claim it gave Gruffudd to the blood – if not the rights – of the southern branch of the House of Merfyn, resembles the marriages claimed for early members of the House of Merfyn: however, unlike the latter, it is likely to be genuine, as it is recorded in sources rather closer in time to Gruffudd's life. It is difficult to know if Gruffudd made much – or any – use of this tie: insofar as we can judge, his power was largely based on rights of conquest and on simple effectiveness. As with his father, there is no trace in any of the contemporary sources that he was regarded as in any way an 'intrusive' or illegitimate ruler. (Indeed, during the twelfth century a connection to Gruffudd was part of the material gathered by the biographer of the later eleventh and early twelfth century king of Gwynedd, Gruffudd ap Cynan, to justify this later Gruffudd's claim to kingship.) Gruffudd ap Llywelyn spent the 1040s and part of the 1050s concentrating on Deheubarth, first killing Hywel ab Edwin (1044) and then fighting and eventually killing Gruffudd, son of Rhydderch ab Iestyn (in 1055/6), who had imposed himself over Deheubarth on the death of Hywel. This second Gruffudd was a major force in his own right, who represented both a challenge to Gruffudd ap Llywelyn and a serious threat to the south-eastern English border: it is no surprise that it is in the time of the two Gruffudds that the leaders of Anglo-Saxon England had again to take notice of Wales.

The king of Anglo-Saxon England was Edward the Confessor, whose reign was dominated by power struggles between his nobility, and especially between the earls of Wessex (Godwine, and later his son Harold) and the earls of Mercia (Leofric and his son Aelfgar). Earl Godwine had a large number of sons, and he sought to have major lands bestowed on as many of them as possible: this threatened the rest of the nobility, and particularly that of Mercia. Godwine was not always in favour with Edward, and in 1051/2 he and his sons were briefly exiled. Harold Godwinesson's lands were temporarily given to Aelfgar, son of Earl Leofric of Mercia, but when Godwine and his sons were reinstated, Aelfgar lost the lands. Mercia had considerable borders with Wales, and throughout the early medieval period Mercian kings and earls had had considerable dealing with the Welsh: Aelfgar and Leofric were doubtless well aware of Gruffudd ap Llywelyn (who had attacked their lands and killed a family member in 1039). Gruffudd, with his widespread power in Wales, was a force to be reckoned with, and Aelfgar in particular did not need another enemy. At some point before 1055, Aelfgar formed an alliance with his neighbour, which would endure into the next generation. We do not know from which party the impetus for this alliance came, although

Aelfgar is the more likely. Godwine had died in 1053, but his sons, and particularly Harold and Tostig, were ambitious. Aelfgar probably feared the loss of his patrimony, and the erosion of his rank at court, and sought to find a powerful friend with whom he could build a power bloc to balance that of Harold. Gruffudd must have appeared an ideal candidate. He had already made one, brief, alliance with an English earl, Swegn, the erratic and difficult eldest son of Godwine, in 1046/7, as part of the campaign to seize Deheubarth. The alliance had not lasted, driven probably by expedience and pragmatism. By 1055, Gruffudd's position in Wales was secure, and he was looking to his eastern boundaries for new lands. Aelfgar was the heir to Mercia, on that eastern border, and thus in a position to confirm or ease expansion (or to resist it, although this did not, in fact, happen). Aelfgar held a high position at the English court, and could be expected to have influence with Edward. Gruffudd and Aelfgar possessed a common enemy in Harold (who also had some lands abutting Wales). An alliance had practical advantages for both in theory, and also, as it was to turn out, in practice. While we do not know exactly when it began, it was in place by 1055 at the latest, in which year Aelfgar was exiled from England temporarily. Together with Gruffudd, he struck at lands in Herefordshire, defeated the local levy, evaded a second army led by Harold and forced Edward to come to terms and reinstate him. Gruffudd benefited by, probably, being granted the rights to lands which had been debated between England and Wales in the border. They repeated this manoeuvre in 1057 (by which time Aelfgar was earl of Mercia), again to their mutual benefit (and the disadvantage of Harold), and at some point sealed the alliance by the wedding of Aelfgar's daughter Ealdgyth to Gruffudd. As part of the peace – negotiations, Gruffudd had accepted Edward as his overlord, but this seems to have been merely nominal: unlike Hywel Dda, Gruffudd never attended the English court or witnessed Edward's grants, and Edward had no effective sanctions against him while Aelfgar lived. By 1060 at the latest, Gruffudd held all of Wales (most of it directly) plus considerable lands in the border, and he had no rivals.

The alliance of Gruffudd and Aelfgar served to bolster the position of both men, and seems to have been important to both of them. When Aelfgar died (before 1063), Harold Godwincsson seems to have been well aware that Gruffudd continued to be a threat – and that Gruffudd might well support Aelfgar's son and heir, Edwin, who might be expected to form part of the faction opposed to Harold. Edward the Confessor had no sons: Harold had ambitions to inherit the throne from him, and thus wanted as much support within England as possible. He may also have born a grudge against Gruffudd for the defeats inflicted on him in 1055 and 1057 (in 1056, indeed, Harold had set up an ineffective plot to damage Gruffudd). Aelfgar's death left Gruffudd more vulnerable, and, with his brother Tostig, Harold led an attack on Wales, aimed at restricting or overthrowing Gruffudd. Gruffudd by this time was no longer young, and his rise to power in Wales was to be remembered in legend as ruthless: he had enemies. Harassed by Harold and Tostig, his power began to collapse. At some point in *c*.1062/3, he was killed by his own household. It is probable that this murder was the result of long-existing resentment and of Welsh ambition, but Harold's actions contributed to weakening him. His hegemony fell apart. Gwynedd and Powys passed into the hands of his maternal half-brothers, Bleddyn and Rhiwallon sons of Cynfyn (who would found another new dynasty, the Second House of Powys). In the south, Deheubarth became a bone of contention between members of the southern branch of the House of Merfyn, and the grandsons of Rhydderch ab Iestyn. Harold married Gruffudd's widow Ealdgyth in an (unsuccessful) attempt to win her brother Edwin over to his own faction.

No other king would ever enjoy such wide power as Gruffudd, who held Gwynedd, Powys and Deheubarth directly and had at the very least overlordship over Morgannwg. His reign impacted the English polity and helped maintain the balance of power between Edward's earls. It also left a memory of Wales as a home of dangerous and powerful kings who could threaten the security of England, a situation which affected the way in which William the Conqueror and his heirs reacted to the Welsh. His half-brothers continued his Mercian alliance until Earl Edwin died in 1072, and this too played a role in Norman perceptions of the Welsh. On the eve of the Norman conquest, Wales had lost its greatest leader.

CONCLUSION

The period between the end of Roman rule and the coming of the Normans saw many changes for Wales. Early, small kingdoms slowly coalesced into or were absorbed by larger units, and the number of dominant royal lines decreased. The rise of the House of Merfyn from the ninth century both created new overkingships and left an indelible mark on Welsh historiography, with its members dominating contemporary historical records. The dawn of the Viking age, corresponding with the rise of this new dynasty, also had a major impact on Wales: with the fall of most of the old Anglo-Saxon kingdoms and the rise of Wessex to dominate all England, later Welsh kings had to learn to deal with powerful and ambitious English kings who sought overlordship throughout Britain. Anglo-Welsh relations had begun in conflict, but developed through raids, wars, alliance and submissions to a point where a king of Wales could play a significant part in shaping English political life. When the Normans arrived in Britain in 1066, the kingdoms of Wales possessed a strong sense of their own ethnicity, identity, culture and, above all, independence.

3

FRONTIER WALES
c.1063 – 1282

A. Huw Pryce

From the late eleventh to the late thirteenth centuries Wales became both more Welsh and more cosmopolitan than it had ever been before. Though a sense of Welsh identity, linked to a particular language and territory, certainly already existed earlier in the Middle Ages, it is only from the period beginning with the first Norman conquests in Wales that we find this identity articulated extensively in the surviving sources and mobilized as a political force by the most ambitious native rulers. In part, this represented a reaction to conquest and settlement by Normans, English, Bretons and Flemings together with attempts at domination by the kings of England. As a result, substantial areas of the country, especially along the southern lowlands from Monmouth to Pembroke but also in the border regions of mid-Wales, came to be ruled and colonized by outsiders. Apart from contributing to demographic growth (which was accompanied by an increase in the size of the native Welsh population), colonization acted as a major catalyst in the dissemination of new influences from England and the Continent, some of which left a permanent mark on the landscape in the form of abbeys, castles and towns.

Unlike England after 1066, however, these conquests were piecemeal and in some cases temporary, only extending to cover the greater part of the surface of Wales in 1277, with the rest falling to Edward I in the war of 1282-3. Welsh dynasties therefore survived alongside the new order and indeed the most powerful of them, in particular the rulers of Gwynedd, made considerable efforts to strengthen their kingdoms. In so doing they not only resisted Norman and, later, English territorial expansion and political subordination but also assimilated aspects of English and European military technology, modes of governance and culture. The last centuries of Welsh political independence therefore present something more complex than a narrative of foreign conquest and native resistance, important though that was. Instead, these political conflicts belonged to a wider process of interaction between different peoples and cultures. In exploring this process I shall begin by sketching in some social and economic background and context before moving on to consider the political, religious and cultural changes of this period.

SOCIETY AND ECONOMY

Wales experienced profound social and economic changes during the two centuries before the Edwardian conquest of 1282-3. The colonization of large areas of the southern coastal lowlands by settlers, mainly from England, introduced by Norman and other lords from the late eleventh century onwards permanently altered the character of areas such as Gwent, the

Vale of Glamorgan, Gower and Pembrokeshire. This settlement not only transformed the ethnic and linguistic composition of substantial parts of Wales, but also brought about urbanization, commercialization and industrialization on a scale unprecedented since the Roman period. Apart from the short-lived early tenth-century Anglo-Saxon *burh* at Rhuddlan, pre-Norman Wales had lacked towns; both the circulation of coin and the use of pottery were minimal. By contrast, between *c*.1070 and 1270 about fifty new towns were established in the country; pottery was not only imported from England and France but also manufactured in the south and north-east; and the use of coin quickened, reflecting a proliferation of markets in town and country. By 1200 the export of wool was already big business, for English lords and Cistercian abbeys alike; by 1250 Welsh cattle were being exported to England by drovers whose successors would continue to ply their trade until the nineteenth century. Moreover, while these changes both originated and were greatest in the areas colonized by settlers from outside Wales, by the thirteenth century they had a significant impact on the territories under Welsh rule too.

Of course, throughout this period Wales remained an overwhelmingly rural country, with a mixed agrarian economy dependent on cereal cultivation and the rearing of livestock, especially cattle and sheep, supplemented by fishing. Yet rural society was neither uniform nor static. The countryside of the most heavily Anglicized areas of south Wales was organized on manorial lines in a similar way to lowland England, with nucleated villages and fields measured by the customary acres of Devon. In native Wales the pattern was more complex. There, too, we find nucleation: around churches and at the bond townships (Welsh: *maerdrefi*) that supported the courts of rulers as they travelled round their lands. Part of one such court site, belonging to the thirteenth-century princes of Gwynedd, has recently been excavated at Rhosyr in south-west Anglesey. The free population, on the other hand, lived in dispersed homesteads such as the farm excavated at Cefn Graeanog near Clynnog Fawr (Caernarfonshire). Moreover, native Wales seems to provide an exception to the strong trend in western Europe at this period towards the erosion of peasant freedom through the spread of serfdom. True, serfs or bondmen and -women were numerous in Welsh society, perhaps accounting for around a third of the population by the thirteenth century; but this probably marked a significant reduction by comparison with the pre-Norman period. While certainly exaggerated, Gerald of Wales's emphasis on the freedom of Welsh society at the end of the twelfth century may not have been entirely wide of the mark. By comparison with the more hierarchical and politically centralized societies of England and northern France, which served as benchmarks for Gerald and his intended readers, native society in Wales not only witnessed an increase in the proportion of those enjoying free status as previously bond townships were enfranchised, but also suffered from less burdensome demands from lords for renders or labour services.

For Gerald, the most striking facet of Welsh freedom was its militarism: the society he portrays so brilliantly, if also misleadingly, in his *Description of Wales* (1194), was a society geared above all else to war. The same was true of the March, where settlers were required to contribute to their lords' defensive needs. Thus, while the burgesses of many Welsh towns were granted the urban privileges known as the laws of Breteuil, they were also expected to perform castle guard, in contrast to normal practice in England. Indeed, the majority of the towns established by Norman and English lords in Wales owed their very existence to military priorities, being sited adjacent to the castles, such as Monmouth, Cardiff, Brecon and Pembroke, that secured the conquerors' hold on the surrounding territory. Nor were native rulers as averse to such castle boroughs as we might infer from Gerald's claim that the

35. Cae Llys, Rhosyr, near Newborough, Anglesey: excavations of court buildings of the thirteenth-century princes of Gwynedd.
36. Clun Castle, Shropshire.

Welsh lived not in towns or villages but only in wattle huts on the edges of forests. The Lord Rhys (d. 1197) retained Llandovery and Cardigan after he had captured them, no doubt appreciating their economic as well as military value; indeed, he made Cardigan, with its settler community including men from Bristol, the effective capital of his reconstituted principality of Deheubarth, symbolized by the rebuilding of its castle in stone in 1171 and the holding of a festival of poetic and musical competitions there five years later. In the thirteenth century, Welsh rulers founded towns from scratch: Rhys's descendant, Rhys ap Maredudd (d. 1291), established towns at Dinefwr, Dryslwyn and Lampeter in the 1270s, while Llywelyn ap Gruffudd (d. 1282), prince of Gwynedd and Wales, planned to set up a borough adjacent to the new castle he began to build at Dolforwyn near Welshpool in 1273.

Gerald's assertion that the Welsh took no interest in trade was inaccurate when he wrote in the 1190s and became even more so during the following century. The militarism which he highlighted itself became a saleable commodity from the mid-twelfth century: Welshmen served as mercenaries in England during the civil war of Stephen's reign (1135-54) and on the Continent from the 1160s onwards. Moreover, Gerald implies that there must have been commercial exchange with England in his observation that the Welsh depended on English imports for supplies of salt, iron, cloth and also corn when harvests failed. In the early thirteenth century Llywelyn ap Iorwerth (d. 1240) of Gwynedd employed merchants and probably also stimulated the transformation of the princely bond settlements at Pwllheli, Nefyn and, above all, Llan-faes on Anglesey into commercial centres. Recent discoveries have unearthed substantial numbers of coins at Llan-faes, some of them minted at Rhuddlan in the first half of the thirteenth century; since Rhuddlan was in Welsh hands for most of this period, this may indicate that the coins, though English in type, were imitations produced at the behest of the prince of Gwynedd as one means of increasing the supply of coinage at a time when renders in kind at centres such as Llan-faes were being commuted into money payments. By 1282 it seems that about thirty ships a year frequented Llan-faes, bringing the prince valuable tolls; in that year Llywelyn ap Gruffudd complained that one of these vessels had been detained at Liverpool and had its goods seized by the justice of Chester. Nor was the export of soldiers and other merchandise the only source of cash. From the late twelfth century Welsh freemen granted land to religious houses in return for rents or lump sums of silver, and there is evidence that some laymen bought land in Gwynedd in the thirteenth century. Admittedly, the scale of commercialization remained very limited in native Wales by comparison with the Marcher lordships of the south, let alone lowland England. But, however great the variations in economic development between different regions of Wales, the trend towards a more widespread use of coin, dependent on a more complex pattern of exchange, is unmistakable.

POLITICS AND POWER

Welsh Rulers, Marcher Lords and English Kings

On Thursday, 29 September 1267 Llywelyn ap Gruffudd, ruler of Gwynedd arrived at Rhyd Chwima, a ford on the River Severn near Montgomery, gave fealty and homage to King Henry III of England, and ratified the peace which his representatives had agreed with the king four days earlier. That peace, known as the Treaty of Montgomery, legitimized the extensive hegemony which Llywelyn had established in Wales over the previous decade or so by granting him and his heirs 'the principality of Wales' together with the title 'prince of

Wales'. Although Llywelyn had already been using this title since 1262, and although it and similar titles had occasionally been deployed by his uncle, Dafydd ap Llywelyn (ruler of Gwynedd, 1240-6) and by the powerful twelfth-century rulers, Owain Gwynedd (d. 1170) and the Lord Rhys of Deheubarth, the English crown had never before recognized either a prince or a principality of Wales. Llywelyn, it seemed, had achieved the goal which had eluded even his most powerful predecessors over the past two centuries: the creation of an extensive native polity in Wales which overshadowed the Marcher lordships established by Norman and English conquerors from the late eleventh century onwards.

Yet if the Treaty of Montgomery represented a triumph for Llywelyn, the principality it legitimized was short-lived. Ten years later, after Edward I's first Welsh war in 1277, it was severely curtailed (Llywelyn, though still acknowledged as 'prince of Wales', had his authority restricted to Gwynedd west of the Conwy). Finally, on 11 December 1282 the prince was killed in a second war with the king which resulted in the annexation of Gwynedd by the English crown. Indeed, the sixteen clauses of the Treaty of Montgomery highlight weaknesses and ambiguities in the political edifice Llywelyn had built and may serve as an introduction to the complexities of power in Wales in the period covered by this chapter.

First, while his territorial hegemony had been forged through military successes, in alliance with native dynasties outside Gwynedd, its constitutional status as a principality was an English creation. It was Henry III who granted the principality to Llywelyn, along with the homages of what the treaty called 'the Welsh barons of Wales', that is, the other Welsh lords whose lands had resisted, or been recovered from, conquest by the Marchers. Moreover, the prince was required, not only to give homage to the king for his principality, but also to pay him the substantial sum of 25,000 marks (over £16,600) in return for this and other grants made in the treaty and 'so that the prince may more fully have the grace of the king and his sons and obtain their good will'. Although Anglo-Saxon kings had intervened militarily in Wales – Harold and Tostig had, after all, led their campaigns against Gruffudd ap Llywelyn as earls appointed by Edward the Confessor – and some, like Edgar (d. 975), had claimed overlordship over Welsh kings, their impact was less profound and durable than that of their Norman and Plantagenet successors, who were not only determined to tighten royal overlordship in Wales but also helped to create and sustain the Marcher lordships.

Second, two clauses offer glimpses of the way that the crown could exploit tensions between Llywelyn and other leading figures of his principality. Gruffudd ap Gwenwynwyn (d. 1286), prince of southern Powys, was not obliged to restore land 'he held while he was with the king, before he went to the fealty and side of Llywelyn' – a switch of allegiance which occurred in 1263 – although claimants could take legal action against him according to the customs of the March; while Llywelyn's brother, Dafydd ap Gruffudd (d. 1283), was to be restored to all the lands he had held before he went over to the king in 1263. Later, in 1274, both men entered into an abortive conspiracy to assassinate Llywelyn and proclaim Dafydd prince in his place, and Edward I's subsequent sheltering of the conspirators became a major bone of contention between the prince and the king. The formation of a Welsh polity under a single prince could not be achieved without conflict both between and within the various dynasties ruling a plural and fluctuating political landscape. One major issue in the history of the period from the death of Gruffudd ap Llywelyn to that of Llywelyn ap Gruffudd is the extent to which Welsh rulers were able to overcome the strong tendencies towards the fragmentation of power.

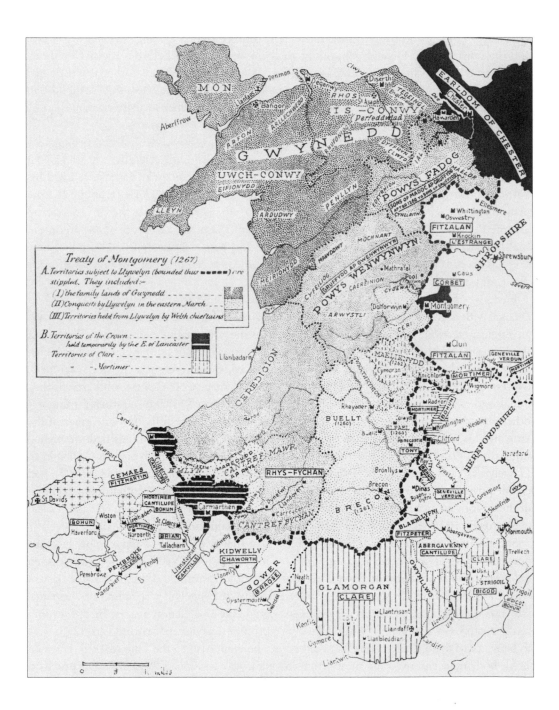

37. Map of Wales in 1267: the Treaty of Montgomery.

This brings us, thirdly, to the contested and fragmented character of the Wales envisaged by the Treaty of Montgomery. Nowhere in the agreement are the boundaries of the new principality precisely defined, although its wide extent, covering three-quarters of the country, is not in doubt. Essentially, it consisted of those areas under either the direct rule of Llywelyn (Gwynedd) or under his overlordship (Powys, the remnants of Deheubarth, territories recovered from the Marchers in mid-Wales), excluding the securely held Marcher lordships in the southern lowlands from Monmouth through Glamorgan to Dyfed. Just over two centuries earlier the brief hegemony of Gruffudd ap Llywelyn, who recovered a broad swathe of territory along the Anglo-Welsh border and whose poet, Berddig, held land in Gwent, was significantly more extensive. The Treaty of Montgomery thus reinforced, even if it also readjusted, the fundamental division between native Wales (*pura Wallia*) and the March which features prominently in a variety of sources from the early thirteenth century onwards. At the same time, however, it reveals that territorial fragmentation and uncertainty were far greater than that formula of binary division might suggest. The focus of the peace negotiators was on particular territories. Thus, of the lands recently conquered by Llywelyn, the prince was to keep the Marcher lordships of Brecon, Gwerthrynion, Builth as well as Cedewain and Ceri, previously ruled by native dynasties of their own. Maelienydd, on the other hand, would be held by Roger Mortimer (d. 1282), lord of Wigmore, until Llywelyn could prove his right to it, while justice would be done according to the customs of the March to anyone claiming lands held by the prince. Far from ensuring territorial stability, the treaty sanctioned a continuation of territorial disputes.

Frontiers and Hegemonies

The Wales of 1267 was, then, a country of many frontiers. In itself, of course, this was nothing new: the same had been true since the Iron Age, and no doubt before that, too. In a medieval context, however, the continuing political fragmentation of Wales (as also of Ireland) through to the late thirteenth century, a fragmentation merely reconfigured by the Edwardian conquest and finally ended only by the union with England in the reign of Henry VIII, ran counter to trends elsewhere in Latin Christendom towards the consolidation and centralization of kingdoms and principalities. True, these trends, exemplified across western Europe from Scotland to Sicily, did not completely pass Wales by. However, they came from two very different, and ultimately mutually incompatible, directions that only served to perpetuate and deepen divisions. On the one hand, the thirteenth-century princes of Gwynedd, especially Llywelyn ap Gruffudd, tried to create a polity embracing native Wales; on the other, kings of England, especially from John (1199-1216) onwards, demanded more precisely defined recognition of their overlordship from Welsh rulers as part of a more general expansion of English royal power in Britain that culminated, in Wales, with Edward I's conquest of 1282-3.

There can be no doubt that the Norman and, in some cases, Breton lords and knights who began to seek their fortunes in Wales within a few years of William the Conqueror's victory at Hastings in 1066 had a profound impact on the political map of medieval Wales. As a result of their conquests, which gathered considerable momentum after the killing of Rhys ap Tewdwr, king of Deheubarth, in the spring of 1093, old divisions were reinforced and new ones created. In the south-west, Dyfed became a land of many lords, some, in the west, ruling territories corresponding to pre-existing administrative districts (*cantrefi*), others, especially in the east, establishing lordships that were new territorial conglomerations, including the king's own lordship of Carmarthen. Ceredigion, on the other hand, remained largely intact, albeit passing to and fro between the Clares, first installed there by Henry I (1100-35), at the expense of the rulers of Powys and the native dynasties of Gwynedd and Deheubarth; from 1165 it formed a core component of the reconstituted Deheubarth of the Lord Rhys. In the north-west, Hugh of Avranches (d. 1101), earl of Chester – one of three border earldoms established by William the Conqueror, the others being at Shrewsbury and Hereford, first held respectively by Roger of Montgomery (d. 1094) and William fitz Osbern (d. 1071) – together with his cousin, Robert of Rhuddlan, took over the kingdom of Gwynedd for some two decades, until the Normans were eventually expelled in 1098. By contrast, the early Welsh kingdoms of Brycheiniog and Buellt were transformed into more durable Norman lordships, Brecon and Builth, and the same was true, up to a point, of the kingdom of Morgannwg, whose successor was the lordship of Glamorgan. However, the authority of the lord of Glamorgan was by no means uniform throughout his lordship; rather, it was concentrated in the lowland 'shire fee' controlled from Cardiff castle and it was only from the mid-thirteenth century that it became truly effective in the theoretically subordinate lordships of the uplands such as Senghennydd and Afan, which until then had largely remained in the hands of native lords.

While the pattern of Norman conquest and settlement in Wales was based to a considerable extent on existing territorial units, it is likely that those units were respected only insofar as they provided a serviceable framework for the exercise of power. After all, men like Earl Hugh of Chester, originally from Avranches near the Norman border with Brittany, were familiar with frontier zones whose boundaries fluctuated. Wherever it occurred, moreover, the essential tool of domination was not the native kingdom, *cantref* or commote, but the Norman castle. Early Norman lordships in Wales, like the 'bannal lordships' held by castellans in eleventh-century France, consisted first and foremost of regions that could be dominated from a castle. This is clear, for example, from the way that some lordships along the Anglo-Welsh border in the late eleventh and twelfth centuries, such as Caerleon, Clun and Montgomery, were referred to as castleries; likewise, the Welsh chronicle's account of the conquest of Ceredigion and Dyfed by the Normans in 1093 was careful to add that they built and fortified castles there. Generally built of timber, as, for example, at Hen Domen (Old Montgomery) – though William fitz Osbern erected a formidable stone castle at Chepstow – and consisting of a defensive tower on an earth mound or motte together with living accommodation in an adjacent bailey, all surrounded by an outer palisade, early Norman castles were relatively quick and easy to build and provided bases for further attacks as well as protection from counter-offensives by the Welsh. They were all the more effective because the Welsh had no castles of their own until the second decade of the twelfth century, and only began to make significant use of them from the middle of that century.

Yet the Normans (or, as their descendants had become by the second half of the twelfth century, the English) were not invincible. The conquerors' advances in Wales were resisted and sometimes reversed. The twelfth century witnessed two major periods of Welsh recovery, the first beginning in 1136, the second in 1164. On 15 April 1136 Richard fitz Gilbert de Clare, lord of Ceredigion, was ambushed and killed in a wooded pass near Abergavenny by Iorwerth and Morgan, sons of Owain Wan, who went on to seize Caerleon, making it the centre of a restored Welsh kingdom that extended over much of lowland Gwent as well as Gwynllŵg

38. Chepstow Castle, Monmouthshire, showing the keep first built by William fitz Osbern (d. 1071).

39. Montgomery Castle, built on Hubert de Burgh's instructions for Henry III in 1223 to curb the power of Llywelyn ap Iorwerth (d. 1240), prince of Gwynedd.

40. Caerphilly Castle, Glamorgan. Watercolour by Henry de Cort (1742–1810).

(Wentloog). Ceredigion succumbed to a combined assault by the leaders of Gwynedd and Deheubarth, namely Owain Gwynedd and his brother, Cadwaladr, sons of Gruffudd ap Cynan (d. 1137), and Gruffudd ap Rhys (d. 1137) and his sons. These and other Welsh successes were facilitated by the unwillingness of King Stephen (1135-54) to come to the aid of the Marchers, many of whom, including the powerful earl Robert of Gloucester (d. 1147), lord of Glamorgan, supported his rival for the throne, Henry I's daughter, Matilda.

Stephen's successor (and Matilda's son), Henry II (1154-89), was determined to restore royal authority in Wales, as elsewhere, to what it had been in the time of his grandfather, Henry I. Royal campaigns brought the Welsh rulers to submission and a temporary return of English rule in Ceredigion and the lordship of Llandovery (Cantref Bychan) as well as Tegeingl in the north-east. But neither of the two most powerful native kings, Owain Gwynedd (d. 1170) and the Lord Rhys (d. 1197), who had assumed sole rule of Deheubarth in 1155, were willing permanently to relinquish their earlier territorial gains, even if they were compelled to submit to the king on occasion, for example, by giving homage and fealty at Woodstock in 1163. Late in 1164, according to a Welsh annalist, the Lord Rhys led an assault on Roger de Clare in Ceredigion and then 'all the Welsh of Gwynedd, Deheubarth and Powys unanimously threw off the yoke of the French' (as Welsh sources continued to call the settlers). The following summer, Owain Gwynedd mustered an army at Corwen that included forces from Deheubarth and Powys as well as Gwynedd, ready to face Henry II's fourth and largest campaign against Wales. In the event, the campaign was, literally, a wash-out, as unseasonably cold weather and rain incapacitated the king's forces as they tried to cross the Berwyn Mountains in August, forcing Henry to retreat. He vented his anger on his Welsh hostages, whom he killed or mutilated; but he led no more campaigns into Wales. Rhys completed the reconquest of Ceredigion and Llandovery, and also joined with his uncle, Owain, in recovering lands in north-east Wales.

In 1171-2 Henry II made agreements with the Lord Rhys, the most powerful Welsh ruler since the death of Owain Gwynedd in November 1170, which recognized Rhys's extensive territorial gains in south Wales. From the later twelfth century the balance of power between the Welsh and English in Wales was significantly more favourable to the former than it had been in the heyday of Norman supremacy under Henry I (1100-35). Yet conflicts between the two peoples had by no means ended: witness the massacre of Welsh lords at Abergavenny in 1175, the Lord Rhys's attacks on Marcher and royal castles from 1189 until his death in 1197, or Roger Mortimer's completion of the conquest of Maelienydd in 1195. Such conflicts are a dominant theme in the thirteenth century. At their heart lay the mutually contradictory state-building aims of, on the one hand, the princes of Gwynedd, determined to establish their supremacy over the other Welsh rulers in a polity embracing the whole of native Wales, and, on the other, the kings of England, who wished to retain direct lordship over all Welsh rulers and curb Gwynedd's hegemonic ambitions.

Nor were rulers such as Llywelyn ap Iorwerth (Llywelyn the Great) (d. 1240) or Llywelyn ap Gruffudd, content to limit their ambitions to the areas already under native rule; as in the twelfth century, the assertion of leadership over the Welsh involved waging war in the March. Thus Llywelyn ap Iorwerth, in a series of campaigns between 1212 and 1218 that established him as the dominant power in Wales for the rest of his life, led his forces deep into the south and seized the two main centres of royal power there, Carmarthen and Cardigan. Although Llywelyn's gains in the southern March were short-lived – the Welsh lost control of Carmarthen and Cardigan in 1223 – the scale of his ambition is striking, none the less; at the height of his power he had authority over more of Wales than any ruler since Gruffudd ap

Llywelyn. His grandson, Llywelyn ap Gruffudd, enjoyed greater success, conquering a substantial bloc of territory in the Middle March, including the lordships of Brecon and Builth, in the early 1260s. The occupation of Brecon threatened the authority of Earl Gilbert de Clare (Gilbert the Red, d. 1295), lord of Glamorgan, over the Welsh of the uplands of Senghennydd (whose native dynasty Gilbert expropriated in 1267), a threat illustrated by Llywelyn's assault in 1270 on the castle which the earl had started to build at Caerphilly in 1268 in order to consolidate his hold on Senghennydd and also protect the chief centre of his lordship a few miles to the south at Cardiff.

Cultures of Power

Though their duration and geographical extent varied over this period, Norman and English conquests in Wales clearly reduced the amount of territory held by Welsh rulers and also planted new settlers who helped to transform the society and economy. In addition, however, the nature of the power exercised by Marcher lords differed in several significant respects from that of the native kings and princes. True, these differences should not be exaggerated. As elsewhere in Europe in this period, all those contending for power in Wales were engaged in a struggle for land and thus for the surplus extracted from its agrarian producers. Moreover, that struggle was often violent. Competition within and between a plurality of political units, combined with the lack of any overarching authority powerful enough to compel the peaceful resolution of disputes, ensured that Wales remained a land of war throughout the two centuries before the Edwardian conquest. Of course, war was central to the ethos of kings and aristocrats throughout Latin Christendom. In Wales, however, its prosecution was largely untrammelled by the restrictions imposed by centralizing monarchies in, say, England or France. Marcher lords could wage war without authorization from the English king and demanded castle guard and other military service from their tenants occasionally even as late as the thirteenth century, long after such demands had ceased to be made in England. Native society, too, was exuberantly militaristic: court poets praised bravery and victory in war as essential attributes of Welsh rulers, while Gerald of Wales was struck by the readiness of the whole free population to take up arms and the emphasis it placed on military training.

It is also true that interaction between Welsh rulers, Marcher lords and English kings resulted in imitation and assimilation that reduced the differences between them. Thus Gerald recommended his Marcher kinsmen in Dyfed as the ideal troops to complete the conquest of Wales on account of their familiarity with the terrain and their adaptation to Welsh methods of warfare. But such borrowings were mainly in the other direction. From the twelfth century onwards, Welsh rulers adopted elements of Norman and English military technology, notably castles, siege engines and the greater use of armour; in the early 1260s the forces led by Llywelyn ap Gruffudd in his conquests in the Middle March included siege engines and barded (armoured) horses. In addition, the thirteenth-century princes of Gwynedd, increasingly exposed to the bureaucratic practices of the English state, not least the definition of Anglo-Welsh relations in written agreements, sought in turn, albeit on a limited scale, to exploit the potential of parchment as a means of securing their hegemony over other Welsh lords. The princes also replaced traditional Welsh methods of proof (the practice of compurgation whereby oath-helpers simply swore in support of a defendant's denial) by the inquest or jury of twelve men normal in English common law, whose task it was to give their verdict on the specific details of a case. These changes belonged to a wider process of acculturation reflected, and reinforced, especially from the later twelfth century onwards, by marriage alliances with Marcher families and even with the Plantagenets: Dafydd ab Owain Gwynedd (d. 1203) and his nephew, Llywelyn ap Iorwerth, married respectively Emma, a half-sister of Henry II, and Joan, illegitimate daughter of King John.

Nevertheless, important contrasts remained between the power of Welsh rulers and that of Marcher lords. While lordship over land and military leadership were essential attributes of both groups, their ideological and constitutional positions differed. For all their independence from the English king, an independence reflected in their right to wage private war and exemption from the normal machinery of royal administration, Marcher lords were still the king's subjects and vulnerable to royal authority. Their lordships came into royal custody during the minorities of heirs or during the wardship of heiresses prior to their marriages, escheated to the crown if there were no heirs and could also be confiscated for political offences, as happened to the earldom of Shrewsbury after Robert de Bellême's revolt was crushed by Henry I in 1102. Indeed, Henry exploited to the full the opportunities provided by failure of heirs and confiscation to place new men in the March, notably his illegitimate son, Robert of Gloucester, granted Robert fitz Hamon's heiress, Mabel, in marriage and with her the lordship of Glamorgan.

Native rulers, on the other hand, were themselves of royal status. Admittedly theirs was an attenuated royalty by comparison with the kings of England, France, Germany or Sicily, not only on account of the small scale of Welsh kingdoms but also because of the apparent absence of any strong sacral element. Welsh kings or princes do not seem to have been anointed and crowned by bishops nor did they normally claim to rule by the grace of God, although on his visit to Henry III's court at Gloucester in May 1240 Dafydd ap Llywelyn wore a coronet – known, significantly, by the French term *garlonde* – described as the insignia of the principality of Gwynedd. An awareness that Welsh kingship was small beer by comparison with kingship in England and elsewhere in Europe may help to explain why, from the latter half of the twelfth century, the most powerful native rulers abandoned the title 'king' (Latin: *rex*) in favour of 'prince' (Latin: *princeps*). To begin with, at least, 'prince', a conveniently elastic title for a ruler that had been adopted by no lesser figures than the Roman emperors, probably expressed an assertion of an authority superior to, and subsuming, that of a mere 'king': after all, Hywel ab Ieuaf (d. 1185) had called himself 'king' in the mid-twelfth century, even though he ruled no more than the single *cantref* of Arwystli in mid-Wales.

However, the most important difference between native rulers and Marcher lords lay in their practices with regard to inheritance and succession. The norms followed in the March were those which had gained acceptance in aristocratic society in England and northern France by the early twelfth century. Their aim was simple: to guarantee the transmission of lordship intact from one generation to the next. Thus a Marcher lord was succeeded by a single heir – a son (the eldest son if the lordship formed the whole or part of the lord's principal estates) or, failing that, a daughter, who would normally be given in marriage to a member of another family who would then inherit the land. Moreover, the heir had to be legitimate, that is, born of a marriage considered lawful by the Church. This principle was probably accepted by the lay aristocracy as a means of reducing the number of potential heirs. Its importance is vividly illustrated by Gerald of Wales in a story – admittedly uncorroborated by other sources – he tells about Nest, the wife of Bernard of Neufmarché (d. *c*.1125),

Norman conqueror of Brecon. Nest took vengeance on her son, Mahel, after he had beaten up the lover with whom she was having an affair, by alleging before Henry I's court that Mahel was illegitimate, even though Bernard was in fact his father; as a result, the king deprived the son of his inheritance and granted Bernard's eldest daughter in marriage to Miles fitz Walter along with the lordship of Brecon.

Among native rulers, too, there seems to have been a general assumption that there should be one heir and that kingdoms should be transmitted intact. In practice, however, succession struggles were common. It was as a result of these that Powys never recovered its unity after the death of Madog ap Maredudd in 1160 and Deheubarth imploded after the Lord Rhys's death in 1197. This was not the application of the principle of partibility that governed the inheritance of land or patrimony among freemen in Welsh society, although the principle may well have helped to sustain the expectations of brothers and other kinsmen; indeed, Henry III chose, for obvious reasons, to assert that this was Welsh custom regarding succession in order to impose a territorial division on Gwynedd in 1247. The problem was that there was no effective way of ensuring that one son prevailed over his brothers, whose rivalries were exacerbated by the facts that they were often not all born of the same mother and that they had been brought up by different foster parents. In Gwynedd, where the struggle for the succession to Owain Gwynedd was finally resolved by Llywelyn ap Iorwerth's defeat of his uncles and cousins at the end of the twelfth century, it was his foster brothers who fought alongside Hywel ab Owain Gwynedd when he was killed in 1170 at the battle of Pentraeth by the forces of his half-brothers Dafydd and Rhodri.

The pool of potential contenders for a kingdom was all the greater because legitimate birth remained at best a contested criterion for succession among native dynasties in the period up to the Edwardian conquest. This reflected deeply rooted norms in native society, where all sons were entitled to inherit a share of patrimonial land if they were acknowledged by their father, irrespective of the marital status of their mother. It is true that attempts were made from the late twelfth century onwards to exclude illegitimate sons from dynastic succession. Thus the Lord Rhys seems to have designated his eldest legitimate son, Gruffudd (d. 1201), as his successor in preference to Gruffudd's elder but illegitimate half-brother, Maelgwn (d. 1231), and Llywelyn ap Iorwerth went to the lengths of obtaining papal approval for the succession of Dafydd (d. 1246), his son with his wife, Joan (an illegitimate daughter of King John), rather than his eldest son, Gruffudd (d. 1244), the product of an extramarital relationship with Tangwystl. Maelgwn, nevertheless, fought hard for what he regarded as his rightful inheritance, being allocated substantial territories in Dyfed and Ystrad Tywi when Llywelyn ap Iorwerth partitioned the lands of Deheubarth at Aberdyfi in 1216, while Gruffudd ap Llywelyn, though he failed to prevent Dafydd from succeeding their father in April 1240, enjoyed considerable support in Gwynedd; ironically, it was his son, Llywelyn ap Gruffudd, who was recognized as prince of Wales in 1267.

By 1267 Llywelyn ap Gruffudd was, as we have seen, the most powerful Welsh ruler in the period between the first Norman invasions and Edward I's conquest. Territorially, he had extended Gwynedd's hegemony, not only over the native rulers of Powys and Deheubarth, but also over the lordships of the Middle March, and gained formal recognition of this hegemony from the English crown. His annual ordinary income of perhaps about £3500 compared well with that of the greatest English lords, including Earl Gilbert the Red, who drew only about £1200 from his lordship of Glamorgan, out of a total of £4500-5000 yielded by his estates throughout England, Wales and Ireland. With his stone castles (for example, at

Cricieth, Dolbadarn and Dolforwyn near Welshpool), his nascent urban centres at Nefyn on the Llŷn peninsula and Llan-faes on Anglesey, his university-trained clerks capable of undertaking diplomatic negotiations as well as drafting letters and accounts, a supportive network of Cistercian abbeys and his French wife, Eleanor de Montfort, who finally joined him in Gwynedd in 1278 after a wedding ceremony at Worcester, Llywelyn had much in common with other European potentates of his age.

Yet, significant though his achievements were and open though he was to the political culture of the Anglo-French world, it is salutary to remember that Llywelyn had risen to power in traditional Welsh fashion, through a ruthless struggle against his brothers, and that his political ambitions were thwarted in part precisely because of the resistance they provoked from within native society. In the brief decade of its existence, the principality legitimized by the Treaty of Montgomery possessed neither the cohesion nor the fiscal capacity necessary to ensure its viability in the face of external pressure from Edward I. In committing himself in fulfilment of his treaty obligations at Montgomery in 1267 to an initial outlay of 5000 marks (over £3000), followed by annual payments of 3000 marks (£2000) for seven years, Llywelyn seems to have seriously overestimated his financial resources, and the resulting exactions on his subjects in Gwynedd – he was unable to tax the other lands of his principality – bred disaffection in the heartland of his power. Given these structural weaknesses, it is small wonder that Llywelyn's principality succumbed to the imperialistic ambitions of a vastly wealthier Edward I. With the benefit of hindsight, it is difficult to avoid the conclusion that the movement towards Welsh political unity under the thirteenth-century princes of Gwynedd was a case of too little, too late.

CATHOLIC WALES

The Church played a key role in bringing Wales into closer contact with England and the Continent between the late eleventh and late thirteenth centuries. One indication of the importance of the Church, and thus of Christianity, in Wales was the large amount of land invested in it: major churches were lords in their own right and cannot be ignored in any assessment of the distribution of power. Underlying this ecclesiastical landholding was the assumption that the religious beliefs represented by the Church were essential to the well-being of society. Adherence to Catholic Christianity was a fundamental feature of the mental as much as the physical landscape: apart from Jews, who were very few in Wales at this period, the peoples of Wales, both native and settler, shared a common system of religious belief. At the same time, the structures and character of religious provision in Wales were transformed in this period to a degree that would arguably be unparalleled until the eighteenth century. In part, these changes resulted from conquest and domination; in part, they reflected the growing influence throughout western Christendom from the late eleventh century onwards of the papacy and reformed religious orders.

Ecclesiastical Reorganization

One important development was the integration of the Church in Wales into a wider institutional framework. This is not to imply that the Welsh Church of the early Middle Ages had been completely isolated, still less that it had refused to recognize the authority of Rome. However, before the Gregorian Reform, named after the pontificate of Pope Gregory VII

41. A Welsh king on his throne holding a sceptre.
42. The distain (steward), holding a dish. By the thirteenth century the distain was the most important officer in the courts of Welsh rulers such as the princes of Gwynedd.
43. Bangor Cathedral.

(1073-85), inaugurated a far more interventionist approach to papal government, effective authority in the Church tended to lie at the regional or even local level. This was certainly true of Wales. Ties with the Church in England were likewise loose and lacking in formal definition: Welsh bishops were independent of English archbishops, and no late Anglo-Saxon monastery is known to have held lands or established monasteries in Wales. From the late eleventh and especially the early twelfth century onwards all this changed. The Normans founded nineteen priories in south Wales dependent on Benedictine monasteries in England and France, of which seven, including Abergavenny, Brecon and Pembroke, attained conventual status, forming religious communities rather than merely centres for managing estates. Welsh bishoprics also came under Norman control. Thus a Breton bishop, Hervé, was intruded, albeit only temporarily, into the see of Bangor in 1092, while in 1107 the new bishop of Llandaff (a Welshman, Urban) became the first Welsh bishop known to have sworn a profession of obedience to the archbishop of Canterbury. His example was followed in 1115 by Bernard (d. 1148), a Norman who had been chaplain to Henry I's queen, on his appointment to St David's. Although Bernard later tried to secure papal recognition of St David's as an archbishopric with authority over a separate Welsh ecclesiastical province independent of Canterbury, a campaign revived between 1198 and 1203 by Gerald of Wales, neither attempt succeeded and the authority secured by Canterbury over the four Welsh bishoprics – the fourth, St Asaph, was created in 1141 – in the first half of the twelfth century only ceased with the Disestablishment of 1920.

The subordination of the Welsh bishoprics to Canterbury formed part of a more extensive process of ecclesiastical reorganization which brought Wales into line with ecclesiastical government in England and on the Continent and linked it to a network of law and jurisdiction ultimately dependent on the papacy. Dioceses were given clearly defined boundaries and subdivided into archdeaconries and rural deaneries, while cathedral chapters were established, first at St David's under Bishop Bernard, then at the other Welsh sees in the late twelfth and early thirteenth centuries. The most important organizational change, however, was the formation of parishes. As elsewhere in Europe the parish, that is, an area which owed tithe and other dues to a parish church, provided the key point of contact between the institutional Church and the laity which made up the vast majority of its members. Although much remains uncertain about the precise chronology and causes of parochial development in Wales, three points are clear. First, although based on an earlier pattern of mother-churches and dependent chapels, the definition of parishes in Wales commenced in the twelfth century, beginning in the southern coastal areas settled early by the Normans but continuing probably into the thirteenth century in the upland areas still under native rule. Second, parishes corresponded to secular territorial divisions: compact knights' fees in the Marcher lordships, rural townships, some of them quite extensive, in *pura Wallia*. Third, the resulting system, while subject to later modifications, proved remarkably durable, providing a fundamental framework for religious devotion, rites of passage and social identities until the nineteenth century.

Reform

For the papacy and bishops, territorial dioceses and parishes were not ends in themselves, but rather means by which the Church's teaching could be promulgated in order to ensure that both the clergy and laity led more Christian lives: in other words, as means of promoting ecclesiastical reform. The aims of ecclesiastical reformers in twelfth- and thirteenth-century Wales are best captured in the prolific writings of Gerald of Wales (*c*.1146-*c*.1223), who sought, especially as archdeacon of Brecon (1175-1203), to apply the standards he had learned as a student from the theologians of Paris. In common with other reform-minded churchmen, Gerald was convinced that the Church was superior to secular authority; that ecclesiastical property should remain exclusively under ecclesiastical control; and that the clergy should espouse the highest moral standards so that they could exercise their ministry effectively. He therefore condemned the tendency in parts of Wales, such as at Llanbadarn Fawr in the late twelfth century, for a church's lands to be divided among portioners, many if not all of whom were laymen. Gerald also noted that it was extremely difficult for bishops to appoint clergy to churches against the wishes of their powerful lay kinsmen, who would take revenge on both the incumbent and the bishop who had appointed him without their approval.

In the opinion of reformers like Gerald, however, the biggest obstacle to improving clerical standards was presented not by men, but by women. From the late eleventh century the papacy placed the eradication of clerical marriage, a widespread practice throughout the western Church despite centuries-old prohibitions, at the centre of its reforming agenda. In part this campaign was aimed against the equally widespread practice of hereditary succession to ecclesiastical benefices. But it was also animated by a vision of the priesthood as a sacred office whose purity needed to be safeguarded. Just as the Church as a whole was the bride of Christ, so too each priest was married to his church and should not commit bigamy by entering into carnal marriage; nor should a priest who touched Christ's body in the Eucharist be polluted by having sexual relations with a woman. The celibate and, one suspects, misogynistic Gerald took these attitudes to heart: citing the fourth-century Greek theologian, St John Chrysostom, he urged priests attracted by the physical beauty of women to pause and consider the vileness that lay beneath their skin and in their nostrils and stomachs! He also complained that the costs of raising children born to priests' wives, including the hiring of wet-nurses, wasted resources that could have been spent on improvements to churches or helping the poor.

The criticisms voiced by Gerald were shared by reforming churchmen in England, notably John of Salisbury, who considered the people of Gwynedd to be barely Christian in the 1150s, and John Pecham, archbishop of Canterbury, who conducted a visitation of the Welsh Church in 1284. But how widespread was a commitment to the values of ecclesiastical reform in Wales? We know that some Welsh bishops adopted a reforming agenda. John of Salisbury heard about the situation in Gwynedd from its bishop, Meurig (1140-61), who had fled to Canterbury after condemning Owain Gwynedd's marriage to his first cousin, Cristin, as incestuous according to canon law, much to the prince's displeasure. One of Meurig's successors at Bangor, Bishop Cadwgan (1215-35/36), son of an Irish priest and Welsh mother and the first Cistercian monk to be a bishop in Wales, had received a higher education in the cathedral schools and sought to improve standards of pastoral care in his diocese by composing a treatise instructing priests how to hear confessions, while at St David's Bishop Thomas Wallensis (1248-55) was a noted scholar who had previously been archdeacon under Robert Grosseteste, the reforming bishop of Lincoln. Yet bishops of the calibre of Thomas Wallensis were probably exceptional in Wales. Moreover, episcopal effectiveness was limited by vacancies – Bangor lacked a bishop from *c*.1093 to 1120 and again between 1161 and 1177 – and, more importantly, by absenteeism. One cause of absenteeism was poverty: Peter de Leia, bishop of St David's (1176-98), spent long periods living in wealthy English abbeys, as

44. St Dogmaels Abbey, Pembrokeshire, founded by Robert fitz Martin, lord of Cemais, in 1113 as a priory affiliated to the reformed monastery of Tiron in northern France and elevated to the status of an abbey in 1120. Watercolour by John 'Warwick' Smith (1749-1831) showing the north transept in 1792.

45. Strata Florida Abbey: west doorway.

46. A mid-thirteenth century manuscript of Brut y Brenhinedd, a Welsh translation of Geoffrey of Monmouth's Historia Regum Britanniae (History of the Kings of Britain).

did Godfrey, bishop of St Asaph (1160-75). Several bishops of Bangor were driven from their sees by conflicts with secular rulers: in addition to Meurig in the twelfth century, both Richard (1237-67) and Anian I (1267-1305/6) spent much of their pontificates in exile in England.

Thus, while the closer integration of Wales into the ecclesiastical structures of Latin Christendom exposed it to new norms regarding the Church's place in society and the behaviour of the clergy and laity, the impact of those norms should not be overstated. Indeed, in some respects Wales may have been more resistant to the reformers' agenda than most other parts of western Europe. Take the question of marriage; the Church not only prohibited the clergy from marrying but, from the twelfth century, claimed jurisdiction over the marriages of the laity, forbidding marriage to kinsfolk and insisting that marriage should be indissoluble, a jurisdiction which generally came to be accepted by lay aristocratic society. As elsewhere in western Europe, the campaign for clerical celibacy in Wales was most effective at the episcopal level. Sulien of Llanbadarn Fawr in Ceredigion, twice bishop of St David's before his death in 1091, was both highly educated, including ten years of study in Ireland, and respectably married; his four sons – one of whom, Rhygyfarch, composed the earliest surviving Life of St David – were prominent churchmen, and at least three of them had sons of their own. Likewise in the south-east, Uchdryd (or Uthred), bishop of Llandaff (1140-8), had a son and a daughter. After the mid-twelfth century, however, Welsh bishops appear to have been celibate. By contrast, marriage continued to be normal among the parochial clergy in Wales for the rest of the Middle Ages.

The marriage of the laity came to conform to the requirements of canon law in only a gradual and piecemeal fashion, especially in native Welsh society, where different norms of marriage were given expression and thus justification by the texts of customary law, the 'law of Hywel Dda', compiled in the late twelfth and thirteenth centuries. (Other European customary laws of this period were far readier to accommodate ecclesiastical definitions of and jurisdiction over marriage.) On the eve of the Edwardian conquest Archbishop Pecham complained of the sanction that Welsh law gave to divorce and its acceptance of the legitimacy of children born outside wedlock; over a century earlier, in 1175, a church council of the province of Canterbury discussed a proposal to prohibit the Welsh from 'changing wives'. On the other hand, there can be no doubt that ecclesiastical norms of lawful marriage did have some influence on Wales, especially by the thirteenth century, even if the extent of that influence is difficult to quantify. Thus Llywelyn ap Iorwerth demonstrated his adherence to the Church's notions of marriage in 1222 when he obtained papal confirmation of his ordinance excluding his illegitimate son, Gruffudd, from the succession in favour of his legitimate son, Dafydd (although it is important to note, as mentioned earlier, that Gruffudd still attracted widespread support in Gwynedd, and his illegitimacy did not prevent the political ascent of his son, Llywelyn ap Gruffudd). More significantly, perhaps, couples in the southern dioceses of Llandaff and St David's, in particular, demonstrated their adherence to the requirements of canon law by seeking papal dispensation to marry despite their being related within the prohibited degrees of consanguinity.

Monasticism and Religious Life

If it is uncertain how far organizational changes in the secular church were accompanied by an acceptance of the reforming agenda which those changes were designed to advance, there can be no doubt that Wales was profoundly affected by movements for monastic reform which were such a prominent feature of the western Church from the late eleventh to the thirteenth centuries. As we have seen, the Normans first introduced Benedictine monasticism to the country with their foundation of priories attached to religious houses in England and France. The Normans were also responsible for establishing the first houses belonging to reformed religious orders of continental origin, especially the Cistercians, named after the monastery of Cîteaux in Burgundy. Thus a Savigniac house was founded at Neath by Richard de Granville in 1130 (later to be absorbed into the Cistercian order); the first Welsh Cistercian abbey, Tintern, by Walter fitz Richard, lord of Chepstow, in 1131; and Margam, also Cistercian, by Earl Robert of Gloucester, lord of Glamorgan, in 1147. However, the most influential Welsh Cistercian monastery was Whitland (Carmarthenshire), first established in 1140 by Bishop Bernard of St David's. Though originally a Norman foundation, Whitland attracted the support of the Lord Rhys of Deheubarth, who also acquired the patronage of Whitland's first daughter-house, Strata Florida, after his conquest of Ceredigion in 1165. The support and example of the Lord Rhys were crucial in the spread of the Cistercians into other regions of Wales under native rule in the later twelfth and early thirteenth centuries, as daughters and grand-daughters of Whitland were established at Strata Marcella (1170) and Valle Crucis (1201) in Powys, Cwm-hir (1176) in Maelienydd, Llantarnam or Caerleon (1179) in Gwynllŵg and Aberconwy (1186) and Cymer (1198/9) in Gwynedd.

If the Cistercians were the most widespread and influential religious order in Wales, patronage was also extended to the Augustinian canons and the friars. Augustinians and friars differed from monks such as the Cistercians in that, while they lived in a community according to a rule, they were allowed to leave the cloister to undertake pastoral work among the laity. Augustinian priories were often created by taking over existing churches, as, for example, at Carmarthen, where the pre-Norman church of Llandeulyddog was transferred to the canons, probably by Bishop Bernard of St David's, or at Bardsey, Beddgelert and Penmon, apparently refounded as Augustinian houses by Llywelyn ap Iorwerth. Houses of the two main mendicant orders appeared in a number of Welsh towns in the thirteenth century: the Dominicans at Bangor, Brecon, Cardiff, Haverfordwest and Rhuddlan, the Franciscans at Cardiff, Carmarthen and Llan-faes on Anglesey.

The diversification of religious provision in Wales in the twelfth and thirteenth centuries is significant on several counts. For one thing, it shows that the political élite, both Marcher lords and native princes, were keen to keep up with contemporary European fashions in their religious patronage: the major churches of pre-Norman Wales were no longer deemed adequate, at least on their own, as centres of spiritual power. Yet the ability of the Cistercians in particular to establish new communities also suggests that there was a wider demand in society for the opportunities these provided to live a life of religious devotion, either as monks or lay brothers (*conversi*) who undertook much of the agricultural labour required. At the same time, it should be stressed that these opportunities were largely restricted to men. No more than four nunneries were founded in Wales in this period, all of them small: a Benedictine house at Usk (by 1236), together with Cistercian nunneries at Llanllŷr in Ceredigion (by 1197), Llanllugan in Cedewain in mid-Wales (early thirteenth century) and, possibly, a community at Llansanffraid in Elfael whose brief existence in the 1170s ended after the abbot of Strata Marcella allegedly ran off with one of the nuns. True, some Welsh women lived a solitary religious life as anchoresses, and it is possible that others fulfilled religious vocations in English nunneries – though the only known example of the latter, Llywelyn ap Gruffudd's daughter, Gwenllian, was given no choice in the matter, being taken in her cradle after the Edwardian conquest to the Gilbertine house of Sempringham in

Lincolnshire where she died in 1337. Nevertheless, the impression remains that, in contrast, say, to England or many continental regions, both native and settler society in Wales were reluctant to make organized religious provision for women.

Lay Devotion and Piety

For the majority of the population devotion was focused on local churches and cults of saints rather than on religious houses. Gerald of Wales praised the Welsh for the respect they showed the clergy, suggesting that most people were less troubled than he was by clerical incontinence and other alleged failings. Lay demand for and participation in religious services took various forms. Landholders established new churches to serve their local communities: Herewald, bishop of Llandaff (1056-1104) consecrated numerous churches of this kind in Ergyng (Archenfield), while in Meirionnydd a certain Hoedlyw founded the church of Llanfihangel-y-traethau during the reign of Owain Gwynedd (d. 1170). Lay patrons also no doubt contributed to the costs of a major change in the physical surroundings of worship in twelfth- and thirteenth-century Wales, namely the replacement of timber churches by ones built of stone. It is likely, moreover, that parishioners attended church regularly, on Sundays and feast days of saints, hearing the priest celebrate mass and perhaps also receiving what were known as sacramentals, namely blessed bread and holy water, which were believed to have health-giving properties. By contrast, as was generally the case in Latin Christendom, the laity took communion only rarely: annual communion at Easter, following confession and penance, was the most that the Fourth Lateran Council in Rome considered it realistic to demand in 1215. Baptisms were popular events. Gerald of Wales warned the clergy of the archdeaconry of Brecon of the potentially dangerous repercussions of the desire of numerous relatives and friends of the child's family to be godparents, as they would then be linked by bonds of spiritual kinship which would make marriages between them unlawful in the eyes of the Church. Gerald also reveals that lay fraternities or guilds met in churches, with much eating and drinking.

The late eleventh and twelfth centuries witnessed important developments in the cult of saints. Not only were the earliest surviving Latin Lives of Welsh saints such as Cadog, David and Teilo written down, partly in response to Norman interest in the patron saints of churches they had appropriated, but Norman enterprise and influence introduced new attitudes to saints' relics. The apparent reluctance of the Welsh earlier in the Middle Ages to disturb the bodies of saints ended in the twelfth century, as bones were exhumed and moved to new resting places. Thus in 1120 Bishop Urban had the body of St Dyfrig and the teeth of Elgar, an English hermit, translated to his new cathedral church at Llandaff from Bardsey Island, reputedly the resting place of 20,000 saints; in 1138 monks from Shrewsbury removed the body of St Winifred (Gwenfrewi) from her grave at Gwytherin (Denbighshire) and took it to their abbey; while at the churches of Barry Island and Pennant Melangell the bones of their patron saints were placed in new shrines above ground that would be more accessible to the devout. At the same time, earlier patterns of devotion continued. Gerald of Wales was particularly struck by the veneration shown to secondary relics such as staffs and gospel books believed to have been owned by saints.

Gerald also noted the enthusiasm of the Welsh for pilgrimage, especially to Rome. While there was a strongly local complexion to much devotion, this coexisted with reverence for universal saints such as St Mary, patron both of all Cistercian monasteries and of a new church at the major native ecclesiastical foundation of Meifod in 1156, and pilgrimages to

47. St Mary's Abbey, Bardsey.
48. Penmon Priory, Anglesey.
49. Twelfth-century carved fragments, possibly of a shrine, in St David's Cathedral.

Becket's shrine at Canterbury, Rome or Jerusalem. Morgan ap Cadwgan died in Cyprus in 1128 while returning from a pilgrimage to Jerusalem undertaken as penance for killing his brother during a bitter power struggle in Powys, and in 1235 Ednyfed Fychan, Llywelyn ap Iorwerth's chief official, was granted a safe-conduct through England on his way to the Holy Land. Such journeys serve as a reminder that Wales belonged to the wider world of Latin Christendom. From the late eleventh century onwards important new links were created with that world as the result of ecclesiastical reorganization, the growing influence of the papacy and canon law, and the foundation of several dozen religious houses. At the same time, however, these Europeanizing and Anglicizing influences interacted with long-established institutions, practices and mentalities which ensured that there was still much that was distinctive about the Welsh religious landscape in 1282.

CULTURES AND IDENTITIES

Ethnic Identities

As a result of conquest and settlement from the late eleventh century onwards Wales became an ethnically and culturally far more diverse country than it had been earlier in the Middle Ages. Contemporary sources tend to emphasize the differences between the various peoples of Wales. Thus Henry I (1100-35) greeted the French, English, Flemings and Welsh in a charter for Carmarthen Priory; the English lined up on one side, the Welsh on the other, when Archbishop Baldwin of Canterbury preached the Third Crusade at Llandaff in 1188; Llywelyn ap Iorwerth's agreement with King John in 1201 distinguished between Welsh and English law, Magna Carta (1215) between the law of Wales and the law of the March. These perceptions reflected the existence of self-consciously distinct groups who differed from each other in their origins, language and customs. The English peasants settled by Norman lords on the coastal lowlands of south Wales left their imprint on the landscape: English place-names are found as early as c.1100 in Gwent; they were also common in the vicinity of Margam Abbey in western Glamorgan a century later. By the later twelfth century, moreover, English had become the mother tongue of Anglo-Norman or Marcher lords in Wales, even if they also learned French on account of the prestige it enjoyed in aristocratic society. In addition, Flemish was still spoken in Pembrokeshire in the early thirteenth century by the descendants of colonists planted in Rhos and Daugleddau by Henry I; these Flemings were renowned for their trading skills and also for their custom of divining future events by examining the shoulder bones of rams.

If the period under consideration marked an important stage in the Anglicization of Wales, it was also an age in which a distinctively Welsh identity was given vigorous expression. One element in that identity was pride in descent from the Britons, as we shall see. Another was the Welsh language: a fine grasp of the language featured among the accomplishments for which native princes and noble women were praised by poets, while one late thirteenth-century lawbook numbered 'an alien who does not know how to speak Welsh properly' among those entitled to the services of an advocate in legal actions. Poets and lawyers also stressed the integrity of Wales as a territorial entity. A late eleventh-century poem described a circuit of the country; both Llywelyn ap Iorwerth of Gwynedd and his grandson, Llywelyn ap Gruffudd, were described as 'the true king of Wales' by thirteenth-century poets. Hywel Dda (d. 950) was likewise called king or prince of Wales in the lawbooks, which opened with accounts of how he had allegedly reformed the laws of Wales in an assembly drawn from all over the country, while some legal texts also incorporated traditional descriptions of Wales as extending from Porth Wygyr on Anglesey to Portskewett in Gwent, and located the border with England on Offa's Dyke. This is not to deny, of course, the strength of regional and local solidarities – the poem just mentioned listed over thirty regions in its circuit of Wales – or the significance of variations between different areas. Gerald of Wales was the first of a long line of commentators to highlight contrasts between the north and the south, asserting that the Welsh of Gwynedd excelled in the use of the spear, those of Gwent in the use of the bow, and citing rival opinions on the respective merits of the Welsh spoken in the north compared with that of Ceredigion farther south.

Outside observers, too, had no doubts about the distinctive character of Wales and its people, although the images they projected of these were far from flattering. One important change in this period was the creation by ecclesiastical writers in England of negative stereotypes of the Welsh, like other Celtic peoples in Britain and Ireland, as barbarous, a conceptualization first seen in the writings of the historian William of Malmesbury in the mid-1120s which became widespread from the later 1130s in the wake of the Welsh recovery in Stephen's reign. According to King Stephen's biographer, Wales had been civilized by the Normans, who had turned the areas they had conquered into a 'second England'; but the risings from 1136 onwards had ruined all that, as the bestial Welsh inflicted unheard-of cruelties on the settlers. Welsh methods of warfare, notably the enslavement of non-combatants and the killing, rather than ransoming, of enemies, evoked great horror.

At the root of such condemnations was the increasing social and economic divergence between England and its Celtic neighbours from the early twelfth century onwards. For example, slavery was banned in England at the end of the eleventh century, yet, according to John of Salisbury, a slave trade continued to flourish in Gwynedd, no doubt with Ireland, in the 1150s. Likewise, as we have seen, native Welsh society differed from aristocratic society in England in its disregard for the Church's teaching on marriage. Although the assimilation of behavioural norms common in English or French aristocratic society made thirteenth-century Wales increasingly less susceptible to charges of 'barbarism' – with the demise of slavery, a greater deference to the canon law of marriage and the replacement of mutilation by imprisonment as a means of neutralizing dynastic rivals – this did not prevent John Pecham, archbishop of Canterbury (1279-92), from castigating the Welsh for their alleged cruelty, immorality and indolence at the time of the Edwardian conquest.

Interaction and Assimilation: the March

Yet, tempting though it is to depict Wales during the two centuries before the Edwardian conquest as a land of essentially two peoples and cultures, Welsh and Anglo-Norman or English, this would be an oversimplification. These categories were less uniform and rigid than such a characterization might suggest. Consider the Welsh March. Since all Marcher lords were subjects of the king of England and the wealthier among them also held lands in England, and since their lordships contained substantial numbers of English immigrants or their descendants, it is likely that many of these settlers identified themselves principally with England. This is the impression given, for instance, by the annals compiled at the Cistercian abbey of Margam, whose patrons were the earls and countesses of Gloucester who held the lordship of Glamorgan, and many if not all of whose monks (as distinct from lay brothers) were drawn from England or

50. Llanfihangel-y-traethau, Merioneth: memorial stone erected by Hoedlyw in memory of his mother, Gwleder, which says that he built the church during the reign of 'King Owain'.

51. A woman with a dish. The beginning of the section on the laws of women in a lawbook of the mid-thirteenth century.

52. The rhingyll (serjeant) of a Welsh court holding his lance.

settler families in Glamorgan. Not surprisingly, the monks' view of the past focused largely on the English kings and aristocracy and their connections with France. Thus the annals open in 1066 with the death of Edward the Confessor and the Norman conquest of England, and, apart from local events concerning the abbey and the bishops of Llandaff, barely mention Wales until the thirteenth century, and especially the 1220s, when Llywelyn ap Iorwerth's campaigns in Glamorgan could hardly be ignored.

On the other hand, the frontier societies of the March also offered opportunities for the interaction and cross-fertilization of cultures. Thus it was by adapting and lavishly embroidering Welsh historical traditions that Geoffrey of Monmouth, whose name reveals his origin in one of the first Marcher lordships to have been established in the south-east, wrote his Latin international best-seller, the *History of the Kings of Britain* (*c.*1138), a tale of epic scope and brilliant imagination which shot King Arthur to European stardom as the pivotal figure in a narrative that began with Aeneas's flight from Troy and ended with the Britons' loss of most of Britain to the Saxons in, so Geoffrey held, the seventh century AD. Likewise, it may well have been at Monmouth Priory that an important collection of Welsh saints' Lives was compiled *c.*1130. In addition, it has been suggested that the close contacts between natives and settlers in south-east Wales led to the importation into Welsh prose literature of imagery derived from English and French aristocratic society and also perhaps from French romances.

In the small lordships of Dyfed, moreover, social and cultural interaction seem to have created a new kind of Marcher identity. So, at least, is the impression given by Gerald of Wales, a prolific and pioneering author whom we have already encountered on several occasions in this chapter. Three-quarters Norman and one quarter Welsh by descent, related – primarily through his maternal grandmother, Nest, daughter of Rhys ap Tewdwr, the king of Deheubarth killed in 1093 – to all the major families of south-west Wales, including that of the Lord Rhys, Gerald was keenly aware of his mixed ancestry. In his book *The Conquest of Ireland* (1189), Gerald emphasized the role of his Marcher kinsmen in the English invasion of Ireland from 1167 onwards, claiming that their courage and military skills resulted precisely from their hybrid origins, combining what was best in both the Normans and the Welsh. Gerald's own sense of identity was, admittedly, complex. For a brief period, during his unsuccessful campaign to become archbishop of St David's (1198-1203), he even identified himself principally with the Welsh; and throughout his adult life he was a scholar and churchman above all.

However, as far as his secular identity was concerned, it was probably his mixed ancestry and connections which mattered most. The Marcher society to which he belonged was certainly ready to adopt or sympathize with aspects of native culture such as the cult of St David. But in essence its relationship to Wales was colonialist. Fascinated though he was by Wales, Gerald thought that it should be ruled by the English and in particular by the Marchers; his *Description of Wales* (1194) presented a blueprint for the conquest of the country by the king of England. Cultural integration was limited, then, by the continuous struggle for territory between settlers and natives and also, very probably, by the Marchers' assumptions about the superiority of English and French culture. Whereas the descendants of the Norman conquerors of England, including those who settled in Wales, soon came to speak English, albeit while also continuing to cultivate French-speaking culture, even in Dyfed few if any Marchers learned to speak Welsh.

Conservatism and Innovation: Welsh Culture

From the late eleventh to the late thirteenth century Welsh culture became more diverse, at least at the level of the élite, whose political and ecclesiastical connections with England and the Continent exposed it to wider European fashions and norms without diminishing its attachment to the native inheritance. It was in this period that the prose tales collectively known since the nineteenth century as the *Mabinogion* were committed to writing (although the earliest version of *Culhwch and Olwen* may have first been written *c*.1000); the compendium of traditional lore known as *Trioedd Ynys Prydein* (the Triads of the Island of Britain) was assembled in written form around the middle of the twelfth century; the earliest surviving Welsh lawbooks, though quite possibly deriving in some part from pre-Norman ancestors, were compiled in the late twelfth and thirteenth centuries; and three different Welsh translations were made of Geoffrey of Monmouth's *History* in the thirteenth century. The period also witnessed a flowering of Welsh poetry. Some 12,700 lines survive of work composed in strict metres by the poets of the princes. Most of their compositions sang the praises of native rulers, celebrating their military valour and victories, their generosity and their distinguished ancestry, and were recited in the princes' halls, to the accompaniment of a harp. The symbiotic relationship between poet and princely patron was summed up by Cynddelw Brydydd Mawr in a poem to the Lord Rhys: 'You without me have no voice; I without you have nothing to say'. Cynddelw, a supremely self-confident poet whose career stretched from *c*.1155 to *c*.1195, had sung at the courts of Powys and Gwynedd before he came to the Lord Rhys at Dinefwr. Steeped in the early Welsh poetry of Aneirin and Taliesin, whose verse he echoed, as well as in a whole wealth of other native traditions, Cynddelw was not only a highly skilled craftsman but also a scholar – not in the sense of someone like Gerald of Wales who had received an ecclesiastical education in the schools of Paris – but as a master of Welsh genealogy, history and traditions of places, knowledge he had probably acquired orally rather than by reading texts.

The traditionalism of poets and lawyers, experts in a body of learning known as *cyfarwyddyd*, is a striking feature of Welsh culture in this period. In important respects, native society was strongly, even obsessively, past-orientated, seeking comfort in a recollection of the former glories of the Britons, the ancestors of the Welsh, and in messianic hopes of a deliverer, often identified as King Arthur, who would fulfil the centuries-old prophecies and expel the foreigners from the island of Britain. Gerald of Wales, observing the ubiquity of such notions in Welsh society, insisted that they were mistaken. Henry II went further, encouraging the monks of Glastonbury to exhume Arthur and Guinevere in order to show that the supposed deliverer of the Welsh was well and truly dead; while Edward I implied that he, the conqueror of the Welsh, was the true Arthur when he celebrated his victory by holding a round table at Nefyn in July 1284.

Yet, though an attachment to a British past and potential future remained a vital strand in Welsh identity throughout the Middle Ages and well beyond, it did not prevent the Welsh from absorbing and adapting new cultural influences in the present. One particularly telling example of this is the way that, in the first half of the twelfth century, Welsh writers of Latin stopped calling the Welsh 'Britons' and Wales 'Britain' (Latin: *Britannia*); instead, they started to imitate the practice of writers in England since the Norman conquest by adopting the English terms 'Wales' and 'Welsh' (Latin: *Wallia, Walenses* and so forth). This shift in terminology cannot be explained simply in terms of cultural imperialism, though it clearly did reflect the dominance of the Anglo-Norman world in the international medium of Latin. Rather, the adaptation of English terms can be seen as a means of giving clearer expression to a sense of Welsh identity focused on Wales, and thus as providing more up-to-date Latin equivalents for the Welsh term, *Cymry*, used for both the land and people of Wales, than was offered by the earlier 'British' usage.

External influences helped to conserve and reinvigorate Welsh culture and identity in other ways, too. Thus the competition for poets and musicians hosted by the Lord Rhys at Cardigan castle in 1176, an event often regarded as the first Eisteddfod, may have drawn its inspiration from contemporary French competitions for poets known as *puys*. French loanwords were borrowed into Welsh, reflecting increasing ecclesiastical and social contacts with England and the Continent, and from the thirteenth century Welsh translations began to be made of French literary works. Caroline script, introduced under Norman influence from the twelfth century, thereby displacing the Insular script used in pre-Norman Wales, became a tool for the preservation of Welsh literature in both Latin and the vernacular. Likewise Cistercian monasteries patronized by Welsh rulers, while belonging to a European-wide religious order, did much to promote the native culture. For example, the annals kept at St David's since the early Middle Ages were continued at Strata Florida from *c*.1175, and the same monastery produced, just after the Edwardian conquest, the Latin chronicle, now lost, which formed the basis of the Welsh chronicles known generically as *Brut y Tywysogion* (the Chronicle of the Princes), a narrative of mainly political history in which the native kings and princes of Wales take centre stage.

At the same time the Cistercians played a major part in introducing continental and English styles of ecclesiastical architecture to Wales. Thus the first churches of the early foundations of Tintern, Margam and Whitland reflected the austerity of Cistercian monasteries in Burgundy, notably Fontenay, a model still followed, it seems, in the original building plan for Valle Crucis in the first half of the thirteenth century. By then, however, the churches of Tintern and Margam were being rebuilt in the Gothic style characteristic of west country churches such as Glastonbury and Wells, a style which also influenced Llandaff cathedral, eventually dedicated in 1266 after many decades of work. Earlier, the west country style of Romanesque had penetrated Gwynedd, albeit on a small scale comparable to some contemporary church buildings in Ireland, at Penmon Priory in south-east Anglesey, probably built during the reign, and quite possibly with the patronage, of Owain Gwynedd in the mid-twelfth century. Such architectural fashions, while signalling the growing influence in Wales of cultural norms originating in England and France, are unlikely to have been regarded by the Welsh as unwelcome alien innovations associated with conquest and settlement. Owain Gwynedd may well have appreciated the rich decoration at Penmon as much as the intricate, and perhaps not always intelligible, compositions of his court poets.

The assimilation of new influences, mainly of English and continental origin, is a theme that runs throughout the history of Wales from the late eleventh to the late thirteenth centuries. As a result of such assimilation, manifested not only in the building of stone churches in new architectural styles but in the construction of castles, the foundation of towns, the use of new documentary forms and the patronage of reformed religious orders, the Wales of Llywelyn ap Gruffudd had much stronger connections and resemblances with other parts of an increasingly uniform Latin Christendom than had the Wales of Gruffudd ap Llywelyn two centuries previously. Yet, as we have seen, these Europeanizing trends did

53. Llandaff Cathedral: Romanesque doorway.

54. Early thirteenth-century seal of Lleision ap Morgan ap Caradog, ruler of Afan, showing Lleision kneeling before the enthroned abbot of Margam, an Anglo-Norman foundation also patronized by Lleision's family.

55. The death of Llywelyn ap Gruffudd, 11 December 1282, described by a Welsh chronicler in Brut y Tywysogion.

not sweep all before them. Indeed, from a wider European perspective one of the striking things about native Welsh society in this period is the tenacity of mentalities and practices, be they customs of inheritance and succession, devotion to the staffs and gospel books of early saints or the composition of vernacular praise poetry, whose origins lay in the pre-Norman past. Part of the explanation for this lies in the prestige enjoyed by native men of learning, notably poets and lawyers, whose championing of the traditional and conservative provided an ideological counterweight to the values of the Anglo-French aristocracy and reform-minded clerics. Thus it was that the resilience of the indigenous culture served both to customize English or European templates to Welsh conditions – the Cistercian monasteries affiliated to Whitland are a case in point – and to compromise the modernizing initiatives of rulers such as the Lord Rhys, Llywelyn the Great or Llywelyn ap Gruffudd.

Above all, however, the Wales of Llywelyn ap Gruffudd was far more diverse, ethnically as well as culturally, than that of Gruffudd ap Llywelyn. The most important vehicles of English and continental influences were, after all, the settlers who colonized substantial areas of the country, while the territorial ambitions of Marcher lords, coupled with the determination of English kings to secure hegemony over native rulers, dominated the political struggles of the period. True, a plurality of political units in Wales was nothing new. But Norman and English conquest, completed with Edward I's war of 1282-83, created new kinds of frontiers, which separated not only different spheres of authority but also different peoples and languages. Although those frontiers were neither immovable nor impermeable, they nevertheless mark an important turning-point. Whereas the Irish who conquered parts of south-west and north-west Wales in the post-Roman period eventually lost their distinctive identity, few of those who colonized areas such as Gwent, Glamorgan or Pembrokeshire from the late eleventh century onwards went native. After the arrival of the Normans the history of Wales was not only a history of the Welsh.

4

WALES FROM CONQUEST TO UNION
1282 - 1536

Ralph Griffiths

The two and a half centuries between the death of Llywelyn ap Gruffudd and his brother Dafydd in 1282-83 and the act of Parliament which unified Wales with England in 1536 have puzzled historians and even repelled many of them. From the sixteenth century onwards, English and Welsh writers tended to regard the union imposed by King Henry VIII as thankfully drawing a veil over a period of disorder and confusion, whilst patriotic Welsh writers in the nineteenth and early twentieth centuries focused on little more than the tragic failure of Owain Glyn Dŵr's revolt of 1400 and the inspiring victory and accession of Henry Tudor in 1485 – episodes that at least seemed to provide a link with an independent Welsh past. These are still popular perceptions of the later Middle Ages today; but in order to appreciate the true significance of this period, we need to venture behind these stirring events and penetrate the myths that shroud the experiences of Welsh people.

This, after all, was the age when the short-lived principality of Gwynedd was replaced, in 1301, by a principality that extended more broadly over half the country in the west and north of Wales (and included Flintshire in the north-east) and which was inseparably bound to the English crown; after the act of union, it encompassed the whole of Wales. This was the age when Wales's contacts with the other countries of the British Isles developed even more strongly than had been the case since the Norman conquest – contacts which made its peoples increasingly cosmopolitan in outlook. This was an age when the peoples of England and Wales grew closer together and found much to unite them in their interests and ambitions, even if their habits and customs – and their languages – remained distinct. Not that this transformation was entirely peaceful, for the centuries of resentment and conflict between native and immigrant in Wales, and the long record of resistance to English invasion and conquest created a legacy of intermittent violence that marred the century and a half following 1282-3. Nor were the changes without their social complexities for, as in the case of England, Scotland, and other west European countries, Wales had always been a land of regional differences and multiple loyalties and attitudes, and so it remained: to southerners the north was unfamiliar; Welsh folk were regarded with suspicion by those who lived in border English counties; townsfolk in Wales did not always live harmoniously with rural folk; and lowlanders ventured only gingerly into the hills and highlands. These features of medieval Welsh society were ingrained and were modified only gradually during the course of the later Middle Ages – and, of course, to a degree they are with us still today. And yet by 1536, a noticeably different tone was being sounded compared with that heard in 1282-83:

relations between English and Welsh had so evolved that the union came about peacefully; no significant mass movements of political, religious or social protest occurred in Wales after Owain Glyn Dŵr's revolt collapsed; and Wales and its peoples henceforth became an integral part of the British state and its community of peoples. The later Middle Ages hold the key to understanding this change.

A New Order: 1282-1350

Looking back over 150 years from his abbey near Edinburgh, the Scottish historian, Walter Bower, concluded that 'This king [Edward I] conquered the Welsh and subdued more or less all [of that country] by guile; but he never governed it peacefully'. It was a critical assessment by someone who also recorded his own countrymen's resistance to an English conquest inaugurated by Edward I. In Wales, this masterful monarch had certainly defeated the pretensions of Gwynedd's rulers to be independent princes; yet over the next generation lesser princes in several parts of Wales resisted their own subjugation, and the task of pacifying and governing the whole of Wales taxed the resources and ingenuity of the English crown and the Marcher lords (who were mostly prominent English nobles). The Scots writer might have added that what Edward I had attempted was the completion of a military and political conquest begun long before, with the Norman incursions in Wales towards the end of the eleventh century. Nevertheless, despite all the qualifications that may be sounded about the nature and completeness of Edward I's achievement, his reign opened a new phase in the history of Wales and especially of its relationship with the realm of England and the king's dominions elsewhere.

King Edward was a fearless and determined ruler (1272-1307), famous as a young crusader in the Holy Land, a notable soldier, intelligent, though with a violent and brutal streak to his nature. All of these characteristics were brought to bear in his dealings with Wales and the Welsh. After Llywelyn and Dafydd were killed, he swiftly set about re-organising their principality of Gwynedd and imposing his authority on the rest of the country and its lords, Welsh and English alike. Those who accompanied him, or observed him, on his tour of Wales in 1284 would have had few illusions about his determination to demonstrate his regal power and to stamp his authority on the country and its peoples: it was an epic journey which was not confined to Gwynedd and the safer Anglicised lowlands. No other monarch was to embark on such a tour until modern times.

When he was at Rhuddlan in March 1284, Edward published his blueprint for the future government of Gwynedd. It is sometimes called the statute of Rhuddlan, or even the statute of Wales, in recognition of its importance; but in effect it was a royal ordinance issued by the king with his advisers, not by a Parliament. However, it proved to be a most influential document, promulgated symbolically at one of the new castles which Edward had begun to build after his first war against Prince Llywelyn (1277). This statute described an administrative structure for the future government of north Wales. Following Edward's initial, ringing declaration that 'Divine Providence... hath now of its favour wholly and entirely transferred under our proper dominion the land of Wales with its inhabitants... and hath annexed and united the same unto the Crown of the aforesaid realm [of England]...', its detailed provisions applied specifically to 'our aforesaid land of Snowdon and our other lands in those parts'. These provisions were based on administrative and political experience gained in English shires, the king's lordship of Ireland, his dominions in France and in those lands which Edward already held in west Wales (centred on Carmarthen and Cardigan), as well as on some existing Welsh arrangements which were familiar to the local population and which he wisely adapted (and re-named).

By these means, the framers of the statute hoped to secure and govern Edward's conquests in north Wales. They created three new shires of Anglesey, Caernarfon and Merioneth, and also a separate county of Flint which was attached for convenience to Cheshire, under the control of the king's justiciar (or lieutenant) of Chester. The three north-western counties were together placed in the charge of a new justiciar, who exercised supreme governmental and political power on the king's behalf; Edward enlisted talented and experienced servants for the post after 1284. Financial affairs and the exploitation of these three counties became the responsibility of a chamberlain, usually a dependable cleric in Edward's service, sometimes in the exchequer at Westminster. The king also announced that he had 'caused to be rehearsed before us and the nobles of our realm, the laws and customs of those parts hitherto in use: which being diligently heard and fully understood, we have... abolished certain of them, some thereof we have allowed, and some we have corrected; and we have likewise commanded certain others to be ordained and added thereto...' This skilful blend of English and Welsh, old and new, meant that English law was introduced for criminal cases, though some of its elements were doubtless already familiar in some Welsh quarters, and that Welsh custom and law were retained for civil cases, especially those related to property and inheritance – though even here English law was beginning to attract the interest of landowners in north Wales.

This elaborate and pragmatic structure lasted in its essentials until the act of union, and gave a distinct identity to the royal dominion in north Wales; this and the king's expanding counties of Carmarthen and Cardigan in west Wales formed the new principality of Wales. In 1301 it was given a new prince in the person of King Edward's sixteen-year-old son and heir, Edward, who had been born at Caernarfon in April 1284. The tradition that Edward of Caernarfon, at the time of his birth, had been shown to Welsh people as their new prince is a later, romantic invention, but the creation of a new principality and, in 1301, a new line of princes may have been gestures of conciliation towards the king's Welsh subjects, and may suggest a propagandist flair to Edward's decisions on how best to secure their loyalties. Henceforward, the principality of Wales, north and south, was a royal dominion separate from the other lordships belonging to the king and his nobles in the March of Wales; it was inextricably linked to the crown, even when there was no prince.

Edward's astuteness had a sterner, ruthless aspect. After his first Welsh war in 1276-7, he built several royal castles to consolidate his initial territorial gains: at Llanbadarn (soon to be called Aberystwyth), Builth in the south, and Flint and Rhuddlan in the north-east; the latter especially would serve as bases from which to launch further operations against Prince Llywelyn. The conclusion of the 1282-3 campaigns was followed by the construction of even stronger, more dramatic fortresses to overawe all of Gwynedd . They were part of a bold, strategic plan which was realised at great effort and expense: Caernarfon, Conwy, Harlech and, lastly, Beaumaris were major castles associated with towns and ports to enhance their own security and their key role as bastions of royal rule. Thousands of labourers and craftsmen were recruited in practically every English county,

56. Caernarfon Castle.
57. Rhuddlan Castle.
58. Conwy Castle.

and some of these workers stayed and put down roots in north Wales. This huge building enterprise was put in the charge of the king's talented master mason, James of St George, who was enlisted by Edward in Savoy as 'master of the king's works'; the two men had probably met during the king's foreign travels. It took between five and seven building seasons to complete each of these castles, with the exception of the larger and grander Caernarfon, which seems to have had a special importance.

The total cost of building his fortresses – including the renovated Welsh castle at Criccieth – was about £90,000; it was an investment that proved its worth in helping to ensure virtually uninterrupted royal rule in north Wales thereafter. The castles were garrisoned and kept in reasonable repair until the end of the fifteenth century, and in the early generations at least their constables were usually loyal and experienced commanders of the English crown. These Edwardian castles were comparable with anything to be seen elsewhere in contemporary Europe and the Near East in their design and their modern, concentric construction. The adjacent towns, which were themselves provided with walls linked to the castles, could keep them supplied; and charters of privileges and grants of land and burgages attracted urban settlers as well as traders to sustain the new regime. The local Welsh inhabitants were welcome in the towns, and after the early decades they began to integrate socially with the townsfolk; even if many of the inhabitants of Caernarfon, Conwy and the other new northern boroughs felt their towns to be English in character and therefore attracted some resentment from Welsh rural folk, they did gradually lose their exclusively English and colonial identity.

A sophisticated administration, imposing castles and urban developments guaranteed the survival of the royal principality of Wales and its successful exploitation in the crown's interest. They also underpinned the social and economic development of the countryside as the age of conquest receded, and as immigrants and Welsh folk learned to live side by side, enjoying a measure of self-government, at least at the local levels that touched them most directly.

To Edward, demonstrating mastery was almost as important as achieving it: it certainly was one way of perpetuating it. The king had a personal interest in legends of King Arthur and their associated British traditions; in 1278 he and Queen Eleanor had been present when the supposed tombs of Arthur and Queen Guinevere were opened at Glastonbury Abbey. Edward sought to harness these symbols and myths in order to reflect his mastery in Wales, not least because the English élite was suspicious of the Welsh passion for prophecies and for tales of the Trojan descent of the British and uneasy as to where this passion might lead. So, in July 1284, during his tour of Wales, the king held a celebrated Round Table and tournament at Nefyn, one of the courts of the defeated Llywelyn, which caught the imagination of contemporary chroniclers. Edward also acquired and valued treasured items from Llywelyn's regalia, including what was claimed to be Arthur's crown; and at Conwy the previous year he had been presented with a fragment of the True Cross, Y Groes Naid, which was taken to England and was later venerated by English kings at Windsor castle. Then, when Edward and Eleanor visited St David's later in 1284, he purloined what was said to be the skull of St David himself and other relics, which were carried in solemn procession from the Tower of London to Westminster in 1285. This appropriation of the revered symbols of a conquered people and their rulers underscored the finality of the conquest. At Caernarfon the castle had a similar function, reflecting the imperial dignity of the English ruler in Wales. To the well-travelled, especially on crusade, the distinctive banded stonework and eagle towers of Caernarfon were reminiscent of Constantinople's imposing Roman walls and had a resonance with the Welsh tradition of Magnus Maximus (or Macsen Wledig), allegedly the Emperor Constantine's father whose supposed body was discovered – as if by a miracle – in Caernarfon in 1283.

During his tour in 1284, Edward visited all the new castles, sometimes more than once, granting charters to the new boroughs, often spending weeks on site, and then, in late autumn, travelling south from Gwynedd. The king's detailed personal interest in his settlement of the whole of Wales is clear. In November he crossed the River Dyfi into Ceredigion, making for his new castle and borough at Llanbadarn before moving on to Cardigan and the royal lands in west Wales, whose administration had been reorganised a few years earlier in a way that had provided useful experience in formulating the statute of Rhuddlan: there was a justiciar and, later, a chamberlain for west Wales, and sheriffs for the two counties, with earlier Welsh arrangements surviving at the more local level. Here, too, the arrangements made by Edward would last until the act of union.

Crossing the River Teifi, the king entered the March of Wales, and he and Queen Eleanor, who was with him throughout the tour, went on pilgrimage to St David's, before wheeling southwards to Haverfordwest, one of the largest and most thriving of Wales's towns with an Anglicised population and numerous contacts in the Severn region. Over the next month or so, the king and queen appeared in one marcher lordship after another, confronting a number of English marcher lords (or their representatives) who had to come to terms with the enlarged and reorganised royal dominion in Wales. Thus, after visiting his own castle and borough at Carmarthen, he passed through the lordships of Gower (where the Welsh announced that they would prefer to live under the king than under a marcher lord!), Glamorgan and Chepstow. In Glamorgan 'he was received with the greatest honour, and [an English chronicler noted] conducted to the boundary of his own lands by the earl [of Gloucester] at his own expense'. Honour to the king was matched by the self-importance of the earl within his own domain. Relations between the king and marcher lords like Gloucester might not be easy in the post-conquest world.

Edward's pilgrimage to St David's had been preceded by a visit from the archbishop of Canterbury, John Pecham, a Franciscan friar and intellectual with outspoken opinions, including about the Welsh whom he had met. This visit was part of a wide-ranging visitation (or enquiry) by the archbishop into all four Welsh dioceses, starting with St Asaph in the north and moving westwards and southwards until he reached Llandaff by August 1284. This comprehensive visitation – the first by an archbishop of Canterbury in the history of Wales – complemented the king's settlement by asserting the authority of Canterbury and by reforming various aspects of the Welsh church after the English example. Pecham sought to enforce discipline and good practices among clergy and people; he championed the preaching of the friars, assisted monasteries like Valle Crucis and parish churches like Mold that had been damaged in the recent wars, and he sought to promote reconciliation of Welsh and English as the foundation of future stability. In the course of his visit to St David's, he emphatically rejected Bishop Thomas Bec's pretensions to an authority independent of that of Canterbury; only Owain Glyn Dŵr would raise again the claims of St David's to a special status. Like the king's administrative arrangements, the changes in the Welsh church facilitated a greater closeness between church and state, England and Wales, which was assisted by some latitude conceded under

Edward I and Edward II in the appointment of bishops (most of whom were from Wales) and a certain degree of autonomy. They also affected the crown's relations with several of the marcher lords, who were fully alive to the fact that their domains lay within three of the dioceses, St Asaph, St David's and Llandaff.

Looking back on the year 1284, even a Welsh chronicler concluded that 'thereupon the king went towards England exultantly happy with victory. After that there were four years of continued peace at a stretch, without anything to be recorded for that length of time.' Taking a longer view, the king and the archbishop had established structures of government which effectively lasted for two and a half centuries – though not with 'continued peace'.

Neither Edward nor John Pecham was under any illusion about the difficulties of reconciling the peoples of Wales to the new regime, especially in north Wales, and some of the English nobles who were marcher lords were also distinctly uneasy. The challenge of ensuring stability and fostering prosperity was likely to be more easily met in the Anglicised south and the eastern borderland. A renewed phase of immigration took place in the wake of the conquest, and some of the prominent families of later medieval Wales – the Perrots of Pembrokeshire and the Stradlings of the Vale of Glamorgan spring to mind – were among the new arrivals. Even in Gwynedd the conquest stimulated urban developments around the coast, with migrants bold enough to venture from English shires into an uncertain environment – though not always bold enough to stay beyond the initial years.

During their tours, Edward and John Pecham encountered Welsh people with strong local and family loyalties, fortified by ties of lineage and kinship, and by patterns of landholding and a tradition of taking part in local administration. The new order could embrace these social features and it offered to loyal landowners opportunities at least in minor roles. Nevertheless, it was a volatile society in which the resentful were quick to arms and prowess in the fight was highly regarded by contemporaries. The king, the church and the marcher lords provided the superstructure of authority for such communities whose orderliness and social peace nevertheless depended heavily on self-discipline, self-regulation and self-help. Disputes about land were settled (as the statute of Rhuddlan conceded, within certain limits) 'by good and lawful men of the neighbourhood, chosen by consent of the parties' at odds. Even the king's requests for taxation from his principality were discussed by communities, though when, in 1318, an enthusiastic old man overstepped the mark and consented to more than the rest of his community in west Wales had agreed, it was the higher sum that was paid. Loyalty to king or lord, and to community or lordship, was likely to develop yet firmer roots in circumstances of conciliation and co-operation after 1282-83.

The population of Wales in Edward I's reign was about 300,000, perhaps a third that of Scotland. As Edward and John Pecham discovered, travel from one part of Wales to another between communities was not easy, but it could utilise the Roman roads which, as is now becoming clear from archaeology, penetrated to the west coast and even linked north with south around the central massif. Ports and the ferries across river mouths and between Anglesey and the mainland were often well established, and migration from Ireland, the west country, France and the Low Countries received a further boost as a result of Edward I's victories. It may be that seasonal Welsh labour drifted towards the richer borderland, just as large numbers of labourers and craftsmen were drawn to Wales for the great construction enterprises after 1276-67. It was, too, an age of rising population , which probably created a land hunger in parts of Wales; and although most settlements were small and dispersed, there was an increasing number of small towns emerging – reaching perhaps eighty or ninety by the 1330s.

The economy of Wales was a mixed one, inevitably so in a landscape of open, highland pastures and cultivable valleys and vales. The weather was notorious for its rain and cold – or so it seemed to those newly arrived in Wales or who allowed their prejudices free rein. 'When it is summer elsewhere, it is winter in Wales', commented a myopic Yorkshireman. The rearing of cattle and sheep, and the growing of corn and exploitation of the forests (some of which had been partially cleared recently to ease the passage of English armies), were complemented by the founding of new chartered boroughs alongside northern castles like Conwy and Denbigh that in time stimulated the commercial economy, including manufacture and trade in leather and coarse cloth. It was of course a colonial society, with Englishry and Welshry areas readily identifiable in most lordships and counties, but the integration of peoples was encouraged in many localities by the crafts and businesses of the little towns: no town was without its weekly market and annual fair. Early in the fourteenth century, even the small ecclesiastical town of St David's had two fairs, each lasting seven days, and a market held every Thursday; its burgesses supervised the marketing arrangements, and if access was a privilege, nevertheless rural folk were welcome under the watchful eye of the burgesses. The newer towns of Gwynedd were likely to be more defensive and their burgesses more starkly divided from the surrounding population, but even these communities became more integrated as the generations passed – a phenomenon which Edward might have noticed on his tour if he had compared Cardigan and Haverford with Conwy and Caernarfon; Aberystwyth was a town of Welsh people from the start.

In 1284, king and archbishop could not be expected to have abandoned their jaundiced view of Welsh people. Other contemporary observers thought the Welsh a poor people with peculiar habits and customs. To Lodewyk van Veltham, who encountered Welshmen in Edward I's army in Flanders in 1297:

> *In the very depth of winter they were running about bare-legged. They wore a red robe. They could not have been warm. The money they received from the king was spent on milk and butter. They would eat and drink anywhere. I never saw them wearing armour... Their weapons were bows, arrows and swords. They had also javelins. They wore linen clothing. They were great drinkers... Their pay was too small and so it came about that they took what did not belong to them.*

When fighting in Scotland for Edward, they proved difficult to control and liable to run amok. Convinced of the need to civilise the Welsh at home, John Pecham condemned the incontinence, drunkenness, idleness and ignorance of both clergy and laity; the long hair, bare legs and gaudy clothing of the clergy earned his disapproval as much as did layfolk's lax sexual and marital practices. Poor diet, simple dress and indolent manners were characteristics of the Welsh that stuck in English minds for long after. Differences spawned prejudices that were censorious. It is perhaps not surprising that a north Yorkshire chronicler in Edward I's reign should dislike Wales and the Welsh only a little less than he disliked Scotland and the Scots: 'May Wales be accursed of God and St Simon! For it has always been full of treason... May Wales be sunk deep to the devil.'

The native population of Wales spoke Welsh, although there were several other languages spoken and written in later medieval Wales – English, French and Latin. Despite the shock that events in 1282-83 delivered to poets, writers and the princely courts that patronised them, well-to-do people continued to read and listen to Welsh prose, history and poetry. Efa ferch Maredudd, from turn-of-the-century Cardiganshire, commissioned a Welsh translation of devotional works, one of a number of collections of Welsh prose and verse on literary, religious and historical themes known to have been compiled in the first half of the fourteenth century. The Chronicle of the Princes was turned from Latin into Welsh by mid-century. Understandably perhaps, there was a growing interest in Wales, as there was in England, in the legendary British past which enriched the poetry written for, and in praise of, notable Welshmen and their families. The greatest of Welsh poets, Dafydd ap Gwilym (*c.*1315-50), popularised newer themes illustrated from nature and the human condition as often as traditional musings on the Welsh condition. He wrote of love, the emotions, and old age, as well as to celebrate notable soldiers and successful families whom he knew and were his patrons: his regard for Ifor ap Llywelyn (Ifor Hael, 'the generous') of Bassaleg was lyrical:

> As far away as man may travel,
> As far as turns the orbit of daring summer sun,
> As far afield as what is sown,
> As far as falls the fair [and] sparkling dew,
> As far as clear eyesight sees
> (That's far!), and as far as ear can hear,
> As far as any Welsh is heard,
> And as far as fair seeds grow,
> Fair Ifor of the liveliest kind of custom
> (Long is your sword), your praise(s) will be sown.

French was spoken and read in certain circles, especially in the towns. When witnesses were interviewed in Swansea and Conwy in 1307 about the proposal to canonise Thomas Cantilupe, a former bishop of Hereford, some of those of immigrant stock responded in French, whilst the broadened horizons of Welsh soldiers in English armies implied contact with the French language and French writing. When the possessions of the Glamorgan rebel leader, Llywelyn Bren, were seized in 1316, they included eight books, three in Welsh and one book of French romance. Kings and marcher lords were not necessarily persecutors of the Welsh language; on the contrary, they made available interpreters and translators in official contexts, in early-fourteenth-century Brecon 'because the people there did not know how to do homage in English'. Later medieval Wales was gradually becoming a cosmopolitan and multilingual society.

The new regime was bound to cause some tension, especially when officials of kings and marcher lords were more insensitive or impulsive than the kings and lords themselves. This was at the root of Rhys ap Maredudd's revolt in Carmarthenshire in 1287-88, after Edward I had sailed for Gascony. Welsh princely families which survived the wars between Prince Llywelyn and Edward I were generally rendered powerless; alone among them, Rhys had thrown in his lot with the king and hoped to benefit accordingly. His expectations were not fulfilled and instead the new order in

Carmarthenshire curbed his freedom of action. Yet, for all the alarm that his revolt caused in England, it proved a localised and personal protest confined to south-west Wales; indeed, it was suppressed by armies recruited mainly in Wales, and his castle at Dryslwyn, where they conducted a vigorous siege, was all but demolished. The king did not feel it necessary to return from France and when Rhys was eventually captured in 1292, by some of his own men, he was taken to the king at York for trial and execution.

Things were different in 1294-95. Revolts broke out simultaneously in several parts of Wales and may have been co-ordinated; they were protests by disinherited Welsh lords, one of whom, Madog ap Llywelyn in Merioneth, called himself prince of Wales. The firm and exploitative nature of the new regime in the royal and marcher lands was at the heart of this wider-spread revolt: unprecedented demands for a subsidy (or tax) and repeated conscription for the king's wars in Scotland and on the Continent were experienced throughout Wales. The revolts were crushed, but on this occasion King Edward thought it wise to embark on another tour of pacification and submission in 1295-96 which, though it concentrated on the north-west, also took him to west Wales and over the Black Mountains to Brecon, Builth and the lordships of the Middle March: heavy fines were imposed, restrictions were placed on Welsh people in the new northern boroughs, and the last of the great castle-building enterprises was begun (but never completed), at Beaumaris in Anglesey. Edward adopted a realistic course: he needed to exploit his own lands in Wales for men and money whilst at the same time pacifying the population and securing the obedience and co-operation of marcher lords and their tenants. It was a delicate balance to strike, in an age of major administrative, political and social change in Wales.

In 1314, when Edward of Caernarfon had been on the throne as King Edward II for seven years, the earl of Gloucester was killed by the Scots at Bannockburn His lordship of Glamorgan faced a temporary royal administration whose oppressive regime led to attacks on castles and towns from Neath to Newport. By the beginning of 1316, the unrest had spread to much of upland Glamorgan and had found a leader in a local lord, Llywelyn ap Gruffydd (or Llywelyn Bren, 'of the wood') of Senghennydd, 'a Welshman, a great man and powerful in his own country' (as a contemporary English chronicler conceded). He had little difficulty in 'reviving the memory of oppressions and injuries committed by the English against their fathers'. The consequences of the earl's death, and of the great famine that was sweeping across Europe in 1315-17, sharpened the sense of outrage felt in Glamorgan and provided a context for revolt. The presence of Scottish troops in Ireland in 1315 while Scottish ships were raiding the Welsh coast gave alarming substance to talk of the common sufferings of the Welsh, Irish and Scots, descendants of the Britons, at English hands. The king's preoccupation with Scotland and his need for resources dictated a measure of conciliation, but after Llywelyn Bren surrendered he was brought to Cardiff castle in 1318 and executed by a new lord of Glamorgan, Hugh Despenser, one of the king's friends. Looking back several years later, the well-informed chronicler saw this instance of tension between English and Welsh in an apocalyptic perspective: 'The Welsh…were once noble and owned the whole realm of England; but they were expelled by the oncoming Saxons and lost both name and kingdom. The fertile plains went to the Saxons; the sterile and mountainous districts remained to the Welsh.' His rhetoric concealed the realities that were involved in striving to win acceptance for the new order.

59. Coin of Edward II who, in 1301, at the age of sixteen was given the newly created title 'Prince of Wales' by his father Edward I.

60. Flint Castle.

61. Ludlow castle.

The tensions between the crown and the marcher lords had been apparent in Edward I's reign, especially as a result of border disputes and warfare between the earl of Hereford (who was lord of Brecon) and the earl of Gloucester (who was Hereford's neighbour as lord of Glamorgan). On several occasions, the king confiscated marcher lordships or imprisoned marcher lords or restricted their rights. Then, when Edward II encouraged the vaulting ambitions of the Despenser family in the March, other lords resisted, and so the civil war that destroyed the king (1326-27) spread its turbulence into Wales and strained the loyalty of Welsh landowners and tenants by damaging those opportunities for local advancement in church and administration that enabled them to maintain their standing and status as leaders of their communities at home and in war abroad. Whereas Sir Rhys ap Gruffydd of west Wales and his kinsman in the north, Sir Gruffydd Llwyd, were loyal to the king and his allies, other leading Welshmen like Rhys ap Hywel of Brecon were committed to their own lords in the March, with the striking exception of the landowners of Glamorgan who deserted the Despensers as lords unworthy of their loyalty. When Edward II fled to Glamorgan in 1326, perhaps en route to join the forces of Sir Rhys ap Gruffydd in Carmarthenshire, he was captured near Neath Abbey by his enemies, who were led to the spot by Rhys ap Hywel; Glamorgan's landowners did not intervene.

By mid-century, the tensions had abated somewhat, but should major grievances arise they might burst forth anew. Relations between crown and marcher lords remained uneasy, but the integration of peoples continued in communities, towns and in royal and noble retinues abroad. By the middle of the fourteenth century, Wales was becoming a more cosmopolitan society in touch with Ireland, Scotland, England and the Continent; it was also becoming more integrated socially as descendants of English, Irish, French and Welsh lived in close proximity and slowly came to terms with one another – albeit the pace of integration varied from one part of Wales to another, and was in its earliest stages in recently conquered Gwynedd.

One incident and one contemporary's observation from the early 1340s illustrate the situation. A murder took place near Caernarfon in 1345 – the so-called Shaldeford incident – which revealed the dangerous tensions that lay beneath the surface between English and Welsh, government and governed, colonial towns and the countryside. This murder, which attracted much comment at the time, may not imply widespread and irreducible discontent with the political order or the consequences of social change, even in Gwynedd; and it must be said that our knowledge of the incident comes largely from alarmist – almost hysterical – reports by royal officials and burgesses of the northern boroughs. It is more than likely that fears that a harsher rule by a new prince of Wales after 1343 would threaten their positions prompted certain leading Welshmen, churchmen as well as laymen, to plot an assassination. On St Valentine's day (14 February) 1345, Henry Shaldeford, the newly appointed attorney in north Wales of Edward, the Black Prince, was attacked, robbed and killed by a large affinity of leading Welsh landowners as he was approaching Caernarfon: 'all the great men of North Wales, clerks and others, were parties to the plot'. Reactions from officials and burgesses alike were swift and furious; in the heat of the moment, the murder seemed to them to be an outburst of ethnic violence, though at Denbigh some loyal Welshmen had warned of possible trouble. The Black Prince and his council were reminded that this was no isolated crime: the castle and town of Rhuddlan had been stormed by Welshmen in 1344 and several townsmen were killed; the sheriff of Merioneth had been killed while holding his court; and at Caernarfon the Welsh 'have become so proud and cruel and malicious towards the English...that [the burgesses] dare not go anywhere for fear of death'. 'If redress is not made by the prince and his council, the Welsh will be such that it will be impossible for any Englishman or English official to dwell in these parts.' According to Denbigh's burgesses, 'the Prince's English tenants in these parts hardly dare to go out of the town ... to plough and sow and trade; and his English bailiffs hardly dare to do their work, for fear of being slain and plundered'. 'The Welsh have never since the conquest been so disposed as they are now to rise against their liege lord to conquer the land from him, if they can attain their purpose.' The 'light-headedness' and 'wildness' for which the Welsh were noted seemed capable of being converted into a fury that threatened the entire governmental and social framework in this part of Wales. However, the crisis passed and after a year or two the leading Welsh rioters were back in charge of their communities serving under the prince's authority.

A year or two earlier, Ranulph Higden, chronicler and monk of St Werburgh's Abbey in Chester, recorded his impressions of Welsh folk in everyday circumstances, for Chester, though a military base in wartime for English armies advancing into north Wales, was a thriving port and market to which Welsh traders and others resorted in more peaceful times. Higden noted that the Welsh now 'cultivate gardens and fields; they come together in towns; they ride in coat of mail; they walk shod; they feed decently; they sleep under coverings, so that they might now be deemed rather English than Welsh'. To him what was significant half a century after Prince Llywelyn's death was that the lifestyles of Welsh people here drawing closer to those of the English.

CRISES AND CO-EXISTENCE: 1350-1435

Just as the great European famine had touched Wales in 1315-17 (and played its part in Llywelyn Bren's revolt), so the great Eurasian plagues struck Wales from 1349 and dislocated its communities. Known as 'The Great Mortality' (Y Farwolaeth Fawr) and 'The Great Pestilence', these plagues blighted the population in all parts of Wales. The first outbreak, later universally known as the Black Death, reached the south in March 1349, probably from infected rats on board the ships that plied the Severn and put in at the ports of the estuary that were in contact with English and continental centres. It seems also to have spread overland and northwards along the populous Severn valley and the borderland to Cheshire. According to one chronicler, it exterminated 'two parts of the Welsh people', and the country's population may have fallen to about 200,000 souls before the end of the century.

Among early victims were two customs collectors in the borough of Carmarthen. Further west, the lordship of Pembroke was 'so devastated by the deadly pestilence which lately raged in those parts' that its annual rent was reduced by a quarter in 1350. To the east, as many as thirty-six of the forty tenants living in the manor of Caldicot died about the same time. Nor was the plague a respecter of persons: in March 1349 the lord of Abergavenny died, probably a victim of plague because the disease is known to have raged in Abergavenny by the following month. In north Wales, the leadminers of Holywell in Flintshire were decimated and the frightened survivors refused to work. The boroughs of Rhuddlan and Denbigh were badly affected, and at Ruthin seventy-seven folk died in two

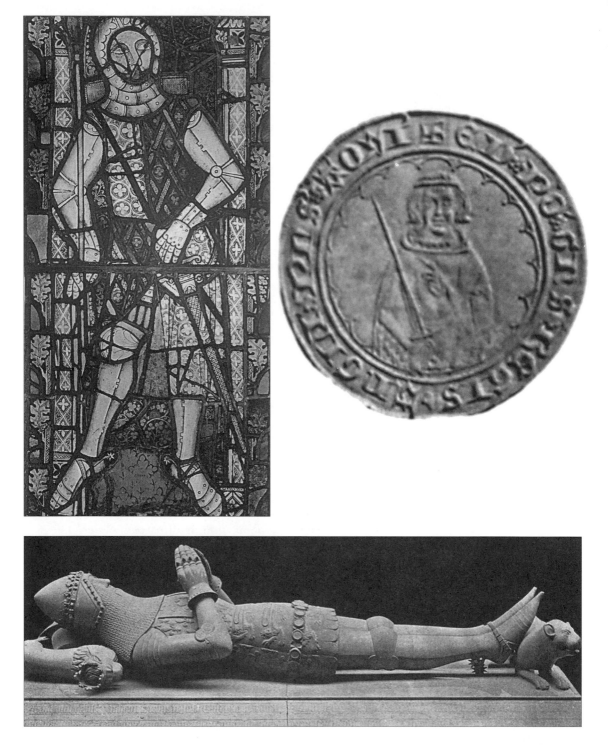

62. Hugh Despenser The Younger. Stained glass, Tewkesbury Abbey, Gloucestershire around
1344 commissioned by his mother, Eleanor de Clare.
63. Coin of Edward the Black Prince.
64. Effigy of Edward the Black Prince, Canterbury Cathedral.

weeks in June 1349. Along the coast, the herring fishery at Beaumaris suspended its operations. The effect on the clergy of Wales, who might be thought especially vulnerable as carers of the sick, is not easy to estimate, but in the adjacent diocese of Hereford 43% of the clergy died in 1349 and the bishop ordained in 1349-50 seven times the average number of clergy on behalf of the absentee bishop of St David's.

Social dislocation and economic disruption were accentuated by sheer fear and frantic efforts to flee the disease and its consequences; some later returned, like the Ruthin man who 'left his land during the Pestilence on account of poverty, but now [in 1354] came and was admitted by the lord's favour to hold the said land by the service due'. The first and subsequent plagues, especially those of 1361-62 (known in Wales as 'the Second Pestilence') and 1369, had the sustained effect of reducing landlords' rents and other incomes because, as was reported of Abergavenny, 'many of the tenements lie empty and derelict for lack of tenants'; they encouraged flight and they cut ties of obligation to perform services and to cultivate the land. Where peasants were unfree or occupied unfree land, some grasped the opportunity to cast off their remaining shackles. The overall impact was severe and lasting, for Wales was hardly entirely free of plague in any year during the 1350s and '60s: one Carmarthenshire official who hailed from Bristol died suddenly in 1361, and so did his mother and his brother. In a brutal fashion, this demographic crisis speeded up the effects of long-term immigration and settlement, of political and administrative developments since Edward I's reign, as well as of the climate changes of the early fourteenth century. It created opportunities for some amid the severe hardship: a thriving land market even for peasantry caused the prince of Wales's officials in west Wales in 1349-50 to create an entirely new office to cope with the disposal of properties that were now thrown onto the market.

The wonder is that the uncertainties of life caused by such turbulence did not lead to deeper social and ethnic antagonisms. But nothing comparable to the Shaldeford incident is known to have taken place in Wales in the decades after 1345. Ethnic hostility was latent and most likely to burst into flame when other factors provided the spark, as the English inhabitants in Wales and those in the border counties well appreciated.

Particular apprehension was felt in the late 1360s at news of the activities in France of the only surviving descendant of the princely house of Gwynedd, Owain ap Thomas ap Rhodri, whose grandfather was the youngest brother of the last Llywelyn; he was known in Wales as Owain Lawgoch (Owain 'of the Red Hand'), and to Jean Froissart, the Low Countries writer who doubtless reflected French attitudes, as Yvein de Galles. Like other adventurous Welshmen, Owain fought in the Anglo-French wars of the mid-fourteenth century, but unlike most of these soldiers he entered the service of the French king and forged a notable career for himself as a mercenary commander in France and Spain. He was, however, aware of his distinguished lineage and Welsh heritage, though he rarely visited Wales and may not have spoken Welsh.

The renewal of the Hundred Years War between England and France in 1369 brought Owain Lawgoch to the attention of the English government when the French planned an invasion with Owain's participation; but the ships were dispersed by storms and a second expedition in 1372 got no further than Guernsey. His declarations that he intended to return to Wales to recover his inheritance seemed hollow and unreal; yet in 1378 he was assassinated by a Scotsman who was later rewarded by the English government. Was he a victim of a covert operation? Owain's name and ancestry had caused a minor stir in Wales, where several poets regarded him as the rightful prince . However, his reputation in Wales was larger after his death than it ever was during his lifetime; he seems a minor link in the chain going back to the disinherited of the 1280s, and hardly capable of generating serious or widespread resistance to the order of things in late fourteenth-century Wales.

By contrast, as the century drew to its close, a number of factors came together to bring the Welsh more generally to a fever pitch of resentment once again. An increasingly harsh economic climate for many of the wretched peasantry in the decades of persistent plague heightened resentment of royal and marcher rule in state and church in many areas of the country and fuelled the smouldering embers of an ethnic hostility which perceived the Welsh to be volatile and untrustworthy. Over a generation (1343-76), Edward, the Black Prince had shown little personal or direct interest in his principality of Wales beyond drawing ruthlessly on its counties for men for his French campaigns and cash for his coffers; he showed little patience with grievances or complaints. Moreover, there was a corrosive strain of inefficiency and corruption in the activities of his officials which had not marked the royal administration in previous decades. The troubled reign of Richard II, who as a boy had briefly been prince of Wales in 1376-7, brought no relief, and his deposition in 1399 may have presented an opportunity to pursue grievances. Some of the marcher lordships outside the more accessible lowlands were also proving difficult to govern; among the Welsh estates belonging to the Black Prince's younger brother, John, duke of Lancaster, it became clear that in the lordship of Kidwelly officials needed to be changed frequently in order to retain the loyalty of the local population. As to the surviving peasantry of Wales, financial burdens imposed on upland communities seemed all the more crushing to a population depleted by plague and yet faced with lords who were anxious to stabilise their incomes by exploiting their rights and their judicial powers to impose fines of various sorts, or by resorting to novel and often oppressive expedients. The economic conditions which produced the Peasants' Revolt in England in 1381 were at work in Wales too, with the added complication that many of its inhabitants felt themselves to be a conquered people. Storm clouds were gathering.

In the Welsh church the division was deepening between those English-speaking clergy who now tended to occupy the higher and more profitable positions, including the bishoprics, and the Welsh clergy who were mostly restricted to the ranks of poor parish priests and monks. The Papacy was almost powerless by the 1370s, and the crown's policy was to promote royal servants as bishops and cathedral canons; mostly non-Welsh, they had little interest in, or sympathy for, their Welsh flocks, and they planned to secure more desirable promotions elsewhere as soon as possible. In 1366 Pope Urban V enquired of the Welsh who were at Bordeaux, the capital of the English domain in Gascony, as to whether the Black Prince's candidate for bishop of Bangor 'so understands the Welsh tongue as to be able to preach it'. The answer was presumably in the negative since Urban preferred another candidate. Such concerns, however, were not repeated. A barrier appeared to be placed before Welshmen, some of them trained at university, especially at Oxford, if they hoped for promotion at home. Monasteries with their vast estates and large sheep flocks were degenerating too, and the numbers of their inmates were depleted in the later fourteenth century: Carmarthen priory and Talley abbey each had only six monks by 1377. Church buildings were difficult to maintain and services were sometimes neglected.

The laity and lesser clergy alike felt increasingly resentful and, as in the Shaldeford incident, were thought likely to take part in conspiracies against the élite and officialdom.

Fears of violence and uprisings in the 1380s led to calls for greater care in garrisoning royal and marcher castles, but harsher government merely made matters worse in the 1390s. Richard II's alleged popularity in Wales is questionable, though in Cheshire he had a cohort of followers – hence, perhaps, he made for Conwy on his return from Ireland in 1399 – and some Welshmen tried to rescue him when he was taken as a captive from Conwy to Flint and on to London. In south Wales, however, the duchy of Lancaster's estates stood loyal to their lord and their castles at Monmouth, Kidwelly and elsewhere were held for Henry of Lancaster, the king's cousin, in 1399 ; indeed, a contingent of men was sent from Brecon to join Duke Henry at Gloucester on his way north to confront Richard II. Locality and lordship still commanded the allegiance of Welsh communities.

Owain Glyn Dŵr (c.1359-c.1415) stepped into an unstable situation in 1400. In the event, his revolt proved to be the most lengthy, dangerous and ambitious rising against English rule to have occurred in Wales since 1283. Although he could trace his descent from Prince Llywelyn's house, and had closer links with the princes of Powys and west Wales who had survived the conquest, Owain combined this princely lineage with the sort of personal grievances of Welsh landowners that had motivated the murderers of Henry Shaldeford. Unlike Owain Lawgoch, he was a wealthy Welsh landowner himself. Capitalising on the dissatisfaction of the times, his rising (1400-10) was arguably the most serious and costly threat to the recently established regime of Henry IV, the usurping Lancastrian king who was also a southern marcher lord in his own right. Paradoxically, Owain's career to date was that of a well-to-do landowner with extensive and profitable contacts in both England and Wales: like others of his kind, he was trained at the Inns of Court in London to learn the common law; he served in Richard II's armies against the Scots in 1384-5, and he became a retainer of the lord of Chirk, who was also the earl of Arundel, one of the richest of marcher lords. He married Margaret, the daughter of Sir David Hanmer, a wealthy landowner like Owain himself and a notable judge of immigrant stock whose forebear had settled in Flintshire in Edward I's reign. In short, Owain Glyn Dŵr (from Glyndyfrdwy, one of his chief residences in eastern Merioneth),was representative of that society of ethnic reconciliation that had emerged in many parts of Wales during the previous century. But in 1400 Wales was ripe for revolt. French meddling and encouragement from Scotland and Irish lords stoked the feelings of resentment, and gave Owain his opportunity.

Owain took the lead in plotting rebellion, partly because of his own grievances against Lord Grey of Ruthin, another important marcher lord, and against Henry IV who denied him justice. It may not have been a precipitate decision without an eye on its wider implications, for in September 1400, at his court at Glyndyfrdwy, he was proclaimed prince of Wales by friends and relatives in an astonishingly bold propagandist move calculated to attract supporters to his cause. He then proceeded to attack Lord Grey's estates and a clutch of towns in the north-east March, from Denbigh to Welshpool, Ruthin to Holt, even though there were Welsh folk living in them. He relied heavily on his kinsmen at the outset, especially on the Tudors of Penmynydd in Anglesey who collaborated with him and overran the borough of Conwy and seized the castle briefly in April 1401. Owain took another strategically and politically important step when he advanced into central Wales following a victory in the Plynlimmon mountains in May 1401, whilst in 1402 his capture of Lord Grey himself (whom he later ransomed for more than £6,500) and then Sir Edmund Mortimer, the uncle of the earl of March, who was claimant to the English crown, were major political *coups*; Mortimer married Owain's daughter the following year.

Like all Welsh risings and incidents of inter-communal violence in the past, Owain's movement did not win universal support in Wales. For one thing, the Severn basin and the Severn channel, focused on towns like Gloucester, Bristol and the ports of Somerset and south Wales, had had a strong Welsh presence of traders and clerics since the thirteenth century and this gave to Severnside society a distinct identity. Welsh families had settled in the English towns and periodically rose to civic office there, and the socil and economic connections between them were not permanently severed by the revolt. The attitude of the peasantry of Wales to Owain is not easy to assess, and outside the north-west loyalties may have responded, weather-like, to the proximity and successes of the military operations of Owain and the king. The Welsh *uchelwyr* (or squirearchy), however, provided leadership, both in support of Owain and, in other cases, in resisting his forces. At the outset, his kinsfolk – the Hanmers and the Tudors – were central to his plans; after he descended on south Wales in 1403, a number of Welsh squires from town and country declared for him, including William Gwyn of Llanstephan and Henry Dwnn (or Don) of Kidwelly. On the other hand, Dafydd Gam of Brecon had a history of staunch service to the earls of Hereford and dukes of Lancaster; during the revolt, he served the king and he died at the battle of Agincourt in 1415 under Henry V's banner. Other families were divided in their attitudes right down the middle. The higher clergy and the monasteries in the north and west generally supported Owain, but in the south the older Anglo-Norman foundations like Margam, Neath and Ewenni were unwelcoming and suffered accordingly.

In what amounts to his autobiography (1377-1421), the lawyer-cleric, Adam of Usk, expressed a southerner's attitude towards Owain and, although his home was in a Mortimer marcher lordship, he was ambivalent about the rising: he could sympathise with 'our men of England' as they tried to combat the rebels, and he later described Henry V as 'our king', as he undoubtedly was. Even Henry IV's attempts to suppress the rising were contrasted favourably by Adam with Owain's brutality and lack of chivalry. Moreover, Adam's loyalties were those of a south-easterner for whom Snowdonia was 'the source of all the evils of Wales'; and when Owain marched south in 1403, Adam regretted the way in which he drove those who resisted him across the River Severn, 'where, being Welsh, they were persecuted by the local people' and thrown into the arms of hostile English communities.

Yet at the height of the hostilities, the common reaction in England to Owain's movement was to see the whole of Wales and all the Welsh as highly dangerous – which may have made the suppression of the revolt more rather than less difficult. Expeditions led by Henry IV himself (1400-03) and, from 1403, by his son Henry (Shakespeare's Prince Hal) achieved little, and Parliament in 1401-02 was panicked, perhaps by the border MPs and by reports of Welsh students leaving the universities and migrant Welsh

65. Opposite: The battle of Shrewsbury 21 July 1403, as depicted in the *Beauchamp Pageant*. The forces of the English king are on the left, on the right is Henry Percy, known as Hotspur, falling backwards after having been pierced through the breast by an arrow, although a contemporary source describes him as having been shot in the face.

ere shewes howe att the batell of Shrevesbury betwen kyng Henr th
e K Henr Percy / Erle Richard there beyng on the kynge party fi
tabley e manly behaued hym self / to his greet laude e Worship p
ich batell was slayne the said S Henr Percy and many other W
And on the kynge party there was slayne in the kynge coteu
of other the Erle of Stafford Erle Richardes aunter Sir w
ny other in greet noumbre on whoos soules god haue mercy An

66. Battle scene depicting a skirmish between Owain Glyn Dŵr and the English forces led by Richard Beauchamp, Earl of Warwick, in 1403 from the *Beauchamp Pageant* a late fifteenth-century manuscript. The claim in the text that the earl captured Owain Glyn Dŵr's banner is not confirmed in any other source.

67. A scene from the *Beauchamp Pageant*, an illustration of the battlefield at Shrewsbury just after the battle, and Prince Henry (the future Henry V), standing to the left with his father on the right.

68. Badge of Richard II, which some on the rebel side wore at the battle of Shrewsbury.

labourers in England deserting their fields, into passing discriminatory legislation to curb the movements and rights of Welsh people, though the king himself was reluctant to assent to them all. Owain had no compunction about seeking allies among the king's other enemies in England, Ireland and Scotland, especially the Percy earls of Northumberland and Worcester, and supporters of the Mortimer earl of March. The king's victory over Henry Hotspur, Northumberland's eldest son, at Shrewsbury in July 1403 was a set-back to this political and military coalition that was partly designed to advance Owain's cause. Owain then focussed on the south , which was necessary if his claims to be prince of Wales were to have any hope of being widely accepted. He captured a number of castles, in particular Harlech and Aberystwyth (1404), which remained in his possession for several years; even Carmarthen was occupied, briefly, in 1403. To secure military and naval assistance and wider recognition, his emissaries, led by his chancellor, the university-trained Gruffydd Young, negotiated a treaty at Paris with King Charles VI of France in July 1404. Equally noteworthy, Owain 'and his hill-men' held assemblies at Machynlleth, Harlech and Pennal (1404-06) which had something of the aspect of a parliament at which ambitious plans were formulated for an independent principality. Owain was consciously acting in the style of a European prince.

His plans show an informed awareness of European political and religious realities, for they included support for the anti-Pope at Avignon whom the English denounced, and whose assistance was sought to create a Welsh church whose metropolitan head would be the bishop of St David's, not the archbishop of Canterbury. Two universities in north and south Wales were intended to provide an educated clergy and a trained civil service, just as the Scots were presently contemplating, and a territorial dominion was outlined that would extend into the English midlands and assist in the dismemberment of the English realm. Such ideas took Owain well beyond the ambitions of all other Welsh rebels since 1282-3 and, through his understanding of intellectual and political developments since the thirteenth century, even beyond the plans of Prince Llywelyn.

Although French troops landed in Milford Haven to help Owain's followers in southern Wales, 1405-06 saw significant military reverses, and his French and Percy allies faded away. His brother Tudur was killed in battle near Usk in May 1405, and his eldest son Gruffydd was captured and transferred to the Tower of London (where he died of plague in 1411). Aberystwyth and Harlech capitulated to English forces in 1408-09, and Owain's wife and two daughters were humiliatingly captured when Harlech fell. Following a raid into Shropshire in 1410, he disappeared from view: he rejected the offer of a pardon from the new king, Henry V, in 1415 and may have died later that year. His place of burial is unknown, although plausible sites still excite attention.

Owain's revolt was remarkably ambitious and his objectives far-reaching and constructive ones; but he lacked consistent support throughout Wales and especially in the south where – as Adam of Usk made plain – his northerners were often resented and his ravaging of towns and countryside alienated opinion. Nevertheless, the revolt was a shock and it preoccupied the English king and the marcher lords for a decade. Henry IV was worsted on his expeditions to Wales because it proved difficult to bring Owain and his followers to battle. English official reactions set back by a generation the evolution of a peaceful society in which migrants (and their descendants) from England and Ireland, France and the Low Countries, and from elsewhere in Wales had been associating in communities, rural as well as urban, for a long time past, even in the north-west heartland of Wales. Owain Glyn Dŵr threatened for a time to put these processes into reverse; his revolt certainly disrupted them and divided regions, communities and some families in Wales.

Glyn Dŵr's failure and the defeat of his Welsh supporters and his allies raised the question of how peace, stability and prosperity could be restored in Wales, and how the various peoples of Wales could be reconciled with one another and with the king's subjects in England. These were similar questions to those which had been posed at the end of the thirteenth century, but they now seemed more acute and more complex because of the developments in the intervening years in Wales and in England. The sheer scale of the revolt and its connections beyond Wales were a threat to the English realm under the Lancastrians beyond anything that Prince Llywelyn had represented: first, because Henry IV was a usurper whose reign was plagued by rebellion and threats from many quarters and, then, because his energetic son re-embarked (1415) on the great war with France on a scale never before attempted, not even by Edward III. The support of Welsh soldiers and Welsh resources was essential if this renewed war were to be won, and so the security of the English realm in the west was vital to Henry V as much as to his father. It took the best part of a generation for contemporaries in Wales and England to come to terms with the consequences of Glyn Dŵr's revolt. The disruption and devastation may have been greatest in the south, where the land was most hotly contested, and from Cardiganshire to Monmouth there were counties and lordships that produced no revenue for their rulers in some years. At Ogmore, Usk and elsewhere mills were destroyed, and in north Cardiganshire former rebels were slow to return to their homes. Many towns, such as Aberystwyth, Kidwelly, Oswestry and Holt, and the suburbs of Chester, were burned or ravaged, and in Chester's case the townsfolk were still claiming sixty years later that the revolt had seriously damaged their livelihoods. But during the reign of Henry V (1413-22), most parts of Wales saw signs of recovery, perhaps more quickly in the upland areas

Born at Monmouth in 1387, King Henry V had a better first-hand knowledge of Wales and its peoples than had any king since Edward I. His grandfather, John of Gaunt, duke of Lancaster, was one of the most prominent marcher lords in southern Wales, and his mother, Mary Bohun, was the daughter of another of them. He was made prince of Wales at the age of twelve soon after his father seized Richard II's crown in 1399, and although Henry IV was careful not to give him the full powers of government in the principality of Wales that the Black Prince had enjoyed (and abused) , the new prince spent much of the decade before his own accession in 1413 coping with the rebellion in Wales. Within days of becoming king, he set about the task of settling Wales with determination. He was under no illusions about the problems, some of which were the heritage of decades. His first priority was to end the disorder, especially in northern Wales and the English borderland, and to this end he adopted an attitude that was at once firm and conciliatory, deploying a calculated clemency tinged with severity. The second priority was the restoration of royal control, underpinned by effective royal authority in the principality shires and the royal lordships (including those of his own duchy of Lancaster in the south) and by shoring up the marcher lords' authority elsewhere. In order to achieve these goals, the quality of government needed to be improved by removing oppressive and corrupt officials who had caused so much resentment before and the rebellion; those leaders of Welsh communities who had supported Glyn Dŵr had to be reconciled at the same time as those who had remained loyal throughout the revolt were rewarded. On the other hand, the king could not ignore the fact that adequate resources to achieve his ends depended in part on resuming the exploitation of his and the marcher lords' estates, and in attempting conciliation he did not shrink from making Welsh communities pay collective and individual fines for pardons, as well as new taxes for the French war.

The commissions which the king appointed in Wales in 1413, headed by his father's staunch marcher supporter, Thomas, earl of Arundel, who had a vested interest in the restoration of order and authority, went about this task with a will. It was far from easy, and in 1417 unrest was still present especially in north-west Wales, where Owain Glyn Dŵr's son Maredudd was at liberty. The escaped lollard knight, Sir John Oldcastle, sought refuge in the lordship of Powys in that year and opened negotiations with Maredudd and the Scots, though the lollard heresy itself attracted few adherents in Wales beyond the English borderland. Arundel's task was made more difficult because some of the greater marcher families were now headed by youngsters, whilst devastation by the rebels had had a crippling effect on their lordships. Moreover, border counties like Hereford and Shropshire continued to be fearful of renewed Welsh raids. In the longer term, the support of Welsh landowners, including former rebels, would be essential if the peaceful integration of peoples were to resume: the fact that Owain's rebellion had not attracted them all helped in the longer term. It was only in 1421 that Owain's son finally accepted the pardon which the king had offered, but nervousness about Wales remained palpable. About 1438, a well-informed but anonymous political analyst wrote the 'Libel of English Policy', which instructed Henry VI' s advisers about the security of the realm: amongst other things, he issued a graphic warning about Wales which reflected the fears that persisted and the concerns which required attention in a decade of famine and poor harvests:

> Beware of Wales, Christ Jesu must us keep,
> That it make not our child's child to weep,
> Nor us also, if so it go this way
> By unwariness; since that many a day
> Men have been afeared of there rebellion
> By great tokens and ostentation.

SELF-GOVERNMENT AND RECONCILIATION: 1435-1536

After Glyn Dŵr's revolt, neither the crown nor many of the marcher lords were able to give to Wales the attention that had been essential during the hostilities: by the mid-1430s the consequences were becoming all too apparent. Welsh landowners, often brothers-in-arms of English gentry and knights at court and in war, were well established as leaders of local society and patrons of the church and monasteries, and of Welsh poets and writers. They enjoyed much of the country's landed wealth, and in some parts they had friendly relations with the townsfolk. Above all, they continued to provide social and political leadership as officials and servants of the crown and the marcher lords, and their role was essential to stability. They were a gregarious, enterprising and ambitious body of men, whose land, lineage and durable ties of kinship fortified their dominance of local affairs. Many of them had been the key to the temporary success of Glyn Dŵr and, after they deserted him, to the ultimate failure of his enterprise. Few could now claim direct descent from Welsh princes, but some, in north and south Wales, like the stock of Abermarlais in Carmarthenshire and of Penrhyn in Caernarfonshire, had ancestors who had served these princes; others, like the Herberts of Raglan and the forebears of Sir Rhys ap Thomas at Dinefwr, sprang from humbler Welsh roots; and yet others had come from England, Ireland or the Continent, notably the Perrots of Pembrokeshire, the Stradlings of St Donat's, and the Boldes and Bulkeleys of Caernarfonshire and Anglesey. Despite the restrictive measures of Henry IV's early Parliaments, the crown realised that it needed these men (and their womenfolk) to administer estates, preserve the peace, collect revenues, and sustain Wales's allegiance. It is true that, as Welshmen, they were excluded from the most important positions in the principality counties: between 1400 and the fall of the Lancastrian dynasty in 1461 no Welshman born of Welsh parents was allowed to be justiciar or chamberlain in north or south Wales. But because these senior officials were usually great English nobles preoccupied elsewhere, men like Gruffudd ap Nicholas in Carmarthenshire and William ap Gwilym ap Gruffudd in Caernarfonshire deputised so regularly for the absentee officials that they enjoyed a high degree of practical power. Both Gruffudd and William took the precaution of securing the king's letters of denizenship (or naturalisation) in the late 1430s in order to secure legal protection against the legislation of 1401-02.

Such Welsh landowners may have been even more essential to the marcher lords. The vast complexes of estates in England, Wales, Ireland and overseas of, for example, Duke Richard of York, Warwick the Kingmaker, and the Stafford dukes of Buckingham were administered by men drawn from a smaller pool of their own retainers and servants than that available to the king. Local men were consequently enlisted as stewards and receivers (or financial officials) of lordships, and not simply as designated deputies: men like William ap Thomas of Raglan and his son, William Herbert, in Usk, Glamorgan and Monmouth exercised the lord's authority for him – even, as in the case of this upwardly mobile family, in more than one lordship and for more than one marcher lord.. As in the past, such men were well placed in their communities to provide peaceful and effective government; equally their selfishness or neglect could create resentment among their neighbours or rivals and provoke violence in their lordships which the crown and the marcher lords might not be able to control. They drew admiring comment from Welsh poets in a tradition of praise-poetry that went back centuries, although as Guto'r Glyn's poem addressed to William ap Thomas on a visit to Raglan makes plain, this admiration was not always disinterested or objective:

> There I received a payment
> To wear your livery, Gwalchmai of Gwent:
> There I received a great welcome,
> And better by far was the respect I received.

The individual histories of these landholding families reveal much about self-advancement, the reputation of individuals in their communities and more broadly, and about reconciliation between Welsh and English. They demonstrate allegiances, interests and ambitions in what was an increasingly Anglo-Welsh world. Only in rare cases was the Glyn Dŵr revolt of long-term damage to the fortunes of such families. Even a scion of the

1. The late Mesolithic human footprints at Uskmouth, near Newport.
2. View of Llyn Cerrig Bach, Anglesey.

3. The Great Orme Copper Mine.

4. The Paulinus stone from Venta Silurum (Caerwent) was erected by the tribal senate of the Silures in about AD 220. It is inscribed to Tiberius Claudius Paulinus, former commander of the Second Augustan Legion.

5. Stone from Llandyfaelog, Powys, showing the figure of a warrior.

6. Decorated slab from Llanhamlach, Powys, showing a female figure on the right.

7. Monument from Llantwit Major, Glamorgan, commemorating Hywel ap Rhys of Glywysing, one of the kings who submitted to Alfred the Great.

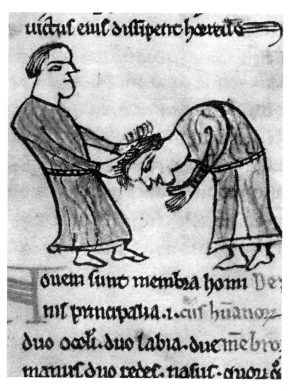

8. *Opposite* A medieval portrait of Macsen Wledig, Magnus Maximus.

9. The Welsh prince as knight: equestrian seal of Gwenwynwyn ab Owain (d. 1216), ruler of southern Powys.

10. The judge of the royal court holding his lawbook.

11. Pulling hair: one of the offences under Welsh law for which the compensation termed *sarhaed* was due.

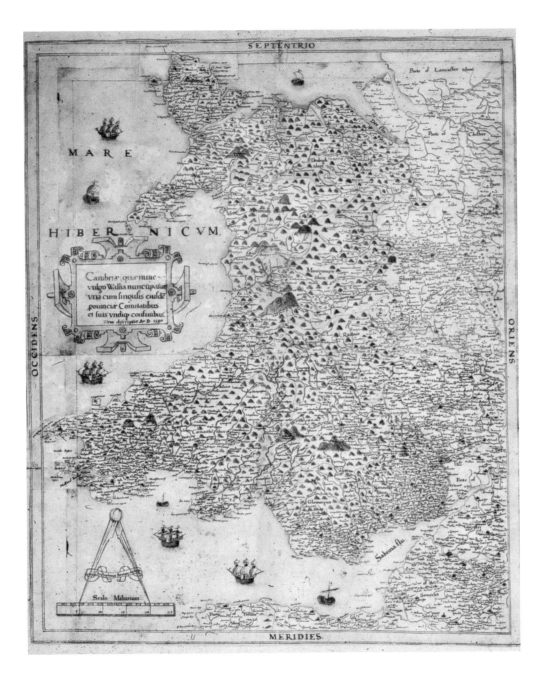

12. *Opposite* Christopher Saxton, Map of Wales 1580.
13. John Speed, Flintshire map incorporating a picture of St Winifred's Well.
14. Shon ap Morgan, William Dicey print, *c.*1747.
15. Wnafred Shones, William Dicey print, *c.*1747.

16. W. Daniell, 'Amlwch Harbour', 1815 aquatint.
17. J. Warwick Smith, 'Parys Copper Mines', watercolour, 1790.

18. J. Ingleby. Dee Bank
19. J. Ingleby. Holywell Cotton Mills, *c.*1792.

20. West View of the Britannia Tubular and the Menai Suspension Bridge, after Hugh Jones, 1850.
21. Richard Wilson, Dinas Bran c.1770.

22. George Delamotte, Mr Howells, preacher, 1810. This is part of a large collection of unpublished watercolours of Swansea characters and Swansea poor.

23. J.M.W. Turner, Dolbadarn Castle, oil 1799.

24. Sketch of Welsh national costumes, 1830, by Lady Llanover.

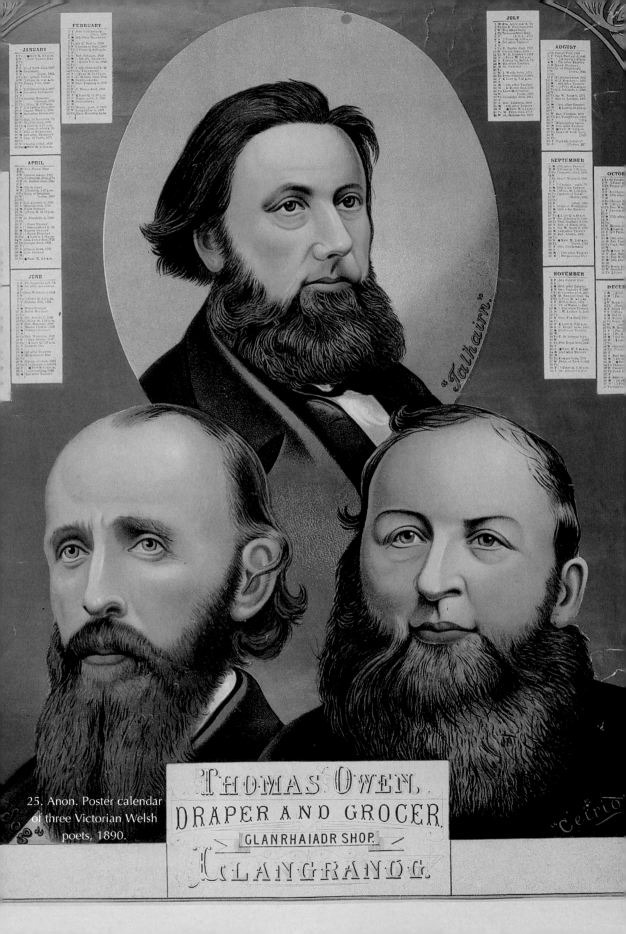

25. Anon. Poster calendar of three Victorian Welsh poets, 1890.

26. South Wales Industrial landscape, Penry Williams c.1825 oil.
27. St David's Cathedral, seen from the ruins of Bishop's Palace.

28. Early medieval brooch from Penycorddyn-mawr, Clwyd.

Tudors of Penmynydd, kinsfolk of Owain Glyn Dŵr himself, was able to do spectacularly well. Owain ap Maredudd ap Tudur seems likely to have fought in France in Henry V's reign, attracted the attention of Henry's widow, Queen Katherine, and eventually married her around 1431-32; two of their sons – a third became a monk at Westminster Abbey – were made earls of Richmond and Pembroke by their half-brother, King Henry VI. This is an extraordinary story, but for a number of Welsh landowners (or their sons) the opportunity to serve in the wars in France was a gateway to fame, which the poets at home lauded. Of Matthew Gough (or Goch, 'the red'), whose family came from the lower Dee valley and who had a notable career in Normandy, the poet Guto'r Glyn wrote admiringly:

> He is an eagle (soaring) over young men
> With Arthur's countenance facing the French battles,
> The soul of the good captains,
> And the leader of the men there.

When he died defending London from John Cade's insurgents in 1450 the elegies turned into eulogies. 'Whenever there is mention in our time/ Of any one in Normandy/ It is of Mathau Goch', but he was not alone. He could have met William ap Thomas there and his son William, who took the Anglicised surname of Herbert whilst winning his spurs with the duke of York in France. Thereafter Herbert attached himself to his lord in the Welsh March, entered the circle of Welsh and border gentry and became a friend of York's son, Edward IV. Sir Gruffudd Fychan of Powys made his name – and secured his knighthood – by capturing the lollard fugitive, Sir John Oldcastle, in 1417; Gruffudd too served in France and was complimented for his prowess. Others did not have to cross the Channel to achieve fame and local power. Gruffudd ap Nicholas of Newton, near Dinefwr, had no princely blood in his veins and did not serve in France; rather did he exploit the needs of a colonial administration whose senior officials were noblemen or absentees. His letter of denizenship in 1437 signalled his ambitions and the crown's trust; his horizons were broadened by relationships struck with Welsh and immigrant families in communities across south-west Wales. He may have been a ruthless and difficult neighbour, yet poets flocked to his household and he presided over a notable eisteddfod at Carmarthen or Newton about 1451. The likes of Gruffudd ap Nicholas did not regard the immigrant families of the lowlands and towns as forming a detached or separate society, for they – and the Perrots and the Stradlings of St Donat's are examples – married into local Welsh families and might even patronise Welsh poets and writers. In north Wales, the Gruffudds of Penrhyn and the Bulkeleys of Beaumaris, the one an indigenous brood with roots among servants of the princes, the other immigrants from Cheshire, tell the same tale of a cosmopolitan society of wide horizons, sometimes – as with the Dons of Kidwelly and the Griffiths of Abermarlais – shifting their main interest from Wales and taking Anglicised surnames whilst maintaining their links with their roots.

The greatest opportunities for Welsh and Anglo-Welsh families arose during Henry VI's reign (1422-61) and the ensuing Wars of the Roses. For several reasons, political control of Wales was weaker then than at any time since the Edwardian conquest. Already in the late fourteenth century, some marcher families were losing their personal involvement in the country and this trend continued in the early fifteenth century. The Bohun inheritance of the earls of Hereford was divided, part going to the king, and the attention of the Mortimer earls of March was diverted elsewhere, especially to Ireland. The Despenser, Mortimer and Stafford families were blighted by minorities at this time: for forty-one of the sixty-five years between 1349 and 1414, the head of the Despenser family was a child; for thirty-four years during 1382-1432 most of the Mortimer estates were in youthful hands, and Humphrey, earl of Stafford and lord of Newport was under age from 1403 to 1423. Some inheritances, like the duchy of Lancaster lordships, the Mortimer lordships, the county of Pembroke, and the immense lordship of Glamorgan, were incorporated in such large landed complexes that their lords, even when they were adults, could devote only a fraction of their time to them. Moreover, the crown's territories in Wales after 1399 were so large and widespread that to supervise them effectively was a very tall order, and probably beyond the resources of a monarchy assailed by noble factions and then overwhelmed by civil war. In 1461 the earldom of March was added to them, and later on much of Pembrokeshire and the Tudor inheritance swelled the number of lordships belonging to the crown. Nor could the burden of government be eased by transferring at least the principality of Wales and Cheshire to a capable young prince of Wales, for between 1413 and 1536 there was a prince for only thirty-seven years and at no time was he an adult.

There was, then, an inevitable distance growing between Welsh society and the lords of Wales, and this was accentuated by continued apprehension in official circles after Glyn Dŵr's revolt and by the difficulties which the crown and the marcher lords experienced in maintaining their incomes from their Welsh estates. This crisis of royal and noble authority in Wales benefited the local landowners. Its dangers could be avoided only if there were effective administrative and political structures operating in a peaceful environment. But even Richard, duke of York (died 1460) rarely visited his Welsh estates except at times of personal crisis when the civil war approached; the interests of Richard, duke of Gloucester (later King Richard III) were usually remote from his lordship of Glamorgan, and at Pembroke Humphrey, duke of Gloucester (died 1447) would have been little more than a tourist. The smaller number of English noble families which, with the crown , lorded it over Wales after Glyn Dŵr's revolt made it impossible for them to give much personal attention to the re-establishment of law and good order.

Warnings about the state of Wales and its potential threat to the English realm were sounded at an unfortunate time, for in 1422 Henry V died and was succeeded by his nine-month-old son, Henry VI. The awesome responsibilities of government (including in France) during the king's minority fell to the English lords, several of whom also had lordships and responsibilities in Wales. The situations in Ireland and Wales seemed comparable to the author of the 'Libel of English Policy', and if Ireland were to be lost, the pessimists argued, 'Farewell Wales'. Greatest alarm was sounded along the English border, where several manors scarcely recovered from Glyn Dŵr's attacks: there were appeals from the inhabitants of royal and noble lordships, as well as complaints from MPs in Parliament. Some of the northern colonial towns and their burgesses – still largely of English extraction – were alarmed, and they protested in 1445 about the number of Welshmen who had received letters of denizenship. The border shires complained about raids, cattle rustling, river piracy and holding to ransom, whilst the patchwork of jurisdictions that was the Welsh March meant that criminals might be able to escape their just deserts in one lordship by escaping to another. The customary means of curbing such lawlessness – 'love days', 'parliament days', 'days of redress' and 'days of the March' between neighbouring lordships – still operated, but they could be subverted by ruthless landowners with powerful kins and by negligent or self-interested officials beyond the reach of a distant king and distracted lords.

In Hereford by 1450 there were English and Welsh factions that bitterly divided the city. In Carmarthenshire and Cardiganshire, an aggrieved landowner in 1435 reported that he was afraid to go to law because one recent royal official 'draweth unto him outlaws and divers misruled men the which obey not [the king's] law there neither your officers'. In the former heartland of Glyn Dŵr's power, Merioneth was virtually ungovernable: it produced little revenue for the crown after the revolt, and its tenants were said to be a plague on the neighbouring lordships of Powys and Mawddwy. A petition presented to Parliament in 1449 claimed that even in the royal territories the people 'daily abundeth and increaseth in misgovernance'. The crown was the only superior authority which could re-establish order and stability in Wales: but conditions at Westminster in Henry VI's reign were not helpful, whilst in Wales those landowners who were given the power seemed less inclined to use it if their own interests were at stake.

Soon after he took up the reins of government, in 1436-7, Henry VI with his councillors tried to make the existing machinery for law enforcement work, putting their faith in the marcher lords and the king's own lieutenants. In November 1436 the constables of royal castles and senior royal officials were sent to their posts, and the marcher lords were told to attend to their lordships and hold their courts regularly. That might at least provide some supervision of Wales's localities. More radically, in November 1437 it was decided to take collective and co-ordinated action: the marcher lords were summoned to a meeting that should take advice from their leading local landowners. It was an imaginative move and the meeting produced 'articles of Wales' in May 1438; we do not know what they contained because they have since disappeared. Little, however, seems to have been achieved, for in October 1442 the king's council decided to examine Edward I's statutes for guidance, and again the marcher lords and their leading tenants were summoned to London in order to produce a solution by Christmas to the problem of disorder in Wales. If nothing had emerged by then, the king gave them an ultimatum: he would intervene himself in the marcher lordships – a radical suggestion indeed. Again, little of permanent value resulted, and in the event the king showed reluctance to tamper with custom and existing practice. In 1448 several marcher lords (or their officials) and the king's justiciar and chamberlain of north Wales were ordered to stop the thieving which was inflaming the borderland between Merioneth and Caernarfonshire and the lordships of Powys and Mawddwy. In 1453 a major enquiry was needed into officers' negligence and extortions in the three northern counties of the principality. Yet when Parliament proposed to give JPs in border English shires the authority to intervene in neighbouring marcher lordships, the king balked at giving them full powers.

The likelihood of being able to re-assert authority over Wales became even more remote when the Lancastrian monarchy was engulfed by the Wars of the Roses (1455-87), which involved Wales as well as the other dominions of the crown. The dynastic disputes within the English royal family, ending with the accession of Henry Tudor in 1485, affected Wales because the crown and so many of the leading protagonists had lordships or lands there. This fact led G.M. Trevelyan to conclude that 'the Wars of the Roses were to a large extent a quarrel between Welsh Marcher lords, who were also great English nobles, closely related to the English throne', and he was partly right. At the same time, the fractured loyalties and bitter noble rivalries that littered the civil wars had a profound effect on Welsh society and encouraged the ambitious, ruthless or self-interested to re-focus their loyalties even more decisively on their own concerns and power. Welsh shires and lordships changed hands (and therefore their political allegiance) between the 1450s and 1500 with bewildering frequency. The lordship of Glamorgan, for example, passed, from the Beauchamp earls of Warwick to the Nevilles in 1449, and then, in 1474, to Richard, duke of Gloucester, to Jasper Tudor, earl of Pembroke, the son of Owain Tudor and Queen Katherine, in 1486, and then to Jasper's great-nephew, Prince Henry who became Henry VIII. The crown's own principality in north and south Wales experienced similar shifts of lordship from Lancaster to York in 1461 and to Tudor in 1485, with five boy-princes along the way.

When the fighting between Lancaster and York took place intermittently in Wales and the borderland, Welsh landowners and their retinues took the part of their respective lords. In the 1450s, King Henry VI relied on his half-brothers, Edmund Tudor, earl of Richmond, and Jasper Tudor, earl of Pembroke, to sustain Lancastrian power in the principality counties and Pembrokeshire, in the knowledge that Richard, duke of York and Richard Neville, earl of Warwick, with their local supporters, the Herberts of Raglan and the Devereux of Herefordshire, had castles, men and resources in the eastern march. When York and his sons were put to flight at Ludford Bridge, near Ludlow, in October 1459, Earl Jasper set about extending his power to Denbigh and the march, with the aid of the Perrots of Pembrokeshire and the sons of Gruffudd ap Nicholas from Carmarthenshire. At Mortimer's Cross in February 1461, Jasper's Welsh army and his allies were defeated by the larger force of the duke of York's son, Edward, earl of March, who was accompanied by the south-eastern retinues of the Herberts and Devereux, and the Vaughans of Brecon. This battle, fought mainly between Welsh retinues on behalf of Lancaster and York, was decisive in enabling Edward of March to seize the crown as King Edward IV.

Edward's most urgent need in 1461 was not for experiment which might antagonise his noble allies but for an effective regime in a traditional setting that would enable him to establish his authority in Lancastrian Wales. Such a regime was provided by a Welsh landowner, William Herbert, the son of Sir William ap Thomas of Raglan and Gwladus Ddu, daughter of Henry V's famous commander, Dafydd Gam, It was a novel choice, though one that illustrated the influence which leading figures in Wales had achieved over the past century. With his Welsh lineage and upbringing, it is not surprising that Herbert inspired Welsh poets and propagandists, moved in a circle of family and friends much like himself in Herefordshire and the March, and served his Yorkist lords at home and in France, and became the new king's confidant. By 1468, when he was created earl of Pembroke in place of Jasper Tudor, there were few areas in Wales of which Herbert was not either lord, custodian, or principal official: according to one poet he was 'King Edward's master-lock' in Wales. In that year he captured the last Lancastrian outpost in Wales, Harlech castle, from Jasper Tudor and a local retinue led by Gruffudd Fychan of Corsygedol. It was far from the king's mind to undermine marcher privilege, for he created two new marcher lordships (including Raglan) for Herbert; rather was he enlisting the talents of one of the ablest and best known Welshmen: Jasper Tudor was the son of a Welsh squire and a French princess, but it was William Herbert who was the first to enter the English peerage with both parents of impeccably Welsh birth.

Herbert's death at the battle of Edgecote in 1469, when the defeat of his large Welsh retinue was much lamented in Wales, created a vacuum in which 'the outrageous demeaning of Welshmen' continued. This, and Warwick the Kingmaker's rebellion against Edward IV which allowed the brief restoration of Henry VI to the English throne (1470-1), gave Jasper Tudor a further opportunity to return to Wales and raise a Lancastrian army from among his loyal Welshmen – and to take charge of his young nephew, Henry Tudor, who had been brought up by the Herberts since 1461. But while he was bringing his forces from south Wales to support the Lancastrian queen, at Chepstow Jasper learned that she had been defeated by Edward IV at Tewkesbury on 4 May 1471. That ended the restored Lancastrian monarchy, but it did not necessarily change residual loyalties in Wales – and as Welsh poets reminded their patrons, Jasper and Henry Tudor were safely in exile and might return.

During the 1470s, therefore, Edward IV, like Henry VI before him, was driven to seek a constructive and lasting solution to the problem of order, and he did so by bringing the king's sovereignty to the fore. He and his councillors approached the matter pragmatically, and it took time. His baby son was created prince of Wales in June 1471, and over the next four years a council managed the affairs of his principality very much as councils had done for princes in the past. In the meantime, MPs from border shires made plain to Parliament how disorderly conditions were in Wales. Like Henry VI, in 1473 Edward IV conferred with the marcher lords, at Shrewsbury, and he made them promise to fulfil their particular responsibilities. Then, in 1476 the prince's council was given authority to ensure that these promises were kept: at Ludlow in March a meeting with the marcher lords addressed the matter of punishing crime throughout Wales and the March, and the prince's council was given the backing of a retinue to punish criminals and investigate negligent officials. This amounted to devolution of the crown's supervisory power to the prince's council and it was extended to the border shires too. It gave Wales an official body with full powers of government in the principality and the royal lordships, and a supervisory authority in the border shires and the remaining marcher lordships.

Of course, what was seen as a problem by the government and border communities was regarded as an opportunity by ambitious landowners in Wales. While officials and councillors were preoccupied with maintaining order and security, these families were bent on advancing their own fortunes and enhancing their lifestyles. Later in the fifteenth century, economic prosperity revived and one symptom of that is the return of Welsh drovers, clothiers and other traders to the thriving border centres of Chester, Oswestry, Shrewsbury, Ludlow, Gloucester, and Hereford by the 1460s, and the growing prominence of Welsh settlers and merchants in Bristol and the north Somerset ports. Moreover, opportunities for apprenticeships, training in the law and a university education seem to have increased during the second half of the century as larger numbers of Welsh youngsters especially found their way to Oxford, London and cloth centres on the drover routes through southern and central England. Like the landowners who – the Dons of Kidwelly and the Stradlings of St Donats among them – made a name for themselves at court and in the king's service in England and abroad, a number of Welshmen – like the Vaughan kin in Bristol – became citizens of English towns, where they could reach the highest civic and gild offices. The accession of the quarter-Welsh Henry Tudor in August 1485, as the best available alternative to the usurper, Richard III, may have quickened the stream but did not begin it.

69. Stained glass of figure of King Sadoc, from a Tree of Jesse, Llanrhaiadr, North Wales, dated 1533.

In Wales itself, the impoverished state of the cathedrals, greater churches and monasteries after Glyn Dŵr's revolt, and the reduced ranks of their personnel, meant that ecclesiastical estates were leased to the likes of Sir Rhys ap Thomas or else managed by Welsh landowners, frequently in their own interests. That is not to say that religion was dead, for the later fifteenth and early sixteenth centuries were an age of lively personal faith which revealed itself in pilgrimages, the veneration of saints and images, the rebuilding and beautifying of churches and the patronage of religious poetry and verse – albeit their themes had a pessimistic tone that dwelt on Christ's suffering and redemption. Welsh landowners and townsmen took the lead, as anyone viewing the array of Herbert tombs in Abergavenny's priory church, or Sir Rhys ap Thomas's effigy in Carmarthen, or the elegant, perpendicular additions to the churches of Haverfordwest and Tenby can readily testify. A number of these squires and townsfolk – even from families of part-immigrant descent – sponsored the literary culture of poetry and prose in Welsh. Poets who could praise Edward IV and William Herbert, Henry Tudor and Rhys ap Thomas and his son, and Sir William Gruffudd of Penrhyn and Lord Stanley in the same breath were welcome in self-regarding households across Wales:

> Edward the conqueror, in place of Edwin,
> Is Julius Caesar over the English host;
> Herbert is brave on a wheeling charger
> Measuring Wales in his commission
> Edward is Charlemagne, by St Martin's grave!
> Herbert is Roland to the generous;
> Edward is Arthur, as is fitting,
> Herbert is Gwalchmai with the broken spear.

Thus Lewis Glyn Cothi, a poet at home in court and household right across south and central Wales and to the English border – even occasionally in Gwynedd too. The houses of these wealthier Welshmen seem to have been metamorphosed in the century and a half before the union, just as the fortunes of their families were transformed. Whatever the quality of their houses in the fourteenth century (and Iolo Goch found much to admire at Owain Glyn Dŵr's house at Sycharth), there was a spate of rebuilding following the revolt's trail of burning and destruction: the stone buildings of Pembrokeshire and southern towns had much in common with buildings in the west country, just as the timber halls of north Wales and the March were reminiscent of those of the English midlands. Tretower Court, civilian in style, reflects the standing of the Vaughans of Brecon in the later fifteenth century; scarcely earlier, the large and elaborate Bryndraenog hall in the lordship of Maelienydd was described by one enthusiastic poet as 'the work of angels'.

From the standpoint of Ludlow and Westminster, however, political order and social stability were paramount, and they rested upon those who staffed the prince's council and those who were required to implement its decisions in the localities of Wales. But Edward IV's death and Richard III's usurpation in 1483, and Henry Tudor's victory over Richard at Bosworth in 1485, demonstrated that the council's very existence depended on there being a prince of Wales. It was Henry VII who decided, when Prince Arthur died in 1502, that a council should remain in existence, under the king's control. How to ensure

70. Henry VIII by Hans Holbein.

implementation of its decisions was a more deep-seated problem. Whatever the council under Edward IV and Henry VII intermittently achieved, and despite the fact that a majority of marcher lordships belonged to the king by 1485, disorders were not eliminated: rebels attacked Brecon castle in 1486 and there was insurrection in Merioneth in 1498 which seized Harlech castle. Henry sought to pacify opinion in the northern counties of the principality and the north-east lordships (1504-7) by assuring their inhabitants of full access to the law and by annulling Henry IV's penal laws, though burgesses of the northern colonial towns were outraged. This permanent delegation of royal authority to a council in the March, based at Ludlow from the mid-1470s, was little altered even after Henry VII died in 1509. This was because, first, Jasper Tudor, earl of Pembroke and the king's revered uncle (who died in 1495), and then Sir Rhys ap Thomas and Sir William Gruffudd of Penrhyn who, like William Herbert before them, were Welsh landowners, were trusted and assisted the council. When Sir Rhys died in 1525, Cardinal Wolsey placed the council in the nominal charge of Princess Mary, though with no new powers: the existing machinery was expected to work, though within a few years more radical proposals were in the air at both Ludlow and Westminster, and these eventually, in 1536, transformed the administrative structure and clarified the constitutional relationship between Wales and England – and confirmed to the leading inhabitants of Wales an even greater measure of control over the affairs of Wales.

According to the terms of the act of 1536, Wales was 'incorporated, united and annexed' to the English realm on principles whereby 'laws and justice [were] to be administered in Wales in like form as it is in this realm'. This legislation recognised the closer political, judicial and administrative relationship that had gradually developed since 1283, building on social, economic and cultural changes taking place at the same time.

More immediately, the union sprang from the circumstances of Henry VIII's reign, especially the death of Sir Rhys ap Thomas in 1525. His son, Sir Gruffudd ap Rhys, who was well qualified to step into his father's shoes, died prematurely in 1521, whilst Sir Rhys's grandson, Rhys ap Gruffudd, was too young to be trusted and reacted wildly to being bypassed. The latter's show-trial and execution in 1531 coincided with the discussions about reform of Welsh government to ensure order and justice, although under Bishop Rowland Lee (1534-43) the council in the March was doubtful of the wisdom of assigning further powers to Welsh landowners. The discussions were overtaken by Henry VIII's marital and succession problems, the consequent breach with Rome and the declaration of the royal supremacy over the church in England and Wales, and the related issues of security and defence which obsessed the king's ministers. Preliminary statutes in 1534-35 emphasised that there should be effective justice and administration throughout Wales in the hands by the local landowners and townsmen; for a short time JPs from the border English counties were allowed to extend their activities into the March, pending the creation of JPs in Wales itself. These reforms of the 1530s, culminating in the act of 1536, were part of a wider policy of achieving uniform control of provincial government by curbing independent franchises in England, Wales, Ireland and Calais. The act of union marked no practical change in the use of the Welsh language in courts and elsewhere, although English had made inroads in Wales over the centuries, not least in administration and justice. Not surprisingly, the union was welcomed by influential Welshmen, some of whom had petitioned for reform, and also by English observers, though hard-headed officials at Ludlow like

Bishop Lee retained their doubts. Until the nineteenth century, Henry VIII was praised for his measure which was regarded as being of great benefit to Wales, and most contemporary Welsh households would have agreed.

On the eve of the union, leading Welsh men and women, whatever their origins, enjoyed a large measure of local self-government and self-advancement comparable to that of the English gentry – perhaps even with fewer restrictions because of the absence of lordship and the distance from Westminster. At the same time, enterprising Welsh landowners and townsmen, merchants and intellectuals, had forged close links with other communities in Wales and with the prosperous towns and countryside of the border and southern England, especially from the mid-fifteenth century; they had done so by marriage and education, war and presence at the king's court, by trade and business. Glyn Dŵr's revolt had poisoned relationships for a season, and contrasts between the north-west and the rest of Wales were still marked (as rivalries among fifteenth-century Welsh poets testified), yet reconciliation was gathering speed. The union confirmed the dominance of the leaders of Welsh opinion, and it confirmed the emergence of a breed of Anglo-Welsh gentle families of knights, esquires and gentlemen who were equally at home in both countries. The union accordingly roused little resistance from the people of Wales or the people of England.

5

FROM REFORMATION TO METHODISM 1536 – c.1750

Geraint H. Jenkins

The early modern period is the Cinderella of historical studies in Wales. Part of the reason for this neglect lies in the unfortunate tendency to judge the Welsh experience against the English model and to be beguiled by the unflattering images of Wales as a 'barren', 'comatose' and 'benighted' land painted by external observers from the Tudor period onwards. Some historians have simply presumed that the political assimilation of Wales by England necessarily meant that the history of this 'internal colony' was no more than a tranquil and uneventful interlude between the rebellions of the fifteenth century and the epoch-making industrial revolution. The cult of writing 'British history' or subsuming Wales within what is vaguely described as 'the peoples of the Atlantic archipelago' have also served to obscure the sociocultural experience of the Welsh within this period, and not even recent attempts to highlight multiple identities within a Celtic framework have succeeded in rehabilitating early modern Wales. The approach adopted in this chapter is to focus on the diversity of the social experiences of the Welsh and the continuities and discontinuities which characterized the period as a whole. It should be emphasized from the outset that the overwhelming majority of people were less concerned about the forging of a British identity or by the ideologies constructed by Crown, Parliament and the rule of law than about making sense of their lives and making ends meet.

MAKING SENSE OF THE WORLD

The lifestyles, structures, values and cultures of people in early modern Wales are light years away from those of the early twenty-first century and to penetrate their mind-set requires a considerable degree of imaginative effort. Our forebears knew nothing of mechanization, complex technology, the silicon chip, high-speed transport, electricity cables, fibre-optic links, phone lines, radios, televisions and videos, and the rhythm and tempo of their lives were appreciably slower. They did not suffer, as do we, from the tyranny of numbers, and official counts of the population did not begin until 1801. By modern standards, the population was small and widely dispersed, towns were tiny, industries were underdeveloped and roads were rudimentary and often impassable. Wales possessed no institutions of statehood, no universities or museums, no capital city or any major recognizable sociocultural focal point. As the humanist William Salesbury confessed in one of the first Welsh printed books in 1547, 'a Welshman today does not know what patriotism consists of'. Outside Wales itself, the Welsh were cruelly caricatured in lampoons, parodies and squibs as a backward, feckless, garrulous and larcenous people who wore coarse frieze, ate flummery, leeks and cheese, strummed harps, kept flea-ridden goats and sheep, and spoke a guttural tongue which resembled 'the gobbling of geese and turkeys'. In short, the Welsh, in common with other Celtic-speaking peoples, were viewed by the English as lesser beings to be pitied or derided.

Early modern Wales becomes more intelligible if we view it as a federation of small communities or an assemblage of tiny localities in which people thought in terms of counties rather than nations or kingdoms and in which face-to-face contacts were more important than printed culture. Within this mosaic of local units people nursed a rich and varied cultural inheritance suffused with rituals, images, symbols, myths and customs which we would find difficult to understand or appreciate. Geography was a major divider: powerful contrasts existed between the thinly peopled rugged upland heartlands and the more heavily populated fertile lowland and coastal plains. North and south Wales were deeply divided by the nature of the terrain and the lack of decent communications, and manuscript and printed records abound with scathing comments about poorly maintained roads and unreliable carriages. Sir John Wynn of Gwydir used to describe the route across Snowdonia as 'the devil's bowling-green' and Breconshire was known to English travellers as 'Breakneckshire'. 'God be praised!' was a common epithet used by weary travellers whenever they arrived more or less intact at their destinations. There were also long-standing historical demarcations, notably between west and east Denbighshire and the Welshry and Englishry of Gower. Welsh speakers from north Pembrokeshire who summoned sufficient courage to cross the *landsker* into 'Little England beyond Wales' were often greeted with the derisive cry 'looke there goeth a Welshman'. The power of localism meant that the first loyalty of people was to their 'county', i.e. the county, region or parish where they had been born, raised or settled. 'Wherever the Welshman is raised, therein he chooses to tarry', wrote the poet-cum-drover Edward Morris, and this had the effect of nurturing a powerful sense of communal and cultural solidarity. Love of locality prompted George Owen of Henllys to prepare his celebrated *The Description of Penbrokshire* at the end of Elizabeth's reign and Henry Rowlands of Llanidan to raise funds from his fellow antiquarians in Anglesey to subsidise the publication of *Mona Antiqua Restaurata* in 1723. The fact that we speak of Griffith Jones *Llanddowror*, William Williams *Pantycelyn* and Dafydd Jones *Caio* reveals that celebrated figures as well as faceless people who seldom figure in the historical record were closely identified with their place of birth or abode.

Yet it would be foolish to believe that all small communities were static and that geographical mobility was low. Even those who lived out their lives within the boundaries of their parish or county were able to travel distances of up to twenty miles. Tradesmen, craftsmen and harvest workers travelled much longer distances and there were always 'masterless' men who travelled far and wide in search of food or work and who were often forced into petty crime by economic hardship. Many people took the long road to London, never to return. Wealthy young gentlemen embarked on the Grand Tour of Europe, Catholic exiles studied in France, Spain and Italy, and peasants relied on soldiers and sailors to keep them abreast of wondrous events in the outside world. Some Welshmen became iconic figures abroad. John Owen, the Caernarfonshire-born epigrammatist, was better known in seventeenth-century Europe than was Shakespeare, and Sir Henry Morgan, formerly a Monmouthshire labourer, became the most celebrated buccaneer in the world.

Each locality within Wales jealously guarded its own socio-economic practices, including customary laws, weight and measures, price structures, domestic architecture, folk customs

71. Sir John Wynn, Gwydir. Engraving by Robert Vaughan.
72. Sir Henry Morgan. Engraving.

and dialects. These, in turn, strengthened the networks of kinship, mutual loyalties and good neighbourliness. Poets often referred to 'roots', 'ties of blood' and 'the nature of kindred'. People who inhabited the world we have lost possessed skills and attributes of which we have either no experience or seldom practise. In particular, they had a much greater awareness of the benefits and perils of natural phenomena. Untroubled by hurry sickness, they pondered long and hard over the natural world around them and were deeply versed in the properties of plants and flowers, the movement of the stars and the behaviour of animals. Their eyesight and hearing were sharper than ours and their memories longer. Since the expectation of a long life was low, people relied heavily on their memories and passed on local lore. During a Pembrokeshire court case in 1637 the lineage of a coroner's wife was traced back to the time of Owain Glyndŵr in order to prove her descent from the same family as the plaintiff. Local oracles with elephantine memories were highly cherished and in the eighteenth century Lewis Morris never ceased to marvel at the ability of his father (an Anglesey craftsman) to recount hundreds of tales from his childhood onwards. We must always remember that what survives in the written record is simply a small segment of long-forgotten traditions which once had a vitality of their own in small communities. Even maypole customs and brutal popular recreations like knappan and bando demonstrated the singularity of individual parishes, as indeed did shaming rituals like *y ceffyl pren* (the Welsh equivalent of the skimmington ride) which heaped public ridicule on those who violated marital and communal obligations. The distribution of poor relief stiffened communal harmony and the rigours of a generally harsh legal code were softened by tacit compromises made by local administrators and jurors.

The absence of an overarching national spoken language meant that a rich and colourful variety of local dialects and speech patterns flourished, so much so that there were constant, though exaggerated, claims that the language and dialects of north and south Wales were mutually incomprehensible. In the late sixteenth century George Owen of Pembrokeshire claimed that southerners looked down on the 'mountain men' of north Wales because they lacked English civility, but by the eighteenth century Lewis Morris of Anglesey was able to turn the tables by deploring the clicking Welsh speech of the Anglicizing 'Hottentots' of south Wales. Over the period as a whole probably as many as nine of every ten persons spoke only Welsh, and although English words and phrases were increasingly infiltrating domains such as the law, commerce and fashion, Welsh was the natural daily medium of communication for the overwhelming majority. People blessed, cursed, prayed, quarrelled, made love and grieved in Welsh, and oral exchanges were far more robust, colourful and vulgar than common discourse is today. Without question, the native language was the most distinctive badge of the national identity of Welsh people.

Yet the fact that the bulk of rural dwellers spent almost the whole of their lives within their monoglot native parishes insulated them from the wider world. Although Renaissance scholars freely used the words 'Europa' or 'Ewrop' in their sixteenth-century treatises, only the educated few appreciated the significance of cultural developments on the Continent. Throughout this period most people believed that the earth was the solid motionless focal point around which all the other planets and stars turned. When the historic Julian calendar, which divided the year in December and June into ritualistic halves, was replaced by the new Gregorian calendar in 1752 which separated the year in October and April, common people angrily complained of having been robbed of eleven days of their lifespan by the educated few. 'Give us our eleven days!' was the popular cry. When George I died in 1727 a woman asked the local schoolmaster at Llanfor, Caernarfonshire: 'Who will they have in his place? I hope they won't ask my husband Siôn; he was parish overseer last year and overseer of the roads the year before; this year he deserves to be left alone.' Sufferers from scrofula knew that the 'Royal Touch' could effect a cure, but, apart from that, peasants had little inkling of the nature of kingship.

Within small, tightly-knit communities people were naturally inquisitive and court records reveal the prevalence of informers who delighted in keeping their neighbours under close surveillance. It was virtually impossible to maintain privacy or keep secrets. Rumour and gossip, some of which was leavened with a grain of truth, spread swiftly. Strangers were received with cool suspicion, especially if they spoke no Welsh or posed a threat to local employment and communal stability. During the civil wars Welsh foot soldiers despised 'alien' royalist commanders and were reputed to 'love not a stranger longer than he can tell them the news'. Welsh jurors were allegedly more lenient towards their own than towards outsiders. The arrival of appreciable numbers of colliers, tin miners and woollen workers from England invariably caused tensions, and several Scottish pedlars were murdered during the early decades of the eighteenth century.

It would be foolish, therefore, to portray rural communities as harmonious entities; they were often riddled with petty conflicts, feuds, bickering, quarrels and antagonisms. This was partly the result of the hazards of the environment in which people lived. Fires could prove catastrophic: draughty candle-lit timber buildings were extremely vulnerable and where houses were located in close proximity high winds could spread a blaze with swift and devastating consequences. Local populations were also pruned by successive harvest failures, food shortages and infectious diseases. The virulence of the bubonic plague, closely followed by smallpox, typhus and dysentery, all of which were encouraged by insanitary dwellings and the rudimentary state of medical knowledge, exacted a heavy toll of life. Inns, taverns and even churches reeked of stale sweat and noxious odours, and during periods of subsistence crises and pestilence no one needed reminding of the fragility of human existence. Preachers sought to reassure their flocks by drawing their attention to the biblical promise that man's allotted lifespan was three score years and ten, but the average expectation of life at birth in the seventeenth century was thirty-five. Disease struck down even the offspring of the well-to-do. Only one of the nine children of Sir Richard Bulkeley III (d. 1621) survived, and five of the eleven children sired by the Puritan Morgan Llwyd died. Special intercessions for preservation from sudden death were included in the Book of Common Prayer, and the Welsh proverb 'Death comes in every guise' was on many lips. Most unlettered folk seem to have accepted their lot with stoic indifference, believing their fate to be 'as natural and unavoidable as the course of the sun and river, or the growth of the grass in the field'.

Even so, life-threatening hazards tested the patience of even the most law-abiding subjects. During years of scarcity poor people stole cheese, butter, oatmeal and bread, took part in food riots, and fed their families on the ill-gotten spoils of smuggling and wrecking. Magistrates dealt harshly with serious offenders but were not disposed to incur the cost and trouble of bringing pilferers and mischief-makers to the courts to face inordinately severe punishments. Petty offences were winked at and the brutality of the penal system was tempered by a wide range of informal sanctions such as mediation, arbitration and even private humiliation. Since anything between a third and a half of the population hovered precariously on or below the level of subsistence, it was thought prudent to ignore statutes, delay or circumvent justice, and soften the rigours of the legal system.

This was certainly the case in matters relating to witchcraft. Although people deployed a wide range of devices such as charms, cures and rituals to protect themselves against daily misfortunes and the depredations of evil spirits and witches, prosecutions for witchcraft were extremely rare. Unlike many countries in Europe, Wales was spared the horrors of the witchcraft craze. Most trials occurred in the seventeenth century and only five suspected witches were put to death. The most common explanation for the reluctance to bring prosecutions for witchcraft is the strong tradition of good neighbourliness in Wales, but it has also been suggested that the state was much more interested in prosecuting and hanging thieves (around 4,000 male thieves were executed before the end of the Tudor period) than in sponsoring a bloody witch-hunt against relatively harmless women. People were more likely to vent their spleen on sowers of discord and strife, and the heyday of cases of verbal and written slander (cheat, knave, rogue, villain, whore and bastard were the most popular epithets) was between 1570 and 1670. Belief in witchcraft, of course, never faded, and common people had recourse to the cunning man, the wise woman and the conjurer until well into the twentieth century because they fulfilled critical roles as healers, lost-property offices, marriage bureaux and as intermediaries between a witch and her victim. Well versed in local gossip and the personal histories of their clients, cunning men impressed them with fortune-telling manuals, indecipherable charms and legerdemain tricks calculated to win their trust. The conservatism and inertia of peasant life, the dearth of medical knowledge and the inability of Protestant reformers to eliminate the ingrained habits of hundreds of years of Catholic piety and devotions meant that superstition and magic retained their appeal throughout this period.

A rich oral culture of storytelling (based on earthy humour), poetry and singing flourished throughout these years among 'the witty common people' and was sustained on the hearth and in taverns by humble rhymesters and remembrancers. Elis Gruffydd, a multilingual soldier and chronicler in Tudor Flintshire, was a wonderful spinner of tales: 'Bring him a stool to sit on', he once wrote of himself, 'and a mugful of beer warmed up and a piece of burnt bread to clear his throat, so that he can talk of his exploits at Therouanne and Tournay.' Ballad-mongers sang catchy songs in fairs, markets and alehouses, 'Buy your Welsh almanac' became a popular cry after 1680, and crudely performed interludes were held – to raucous and abusive heckling – on makeshift wagons in public places. Those with hard-earned pennies to spare drowned their sorrows in drink or gambled at dice and cards. Sturdy youths displayed their athletic prowess in violent ball games and large crowds attended cockfights, wrestling matches and cross-country races in which the matchless Griffith Morgan (Guto Nyth Brân) excelled. Sundays, wakes and festivals were days of boisterous merrymaking which provided a release from the stresses and strains of daily toil. Any kind of light-hearted frivolity or rowdy behaviour was, of course, anathema to Puritan and Methodist reformers, but their exhortations fell on deaf ears among large sections of the rural community.

THE PECKING ORDER

Poets and writers throughout this period often referred to *bonedd a gwrêng* (gentry and commonalty), a popular epithet which signified the deep-seated distinction between the propertied élite and landless peasants. The former group comprised less than 5% of the total population but all its members believed that their privileged status was a God-given blessing and that 'inferior' or 'vulgar' sorts should treat them with unswerving respect and

73. Will (partly in Welsh) of Thomas David, Puncheston, Pembs., 1718. In the hand of William Gambold.
74. Title-page of Thomas Jones's almanac *Newydd oddiwrth y Ser* (1683).
75. John Speed's map of Flint 1610 showing a body hanging from a gibbet.

deference. Over the period as a whole the gap between rich and poor widened. Indeed, compared with the affluence, domination and control of the great gentry, the lower orders at the bottom of the heap were simply 'low-born clods of brute earth'. In no period was the chasm between the 'haves' and 'have nots' more apparent, and every landless person was expected to recognize that landowners were superior people of distinction. But although the fundamental social division was between *bonedd a gwrêng*, communities were composed of finely graded hierarchical groups ranging from the aristocracy and the gentry at the top of the scale, through the middling sorts, and down to the dependent poor at the foot of the social pyramid.

Unlike England, Wales was not an aristocratic society and most of the great magnates who held estates in Welsh shires were absentees. The natural leaders and shapers of opinion within society were the gentry, the most prosperous and robust of whom could boast extensive acres of land as well as reputable ancestry. Those who were convinced that nature had intended them to bear 'the port and countenance of a gentleman' and who could withstand the gibes of English lampoonists were expected to provide abundant visible proof of their privileged position and, as inflation began to bite from the mid-Tudor period onwards, many of them embarked on a variety of stratagems, not all of them legal, designed to extend their domains and fill their coffers. The acquisition and misappropriation of monastic land, judiciously arranged marriages (the feisty Katheryn of Berain married four times!), opportunistic forays into the land market, and the enclosure of extensive pieces of waste, forest and common land all helped to enhance their patrimonies and strengthen their authority and prestige in local circles. The rise of the Welsh gentry was also facilitated by the abolition of gavelkind in 1543 which eliminated the dangers associated with the minute subdivision of holdings. Progressive gentlemen were strongly in favour of primogeniture, whereby the eldest son inherited property intact, and the overwhelming trend was towards the building of large estates. This coincided with a building boom as the richest Tudor and early Stuart families sought not only greater privacy and comfort in great houses but also visible proof of their supremacy. Those who laid claim to gentry status and whose rentrolls exceeded £1,000 per annum could afford a reasonably comfortable lifestyle: they dressed in fashionable clothes, ate and drank well, and generally travelled on horseback or in carriages. Bards would sing their praises, their sons would be dispatched to public schools, the universities and the inns of court, and scholars would seek their bountiful patronage. As might be expected, the gentry were a mixed lot. Some, like Sir Edward Stradling of St Donats, were men of considerable learning and wisdom, whilst others chronicled and cherished the nation's history. But there were also bullies, spendthrifts and rakes among them. As the years rolled by, too, they set less store by the native tongue and became increasingly enchanted by the glittering lights of London and the company of the chattering classes. Welsh bards soon discovered that the number of genuine patrons was dwindling swiftly as the effects of inflation prompted them to tighten their purse-strings. The Anglicization of the gentry proved to be a long process, stretching well into the eighteenth century, but there were clear signs long before the civil wars that the landed élite believed that English was a prestigious tongue, entirely suited to government, law and administration, whereas Welsh was a barley bread tongue fit only for the hearth, the fair and the market.

Yet, all was not plain sailing for the gentry. Inflationary pressures meant that for every progressive capitalist landowner who prospered there were many others who went to the wall. The civil wars, too, brought further upheaval, and during the Interregnum many traditional families temporarily found themselves unseated by upstarts, low-born strangers and traffickers in sequestered lands. The Welsh version of the world turned upside down was neatly encapsulated in verse: 'Placing the head where the tail should be, and placing the tail where the head should be.' In many ways, however, the most decisive shift in the pattern of Welsh landownership occurred after the Restoration in 1660. This was the age of the Great Leviathans, remarkably wealthy landowners with annual rentals in excess of £3,000, who accumulated and consolidated such large estates that they provoked a massive change in the balance of wealth and power. The trend was towards the concentration of landed estates into fewer and wealthier hands. Weakened by their curious failure to produce male heirs and burdened by insoluble debts brought on by addiction to the bottle, the chase and the gambling table, the smaller gentry slipped down the social scale. Small estates were snapped up by new parasites and Wales became pockmarked with deserted mansions. In Tudor times poets had admired resident and munificent landlords but by the mid-eighteenth century the new breed of absentee landowners were radically different from the *uchelwyr* who had been the linchpins of the traditional order. In no Welsh county was this process more evident than the highly gentrified shire of Glamorgan where many of the élite were more prosperous than the nobility of France and Italy. Between 1720 and 1750 the male line died out in some of the most affluent families – Cefn-mabli, Dunraven, Friars, Hensol, Margam, St Donats and Y Fan – and their properties fell into the hands of powerful alien Titans who had neither sympathy nor patience with the social habits and culture of the native Welsh-speaking community. The Great Leviathans were therefore the main beneficiaries of the demographic crisis in the ranks of the gentry. Just as minority languages like Basque and Breton were deemed 'barbarous' and 'contemptible' by the upper classes of Europe, so was the Welsh language viewed as an 'uncouth ungenteel lingua' by the Anglicized élite in Wales.

Below the landed gentry came the rural and urban middling sorts. Yeomen were robust substantial farmers who lived in modest vernacular storeyed houses and who prospered particularly well in 'open' parishes where resident gentry families were absent. They oiled the machinery of local government by providing most of the jurors who served the courts of great and quarter sessions and they also filled the posts of overseers of the highways and the poor as well as high constables and churchwardens. Until the economic slump of the Napoleonic wars they fared pretty well. The quickening pace of economic change also enabled urban middling sorts to expand and prosper. Although numerically small, this group, which included shopkeepers, merchants, civil servants, attorneys, medical practitioners, schoolmasters and excisemen, took advantage of trading and professional opportunities and, by the second half of this period, they were also responding to the growing sense of cultural malaise by promoting godly reformation and revivalism, popular education and literacy. Industrious yeomen in rural communities and well-to-do members of the mercantile community in towns formed the backbone of Dissenting congregations and Methodist society meetings. In fertile, low-lying areas prosperous gentry families were able to keep their tenants docile and obedient, but there was a tradition of cussed independence among hill-farmers. Protestant reformers found them receptive people and the inventories of deceased yeomen often contained references to Welsh bibles and other pious devotional books.

Husbandmen were far more numerous and hard-pressed than yeomen. They dwelt on a knife-edge margin between subsistence and ruin, and most of their waking hours was spent eking out a bare living on small and unproductive farms. Constantly at the mercy of the weather, infectious diseases and the disposition of their landlords, their lot was hazardous in the extreme. Successive harvest failures prompted them to deplete their seed-corn in order to feed their families and they survived only by growing enough food for their own use and a sufficient surplus to enable them to pay rents, tithes and local rates. Ready cash was extremely scarce in their households and they were often forced to sell off their livestock in order to subsist. The most adaptable of them found part-time or seasonal work in the craft, woollen, fishing or mining industries, where extra pennies and shillings were available to placate rent-collectors. The size and viability of their farms varied wildly, and risk-taking was out of the question. Indeed, at times of population pressure, inflation and land shortage, small farmers were often reduced to the ranks of landless labourers with little or no prospects of recovery.

Anything between a third and a quarter of the population constituted the labouring classes or the 'common sort of people'. At this level, life was assuredly nasty, brutish and short. Agricultural and industrial labourers lived in tiny, verminous hovels which had no running water, lavatories or privacy. Dearth, disease and death were constant companions. Condemned to a life of backbreaking toil, peasants worked on the land from dawn to dusk. According to George Owen, they were 'forced to endure the heat of the sun in his greatest extremity to parch and burn their faces, hands, legs, feet and breasts in such sort as they seem more like Tawny Moors than people of this land'. Women, too, worked on the land, helped with brewing and in the dairy, and spun wool and knitted stockings at night. Their diet comprised bread, stale cheese, porridge, flummery and oatmeal, and any rabbits, hares or birds they managed to poach secretly. They had few, if any, rights and they took great delight in giving zealous religious reformers a dusty time. Their lot was accurately described by an early eighteenth-century clergyman: 'What is poverty, but having to wear homespun clothes, live on modest fare, eat frugally, drink water from wooden bowls, earn bread by the sweat of one's brow, sit at the lowest end of the table, and tug one's forelock in gentle company?'

There seems to have been a genuine sense of concern and sympathy for the plight of the deserving poor. The ancient Welsh custom of *cymorth* prevailed throughout this period and Thomas Pennant rightly admired 'the warmth of human affection' which eased the burdens of poor people. In periods of dearth even vagrants were provided for in informal ways and even in early eighteenth-century Wales there were many parts where the poor rate remained unlevied. However, the general policy towards 'masterless' beggars, vagabonds and ne'er do wells was positively draconian. From the Elizabethan period onwards they were liable to be arrested, whipped, locked up in a gloomy 'House of Correction' or, after a severe beating, escorted back to their parish of birth or last known place of settlement. Governments encouraged immobility and inertia, and rootless elements within society were frowned upon. The preservation of hierarchy and a properly constituted pecking order was of paramount importance to the governors of early modern Wales.

ECONOMIC ACTIVITY

It is impossible to extract precise and accurate demographic information for the period before the first decennial census of 1801. We are forced to make educated guesses on the basis of fragmentary and unreliable information and our estimates therefore often fluctuate wildly. What we can safely say is that the population, though it never exceeded that of London, was growing and that it more than doubled between 1530 and 1750. The basic trends show a rise from *c*.230,000 (1530) to 370,000 (1670) to 489,000 (1750) and this demographic growth was unquestionably the principal engine of socio-economic change. It was reflected, for instance, in the landscape. In order to accommodate the rising population, among the major changes in train in post-Union Wales were the clearance of woodland to create new farmland and the enclosure of arable fields. By the end of the sixteenth century, the traditional manorial lowlands had been hedged and the Welsh clanlands had virtually disappeared. Elizabethan commentators as different from one another as Thomas Churchyard and George Owen (as well as countless poets) gloomily bemoaned the assaults on woods and forests by cultivators, enclosers and industrialists, and since sheep were already more numerous than cattle on upland pastures young trees were swiftly and remorselessly destroyed. By the eve of the industrial revolution travellers were forcibly struck by the deforested nature of the landscape and most of the surviving woodland lay on the middle slopes of valley sites. Closely linked with this major ecological change was the threat to the ancient practice of transhumance. By the eighteenth century the traditional *hafod* and *lluest*, smallholdings which had served as temporary upland pastures, had become permanent homes in order to meet the growing needs of the livestock economy. Colonizing waste and common land had become rampant and the familiar landmark of the *tŷ unnos* would soon pepper the uplands. Unlike England, however, Wales remained unaffected by the large-scale process of enclosure by parliamentary legislation or by the making of landscape parks and gardens.

The Welsh economy was predominantly agrarian and well beyond this period the most significant element in the farming calendar was the condition of the annual harvest. Harvest failure could lead to severe malnutrition and death, and growing efforts were made, especially in the more fertile low-lying valleys and coastal plains, to improve soils by using fertilizers like lime, seaweed and marl. In many counties land was cleared by folding or by beating and burning in order to facilitate crops like oats, rye and barley. In the rugged uplands the acidic soil, unfriendly climate and ramshackle farm implements conspired against the improver, and even in more fertile areas new patterns of cultivation were slow to establish themselves. Only from around the 1740s did root crops for domestic and animal consumption, as well as more sophisticated lowland cropping patterns, begin to emerge.

The rearing of sheep and cattle was clearly the mainstay of the economy, and the driving of livestock to lowland England for fattening and their subsequent sale in the great markets of Barnet and Smithfield was absolutely critical to the livelihood of Welsh farmers. Welsh drovers – the celebrated 'Spanish fleet of Wales' – were substantial and resourceful middlemen who struck hard bargains, negotiated bills and carried large sums of cash back to under-capitalized Welsh communities. Some drovers were unscrupulous and dishonest – the interlude-writer Twm o'r Nant reckoned that hanging was too good for them – but they were an integral part of the economy throughout this period. Their return (not always assured since they had a reputation for absconding) was always eagerly awaited because farmers required gold and silver coins to pay rents, taxes, tithes and dues. Livestock sales ensured ready cash, especially after the passing of the Irish Cattle Act of 1666 which, by denying entry to Irish livestock, ushered in welcome price rises for the sale of store cattle.

The fact that so much anecdotal information about drovers is available has obscured the plain fact that sheep were more numerous than cattle from the Tudor period onwards. Large flocks of sheep were kept on upland farms and communal pastures, though Lewis Morris was probably exaggerating when he claimed that hill-farmers in early eighteenth-century Cardiganshire kept 'many thousands, even to fifteen or twenty thousand, which is more than Job had'. Sheep were kept mainly for their wool. Cloth manufacturing migrated during the

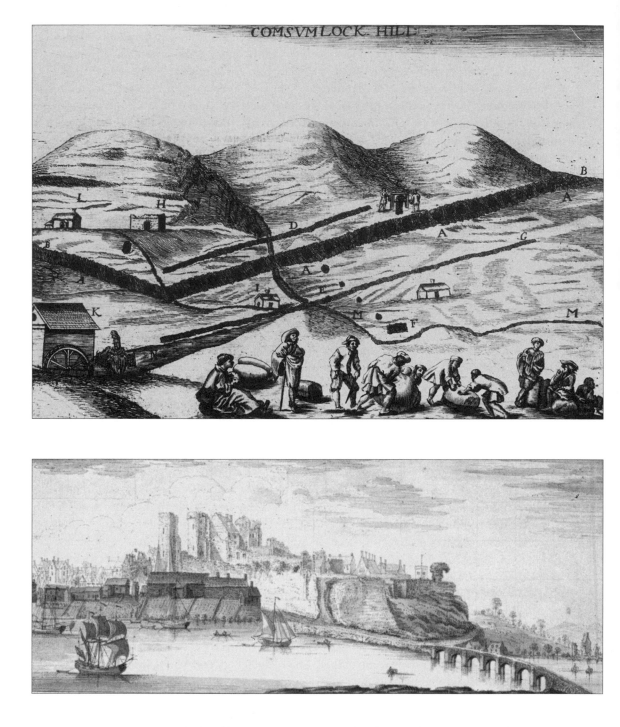

76. 'Comsumlock Hill', showing old lead works of Sir Hugh Myddelton and
Sir Thomas Bushell. In John Pettus, *Fodinae Regales* (1670).
77 Nathaniel and Samuel Buck, *The South View of Caermarthen Castle and Town,* 1740.

mid-sixteenth century to mid and north Wales and a flourishing domestic industry was established wherever there were fast-flowing streams and rivers. Few parishes were without spinners, carders, weavers and fullers who busily prepared copious supplies of coarse Welsh cloth, gloves, socks, caps and wigs in their small cottages and outhouses. The woollen trade prospered best in mid-Wales, where the drapers of Shrewsbury exercised a tight monopoly over the production and sale of woollen products from 1562 onwards. This caused considerable resentment among the workforce since it brought little reward for poor cottagers, and not until the latter half of the eighteenth century did the demand for 'Welsh plains and cottons' increase sharply on the international market. Until then the industry was run on a shoestring in tiny domestic units.

By modern standards, Welsh industries were decidedly small-scale and undercapitalized. Yet, over the period as a whole modest but significant developments occurred in the production of coal, iron and lead. Some commentators castigated the Welsh for their lack of enterprise, but want of capital was the Achilles heel of most gentry families and aspiring industrialists. Much of the stimulus, therefore, came from affluent or skilled outsiders or well-endowed companies. In the Elizabethan period chartered companies imported enterprising engineers like Christopher Schutz and Ulrich Frosse to iron and wireworks at Tintern and Neath, while in the early Stuart period the hard-headed entrepreneur Sir Hugh Myddelton was reputed to be milking monthly profits of £2,000 from Cardiganshire lead mines leased from the Society of Mines Royal which had held monopoly rights in every Welsh county except Monmouthshire from 1568 onwards. The most critical breakthrough, however, occurred in the 1690s when Sir Humphrey Mackworth, a Shropshire-born technophile with autocratic tendencies, brought the lead mines of Cardiganshire out of stagnation and seized the opportunity to develop coal-mining and the smelting of imported lead and copper in the Neath / Swansea area, thereby ensuring that by the 1730s it had become the greatest metallurgical centre in the world. The brass and copper works of Holywell were reckoned to be superior to any in eighteenth-century Britain and when, in 1709, Abraham Darby of Coalbrookdale discovered that coke could smelt iron ore more swiftly and cost-effectively than charcoal coal-mining began to thrive as never before. Even so, units of production in early modern Wales were generally small and widely scattered. Native capital was at a premium, working conditions were lamentable, and poor communications were a deterrent even to the most audacious risk-taker. There were few obvious indications of the massive socio-economic transformation which occurred swiftly and decisively after 1760.

Since the transport of goods by land was not only slow but also cripplingly expensive, the sea offered a swifter and cheaper alternative. From the mid-sixteenth century onwards an appreciable number of ships plied along the coastline, carrying coal, grain, dairy produce, copper, timber and slates, and venturing as far as Ireland, France, Spain and Portugal. The expansion, however modest, of coastal trade reflected the growing importance of livestock, agricultural and industrial produce, and the key role played by merchants, tradesmen and craftsmen in urban centres. As George Owen noted, several counties were 'much fallen to trade by sea' and by the early eighteenth century seafaring had become a full-time occupation for fishermen on the west coast. Indeed, the prosperity of ports like Beaumaris, Barmouth, Aberystwyth and Swansea was closely associated with growing Atlantic trade. But as local people became familiar with the mouth-watering range of luxury goods carried by local and foreign vessels, smuggling and pillaging – both of which were considered to be entirely legitimate practices (at least by common people) – became a way of life along the coastline. We should not, however, romanticize these activities: smuggling gangs were invariably ruthless thugs who treated their prey with merciless ill humour.

At the beginning of this period few people were town-dwellers and even as late as 1801 less than 15% of the total population lived in towns of over a thousand inhabitants. Most towns bore a rural complexion and some of them were scarcely more than glorified villages with their own meadows, pastures, wastes and gardens in which pigs, boars and sheep roamed freely. During the Tudor and early Stuart period only those with robust economic and administrative functions could boast populations in excess of 1,500 people. Surviving maps and plans reveal that few towns had changed the configuration of streets since medieval times and the very smallest urban centres were so shabby, foul-smelling and fragile in their prospects that they could not begin to compete with major regional centres like Brecon, Carmarthen, Haverfordwest or Wrexham. But in the longer perspective we should not underestimate the vigour and verve of urban life. Towns held fairs and markets at which agricultural produce was bought and sold, offered shopping facilities at general stores run by mercers, and provided a range of legal, educational and recreational services. Although life in the towns was governed by an élite of gentry families and professional classes, there was also room for upwardly mobile tradesmen, skilled craftsmen and artisans, and even the rootless pool of poor people discovered that employment prospects were more numerous and varied. Several of the bigger towns experienced a period of expansion after 1660. Carmarthen, a populous town with over 3,000 inhabitants and a well-regarded grammar school, academy, printing press and well-stocked shops, was dubbed 'the London of Wales' by an early eighteenth-century visitor, while Wrexham, the capital of north Wales, prided itself on its prosperous streets and wide range of amenities. Their strongest challenger was Swansea which, even by the 1730s, had acquired a strong industrial profile and an enviable reputation as a major exporter to America, Africa and the Caribbean. Daniel Defoe found its inhabitants 'more civilized and more courteous than in the more mountainous parts' and, as the pace of economic change began to quicken, it was well placed to become the principal urban centre in Wales. Swansea's success was simply the prelude to industrial and urban growth of undreamed-of magnitude in future years.

ASSIMILATING WALES INTO ENGLAND

To English eyes, Wales at the beginning of this period was a major security risk. It was perceived as a disorderly, backward region whose unprotected coastline was a tempting prospect for potential invaders and whose marcher lordships were hives of lawlessness in which violent assaults, ambushes, cattle-stealing, the suborning of juries and the misuse of *arddel* and *cymortha* prevailed. Initially it was felt that the Welsh 'problem' could only be solved by naked force and this led in 1534 to the appointment of a draconian bishop, Rowland Lee, to the Presidency of the Council in the Marches. It would be hard to imagine a less congenial governor than Lee. A man of limited vision, he took sadistic delight in intimidating and hanging offenders, and it is easy to believe contemporary reports that wrongdoers quaked with fear whenever he rode into view. A raft of statutes in 1534-35 strengthened his determination to bring order to unruly parts, but strong-arm tactics did not begin to address the problem of disunity within Wales. Short-termism of this kind, however, was swiftly overtaken by more radical initiatives designed to incorporate Wales into the English state and to modernize its government and administration. The aim of the chief policy-maker Thomas Cromwell was to establish a 'unitary realm' of England and the model of assimilation devised for Wales formed part of a radical programme designed to ensure that the king's writ ran effectively in vulnerable peripheries like Ireland, Calais and counties palatinate such as Durham.

In 1536 Cromwell began the process of extending English political hegemony which was completed in this period by the Act of Union with Scotland in 1707. Unity, uniformity and administrative efficiency were central to the Tudor settlement of 1536-43 which historians have traditionally called the Acts of Union, though it could just as plausibly be argued that the 'Acts of Assimilation' would provide a more accurate indication of the integrative process at work. Both administratively and politically, Wales was made part and parcel of England. So entrenched did this integration become over this period that in 1746 Parliament could declare, without fear of offending the Welsh, that whenever the word 'England' appeared in any piece of legislation it should be read as including 'Wales' also. Although twentieth-century nationalists have vilified Henry VIII and Cromwell for allegedly destroying an ancient nation by integrating it into the English system, it is hard to see what possible alternative presented itself at that particular time. Although Union was a crude piece of annexation it is inconceivable that the destabilizing jurisdiction of the Marcher lords and the *morcellation* of the border counties could have been allowed to persist at a time when unified and powerful states were all the rage on the Continent. Cromwell's ideals also happened to coincide with the shopping list of the rising Welsh gentry who were perfectly happy to sell their national birthright (Welsh laws, gavelkind and a cultural identity) for a mess of English pottage (English laws, primogeniture and a voice at Westminster).

In many ways, Union was a thing of threads and patches. In creating a new map of Wales, the arbitrary settlement of the political boundary isolated several robust pockets of Welsh speakers on the English side of Offa's Dyke. The headquarters of the Council in the Marches was located outside Wales, at Ludlow in Shropshire, and by adding Monmouthshire to the Oxford circuit of the English assize courts a new anomaly was created which necessitated in many subsequent statutes the use of the irritating phrase 'Wales and Monmouthshire'. Internal unification was established through shire government. Wales was divided into thirteen shires, six of which (Anglesey, Caernarfonshire, Merioneth, Flintshire, Carmarthenshire and Cardiganshire) had already been in existence since the Statute of Wales in 1284. The seven new counties, carved out of Marcher lordships, were Denbighshire, Montgomeryshire, Breconshire, Radnorshire, Monmouthshire, Glamorgan and Pembroke-shire. English common law displaced *Cyfraith Hywel*, English principles of land tenure replaced partible inheritance, and the English language became the official tongue of law and administration. Parliamentary representation was extended to the shires and boroughs of Wales, thus permitting twenty-seven voices to be heard at Westminster.

The practice of law and administration was entrusted to three major courts. The Court of Great Sessions was established to hear criminal, civil and equity cases. Four circuits were set up in each corner of Wales and the courts were charged to administer English law in six-day sessions held twice a year. Although complaints were regularly aired regarding the Court's procedure and personnel (judges were invariably monoglot English speakers), the proceedings were generally acceptable to the Welsh because justice was swift and cheap. Indeed, the Court won such respect that when its abolition was recommended in 1829 *Seren Gomer* reckoned that its demise would 'remove the Welsh nation from the face of the earth'.

78. Map of post-Union Wales.

The Council in the Marches, first established in 1471 and granted statutory authority in 1543, possessed considerable administrative and legal powers. Dissolved in 1641, it was reconstituted in the Restoration period, only to be abolished in 1689. The most popular court, however, was the Court of Quarter Sessions which became a fiefdom of local justices of gentry or clerical stock. Local magistrates tried all persons whose offences did not require a jury, and their administrative burdens ranged from supervising the provision of poor relief to the maintenance of bridges, highways and gaols. In the first instance, eight justices were to serve in each shire, but as the volume of work increased so did the number of officers multiply. Often described as 'maids of all work', local office-holders were hardly paragons of virtue and some of the worst enemies to good order and government were the gentry themselves. As Bishop Richard Davies bitterly complained in 1567: 'For what is office in Wales today but a hook to draw to himself the fleece and crop of his neighbour?' Countless examples of bribery, corruption and jury-rigging figure in court records and feuds between gentry factions often culminated in fierce skirmishes, duels and riotous behaviour on the streets. Yet, although the gentry were no angels, their attitudes to office and the law were changing by the end of Elizabeth's reign. Thomas Cromwell had shrewdly calculated that those who gained benefits from the Tudor settlement would happily implement the process of assimilation. Whereas the English élite in Ireland gibbed at the intrusiveness of centralized bureaucracy, the Welsh gentry co-operated fully in the campaign to bring Wales fully into the unitary state. In 1594 George Owen referred to Wales as 'a perfect well-governed commonwealth' and there were other Welsh commentators, too, who believed that the Acts of Union had ushered in a new and more civilized era. Their fulsome praise to the Tudors, however, simply voiced the opinion of a landed élite who had benefited most from the epoch-making legislation of 1536-43.

Unlike the rebellious Irish, the Welsh remained tranquil from the Union to the civil wars. The practice of politics was dominated by the landed gentry, few of whom acquired a high profile in Parliament. Although they were not uncritical of royal policy under the early Stuarts, they never quite managed to form a clearly defined caucus capable of protecting Welsh interests on matters such as parliamentary subsidies, cattle prices, ship money and the sale of monopolies. Yet, as England and Wales drifted almost unwittingly into civil war in the summer of 1642, a large body of the population, led by the gentry, felt strong ties of duty towards, and affection for, their anointed monarch, Charles I. A sheaf of decisively pro-royalist petitions, promising loyalty and support, was forwarded by Welsh counties to the king and in the initial years of war the Welsh ruling élite were not found wanting. From a strategic viewpoint and as an accessible recruiting field for men, victuals and arms, Wales was a vital cog in the Royalist war machine. Although there was robust support for Parliament in south-west and north-east Wales, Royalist sentiments prevailed for the most part. Yet tensions clearly simmered beneath the surface. In Glamorgan, for instance, 'ultra-royalists', much influenced by the immensely rich and powerful Earl of Worcester, were more heavily committed to the king than were the moderate gentry. And as the Royalist war machine faltered, many of the gentry either trimmed shamelessly or concentrated their energies on shielding their families and estates from the brutal depredations of marauding troops. Neutralists and peacemakers revolted against pillaging Royalist armies who disrupted the paths of drovers and clothiers and, as superior Parliamentary forces laid siege to Welsh castles, there were large-scale defections. Mercifully, Wales was spared the sustained battles and heavy casualties which featured in England, but the much derided Welsh foot soldiers who trudged reluctantly beyond the Welsh borders to serve the king told harrowing tales of atrocities. The Second Civil War in 1648, in which insurgents in Pembrokeshire and Anglesey took part, incensed Oliver Cromwell and probably sealed the fate of the king.

In January 1649 Charles I was publicly beheaded outside the Banqueting House in London. The Welsh Presbyterian Philip Henry, who witnessed the execution, never forgot the response of the horror-struck crowd: 'such a groan as I never heard before'. A deep sense of desolation fell over much of Wales in the wake of this cataclysmic event and the ensuing republican rule cast a shadow over Welsh life for many generations. Never had the gentry been more bruised and battered. County committees – purged of Royalists – were set up to sequester or milk their estates. A Gideon's army of armed blacksmiths, millers and tailors took over local administration, expelled the old liturgy, and established a joyless Puritan regime. Voicing the despair of landed families, Welsh poets poured vitriol on arrivistes, aliens and strangers whose sharp swords and short tempers had made life so unbearable. For the majority, the Cromwellian republic proved to be 'a monster without a head'.

Two decades of civil strife, revolution and republican rule left their mark on people's minds far more than any other political event in early modern Wales. Even in the mid-eighteenth century commentators referred to the 'late troubled times' as if they had occurred the previous day. The possibility of further turmoil chilled the marrow of those with vested interests in the established order and William Lloyd, bishop of St Asaph, feared that rebellion 'leaves an odious scent to posterity'. John Jones Maesygarnedd, one of the Welsh regicides, was hanged, drawn and quartered following a show trial in 1660 and scurrilous Welsh churchmen seized their opportunity to blacken the name of Dissent. Yet we should bear in mind that although gentry families had suffered a blow to their pockets and prestige most of them weathered the storm and recovered their social pre-eminence in the Restoration years.

Oligarchic government by the privileged few – families like the Vaughans (Cards.), Harleys (Radnor), Mansels (Glam.), Bulkeleys (Anglesey), Owens (Pembs.) and Myddeltons (Denbs.) – was restored after 1660 and their wealth ensured that their domination as MPs and local governors remained virtually unchallenged until the democratic revolutions of the late eighteenth century. Protecting property rights and defending the Protestant establishment were their chief goals and there was no sign in the manifestos or speeches of parliamentary candidates of either political nationalism or radicalism. Electorates were tiny, ranging from 500 to 2,000 people, and contested elections were frowned upon because they entailed prohibitive costs and disturbed 'the peace of the county'. A subtle mix of paternalism and coercion oiled the wheels of politics and, whenever necessary, the use of bribery, corruption and brute force by bullying agents, acting on behalf of powerful landlords, ensured that even the most recalcitrant voters obeyed their masters at the polling booths. Although several gifted Welshmen rose to high office during the reigns of Charles II and James II – Sir John Trevor of Bryncunallt and Sir William Williams of Anglesey became Speaker of the House of Commons, Sir John Vaughan of Trawsgoed became Chief Justice of Common Pleas, and Judge George Jeffreys of Acton, Wrexham, served as Lord Chancellor – most Welsh politicians were conspicuous by their silence in, or absence from, the parliamentary bear-pit. Party passions seldom ran high and ideological principles which caused deep divisions in England never surfaced in Wales. There is little evidence of a struggle between Whigs and Tories, and most local elections were a trial of strength between rival personalities or factions.

Even the long-awaited Jacobite rebellions of 1715 and 1745 caused hardly a stir in Wales. Welsh Jacobites, led by the Pryses of Gogerddan and the powerful 'Prince of North Wales'

Sir Watkin Williams Wynn of Wynnstay, shrouded their activities in secrecy and privately expressed their disaffection towards the Hanoverians in smoke-filled rooms. The premier Jacobite societies – the Cycle of the White Rose in north Wales and the Sea Serjeants in south-west Wales – never attracted large numbers of Stuart loyalists, and more time was spent singing romantic songs and toasting the Pretender than planning ways and means of bringing about a second Stuart Restoration. When the acid tests came in 1715 and especially in 1745 leading Welsh Jacobites refused to risk either their lives or their property. Jacobitism in Wales is the tale of the dog which barked a good deal but never bit. For most Welsh MPs politics was an engaging hobby rather than a matter of deeply-held principles. Small wonder that the practice of politics in the Wales of the *ancien régime* rarely causes the historian's heart to skip a beat.

THE SLOW REFORMATION

At the beginning of this period the Welsh people were nominally Roman Catholics, but by the mid-eighteenth century they either worshipped in Anglican churches or, in the case of a small minority, in Dissenting chapels and meeting houses. Over a long period of time there occurred a struggle to win the hearts and minds of the Welsh to a new 'official' culture of Protestant Christianity. Initially it was imposed by act of state. A series of legislative changes, beginning in the 1530s, were driven through Parliament by monarchs and powerful élites and were foisted upon reluctant and often aggrieved plebeian folk who neither understood nor revered a new religion which laid so much store by bible-reading, literacy, discipline and respectability. The doctrines of Luther and Calvin won grudging acceptance only over a prolonged period of time and not until the civil wars does strong evidence emerge of widespread popular affection for the Anglican liturgy. Nowadays historians rightly refer to a slow reformation, promoted by growing numbers of enthusiastic advanced Protestants, which never reached its fulfilment until the late eighteenth century. It is important to bear in mind that the 'magical' aspects of the Catholic faith survived and retained their appeal over the whole of this period. Amulets and charms were worn, prayers and vigils were held for departed souls, healing wells like St Winifred at Holywell were frequented by the sick and the infirm, and even those who attended church only for baptisms, marriages and burials did so because they enjoyed the ritual and ceremony involved. In turn, godly Protestants, Puritans and Methodists noted, often despairingly, that spreading God's word among such a credulous and often hostile people was very much an uphill struggle.

In the light of this, it is difficult not to conclude that during the Tudor period and also during the controversial Puritan regime of the 1650s the doctrines of the Reformation were imposed upon Wales. There are good reasons for believing that the richness and vigour of late medieval religion have been underestimated and that the changes which occurred in the 1530s came about less because people were dissatisfied with medieval Christianity than because of the political and financial needs of Henry VIII. The first decisive change occurred in 1533-4 when the king severed ties with Rome and made himself, by the will of Parliament, Supreme Head of the Church in England. Anxious to restore the Crown's finances he then cast his beady eye on the monasteries and friaries which, in their heyday, had been an integral part of 'the garden of the Catholic faith' and which contained estates and property which could save him from bankruptcy. When his chief minister Thomas Cromwell dispatched hit-squads in 1536 to report, in a heavily loaded manner, on the state of discipline within cathedrals and monasteries several contemporaries, informed and otherwise, predicted that the Welsh would rise in rebellion on behalf of the inmates of the beleaguered monastic houses. But the decline of magnate power and the fact that the Welsh gentry were so fervently devoted to the Tudor dynasty and eager to acquire monastic estates at favourable prices meant that there was no Welsh version of the Pilgrimage of Grace or even much evidence of popular discontent let alone rebellion. Like the Taliban in our times, Cromwell's servants embarked on an orgy of licensed vandalism which included the destruction of wonderful Gothic buildings, the mutilation of church property, the melting down of metalwork and jewellery, and the sacking of richly stocked libraries. By 1540 the entire Welsh complement of forty-seven monastic houses had been dissolved and an age-old way of life had come to an end. But the passing of the monasteries does not seem to have occasioned much breast-beating, pangs of conscience or anger, largely because they had lost their *raison d'être* and also the affection of the populace. No families were more eager to demand a share of the booty than well-established Catholic families. In short, neither the will nor the means to reform the monasteries existed in Wales. Given the political climate of the times and the king's urgent need of new sources of wealth, nothing could save them.

Much more serious misgivings were voiced at a popular level when, in 1538, orders were issued for the suppression of shrines and centres of pilgrimage associated with monasteries and cathedrals. These were deeply cherished foci of public worship among the Welsh and the authorities were evidently fearful of a backlash. For instance, when the wholesale removal of the popular shrine of the Virgin Mary at Pen-rhys in the Rhondda was organized, the despoilers were ordered to carry out the deed secretly at night in case it provided local people with a rallying point for more widespread disturbances or riots. At Llandderfel, Merioneth, the most celebrated local landmark was a wooden statue of Derfel Gadarn, a sixth-century saint, mounted on a horse and holding a staff. It was reported to Cromwell in 1538 that 'the innocent people hath been sore allured and enticed to worship the said image' and when the effigy was dismantled it was transported to London and tossed onto a bonfire on which a Franciscan friar was executed. It is hard to believe that the fawning poet Lewys Morgannwg was expressing the sentiments of the entire Welsh populace when he praised Henry VIII for having consigned the monastic houses and popular shrines 'to the flames and burnt their dead bones to the marrow'.

In the event, however, the worst excesses of the Henrician assault on the old order proved to be only a curtain-raiser for even more wanton destruction in the Edwardian period. Even though he had spurned Rome, Henry VIII remained a Catholic until his death in 1547 and in many ways the religious revolution which occurred during the brief six-year reign of his young son Edward VI was much more long-lasting. The boy-king's advisers were determined to eliminate as many traces of Catholicism as possible. Church property, especially chantries and colleges, was pillaged, altars were replaced by tables, images, roodlofts, pictures were destroyed, and saints' days were abolished. All decorations on the walls of Welsh parish churches were either mutilated or covered with whitewash. Of equal significance was the introduction of the Protestant English Book of Common Prayer (in 1549 and 1552) at the expense of the familiar Latin and Catholic liturgy. Such wholesale changes, carried out so swiftly and without consultation, provoked widespread bitterness and resentment. Poets fulminated against 'the faith of the English' and yearned for the old ways. Apart from a small minority of middling sorts in towns like Brecon and Carmarthen, few people pledged their support to the new Protestant doctrines and there was genuine rejoicing throughout Wales when Mary, the Catholic daughter of Catherine of Aragon, succeeded to the throne in 1553. She promptly returned her people to the familiar Catholic fold and instigated a policy of zealous persecution which led to the martyrdom of three courageous Welsh Protestants for heresy. The Welsh version of the Marian reign of terror, however, was relatively mild and most Protestant enthusiasts either discreetly awaited better times or emigrated to the great Protestant centres of Frankfurt, Zurich and Geneva to deepen their learning and organize powerful anti-Catholic propaganda. Yet Catholicism was once more on the offensive in Wales and might even have triumphed for good had Mary not died in November 1558. Her five-year reign proved insufficient to recover lost ground and, while poets continued to anathematize the Protestant cause, the inert mass of the population clung to Catholic beliefs mediated through folk religion and healing rituals and dreaded the reimposition of an 'English' and 'alien' liturgy.

In the event, that is precisely where the future lay, though with the important caveat that the Elizabethan Settlement of 1559 was implemented in a Cymricized manner which invigorated the Protestant mission. Unlike her immediate predecessors, Elizabeth I had the good sense (and fortune) to live long. This enabled her to win support, however grudging in the first instance, for the cautious and moderate Anglican church settlement, to appoint high-calibre Welsh bishops to further the work of godly reformation, and to make life increasingly unbearable for Catholic recusants. The most significant and extraordinary change, however, was the recognition by the government that the Reformation in Wales could never succeed unless Welsh became the language of worship. That this should have occurred owed less to the political initiative of Elizabeth and her advisers than to the determination and acumen of a progressive group of Welsh ecclesiastics, led by Richard Davies, bishop of St David's, who persuaded them that religious unity was infinitely more important than linguistic unity and that Protestantism would be an alien plant unless its doctrines were disseminated in the vernacular. The result was an Act of Parliament in 1563 which authorized the translation of the Bible and the Book of Common Prayer into Welsh and which thereby permitted Welsh to become the official language of public worship in all parts of Wales. This statute drove a coach and horses through the programme of 'unity' and 'uniformity' prescribed in the Acts of Union. Although the drive towards political unity remained firmly on the agenda, it would be achieved only at the price of empowering and energizing the 'contemptible' Welsh tongue in the religious domain. The native language was given the priceless advantage of becoming the medium of religion, a common and durable linking between parson and parishioner.

Genuinely enthused by the prospect of making the Reformation a living, regenerative faith among their fellow countrymen, a triumvirate of gifted scholars – Richard Davies, William Salesbury and William Morgan – embarked on the arduous task of translating the Scriptures into Welsh, thereby ensuring that Protestantism became associated with the vernacular, patriotism and security. Salesbury's archaic and flawed version of the Welsh New Testament in 1567 received a dusty reception in Welsh churches, but Morgan's complete version of the Welsh Bible, published in 1588, proved to be a huge success, not least because it was relatively easy for congregations to listen to, to read and understand. It also set a benchmark for future generations of Anglican and Dissenting prose-writers until the twilight of the Victorian era. Without these critically important texts, Protestantism would never have taken root among the Welsh-speaking population. Welsh became the official voice of Protestantism in Wales and, within the religious domain, it signified the 'otherness' of Wales. By contrast, in Scotland and Ireland the vernacular was scarcely used in the churches and the native tongues were tainted (in English eyes) with Popery and subversion. Without question, therefore, the jewel in the crown of Welsh Protestant reformers was the magnificent Welsh

Bible of 1588. In England any mention of the year 1588 conjures up images of the Spanish Armada dispersing in alarm and confusion, but in Wales the date is indelibly associated with the achievement of the humble incumbent of Llanrhaeadr-ym-Mochnant, who produced, in the words of Morris Kyffin, a translation 'for which Wales can never repay or thank him as much as he deserves'. Without it, the Welsh language would not have survived.

Hand in hand with the Protestant mission came efforts to outwit, silence and bludgeon Roman Catholics into submission. Welsh Catholic exiles based in Douai, Paris, Milan and Rome, never abandoned their dream of making Wales a Catholic country once more and continued to liaise with influential recusant gentry families in north-west Wales and along the borders, especially Monmouthshire. But powerful factors militated against them and isolated them. Following Pope Pius V's bull *Regnans in Excelsis* (1570), Catholics were judged to be potential traitors and brutal punishments awaited Catholic priests, conspirators and recusants. From 1581 a Catholic layman was liable to a fine of £20 per month for not attending church. Clandestine printing presses, poorly financed and vulnerable to swift and catastrophic detection, never sprouted many books and only a small number of Catholic priests trained on the Continent were smuggled back into Wales. An army of magistrates and informers kept them under constant surveillance, especially those who were believed to be linked to treasonable invasion plans. Even those who maintained that their mission was purely pastoral were brutally treated before being put to death. Richard Gwyn, a Llanidloes-born schoolmaster, spent four years under torture before he was hanged, drawn and quartered in 1584. The first Catholic martyr in Wales, he was canonized by Pope Paul VI in 1970. Slowly but surely, the process of attrition against the Counter-Reformation began to pay dividends. Thanks to the powerful propaganda of John Foxe's *Acts and Monuments* (popularly known as the 'Book of Martyrs'), first published in 1563, Catholicism was becoming increasingly associated with foreign rule, oppression and intolerance. One Welsh sailor, involved in skirmishes with the Spaniards in the 1580s, described his Catholic enemies as 'devilish curs of fierce, rough physique, their skins painted and looking like Satan; wire in their noses like boars and rascals with their lips foaming froth'. The legend of the Romish Antichrist grew stronger with each passing decade and most Welsh people, especially the gentry, preferred to be loyal to Elizabeth I than to the Pope in Rome. At the end of the Elizabethan age it was estimated that there were only 808 recusants as opposed to 212,450 regular Anglican churchgoers in Wales. Protestant reformers enjoyed significant advantages denied to the dwindling body of Catholic recusants and although many of the latter still dreamed of restoring the 'old faith' they must have realized by the early seventeenth century that the die was cast against them. By the 1630s only octogenarians would have retained even the faintest memory of life under a Catholic ruler. With the aid of the coercive power of the state and the widespread appeal of the Welsh Scriptures, Welsh Protestants (so they believed) had led their countrymen out of bondage in Egypt to the Promised Land of the true Word of God.

But there were also by this stage increasingly vocal groups of advanced Protestants whose affection for the Anglican church was tempered by their hatred of its abuses. These godly people were known as Puritans and their principal aim was to reform the Church of England, spread the Word of God among the masses, and nurture a society which prized hard work, discipline, thrift and moderation. Indeed, Puritanism has been rather harshly described as 'the haunting fear that someone somewhere may be happy'. Its leading advocate in Elizabethan Wales was John Penry, a Breconshire man who, following his conversion to Calvinism, became so disaffected by the failure of the Church to disseminate 'saving

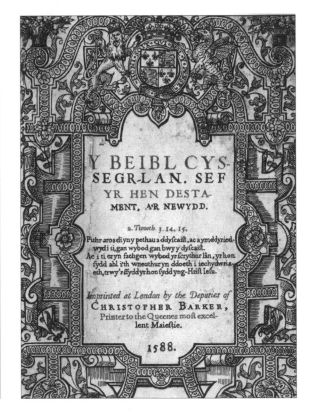

A treatife containing the aeqvity of an hvmble fvpplication which is to be ex/hibited vnto hir Graciovs Maiefty and this high Court of Parliament in the be/halfe of the Countrey of Wales, that fome order may be taken for the preaching of the Gofpell among thofe people

Wherein alfo is fet downe as much of the eftate of our people as without offence could be made known, to the end that our cafe (if it pleafe God) may be pitied by them who are not of this affembly, and fo they alfo may bee driuen to labour on our behalfe ·

AT OXFORD,
Printed by IOSEPH BARNES, and are to be sold in Pauls Church/yard at the figne of the Tygers/head. 1587

79. Portrait of King Henry VIII in the capital 'P' at the beginning of the word Placita in the first plea roll of the Court of Great Sessions for Breconshire in 1543.
80. A Welsh monastery, Valle Crucis. Watercolour by Julius Godet, *c*.1870.
81. Title-page John Penry, *Aequity* (1587).
82. Title-page Welsh Bible (1588).

knowledge' that he became a strident anti-episcopalian and a separatist. In 1587-8 he published several outspoken tracts in which he described bishops as 'murderers and stranglers of men's souls' and the parish clergy as 'dumb and greedy dogs', and his links with the Martin Marprelate tracts which poked fun at the episcopacy made him a marked man. In May 1593, at the age of thirty, Penry was executed for treason. He left behind him his widow Eleanor and four small daughters called Safety, Comfort, Sure Hope and Deliverance (a rare example of the use of 'virtue-names' in Wales). Shortly before he died this first martyr for the Puritan cause in Wales had claimed in a last-minute appeal to Lord Burghley that his sole aim had been to sow 'the blessed seed of the Gospel' in his native land. 'Imprisonment, judgement, yea, death itself', he informed his accusers, 'are not meet weapons to convince men's consciences, grounded on the word of God.' Early Puritans like Penry were never numerous in Wales but by the early Stuart period those who were most discontented with the track record of Anglicanism were convinced that separation from the Church, rather than wholescale presbyterian reform from within, was the only feasible solution.

The second phase of the slow Reformation thus involved the emergence of godly Puritan discipline within the Established Church and the promotion of the idea of independent congregations which rejected church government. The former ideal was personified in the small octavo Welsh bibles which London-Welsh Puritans sponsored in 1630 or in the rough and ready popular religious verses of Rees Prichard, vicar of Llandovery, whose extraordinarily influential *Canwyll y Cymru* ran to fifty-two editions between 1658 and 1820. The Old Vicar's homely version of Puritan values in free-metre forms became the song-book of the common people in the pre-Methodist era and it helped to combat the influence of Arminian innovations after 1625. The first separatist congregation in Wales was the Congregational church of Llanfaches, Monmouthshire, founded in 1639 as the 'mother' church of the Puritan cause. This was the headquarters at which William Wroth, rector of the parish, masterminded a vigorous programme of reformation led by gifted young preachers in the border counties whose names – Walter Cradock, Morgan Llwyd and Vavasor Powell – figure prominently in the annals of Welsh Dissent. Yet it would be foolish to believe that Puritanism was greeted with general enthusiasm in pre-civil war Wales. Its doctrines and lifestyle were known to very few and endorsed by still fewer. The lack of a preaching ministry and effective schooling meant that only the educated élite were familiar with the meaning of favourite Puritan words like 'predestination', 'election' and 'grace'. Only among the articulate well-to-do 'industrious sorts' along the Welsh borders, in trading centres in Glamorgan and Monmouth, and in mercantile communities in south Pembrokeshire did Puritanism gain a secure foothold. Whatever its merits, Puritanism, like early Protestantism, was viewed by the Welsh as an alien plant.

The peculiar circumstances of the 1640s offered a new opportunity for Puritans to press the case for reform. The turmoil of civil war, the abolition of episcopal government and the collapse of censorship permitted Puritan ministers and soldiers to desecrate churches, eject unsatisfactory clergymen and preach freely. The pace of change accelerated sharply with the passing of the Act for the Better Propagation for the Gospel in Wales (1650), a piece of legislation which led over a period of three years to the replacement of 278 so-called unfit clergymen by zealous preaching ministers bent on inspiring a genuine spiritual revolution. Supported by sword-waving soldiers, bureaucrats and sequestrators, Puritan saints like Cradock, Llwyd and Powell strove unstintingly to introduce the people of Wales to the civilizing benefits of the Puritan gospel. The strongly libertarian and millenarian mood of the times also encouraged sectarian activity and a host of new teachings, peddled by Baptists, Fifth Monarchists, Quakers and Ranters, both mystified and exasperated conservative elements in society. For Royalists and Churchmen, these were 'distempered and bedlam times' in which their traditional supremacy was challenged for the first time. The most extreme sect were the Quakers, whose anti-establishment views and behaviour brought colour and vitality to the religious mission of the 1650s but who also provoked more fear and hostility than any other religious group. 'Get thee behind me Satan' was a common retort by angry Anglicans and Puritans as Quaker missionaries, both male and female, harangued them mercilessly. Even though Morgan Llwyd, in a series of remarkable prose works the best known of which is *Llyfr y Tri Aderyn* (1653), pleaded with the Welsh to embrace the Puritan faith, the explosion of sectarian activity and the rigid Calvinism of the Puritan saints were deeply unpopular. The bulk of the populace resented having their ecclesiastical and social world turned upside down, and it was widely believed that Puritan propagators were laundering public moneys and enabling 'upstart' base sorts to undermine the spiritual authority of the learned. Whereas Puritan apologists believed that a vigorous and successful missionary campaign had been sustained during the Interregnum, most of the Welsh shared the view of the Metaphysical poet Henry Vaughan 'Silurist', who feared that it represented 'a thick black night' rather than a 'glorious day-spring'. Yet even at this stage it was clear that religious pluralism was likely to become a permanent fixture, and had Oliver Cromwell not died in 1658 the growth of sectarian communities would have been even more marked. In the event, however, the restoration of the monarchy and an episcopal Church of England in 1660 was greeted with joyous relief. Never were church bells rung with such vigorous glee.

Charles II set himself the goal of making the restored Church of England acceptable to moderate Puritans, but vengeful Anglicans thwarted him. The Act of Uniformity of 1662 turned Anglicanism into a monopoly and the Puritan who chose not to conform became known as a Dissenter. 'Ah, thou old whore of Babylon', cried the Welsh Puritan Jenkin Jones as he fired bullets into the door of Llanddeti church in Breconshire, 'thou wilt have it all thy own way now!' For at least a generation that proved to be the case, for all Dissenters, especially the most unorthodox and also those with a reputation for social radicalism, were at the mercy of punitive measures implemented by angry royalists. A series of draconian penal statutes, passed between 1661 and 1673 and collectively known as the Clarendon Code, ushered in an age of repression. The aim of this battery of laws was to inflict upon past and present enemies as much pain, suffering and humiliation as possible. Indeed, had the Code been enforced thoroughly over a period of time Dissent in Wales might well have been snuffed out. In practice, however, magistrates were neither able nor willing to implement the law, and even those who did soon discovered that Dissenters had devised several wily stratagems which enabled them to outwit their persecutors. Yet it was not a pleasant experience for any Dissenters to worship in fear in barns, hay-lofts and caves. The brunt of persecution was borne by Catholics and Quakers, the latter of whom had adopted pacifism as an article of faith by 1660 and who now accepted that both mental and physical suffering was an integral part of the 'Lamb's War'. Enfeebled by having to languish in foul prisons and dungeons, Quakers lost many of their best people when hundreds of them joined a major exodus of Friends to William Penn's 'Holy Experiment' in Pennsylvania between 1682 and 1700. Henceforward, their depleted brethren in Wales poignantly referred to themselves as 'the remnant'. Not until the passing of the Toleration Act in 1689 did old enmities begin to soften, but Dissenters remained barred from municipal administration, political office and the universities throughout the eighteenth century. As a disadvantaged minority, they wore the badges of civic inferiority. Even by the mid-eighteenth century 'the Lord's free people' constituted less than 5% of the population. Yet they were a lively and influential leaven in the lump, especially in busy urban communities and in rural parishes where pastoral oversight by the Anglican clergy was defective. Dissenting meeting houses might have been rickety edifices, made of stone, timber, mud and thatched roofs, but they were deliberately located in the post-Toleration period within easy walking or riding distance of the local population. Thus, although the Anglican majority continued to hold all the political trump cards, Dissenting ministers took advantage of the inadequate administrative and parochial structure of the Established Church.

This brings us to the third and final phase of the slow Reformation: the arrival of the religion of enthusiasm and opportunities for widespread schooling and literacy. During the 1730s the so-called Methodist revival formed part of a much wider international programme of religious renewal within countries stretching from eastern Europe to the American colonies. Although Methodist historians have always emphasized the alleged novelty of the movement, it was essentially an amalgam of the old and the new, of Churchmen and Dissenters, of the printed word as well as rousing field preaching. Historians have abandoned the notion that it spread like wildfire throughout the whole of Wales and, as countless examples of mob violence reveal, many people were hostile (or indifferent) to the new enthusiasts. During its first fifteen years Methodism was a spontaneous, inchoate and sometimes fractious group of reformers rather than a robust nation wide movement. Yet it weathered early persecution and unleashed powerful spiritual forces which greatly strengthened the work of Reformation.

One of the great advantages of Welsh Calvinistic Methodism was that, unlike early Puritanism, it could legitimately claim to be 'of the people'. The commander-in-chief of the movement was Howel Harris, a carpenter's son from Trefeca in Breconshire and an inveterate social climber who thirsted for self-improvement. Although he despised poor countryfolk for being 'so Welchy', he was just as critical of non-Welsh-speaking absentee bishops and their time-serving favourites. In the company of Daniel Rowland, a young Cardiganshire cleric, he led a new generation of eloquent preachers who delighted in striking 'bright and fiery sparks' in the hearts of their followers. Appealing to people's emotions rather than to their intellect, Methodists preached to sizeable crowds in the open air and gathered converts together in exclusive, tightly-knit society meetings in which young people were encouraged to indulge in spiritual small-group therapy under the watchful eye of stewards. Within these tiny cells the struggle against Satan was enacted with unremitting and often tearful zeal, and the manner in which converts unburdened themselves became the theme of many memorable poems, hymns and prose works by William Williams, Pantycelyn, who by mid-century had become the movement's much-loved 'Sweet Singer'. Methodism's attractive combination of open-air sermons, individual introspection and fervent hymn-singing appealed principally to yeomen farmers, tradesmen, craftsmen, artisans and women. Young married women were often in the majority in rural-based society meetings and they thrived on the opportunity to socialize with like-minded males and to deepen their spiritual experiences. Scenes of ecstasy (often described as 'wild pranks' by their enemies) accompanied the spirit-filled ministry of the itinerant preachers and the intense enthusiasm of Methodism not only set it apart from the mores of the raw multitude but also prompted old-style clergymen and pious Dissenters to embark on fervent evangelical preaching. The

83. Extract from Howel Harris's Diary.
84. Morgan Llwyd Window in Ffestiniog Church by Christopher C. Powell.
85. First Welsh Methodist Association at Watford, Caerphilly, January 1743.

physical manifestations of revivalism-catatonic trances, convulsions, paroxysms-were best seen at Llangeitho in Cardiganshire, where Daniel Rowland provoked recurrent waves of emotion among pilgrims who regularly travelled on foot, on horseback and by boat from all quarters of Wales in order to hear him preach and to attend monthly communion. In 1743 Howel Harris was astonished by scenes of public praise at Llangeitho: 'Such Crying out and Heart Breaking Groans, Silent Weeping and Holy Joy, and shouts of Rejoicing I never saw.' Such febrile excitement had never been witnessed before in the somnolent rural communities of south-west Wales and, by 1750, 81% of the 428 societies were located in the six counties of south Wales. Not until after 1780 did Methodism gain a popular foothold in north Wales and we should beware of exaggerating the achievements of the first generation of enthusiasts. Internal divisions and factionalism hampered the development of the movement and Harris's gargantuan ego and selfish foibles drew him into a damaging theological and personal scandal which split the movement in 1750.

By emphasizing bible-reading, a profound consciousness of individual and collective piety, and the subjective awareness of sin, Methodist reformers pushed the doctrines of sixteenth-century reformers to their logical conclusion and helped to meet the spiritual and psychological needs of those who yearned for more effective pastoral care. Young people were impressed by the sheer dynamism of revivalist missions and seized new niches of opportunity within its lay-based cells. Methodism, of course, was not without its faults. It did not promote fresh critical thinking about the past and it elevated the heart above the head. It also gained a reputation for bigotry, philistinism and a holier-than-thou sense of superiority. Yet its army of exhorters and supporters was never less than energetically dedicated to the cause of spreading the Gospel as widely as possible. When religious revivalism penetrated the whole of Wales at the end of the eighteenth century the Welsh Reformation came of age.

It is becoming increasingly clear that Methodism and Dissent could never have prospered without the tremendous impetus provided by the stream of pious Welsh books issued by printing presses and by striking advances in the provision of schooling and literacy. In the mid-sixteenth century Bishop Richard Davies had urged the Welsh to 'go forth and read', but at that time few people had either the means or the opportunity to learn to read and to acquire the habit of buying and reading religious literature. During the Interregnum Morgan Llwyd complained that 'there are not many Welsh books in Wales'. The turning point came in 1695 when printing restrictions were lifted and the opportunity offered to publishers to practise their trade outside London. Thomas Jones, a remarkably enterprising and canny printer and bookseller, turned the flourishing market town of Shrewsbury into the headquarters of the Welsh printing trade. Five years after his death in 1713, the first official printing press on Welsh soil was established in the tiny village of Trerhedyn in the Vale of Teifi. By 1721 Carmarthen, the commercial capital of south-west Wales, had established a thriving printing press which soon threatened the monopoly of the Shrewsbury printers. Statistical evidence reveals the growing strength and popularity of the printing press: whereas 112 Welsh books were published between 1660 and 1699, 614 were published between 1700 and 1749, and the trend was towards an even more rapid and appreciable rise after 1750. The staple source of reading matter was religion, and the overriding priority in this period was to disseminate large numbers of didactic and devotional books to pious middling sorts and as many of the 'vulgar sorts' able to cope with them.

The most noteworthy changes in literacy rates occurred from the 1730s onwards when Griffith Jones, an asthmatic middle-aged clergyman from south Carmarthenshire, publicly distanced himself from the ineffective and discredited policy of the SPCK of imparting a knowledge of English and the three 'Rs' to pupils in its charity schools by launching a strikingly effective system based on peripatetic schooling for the benefit of humble folk, both young and old. A melancholy workaholic, Jones was deeply concerned about the eternal fate of the godless and the illiterate. Determined to save them from 'the dreadful abyss of eternity', he assembled an army of schoolteachers, plied them with bibles and catechisms paid for by well-to-do patrons like his benefactress Madam Bridget Bevan, and bid them instil the reading habit by conducting Welsh-medium tuition over periods of six or eight weeks. *The Welch Piety*, Jones's annual report, reveals that common people, eager to learn their letters, used to carry fuel and candles to draughty church vestries in order to extend their hours of tuition. In 1721 Erasmus Saunders had noted 'the extraordinary Disposition to Religion' among common people and Griffith Jones was the first Welsh educationist to devise a scheme suited to the needs of rural, monoglot folk. Large numbers of underprivileged people, including tenant farmers, craftsmen, labourers, servants and young children, flocked to his circulating schools to master the Scriptures and the fundamental doctrines of the Church catechism. By 1750 parish churches, farmhouses and barns throughout Wales echoed to the sounds of adult and infant voices chanting the alphabet aloud, spelling words, reciting scriptural passages, repeating the catechism, and singing verses from *Canwyll y Cymru*. By the time of the death of Griffith Jones Llanddowror in 1761, 3,325 schools had been established in 1,600 different locations in Wales, and around half the population had learnt to read. There can be no question that the circulating school system was one of the major success stories of eighteenth-century Wales. The upsurge in literacy rates and the injection of new life into dormant or inactive churches greatly strengthened the Evangelical revival and church life in general. Little wonder that so many people paid homage to Jones as an 'old and much honoured soldier', for he had turned the Welsh into one of the most literate peoples in Europe.

HUMANISTS, CAMBRO-BRITONS AND CELTS

In cultural terms, the most difficult challenge facing Welsh scholars in this period was how to sustain the native literary tradition and introduce new ideas and concepts in a land which lacked not only affluent patrons but also universities, colleges, scientific academies, literary clubs and a capital city. Even as early as 1540 a major cultural shift was affecting the distinctive and perhaps unique poetic tradition. The days of the chief poets (*penceirddiaid*) had passed and the traditional *awdl* (ode) and *cywydd* seemed to be out of place and even redundant in the new materialistic age. Poets became increasingly despondent as they contemplated the future of their cherished craft and Wiliam Llŷn spoke for his age when he wrote in 1562 'Judgement Day has come to the art of poetry'. From the point of view of patronage, the problem was compounded by the baneful influence of the so-called 'language clause' in the 1536 Act of Union and the effects of inflation on gentry patterns of getting and spending. From 1536 onwards no person could hold office in Wales without a knowledge of English. This made the Welsh monoglot a second-class subject and offered irresistible inducements to the gentry to view English as the language of opportunity and advancement and to discount their native tongue. It is significant that the stereotypical Dic Siôn Dafydd, the effete Welsh gentleman who affected an English accent and despised the vernacular, entered the historical stage in the immediate post-Union period. By mid-century, too, the number of genuine patrons for family and itinerant bards was dwindling swiftly as the effects of inflation bit deeply into their pockets.

But whilst acknowledging and deploring the malaise, Welsh humanists were also excited by the prospect of being able to translate Renaissance ideals into Welsh poetry and prose. The robust circle of Welsh humanists who were active in the Vale of Clwyd – the cradle of the Welsh Renaissance – were European in their way of thinking and were thus deeply sensible of the intrinsic value of their native tongue. In the words of Edward Kyffin, they were determined to serve their country 'for the glory of God and for the elevation of our language'. Their goal was to render Welsh a 'learned tongue', to modernize it and enhance its intellectual and spiritual authority. The intellectual trendsetter was the remarkably prolific polymath William Salesbury of Llansannan, Denbighshire, whose self-conscious attempt to restore, renew and embellish the native language and literature was an inspiration to the learned élite. The printing press, though located in faraway London, clearly held the key to success, and by publishing works which developed and refined the Welsh vocabulary, standardized the orthography and awakened interest in the nation's historical past the small band of Welsh humanists strengthened the literary tradition of Wales.

But wherever they turned, they confronted an immovable stumbling-block: the unpropitious nature of Welsh society. A mainly pastoral land with no rich endowments or affluent élite groups provided a singularly unfavourable milieu for the courtly, urban-based ideals of the Renaissance. Of the 115 Welsh books published between 1546 and 1642, only sixty-seven might accurately be described as humanist. Most Welsh books were of a religious nature and, although the production of a Welsh Bible was a prodigious achievement, the fact remains that there were no heroic epics, musical compositions, works of art or poetic drama. The heavy emphasis placed on producing the Scriptures in Welsh meant that other rich and interesting subjects which lay at the heart of humanism were neglected. Possibly too much was expected of these pioneers and had some of the hidebound Welsh poets been blessed with more fire in their bellies more might have been done to fashion metrical patterns to suit new tastes. Their reluctance to share the secrets of their craft at a time when the bardic order was in terminal decay bewildered Welsh humanists and for much of the seventeenth century poetic texts continued to be transmitted by manuscript rather than print. As a result poetry became an agreeable hobby rather than a profession, practised by bachelor farmers like Huw Morys or drovers like Edward Morris and disseminated by unskilled itinerant minstrels known as *y glêr* or, more crudely, *clêr y dom* (dung flies). In many ways, Welsh poetry became an open rather than a closed shop and this was reflected in the removal of gender barriers as gifted strict-metre poets like Angharad Jones of Dolwyddelan and Margaret Davies of Trawsfynydd came to the fore during the eighteenth century. Instead of mourning the demise of the bardic order, perhaps historians should celebrate the real sense of liberation felt by those who had traditionally been denied access to the charmed circle. On the other hand, new poets of humble stock never matched the rich quality of the old professional *cywyddwyr*.

The death of the distinguished lexicographer John Davies of Mallwyd in 1644 signalled the end of the humanist effort and in the Restoration period it was left to the smaller Welsh squires to salvage and sustain the nation's memory. John Jones, a calligrapher from Gellilyfdy, Flintshire, copied hundreds of Welsh manuscripts in a hand which remains a feast to the eye, while Robert Vaughan of Hengwrt, Merioneth, assembled the finest collection of rare manuscripts to be found under one roof in seventeenth-century Wales. His magnificent library, though vulnerable to the ravages of mildew and mice, eventually became the corner-

86. Lewis Morris by an unknown painter.
87. Title page of the Constitution of the Honourable Society of Cymmroddorion, London, 1755.
88. Title-page of Edward Lhuyd *Archaeologia Britannica* (1707).

stone of the manuscript collection of the National Library of Wales. But the portents were gloomy. The great landowners showed little enthusiasm for the cultural traditions of 'the mountain Welsh' and placed a much higher premium on 'civilizing' or Anglicizing trends. London creamed off gifted young Welshmen who were expected to adopt a refined English accent, abandon the patronymic article 'ap', and assimilate metropolitan fashions and ideas. Many of the 3,000 students who enrolled at the universities of Oxford and Cambridge and at the Inns of Court between 1545 and 1642 eagerly imbibed the New Learning and viewed it as a passport to polite society and intellectual circles. 'Cambria me genuit' (Wales gave me birth), wrote the great poet Henry Vaughan in 1651 but, unlike Tudor humanists, he and other borderland writers expressed themselves in English. Jokes about the derisory patois of 'Poor Taffy' abounded in English taverns and coffee-houses, and caricatures of Wales as 'the fag-end of Creation' and 'a Country in the World's back-side' flowed from the printing presses. Some of the chickens reared by the Acts of Union were coming home to roost. Gentlemen who had once proudly called themselves 'Ancient Britons' were now self-styled 'True Englishmen'. 'Since the happy incorporation of the Welsh with the English', wrote the historian William Wynne in 1697, 'the History of both Nations as well as the People is united.' A mood of deep pessimism prevailed at the end of the seventeenth century and it was widely felt that Wales was in great danger of losing its literacy and historical inheritance forever.

That this calamity was averted is largely attributable to the development of native printing presses and the emergence of groups of scholars, savants, antiquaries and poets who were determined to rediscover the traditional heritage and revive a sense of national confidence among Welsh speakers and writers. As books poured from the presses, the culture of print helped to disseminate knowledge and create new expectations. A growing number of communities sported charity or circulating schools, book clubs, academies, Methodist societies and a network of booksellers, bookbinders and subscription schemes. Although most publications were works of Protestant piety and devotion, a host of antiquarians, almanacers, ballad-mongers and composers of interludes were staking their claims and appropriating the printing press for popular use. As Lewis Morris wrote in 1735, Caxton's invention was 'the Candle of the World, and the Freedom of Britain's Sons'.

External stimuli also helped the Welsh to bestir themselves. In 1703 Paul-Yves Pezron, a patriotic Breton monk, exercised an important influence on the growth of Celtic consciousness by publishing *L'antiquité de la nation et de la langue des Celtes*. Indeed, his wild and vivid theories about Celticism and the Celtic languages proved much more popular than the sober comparative approach favoured by Edward Lhuyd, the supremely gifted Oxford-based Welsh polymath whose *Archaeologia Britannica* (1707) grouped and classified the Celtic languages. Lhuyd died within two years of the publication of this *magnum opus* and, robbed of his wise guidance, the Welsh took refuge in speculative fantasies and myth-making which reached its apogee with the Ossianic craze and the semi-fictional writings of Iolo Morganwg in the Romantic period. In 1716, at the tender age of twenty-three, Theophilus Evans published the first Welsh history book to achieve real literary status. *Drych y Prif Oesoedd* stoutly defended the legend of the Trojan origins of the ancient Britons as peddled by Geoffrey of Monmouth and also celebrated the native language by linking it to the account in the Book of Genesis of the peopling of the world: 'here is the blood and race of the old Welsh, as exalted as any earthly lineage could be'. Unashamedly Cambro-centric, polemical and partisan, Evans's epic tale greatly stiffened the self-confidence of the Welsh. At least twenty editions of *Drych y Prif Oesoedd* were published by the end of Victoria's reign.

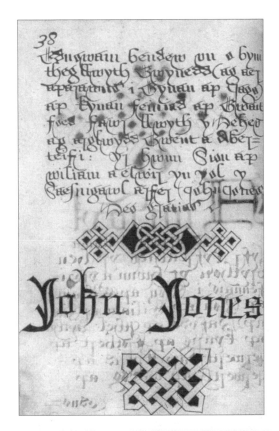

89. John Jones, Gellilyfdy's signature in pen and ink with watercolour, in Peniarth MS 224 folio 45-46.
90. Old Matthews, native of Pembrokshire, aquatint by G. Arnold, 1802.

Finally, the claims of the Welsh to be the 'Earliest Natives' acquired some kind of official status when the Honourable Society of Cymmrodorion was established in London in 1751. As its principal founder Lewis Morris rather grandly put it, the aim of the Society was to transform Welsh cultural life by the 'Cultivation of the British Language, and a Search into Antiquities'. In practice, although the Society provided a focal point for cultural endeavours it promised more than it delivered, and it was left to members of the Morris Circle in Wales, whose 'itch for scribbling' was insatiable, to swell national pride by revealing that Wales had a rich and copious living language and literature. In view of the fact that early modern Wales was bereft of major national institutions, an easily identifiable cultural infrastructure and a robust body of wealthy patrons, it is nothing short of remarkable that so many religious reformers and cultural patriots were prepared to invest so much time and energy in saving souls, extending popular education and keeping alive cherished literary and historical traditions. By 1750 Wales had more reason to be confident about its future than was the case a hundred years earlier and the impending industrial revolution, which would bring about a sharp and decisive break with the past, offered the next challenge to the ingenuity and enterprise of its people.

6

ENGINE OF EMPIRE
c.1750 – 1898

Prys Morgan

For once in its long career Wales becomes in this period a rich country, with a galloping population increase, drawing immense capital resources from outside, attracting vast numbers of immigrants, making the lands around her dependent upon her, and in some ways becoming the engine driving the British Empire. True, the Welsh in this period saw other aspects of their life transformed: this was the period of the 'Nonconformist revolution', a period of rapid advance in popular literacy and eventually the invasion of the English language. a time of great cultural revival through the medium of Welsh too, and, although it was slow to surface, it was an age of profound politicization. All those features are important, and it is the overwhelming impetus of industrialization which makes the period unique, but one should begin with cultural changes because these were most peculiarly Welsh.

FROM WILD WALES TO THE AGE OF RESPECTABILITY

In the middle of the eighteenth century the great mass of the people spoke Welsh, but Wales and things Welsh on the whole had a low status. The hymnwriter Ann Griffiths at the end of the century lived barely ten miles from the English border, and took some English lessons, but was never able to master any of the language. Over the previous generations there had been many complaints by the small number of Welsh scholars that the Welsh were indifferent to their own traditions, that they had lost contact with their own history, that they found it difficult to write their own language. There was little or no sign that Wales was the land of song, and there were few institutions devoted to nurturing Welsh history or traditions. The English regarded the Welsh as poor, rough, old-fashioned country bumpkins, and right up to the end of the eighteenth century published many cartoons of the Welsh as fairly harmless barbarians who ate toasted cheese because unable to afford meat, and rode on goatback because unable to afford a horse. The cartoons became slightly more friendly as the century advanced, but it is as well to remember that the nursery rhyme about ' Taffy was a Welshman, Taffy was a thief' is first recorded in this period. The Welsh knew that their mountain landscape was a harsh one in which to eke out a living, and the English of the period considered its contours repellent: it was 'the rubbish of Noah's Flood'.

Despite all this, there were already many signs of change before 1750, which accelerated greatly as the century advanced. From the late seventeenth century onwards there was a growing sense of a need, among English and Welsh scholars, to understand the earliest parts of British history, and groups of Welsh scholars published works which raised the status of Welsh and Welsh history. Dictionaries and grammars of Welsh began to appear, scholars such as Edward Lhuyd showed that Welsh was not 'gibberish' as English satirists said, but was related to Breton, and Irish and other languages later termed 'Celtic', and had an ancient and honourable history. The work of Edward Lhuyd and his fellow-scholars was popularised by such writers as Theophilus Evans. Other scholars published bibliographies of Welsh books and editions of medieval Welsh laws. By the 1740s some were publishing collections of music to prove that the Welsh had a musical tradition as distinguished as its literature. Groups of scholars had emerged among the London Welsh and in various parts of Wales who were corresponding with each other, trying to piece together the lost history, literature and language of Wales. the most lively and entertaining circle being that of the three Morris brothers of Anglesey, Lewis (who ran the Crown mines in Cardiganshire), Richard (clerk in the Navy Office, London) and William (customs officer at Holyhead).

The Morris brothers raise the question as to why this ferment was happening in the mid-eighteenth century. They were successful middle-class bureaucrats, who wished for noble and gentry patronage for native culture, and where it was found wanting, were prepared to supply a new sort of leadership themselves. They did this partly by correspondence, by encouraging talent in all sorts of Welsh writers, by organising publications, and above all, perhaps by establishing the Honourable Society of Cymmrodorion in London in 1751. This was not the first, but certainly the model of later 'Welsh societies' to encourage the study and discussion of things Welsh. The word Cymmrodorion signified 'the earliest natives of the British Isles', to remind the rest of Britain that British history was not comprehensible without its Ancient British and Welsh dimensions.

It was a propitious time to start to raise the status of things Welsh, because there seems to have been in England a growing sense of Great British unity, possibly to do with the need to bring the Scots and the Welsh to unite in a titanic struggle against France and Spain. The anthem of the Cymmrodorion roared against the French and the Spaniards. Wales's plucky resistance to invaders in the mountain fastnesses seemed more and more symbolic of British determination to resist every attacker from Europe. In a quite different way, there was a growing realisation that Wales was a country potentially of great riches: its mountainous geology showed more obviously the hand of the Creator than any other that was within reach, and beneath there lay unbelievable treasure troves of ores.

The image of Wales as a country began to change with the spread of prints and engravings of Welsh antiquities (castles, abbeys, historic towns) from the 1740s onwards, with the work of Samuel and Nathaniel Buck, Alderman Boydell (a native of Hawarden, in Flintshire), then the work of landscape painters such as Richard Wilson (a native of Montgomeryshire) in the 1760s, who painted not only antiquities such as Caernarfon Castle, but also made the wild mountains look splendidly sublime, and finally, the prints and paintings and guidebooks of hundreds of travellers who began to trickle into Wales from 1770 onwards, becoming a huge flood in the 1790s. The travellers made considerable demands on the native Welsh, demanding accommodation and guiding, and gradually made them see their own country in a new light. The Welsh were at first puzzled, asking 'Have you no waterfalls in your own country?'; Samuel Taylor Coleridge said the marvellous mountainscape of Wales was in the eyes of the Welsh just music to the deaf and pictures to the blind. But gradually in the early nineteenth century the Welsh themselves changed and came to be proud of their landscape, until by the 1840s and 1850s, the beauty of mountains had become a central part of the national mythology and image.

91. T. Rowlandson, Penillion singers, engraving, 1802.
92. J. Lewis, Pistyll Rhaiadr Waterfall, engraved, c.1736.
93. Cwmdwyfran Works, Carmarthen, 1750 by JCD.

The process of reestablishing the status of Welsh as a language had already started before 1750, but it was greatly helped by publishing dictionaries and grammar books. For example in 1753 Thomas Richards of Coychurch, Glamorgan, published a substantial grammar and dictionary, which in turn was dwarfed by the immensely long English-Welsh dictionary of John Walters of nearby Llandough (which took virtually every English expression and gave it a Welsh equivalent). Several works were published to try to prove that Welsh was a language of great status because it was the language of the Patriarchs, or because it was the language of the Ancient Druids, or yet others who said that it had unique status because its particles formed the bases of all European languages. The largest store of Welsh words was provided by the Welsh dictionary of William Owen Pughe (1803), ancient words drawn from his detailed reading of manuscripts, and thousands of words made up from the separate particles or phonemes of Welsh words. Most of his inventions remained mere dictionary-words, but plenty of them came into common use. This reminds us that the language developed in the period from the first numbers of Walters's dictionary in the 1770s to the mid-nineteenth century, into a modem language with a rich and complex vocabulary.

What happened in the field of polite literature was not quite the same as that of language. The members of the Cymmrodorion society probably greatly enjoyed the lyrical or moralistic ballads which had been in vogue in Welsh for the previous hundred years, indeed Lewis Morris was a master at composing these himself, and he believed Welsh literature 'took a Nap' since the death of Queen Elizabeth, and he and others wished to awaken it, by teaching poets the elaborate rules of correct prosody, and by teaching them to compose 'heroic poetry'. The Morrises encouraged others to publish collections of popular Welsh poetry in 1759 and 1763, and in 1764 helped their protégé Evan Evans to publish *Some Specimens of Antient Welsh Poetry,* partly to show the Welsh themselves that they had a corpus of serious bardic verse going back to the early middle ages, and partly to prove that the Welsh had a genuine corpus of poems which were in contrast to the dubious texts of Gaelic poetry of Ossian recently published by James Macpherson. In the same period they encouraged another protégé Goronwy Owen to master the medieval rules of Welsh verse and to compose verse of a more serious or epic quality. Later in the eighteenth century Welsh scholars managed to get a good deal of ancient Welsh literature into print, the fourteenth-century lyrical poetry of Dafydd ap Gwilym in 1789, the early poems named after Llywarch the Old in 1792, and then from 1801 to 1807 the three volumes of the *Myvyrian Archaiology of Wales,* a compendium of medieval Welsh literature .There was however a fly in the ointment, and that was the tendency of one important scholar to indulge his fancy in inventing ancient Welsh literature and passing it off as genuine. Although the element of invention is to be found in other fields, it is in literary and historical texts that we see the hand of a forger of genius, Edward Williams 'Iolo Morganwg' (1747-1826). To the 1789 edition of Dafydd ap Gwilym's poems he contributed a collection of bogus poems, to the book on Llywarch the Old in 1792 he contributed much bogus material on the druidic tradition in Welsh bardism, and much of the third volume of the *Myvyrian Archaiology* (1807) consists of his fabrications. His post-humous publications contain a vast amount of fascinating but bogus lore, a lot of it to prove that he was the last of the Ancient Druids, and that bardo-druidism was a cult which continued down the centuries in the hills of Glamorgan.

In the revival of Welsh music there was also a good deal of Romanticised invention. The three key figures in the establishment of a Welsh musical tradition were John Parry of Ruabon, the blind harpist of Sir Watkin Williams Wynn, in the mid-eighteenth century,

Edward Jones 'Bardd y Brenin' (literally King's Bard, because he was harpist of George, Prince of Wales) late in the century, and third, another John Parry who was a music director in London in the early nineteenth century. They established through their performances and their publications of collections of 'Welsh airs' the idea that the Welsh had an ancient musical tradition. It was also believed that the triple harp which became fashionable in Wales during the eighteenth century was the national instrument. One musical art given much publicity at the end of the eighteenth century, and cultivated as an art peculiarly Welsh, was that of penillion-singing. Short pithy stanzas were extremely popular amongst the common people and sung to the harp in various fashions, but the most esoteric was that where the harpist played the melody while the singer sang words to accompany the instrument as a counterpoint or descant. It seems to have been preserved in only a few limited fastnesses, but was now revived and spread through Wales by means of the eisteddfod movement in the early nineteenth century. The fate of native Welsh dance music was less fortunate. Religious revivalism had one aspect which was puritanical condemnation of worldly and carnal pleasures, and the harp was associated above all with dancing. Gradually in the course of the early nineteenth century the old Welsh dances disappeared, and only a few bold outsiders such as the pioneer eighteenth-century radical William Jones of Llangadfan, ventured to record the steps, figures, and music.

The Welsh scholars always bewailed the fact that the Welsh in previous centuries had lost a sense of their own history: this again was remedied to some extent in the eighteenth and early nineteenth centuries. Societies such as the Cymmrodorion encouraged antiquarians to correspond with each other and this produced in the last quarter of the century a flood of publications about Wales, most of them written in English. Sometimes these were reprints of books of an earlier age such as Sir John Wynn's book on the Gwydir family, at other times they were elaborate history lessons in the form of travel books such as Thomas Pennant's *Tours in North Wales*, while at the end of the century there was a series of county histories on Monmouthshire, Breconshire, Pembrokeshire and other shires, which usually gave attention to recent history. There were also popular history booklets in Welsh, often giving highly Romanticised and sometimes mythical versions of early Welsh history, such as the 'Treason of the Long Knives', or the massacre of the Welsh bards by King Edward I, and history formed an important part of the Welsh magazines which proliferated throughout the early nineteenth century. The American War of Independence greatly excited the Welsh people, and Romantic historians obliged the Welsh of the period by showing how intimately the Welsh were connected with the American past, for they resurrected an almost forgotten legend that America's first discovery by Europeans was not by Columbus but rather by Prince Madoc son of Owain Gwynedd in the twelfth century, and that the descendants of his expedition still lived in the wild West. An expedition was sent to look for these Madocian Indians, and one result of this publicity was to persuade large numbers of Welsh people to emigrate to the infant United States.

We have mentioned the eisteddfod more than once. The ancient institution had ceased to exist in 1567, but had been revived on a very small scale in 1701, but by 1789 it was possible to revive it on a large scale, more or less on lines resembling its modern counterpart. A home-grown bourgeoisie with a good deal of know-how had appeared by then, there were good roads crossing north Wales and hotels beginning to appear which catered for tourists, and above all, there were rich London Welsh who could give subventions for the prizes, and indeed pay for handsome medals designed by men such as Dupré (later official medallist of the French Republic). Three successful eisteddfodau were held at Corwen, Llangollen and Bala in 1789. During the long French wars eisteddfodau had to be in abeyance, but after 1815, they reappeared in various parts with the encouragement of new 'Cambrian' or Cymreigyddion societies, which proliferated rapidly.

The neo-druidic ceremonials which are today associated with the eisteddfod were not originally part of the institution. Edward Williams 'Iolo Morganwg' was fascinated by Stonehenge and amazed that there were esoteric societies of Druids in London, a city where he worked for much of his youth, and he was determined that Wales too should have its druid organisation. With his London Welsh friends he held in 1792 at Primrose Hill the first Welsh druidic moot, termed a *Gorsedd* by Iolo, and subsequently Iolo returned to Wales, setting up groups of supporters who were initiated into the rites and ceremonies of a kind of order or guild of druid bards. It was only in 1819 at the Carmarthen Eisteddfod, held under the presidency of Bishop Burgess, that Iolo persuaded the eisteddfod to make the *Gorsedd* a part of the ceremonies.

The fullblown Romanticism of the end of the eighteenth century continued through the first half of the nineteenth century, as is shown by the career of one of the Welsh cultural leaders of the period, Augusta Hall, Lady Llanover (1802-96), a doughty defender of the Welsh national instrument, the triple harp, and its music, and it was she in the Cardiff Eisteddfod of 1834 who drew attention to the importance of a national costume for women, and on the basis of her detailed study of folk costumes of different areas. invented the homogenised version with the colourful cloak and bedgown and tall black hat. which she herself wore and fixed forever in the imagination as 'The Welsh Costume'. She and her husband were part of a wide circle. containing among others, the historian, Thomas Price 'Camhuanawc', and European scholars such as her brother-in-law Baron Bunsen, all of them with profound and complex plans for the regeneration of the Welsh people. But the Romantic movement in Wales was forced to come to terms with a new Wales growing up around it during the first half of the nineteenth century, with the forces of religious dissent and nonconformity, rapid industrial change and social dislocation, with the spread of political participation, and with the rise of scientific standards. Publicists and preservationists such as Edward Jones, Iolo Morganwg, and William Jones of Llangadfan, believed that Methodism had already killed off a lot of traditional rites, traditions and lore, such as dances, local tales, fiddle and harp music, and in the early nineteenth century collections of fairly innocent ballads were condemned by chapel folk as rude and indecent, while the performances of interludes (*anterliwtiau*) were prosecuted, and came to an end by about 1830, only about twenty years after the death of their most important author Twm o'r Nant. What we see then is a dual process occurring in the second quarter of the nineteenth century, on the one hand the bawdy, rough colourful and even lewd characteristics of popular Welsh cultural life are ruthlessly stamped out by the leaders of Welsh society, and on the other hand, chapel folk gradually come to accept that cultural societies and eisteddfodau were in themselves useful tools to civilise, and by the 1850s only the Methodists stood out against attending them. The religious census of 1851 had proved beyond doubt that the nonconformists formed almost the whole of the worshippers of Wales, and that there was a chance that they could soon convert the remaining half of the population just beyond their embrace. Forming the nation, they felt a responsibility to things Welsh which in previous generations they had left to Church folk. and indeed through the first half of the century Church folk had dominated Welsh cultural life. Romantic Wales also realised that it must come to terms with industrial

94. Phillipp de Loutherbourg, The Last Bard, engraving 1784.
95. Edward Pugh, engraving of Thos. Edwards, Twm o'r Nant, 1800.
96. *Below* Hugh Hughes frontispiece to history book showing Treason of the Long Knives, 1822.

Wales. Its vast impersonal forces broke the Welsh away from their remaining traditions even more effectively than nonconformity and puritanism. The revived and powerful national eisteddfod movement from 1858 to 1868 was a battleground of new and old Welshness, with the balladists and bards of the Gorsedd preserving the merry folksy entertainment of the tavern and alehouse of the eighteenth century, and devotion to the language of the Druids, namely Welsh, while there were powerful forces of modernisation amongst the administrators and middle classes demanding a more relevant syllabus, the establishment of a Social Science Section with seminars and lectures (in English), prizes and medals for essays on geology and industry, and new skills such as photography. A minor musical revolution in the mid-nineteenth century was a sign of profound change, showing how Welsh culture was adapting itself to nonconformity and to industrialisation. The fashion for choral singing appeared in the 1840s, as Wales became more urbanised, and chapels were rebuilt in a style which made possible the disposition of four-part choirs with a conductor, and indeed employers of the period encouraged employees to spend their leisure in joining brass bands and choirs. The temperance and total abstinence movement strongly believed in occupying idle hands by persuading everybody to join a choir and a Sunday school, and to come frequently to singing festivals, so that by the 1870s the *cymanfa ganu* (hymn singing festival) had become a distinctive national institution. Despite puritanical opposition to musical instruments, soon chapels had organs and even small orchestras. The process of industrialisation created a large and comfortable middle class by the mid-nineteenth century, and these people associated the pianoforte with respectability. Hence the army of music teachers, the composers of lyrics for old 'Welsh airs' for the harp, now arranged for voice and piano. The railways made it possible for people from a wide area to attend choir practices, and indeed to travel far and wide to attend the eisteddfod. By the 1870s Wales had large choirs, such as Côr Caradog in Aberdare, and when these won prizes in English choral festivals, it was felt that Welsh culture had really triumphed, and the Welsh choir (a tradition hardly thirty years old) was considered a national symbol.

In the Llangollen national eisteddfod of 1858 a prize was offered for an essay on the veracity of the tale of Madoc's discovery of America. The best entry was a well argued and scholarly debunking of the legend by a chemist from Merthyr, Thomas Stephens. His prize was withheld on the hilarious grounds that the essay had to prove the legend was true, not false. Stephens had already made a name for himself as a new type of analytical scholar, examining the preconceptions of Romantic Wales, and often finding them wanting. On a more general level, in the mid-nineteenth century, at the same time as the Welsh were going through a real social and economic crisis, there was growing disenchantment with Romantic Wales, its Druidism, its Celticism, and its quaintness. Already during the 1830s scholars such as J.C. Prichard had shown the connection of Welsh to other Indo-European languages, and German philologists such as Bopp and Zeuss a few years later, put its study on a scientific basis. During the 1840s we find the rise of modern archaeology, and modern scholarly history, which made it difficult for the views of Iolo Morganwg and other Romantics to go unchallenged. The violence and turbulence of Welsh society in the 1830s and '40s greatly alarmed respectable English opinion, and the Welsh were often coupled with the violent and turbulent Irish, and since the belief in English and Teutonic racial superiority was strong in

97. *Opposite* Archdruid Hwfa Môn in druidic costume.

Victorian England, the Welsh found themselves cast in the role of an inferior race with a backward and irrelevant culture. It is a curious paradox, that as Wales was becoming a rich and powerful economy, of essential value to the running of the British Empire, and as the Welsh gained great self-confidence that they were Europe's most godly and moral people, so also this was a time of crisis of confidence in their secular culture, and the Welsh rapidly adopted a Victorian English mindset or values and rapidly adopted the English language. One should however not exaggerate this tendency: there was a powerful undercurrent of nationalistic feeling in Victorian Wales, shown in the rapid acceptance of *Hen Wlad fy Nhadau* ('Land of My Fathers') as a national anthem fairly soon after its composition in 1856, or in the establishment of a colony in Patagonia on the southern fringes of Argentina in 1865 with Welsh as its official language. There was also a nationalistic dimension to the drive for Welsh institutions, educational and political. in the 1880s and 90s, as our period comes to an end.

From Pastoralism to Industrialism

Several industries, such as lead and iron, had long existed in Wales before the mid-eighteenth century – although it was chiefly an agrarian society throughout the century – but their rapid expansion came from the English commercial classes, together with several Welsh merchants such as Robert Morgan of Carmarthen, realising that the Welsh hills contained vast untapped resources which could supply the growing domestic English demand for products made of lead, tin and copper, iron and slate, and which could supply the constantly growing demands of the British war machine, as it defended a world wide empire against France and Spain. Its hitherto barely-exploited wood and coal resources could make up for the long-used, badly-depleted fuel supplies in England. Welsh landowners were anxious to treat their estates as business concerns and to cooperate with bankers and investors, while the latter began to see that Welsh industry was likely to be a profitable field for investing fortunes made in London or Birmingham or in such enterprises as the slave trade at Bristol and Liverpool. The diseases which had long ravaged the Welsh population abated gradually during the century, the increasing efficiency and modernisation of agricultural estates and farms meant a larger food supply with fewer hands needed to produce it, and the enclosure of great swathes of common pastures and manorial waste, through acts of parliament, all helped to drive an army of unemployed labour to seek work in Welsh industry.

The potential of mid-Wales for lead-mining had been seen as long ago as the Civil Wars, and several estates began to exploit their lead deposits from the mid-eighteenth century onwards: the Myddeltons of Chirk in eastern Denbighshire, Lord Powis in Montgomery-shire, Lord Grosvenor in Flintshire, while the Crown estate developed immensely rich mines in the north Cardiganshire hills. In west Glamorgan coal deposits were easily exploited near the coast, and at Swansea, on the beach itself, and the nearness of Cornish copper mines meant that Swansea and its environs became early on a centre for copper smelting. In 1750 it produced around 50% of Britain's copper and by 1799 about 90%. The old Roman copper workings in Anglesey were rediscovered in 1761, this leading to the discovery seven years later of the immense copper deposits of Parys Mountain near Amlwch. The greatest copper merchant was Thomas Williams of Llanidan (an Anglesey attorney), who transported the ore not only to Swansea but also to the coal-rich Greenfield valley on the Deeside coast in Flintshire, and dominated the world copper market from about 1788 to his death in 1802.

Iron had been mined and smelted through the use of charcoal in many parts, and Carmarthen's prosperity to some extent depended on this heavy industry in a sylvan setting, but the significant development from 1750 onwards lay high in the hills where north Glamorgan and Monmouthshire met Breconshire, where abundant supplies were discovered of iron, coal, limestone, and rapid streams were found, such as the Dowlais brook which gave its name to the iron company founded in 1759 near Merthyr Tydfil. This was in the middle of the Seven Years War. Cyfarthfa, also near Merthyr, was founded in 1765, and within a few years there was a chain of enormous iron works stretching across the bare hills from Hirwaun above Aberdare to Blaenafon north of Pontypool. John Wilkinson from Whitehaven, Cumbria, was one of the partners in Cyfarthfa, but his particular theatre of activity was in Flintshire and east Denbighshire. Barren of food and people, the hills sucked in thousands from the neighbouring Welsh counties. These heavy extractive industries with their immense forges and kilns and elaborate technology, and the innovative infrastructure of roads, tramways and canals to take the finished product out to supply the armies navies and cities of the world, required a stupendous outlay of capital. Pioneering roads were cut in order to reach ports such as Newport and Cardiff, then tramways, and by the end of the eighteenth century, canals, which in a short time would allow Cardiff to become one of the great seaports of the world.

As was the case with iron, tinplate had been made in south Wales long before 1750, around Pontypool in the east and around Swansea and south Carmarthenshire in the west. In the eighteenth century, although the Pontypool area was famous for its wonderful imitation lacquer industry, the 'Pontypool Japan', the great development of tinplate lay in the west where tin could easily be imported and coal easily mined, and indeed easily exported from Swansea and Llanelli and other ports. Tin came to serve all sorts of new uses: from 1825 onwards in the food canning industry, for example, all creating a huge demand for Welsh tin. The whole area came to dominate the British tinplate industry almost unchallenged until the twentieth century.

One industry which was considered more peculiarly Welsh than the others just mentioned was slate, and here the crucial change to a large-scale capitalistic industry took place in the 1780s. The chief centre was in the north west in Merioneth and above all in Caernarfonshire, where Richard Pennant (who had inherited part of the Penrhyn estates) in 1782 used his skills as a Liverpool merchant and his capital from Jamaican sugar estates to unify and transform lots of small-scale slate exploitations, to create a major industry. In 1788 the Dinorwic Slate Quarry Company was founded, and other local families also developed rival companies. In the early nineteenth century the enterprising W.A. Maddocks built the new port of Portmadoc, a harbour linked by tramway (and eventually a narrow-gauge railway) to the quarries at Blaenau Ffestiniog. Before the mid-eighteenth century Wales had been infamous for its poor communications, but there soon developed by the early nineteenth century a network of roads and great bridges (such as those built by Thomas Telford at Conwy and over the Menai Straits), and a fringe of canals served by series of locks and several immense aqueducts (such as those built by Telford at Chirk and Froncysyllte in the north east). Nothing can show more clearly how much Wales had lost its remote backwardness than the fact that in 1804 at Penydarren near Merthyr the world's first steam locomotive was tried out, while a short time afterwards the world's first passenger railway ran from Oystermouth to Swansea. The Pwll Du Tramroad Tunnel near Blaenafon ran for about a mile and a half underground, the longest such structure at that time in the world.

Another sign of modernisation and sophistication was the appearance of Welsh banks, at Aberystwyth in 1762, at Brecon in 1778, the Chester and North Wales Bank in 1792, and a few years later the Bank of the Black Ox at Llandovery and The Bank of the Black Sheep at Aberystwyth and Tregaron, a sure sign of the development of a small middle class in this period – people such as William Williams of Llandygai, the Welsh writer and historian, deputy manager of the vast Penrhyn slate quarries at the end of the eighteenth century, or his friends in Bangor, shipbuilders and merchants of all sorts. One field where a Welsh commercial class appeared was that of printing: the first permanent press on Welsh soil appearing as late as 1718, but within a few decades a network of printers and publishers had appeared the length and breadth of Wales.

What was the effect of all this change on the Welsh population? It is impossible to be certain, but it may be that Wales had about 489,000 people around 1750, increasing rapidly to 530,000 in 1780, and the first census of 1801 gives us 587,000. Agriculture was still buoyant at the time of the Napoleonic Wars, and industries were not yet concentrated in a few small areas. One feature of the early stages of industrialisation in Wales was that certain areas had a great variety of industries, such as Flintshire with its cotton mills at Holywell, its potteries at Buckley, its copper works, as well as its lead and coal mines. The rapid changes are really only visible with the censuses of the nineteenth century, where industrial areas such as Flintshire and above all Monmouthshire, begin to show phenomenal gains, so that Wales's population had doubled to just over a million in 1851 and to almost two million by the end of the century.

With the return of peace in 1815 Welsh industrialists were forced to adapt, and although this period from 1815 to the 1840s was one of the stormiest in industrial relations, it was for most of the time one of great expansion. The industries already mentioned went on expanding: although the copper of Anglesey gradually declined and ended by 1871, there was considerable mining several decades later in neighbouring Caernarfonshire. The lead industry, had declined during the great wars but recovered and its peak year of production in Wales came in 1856. House building had suffered during the great wars, but after 1815 the demand for roofing slates returned, and although there were slate quarries in areas such as the hills of north Pembrokeshire (providing the Palace of Westminster with its roofs), north Wales came to be the world leaders. Nantlle quarries had cornered the Irish market, Penrhyn quarries supplied the USA through the ports of Boston and New Orleans, and fleets took slates to the Cape of Good Hope and Australia, while Port Madoc exported Ffestiniog slates to such places as Hamburg.

Far more striking was the early nineteenth-century expansion of Welsh iron. Welsh pig-iron production rose by 50% from 1823 to 1830, when Dowlais works (under Josiah John Guest) overtook Cyfarthfa as the major producer in the south, sending rails for the railways across Europe and America, though it was the Ebbw Vale works (started in 1789 by Jeremiah Homfray) which in 1825 produced the rails for the historic Stockton to Darlington Railway in England. By 1827 north east Wales also had twelve huge furnaces at work, dwarfed by Dowlais and Cyfarthfa and the others, all calling upon teeming workforces, and drawing in vast capital from outside. It has been said that J.J. Guest by 1847 probably controlled the largest single workforce in the world, and this was in the hands of his widow Lady Charlotte after his death in 1852.

The value of coal had been seen in the eighteenth century as a means of replacing coke in copper and then iron smelting, and its use to drive steam engines of all kinds, and then locomotives, meant that the successful industries of the age needed to be near coalfields, hence the large numbers of lesser industries drawn to the Welsh coalfield such as the potteries and porcelain works of nineteenth-century Swansea, and in 1816 the chain works of Brown Lennox,

98. Engravings of Lady Charlotte Guest and J.J. Guest, 1852.
99. R.T. Crawshay, photo of Penydarren works in ruins *c*.1870.

which moved from Millwall in London to Pontypridd. Even in the late eighteenth century coal owners in west Glamorgan had tried to open up the market for coal. Wales had a great variety of coal, suitable for all types of uses. A few pits were sunk around 1807 in the Rhondda by pioneering mining entrepreneurs such as Walter Coffin, and from 1828 Robert and Lucy Thomas of Abercanaid began to market coal, and soon Welsh coal was used by the fleet of the East India Company, exported to the West Indies and Portugal, and in the 1850s and 60s the Royal Navy used vast quantities of the excellent steam coal of such districts as Aberdare, and the conurbations of Victorian England consumed endless supplies for domestic and commercial use. The Taff Vale Railway was opened in 1841, with lines spreading to all the south Wales valleys in the following decades, making it easy to move coal to Cardiff and other ports for export, and the advances in mining technology meant that deep mines could be sunk in the middle area of the coalfield where coal lay unfathomably deeply underground. The Bute estate experimented with deep coalpits in Treherbert (at the head of the Rhondda Fawr) in 1855, with a rail link to Cardiff in 1856. The Rhondda valleys and valleys to the east and west of them rapidly developed from 1870 onwards. The Bute estate developed ever larger docks in Cardiff, which became the world's greatest coal port, and by the 1880s Wales was exporting about 25% of the world's coal, at a time when the economies of the advanced world ran on coal, so that south Wales was a kind of Victorian Saudi Arabia of the pre-petroleum age. In the 1880s even the vast Cardiff docks were not sufficient, and a rival to the Marquess of Bute, David Davies of Llandinam, opened Barry docks a few miles away, as a port to rival Cardiff in 1884. Steam coal in particular was shipped out by such Cardiff companies as Cory Brothers to coaling stations at Aden and elsewhere, enabling British ships to sail efficiently to colonies, protectorates and dominions of the far-flung British Empire.

During the nineteenth century Swansea and Llanelli and various other towns in the hinterland, and coastal towns such as Briton Ferry and Aberavon, became the home of much of the British tinplate industry. Swansea in addition was the centre over a long period of the British non-ferrous smelting industry. Vivians of Truro came to the area at the opening of the century and in 1809 opened the Hafod Copper Works a mile or so north of Swansea (which had prided itself on being a Welsh Weymouth), and the process used in copper smelting meant the despoliation of the environment, with miles of slag heaps under belching black clouds of poisonous fumes.

Swansea and similar ports had always imported raw materials (save coal), and the economy of Chile was for much of the century dependent on the demands of Swansea copper importers. This dependence on foreign ores was also more and more true of the famous Welsh iron industries. One of many difficulties faced by the old iron works from 1858 to 1867 was that local ironstone mines were worked out, and, while new sources were found in iron ore mines around Bilbao in the Basque Country, and elsewhere, the main disadvantage, however, was the distance of the old-established iron works from the sea, causing several of the old works to close in the mid-nineteenth century. The revolution affecting the whole iron industry was the coming of new techniques to make steel. Bessemer's converter (1858) and Siemens's open-hearth process (1863) were methods adopted by iron works in the following decade, Landore works in Swansea as early as 1868, and in 1888 the great Dowlais works of Merthyr transferred its steel making operations to East Moors on the shore east of Cardiff docks.

What then had been achieved by the industrialisation of Wales by the end of the nineteenth century? At the start of the period the population had been mostly rural, and by the end mostly urban or industrial. Industry had made it possible for Wales to sustain a population of close on two million. Up until the middle of the nineteenth century the surplus population of neighbouring counties had provided the industrial workforce, but later the trend was for large numbers of Irish and then English immigrants to pour in, the 1851 Census showing that about 110,000 of the Welsh population (about one tenth) was born in England, and around 20,000 had recently fled into Wales from the Irish famine. This great change first of all tilted the linguistic balance towards English in Monmouthshire and the large towns such as Cardiff, and then further afield, until only half the population was Welsh-speaking by the time of the first language census in 1891. Industry however had made it possible for the absolute numbers of Welsh-speakers to increase from the mid-eighteenth to the late nineteenth century from possibly 400,000 to somewhere not far from a million. Industry had also gradually changed the whole fabric of Welsh society, creating a new moneyed class of capitalists such as the Vivians in Swansea (Lords Swansea), or W.T. Lewis (Lord Merthyr) or D.A. Thomas (Lord Rhondda), a fairly small though significant middle class, and an immense proletariat of workers in heavy extractive industries. In a few places such as Swansea, Neath and Wrexham industry developed around old-established towns, but generally Welsh industrial settlements were brash new raw work camps, frequently in high wet bald mountain areas hitherto the haunts of shepherds and huntsmen.

In the first decades of industrialisation, the new proletariat lived in small settlements hurriedly flung up near the forges or mines, and indeed this generally remained the pattern in the narrow valleys of south Wales where a large city would have been physically impossible to develop. In the early stages the diet and housing of the workers were said to be terrible, and the absence of retail outlets meant that industrialists were driven to establish company stores or 'truck shops'. In the terrible social conditions plagues such as cholera were rife, and capitalists and the middle classes unwilling to pay higher rates in order to improve social conditions. In the latter half of the nineteenth century however, boards of health were established, the mines and works were subjected to the supervision of inspectors and the grim toll of industrial accidents was somewhat abated, the public health acts meant that workers' housing in the Rhondda, for example, after 1870, was greatly improved, and Wales saw a large number of genuine industrial towns emerge, with mercantile middle classes with a municipal self-consciousness, in such places as Llanelli, Bridgend, Tredegar, Pontypridd and Pontypool.

The process we have just described had not been as early as that in England, but it had come more suddenly, and with more sweeping effect, turning the country around from being one of the poorest parts of Western Europe into one of the richest, catapulting the people without warning from a state of pastoralism into industrialism. The historian Benjamin Heath Malkin, writing of the change he had seen in south Wales in the ten years or so before he wrote in 1803, called it 'a revolution', noting that it would sooner or later also have profound effects on the political stage. So it is to politics that we turn next.

From Oligarchy to Radicalism

One of the greatest of all new experiences in this period was political participation. A tiny proportion of the population took part, except as onlookers, in politics before the Reform Act of 1832, and while a larger minority of people participated after that, and an even larger minority after the second Reform Act of 1867, it is only after 1884 that a large proportion of the male population could vote. The picture is made far more complex because of the growing number of people joining in political activities such as agitating for causes, or reading the press, or taking part in local government bodies such as Boards of Health; and above it is complicated in Wales by a most exceptionally turbulent period of disturbances, riots and rebellions stretching from the 1790s to 1844.

In the 1750s Wales was still governed by the political system set up in the 'Acts of Union' of 1536 and 1543; Welsh counties had, with some exceptions, one shire MP and one burgess MP. In the eighteenth century very few elections took place, the MPs usually being returned unopposed. This is because political power was in the hands of a small number of rich aristocratic families in most cases established in power after the Acts of Union, such as the Mostyns of Mostyn in Flintshire – thirteen generations of the Mostyns represented Flintshire from the sixteenth century up to 1861. The burgess seats should in theory have had elections on a franchise of burgesses of the towns, but in practice these seats too had fallen into the thrall of the great 'county families'.

In certain parts of Wales there had been a realignment of political loyalties after the 1688 Glorious Revolution, with a few Welsh families becoming Whigs – the majority of Welsh families were solidly Tory – so that in Denbighshire there was a rivalry between the decidedly Tory, and immensely rich, Williams Wynns of Wynnstay and the Whig Myddelton family of Chirk – though the Myddeltons and the Williams Wynns appeared to make peace with each other by 1790, in Monmouthshire there was rivalry between the Tory Dukes of Beaufort (whose castle at Raglan was ruined, but whose Raglan estate was not, and the Dukes had houses in Monmouth town and nearby at Troy), and the Whig Morgan family of Tredegar Park near Newport. The magnates of Wales, perhaps six to twelve families in each county, were anxious to avoid electoral contests partly because they knew that beneath the surface there were many rivalries which could turn to violence. Carmarthen Whigs believed that local Tories were Jacobites and fomented discontent and rioting in 1755 and 1758. Jacobitism in any case had divided Welsh Tories into two opposing groups after 1714.

Political disagreement showed itself often at a lower or local level, with families trying to gain power in the Quarter Sessions or by gaining advantages for their localities or their kinsfolk. So tenacious was the hold of the county families on Welsh society that they held on to much of their power until the 1880s. Ideological conflict hardly disturbed Welsh electoral politics in the eighteenth century, though Tories may have used the new masonic lodges spreading through Wales in the mid-eighteenth century as meeting places for opposition, and the gradual growth of political dissenters such as Arians and Anti-Trinitarians meant that there were a few critics here and there demanding political freedoms. Richard Price of Tynton, Llangeinor, Glamorgan, went to London as a dissenting minister and became a famous scientist and political writer, the chief spokesman for the American colonists in their war against Britain, but, although London-based, he spent a good deal of each year in Bridgend and was master of the masonic lodge there. The American war affected Welsh trade considerably, and Welsh dissenters who felt they had a grievance were moved by the struggle of colonists over principles of political representation. The government was discredited over its conduct of the American war, and in the 1780s there were in England several movements demanding political reforms to make the system more representative and to reduce the personal power of the King. There were of course several individuals up and down Wales who adopted radical views: the country doctor William Jones of Llangadfan, Montgomeryshire, was called a 'rank republican and a leveller'. Burke's bill of 1780 proposed as part of the reduction of royal influence to abolish the ancient fiscal unit of the Principality of Wales, but the Welsh politicians opposed this vehemently for their own interests and the clauses were withdrawn in 1782. Wales also saw some amount of the ferment of the county associations for reform to be found in England: the Flintshire Association at one point became very active in publicising demands for reform, though here there was considerable disagreement between Thomas Pennant who only wanted limitation of royal powers and Dean Shipley of St Asaph, an ecclesiastic stormy petrel, who wished for some real democracy. Shipley's publication of the pamphlet *The Principles of Government* by his brother-in-law the judge Sir William Jones (also famous as a philologist) led to his being prosecuted for seditious libel, and his release caused a short-lived furore in north Wales.

It is curious that reformist ideas of Shipley and Jones should have been conveyed to the Welsh public in the form of an *anterliwt,* the real difficulty being faced by the Welsh being their inability to read political discussions in their own language. This was partly resolved by the appearance of several journals in the 1790s, at the beginning of the great wars against France, such as Morgan John Rhys's *Cylchgrawn Cynmraeg* (1793) or David Davies's *Geirgrawn* (1796), which explained politics to them. In the early stages of the great wars it was possible to express reforming political and even pro-French views, which is what Iolo Morganwg did in his *Poems Lyric and Pastoral* (1794), among whose subscribers we find Citizen Brissot. A few Welsh reformist books were published, two by John Jones 'Jac Glan y Gors' explaining the revolutionary views of Thomas Paine to the Welsh in 1795 and 1797. Iolo's friend Thomas Evans 'Tomos Glyn Cothi', the Arian minister at Aberdare, went to prison for his revolutionary views, but other reformists such as Iolo kept their sympathies quiet, and outwardly conformed, Iolo writing ballads for the Glamorgan Volunteers. Morgan John Rhys, who had gone out to Paris to try to make Welsh Baptists out of the French revolutionary crowds, and had returned to hope to make revolutionaries out of the Welsh, despaired by 1796 and left to found a Welsh radical colony in Pennsylvania. Pitt's 'gagging acts' repressed public meetings and even eisteddfodau disappeared. Individual expressions of Jacobinism or revolutionism were punished, meanwhile loyalist associations were set up, and the Welsh joined the Volunteer movement and the local militias. Swansea potteries produced anti-Bonaparte mugs and jugs.

Dissenters and Methodists were at pains to express loyalty, although they were all accused of attracting to the Welsh shores the small and indifferent French Revolutionary army under the command of Colonel Tate which landed near Fishguard in 1797 with the hope of starting a Revolution on the British mainland. The Welsh showed no propensity to revolt, and the invasion, a hopeless fiasco, was swiftly defeated, although the crisis had a serious effect on public confidence in the government and in the Bank of England. In Wales it led the Methodists first to hold services of thanksgiving, and then to write pamphlets to protest their loyalty. The authorities can hardly have felt happy that Iolo Morganwg and his friends had founded the South Wales Unitarian Society in 1802, but it was purportedly a religious organisation. It was several years before the home situation eased, and a few discussion groups, such as the Merthyr Philosophical Society began to peep out from under the repressive blanket.

It was not merely the siege mentality of the wars which caused repression, but fears of industrial strikes and food riots, which flared up in various parts of Wales, in Swansea, for example in 1794 the authorities were reminded of the drastic events in France. But in the main the years of the great wars were years of prosperity and full employment for the Welsh, the farmers selling their produce at high prices to the armed forces, the industrial workers keeping the forces supplied with armaments. It was the return of peace in Europe which brought great instability once again to Wales. Demobilised soldiers and sailors returned home, the farmers found they had no easy market for their produce and had to lay off their agricultural workers, and the foundries took a long time to readjust to peacetime, and to find new markets for different kinds of products, such as pipes, or rails for railways. There were violent strikes all over the Welsh industrial areas and a great deal of hardship in the countryside, the strikes in Tredegar and Merthyr Tydfil being so bad that troops were called in to keep order in 1816. There were also violent strikes in the coalfield in 1822, 1830 and 1832, and at Bagillt on the Flintshire coast in 1830 the strikes were so violent that Sir Watkin Williams Wynn sent in his militia cavalry to keep order, but he and they were unable to prevent English-type trade unionism spreading into north and south Wales. Strikes and protests were particularly bitter in the hill country of south Wales because the ironmasters tended to be extremely autocratic, dismissing men whenever (as frequently happened) there was a sudden downturn in demand, and since the settlements were built in hitherto uninhabited mountain country, the masters had founded truckshops, giving the masters a monopoly over retail sales, which had the effect of keeping the men perpetually in debt to the company. One reaction to the powerlessness felt by the workers was the peculiarly Monmouthshire movement of intimidation of the workers by gangs known as 'Scotch Cattle'. These terrorised workers from about 1820 until they were suppressed by firm government policing in 1835.

The British Reform crisis of 1831 added a further political dimension to a Wales already racked with disturbances, and there were minor election riots in 1831 in Caernarfon, Montgomery, Llanidloes, Haverfordwest; a branch of the Political Union of Working Classes was established by John Frost at Newport, and Carmarthen, as people expected, had violent election riots in June 1831, caused by the failure of the Reform Bill at the end of April. Only in Merthyr Tydfil, the largest town in Wales, was there anything approaching a full scale rising. Since about 1800 there was a tradition of political discussion in Merthyr and a considerable literate and articulate middle class, and great public interest at the end of May in the meetings held to protest at the failure of Reform. Into the midst of this mood of anger came the sudden dismissals of ironworkers by William Crawshay of Cyfarthfa, adding economic misery to political anger, with the result that demagogues brought out a huge mob of workers who then proceeded to take over the town for a week, up to June 8th. The violence, with troops shooting down an unknown number of rioters, divided the protesters into moderates and extremists. Government troops eventually managed to restore order, and the leaders were tried later in the summer in Cardiff, Lewis Lewis 'Lewsyn yr Heliwr' being sent for transportation, and Richard Lewis 'Dic Penderyn' found guilty of injuring a Scottish soldier Donald Black, was hanged in Cardiff. Public opinion in Wales believed he had been hanged unjustly, and his funeral in his home parish of Aberavon, Glamorgan, was attended by unprecedentedly large crowds from all over Glamorgan, indicating that he was a hero or martyr to rural workers as well.

The authorities clamped down on the nascent trade unions in Merthyr and elsewhere, then suppressed the Scotch Cattle with a firm hand in 1834-5. The Merthyr radicals then turned to more peaceful means of protest, founding, for example the newspaper *Y Gweithiwr* (The Worker) in 1834. The actual reforms carried out by the successful Reform Act of 1832 turned out to be a great disappointment, though Merthyr gained its first MP, electing the ironmaster of Dowlais, Josiah John Guest. The electorate created was still small, and largely middle class. The subsequent reforms carried out created a great upheaval in Wales. Humanitarians, dissenters, taxpayers, and the poor, all hated the new workhouses proposed by the New Poor Law of 1834 – Merthyr avoided setting one up for many years, and several workhouses were attacked, Caersws had to be protected by troops in 1838 and Carmarthen workhouse was attacked by a mob in January 1839. The many reforms of the Church of England were of intense interest to the Welsh, most especially since the old Test and Corporation Acts had been abolished in 1828 for dissenters, which encouraged chapel folk in Wales to take some interest in politics. The Tithe Commutation Act of 1836 however infuriated Welsh rural folk once it was seen that farmers would have to pay their dues not in kind but in money, and it became clear that they would end up paying rather more than in the past, at a time when more and more were deserting the Church and joining the chapels. Dissenters also attacked the paying of the Church rate and tried to find ways of dominating local vestry meetings which determined the rate. All through the 1830s, it should be recalled, there was a growth in the Welsh newspaper and periodical press. The first paper had been *The Cambrian* (in Swansea) in 1804, and soon there were regional newspapers, some Tory, some Whig, in English, and also Welsh periodicals – *Seren Gomer* founded in Swansea in 1814 had been the first – which set out both sides of the arguments. *Yr Haul* for example was a Tory Church magazine, and *Y Diwygiwr* a Radical dissenting paper. In addition to all this debate and discussion, there was the argument over state aid to education (from 1833 onwards), and public meetings called on many different matters, such as the abolition of the slave trade. The general run of nonconformists had been previously rather scared of being labelled 'political dissenters' (like the Unitarians), but they were rapidly drawn into the maelstrom of Welsh politics, and although John Elias the 'Methodist Pope' kept the Methodists back from political involvement until 1841, the younger generation of Methodists led by Roger Edwards of Mold were straining at the leash.

If people thought that the Wales of William IV had been turbulent, then worse was to come in the first years of Victoria. As a result of the rapid politicization of the Welsh there was great interest in Chartism in certain parts of Wales: in the woollen towns of mid-Wales, such as Llanidloes, in Carmarthen where the lawyer Hugh Williams was influential, in Merthyr where the Unitarian Morgan Williams worked, and in Llantrisant, home of the eccentric radical Dr William Price, pagan druid, apostle of free love, and later pioneer of cremation, and in Newport, where John Frost was an important radical leader. When the charter organised by the London Working Men's Association was rejected by Parliament in 1838 there was in Wales bitter disappointment, and although rational argument had been the aim of the Chartists, the 'physical force Chartists' gained the upper hand in parts of Wales, and began to organise a secret uprising. The Chartist Uprising of November 1839 is one of the most famous events in nineteenth-century Wales, but its aims are by no means clear. John Frost and the other Chartist leaders secretly armed some five thousand men, who then marched down to capture Newport on 4 November 1839, with the possible aim of triggering similar uprisings in England, and those in turn would cause a revolution to put into force the Chartist aims of political democracy. The march on Newport was a fiasco, mistakes were made, the weather extremely bad, and the full impact of the Chartist army never felt. Thomas Phillips, mayor of Newport, had time to organise the defence of the town, there was a skirmish with the govermnent troops, in which an unknown number of men were killed. The leaders such as John Frost were tried and sentenced to transportation. This was, it is obvious, a terrible blow for Welsh Chartism, yet the movement did not disappear, but regrouped quietly in centres such as Merthyr in the 1840s, turning to influencing popular opinion in favour of political participation and electoral politics.

Meanwhile the rural hinterland of industrial south Wales was rocked by a series of riots and plots lasting from 1839 to 1844, and since Hugh Williams, the Chartist leader, lived in St Clears, near the epicentre of the rioting, it was frequently suspected that this was a rural Chartism. The riots at first took the form of attacks on the tollgates of the turnpike roads in the summer of 1839, and after a period of quiescence, reintensified in the early 1840s, rising to fury in 1842 and 1843, dying away, as mysteriously as they had started, by 1844. They were carried out often at night by armed gangs of horsemen, in disguise, with blackened faces and wearing women's clothes, and, in order to establish their credibility with their crowds of supporters, they enacted traditional horseplay before they burned the gates or tollhouses. The horseplay, called *Ceffyl Pren* (wooden horse), was well-known in most European peasant societies as the charivari, rough music, or skymmetry, would be a mocking drama about the victim, carried in effigy on a wooden horse. The attacks were called The Rebecca Riots possibly because of the verse, well-known to Welsh chapelgoers, in the Book of Genesis about the sons of Rebecca possessing the gates of those which hated them. The tollgates were generally out in the country, a fairly easy target for attack, and they were intensely disliked by farmers of west Wales because the system of turnpike roads had spread so rapidly in the area over previous decades until even tiny lanes had bars and chains across them, and the turnpike trusts had become big business. Farmers, whose industry was in a state of crisis in the late 1830s, especially since the downturn of prosperity in Welsh industrial areas also hit them badly, hated the profiteering of the turnpike trusts. But the farmers and the poor labourers also hated the New Poor Law, and attacked workhouses, the Rebecca movement also sent threatening letters to landowners demanding rent reductions, and lastly, used the riots in order to settle old scores and vendettas. By 1843 many of the respectable farmers who had started the movement felt uncomfortable about the slide into general anarchy, and were frightened by the demands of the labourers, miners and the poor that there should be riots to help the lowest orders to gain fair play. By the Autumn of 1843 west Wales was spreadeagled by an army of 1,600 troops headed by Colonel Love and police forces were established in order to dissuade the civil population from supporting Rebecca. Peace and order were gradually restored, and a government commission examined the whole problem sympathetically, reporting in 1844. They believed that the riots had been spontaneous reactions to real hardships, and recommended the complete reorganisation of the turnpike system, making the enclosure and the workhouse systems less harsh, and so on. These were accepted by the government of the day, and gradually during the later 1840s prosperity and calm returned to west Wales, the improved roads and eventually the new railways bringing new prosperity to the hinterland, taking produce to the markets and moving surplus labourers easily into the industrial districts. The government report of 1844 also said that rural dwellers of Wales, if they were to come into the general run of the politics and prosperity of Britain, they would have to learn English. This was the sting in the tail of the otherwise benign report.

The government did little about this recommendation. William Williams MP for Coventry, an independent-minded radical, and a native of Llanpumsaint in Carmarthenshire, was stung into complaining that the government had done nothing to help the Welsh learn English. His questions led to the commission on Welsh education in 1846, reporting in the

100. Print by T.H. Thomas of John Elias preaching.
101. Protesters at Hirwaun, Merthyr riots of 1831 (engraving).
102. The attack of the Chartists on the Westgate Hotel, Newport, 4 November 1839.
J.F. Mullock, Engraving.

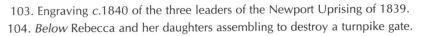

103. Engraving *c.*1840 of the three leaders of the Newport Uprising of 1839.
104. *Below* Rebecca and her daughters assembling to destroy a turnpike gate.

famous Blue Books of 1847. These reports had several, somewhat contradictory, effects on Wales. The furious reactions in Wales to the reports (from Anglicans such as Thomas Phillips, who had been knighted for his defence of Newport against the Chartists, and from a host of dissenters) delayed any state aided education for Wales for a generation, and it also caused public meetings to be held throughout Wales to protest about the calumnies of the Blue Books, which brought to the fore young activists such as Thomas Price of Aberdare and Henry Richard, and also brought the Methodists out of political purdah, causing them to join forces on many issues with the dissenters. Perhaps the nursery of political involvement was the setting up of local boards of health, as a result of the Public Health Act of 1848. This was an unfamiliar field of ad hoc bodies where the old aristocracy had little knowledge, and it helped to give an apprenticeship in government to radicals and dissenters (now usually called nonconformists). The new young leaders attempted to push their members on to the bench of magistrates, into local councils, and in the election of 1852 actually succeeded in getting a Unitarian coal owner, Walter Coffin elected MP for Cardiff. They also joined the local Welsh branches of the Liberation Society (aiming to disestablish the Church), and these were very active after 1862, and set up societies to persuade the public to register as voters, and other societies to extend the franchise, such as the South Wales Liberal Registration Society in 1867 or the Welsh Reform Association in 1868. This was a quiet revolution, transforming Wales from the angry riotousness of the period from 1831-44, to the world of responsible and stolid world of participatory politics. The radical reformers had hoped for a breakthrough in the general election of 1859, but Wales remained still in the hands of the old guard of Tory landed families. The reformers, led by a new breed of politicians such as Thomas Gee of Denbigh, Methodist owner of the influential Welsh paper *Baner ac Amserau Cymru*, seized on the actual and threatened eviction of tenant farmers in some parts such as Merioneth for voting against the will of the landowners, and turned the tenants into martyrs. They also began to play the nationalist card, by arguing that the landowners were not merely Tory, they were un-Welsh. The signs that the ice was cracking came in the 1865 general election when Wales returned eighteen Liberals and only fourteen Tories, but the electorate was still tiny and the MPs were all of the landlord class. A fresh chance for a Liberal and nonconformist impact came at last after Disraeli's Second Reform Act of 1867, which greatly extended the franchise in certain kinds of constituencies, notably in Wales Merthyr Tydfil, which now had several thousand voters, the most 'democratic' seat in Britain. In the general election of 1868 all Welsh eyes, it was said, were upon the Merthyr constituency, which now had two seats. It was expected that the people would elect two industrialists, H.A. Bruce in Merthyr and Richard Fothergill in Aberdare, both Liberals. But the workers went out of their way to adopt Henry Richard, secretary of the International Peace Society, and a noted dissenter and radical, as their preferred candidate. Bruce came bottom of the poll, Richard and Fothergill were elected. amidst great celebration in radical reformist Welsh circles. It was also a portent of things to come that George Osborne Morgan was elected as a radically-minded MP for Denbighshire. The Marquess of Bute was infuriated that his candidate was rejected by Cardiff, and, in order to fight for Welsh conservatism, founded and financed the new paper *The Western Mail* (published from 1 May 1869).

One of Gladstone's government's first tasks was to disestablish the Church of Ireland, achieved in 1869, and the Welsh Radicals (that is, left-wing non-Whig Liberals) tabled a Welsh Church Disestablishment Bill. It was unsuccessful, but again a sign of things to come. The Radicals made a great fuss about the browbeating of Welsh voters by threatened evictions on landed estates such as Rhiwlas near Bala, or dismissals of quarrymen at the Penrhyn quarries, and this strengthened the successful campaign to bring in the Secret Ballot (for the whole of the kingdom) in 1872. One other important issue raised by the Radicals because of the appointment of Judge Homersham-Cox, to serve predominantly Welsh-speaking areas, was the need for Welsh-speakers to be appointed to offices in Wales. The Church had responded to the change of public mood and in 1870 appointed a Welsh-speaking Bishop for the first time in nearly two centuries. The Liberals were in opposition from 1874 to 1880, and when Gladstone returned to power then, the Welsh Radicals had a programme of reforms, the Commission on educational provision in Wales chaired by H.A. Bruce, now Lord Aberdare, and in 1881 the Welsh Sunday Closing Bill, proposed by John Roberts, an extremely prosperous (and teetotaler) Liverpool builder. The Sunday Closing Act was again a pointer of things to come, for it was the first piece of legislation to recognise Wales as a political or ethnic unit. The Radicals felt their programme was gradually being fulfilled by the foundation of university colleges at Cardiff 1883 and at Bangor 1884 and a rescue package was worked out for Aberystwyth college in 1885, and their extra-parliamentary propagandists felt they were keeping up the Radical pressure by supporting tenants who refused to pay their tithes to an 'alien Church', which led to widespread public protests in areas such as north Pembrokeshire, and above all in the hill-country of Denbighshire. The so-called 'Tithe Wars' lasted from about 1880 to 1890, and died down when an Act of 1891 made it compulsory for the landlord rather than the tenant to pay the required tithe charges.

The Third Reform Act of 1884 and Redistribution Act of 1885 extended the franchise further, and in the election of 1885, the Liberals gained thirty of the Welsh seats, and fourteen of the MPs were nonconformists, and of those, some, such as the young T.E. Ellis (MP for Merioneth) avowedly nationalist as well as nonconformist. Liberalism was of course badly split over Irish Home Rule in 1886, after which Gladstone was heavily dependent on MPs in the 'Celtic fringe', so the Welsh Liberals began to think of themselves as a 'Welsh Party' within Liberalism organised by one of their most unusual members, Stuart Rendel, a rich English arms manufacturer and MP for Montgomeryshire. They had a programme of measures on temperance, education, tithe reform and disestablishment of the Church, land reform on the model of the land reforms in Ireland, and a modicum of 'home rule'. It was Stuart Rendel who gained Tory support for his Welsh Intermediate Education Bill in 1889, which provided government help to establish a network of secondary schools through Wales. These were called 'county schools' because administered by the new elected county councils established by the local government act of 1888. The system of Quarter Sessions which had run Welsh local government since the Acts of Union, and which had been dominated by the gentry since then, came to an end, the new county councils being largely in the hands of a nonconformist middle class. A second local government act of 1894 setting up district and parish councils confirmed the rule of the same sort of people in the localities.

In Gladstone's last government of 1892-94 Stuart Rendel (a great friend of Gladstone's) was influential, and T.E. Ellis was deputy chief whip. Ellis and his friends saw the county and local councils as an ideal opportunity to push for a national body or assembly, but in 1892 a National Institutions (Wales) Bill failed. and indeed a Welsh Church Disestablishment Bill also failed. One signal success was the granting of a royal charter to a federation of the university colleges, to be called The University of Wales, in 1893. The Radicals had long argued that Welsh landlords were just as arrogant and oppressive as the Irish variety and that

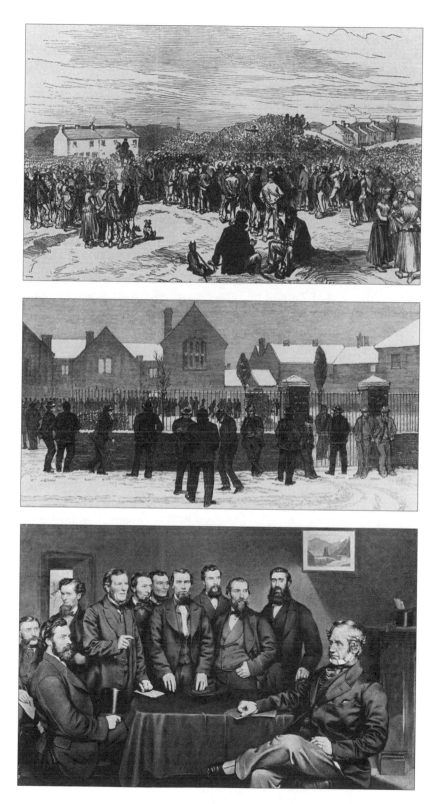

105. South Wales Lock Out Meeting, Merthyr 1875, engraving.
106. Relief at Merthyr Workhouse, engraving 1875.
107. Lord Penrhyn and Strike Committee 1874. Lithograph of 1875.

the grievances of tenant farmers should be addressed. *Pwnc y Tir* (The Land Question) was the burning issue for rural folk, and at last in 1892 a Royal Commission examined the problems of land tenure in Wales, reporting in immense detail by 1896. By then a Conservative government was in power, and the question was mothballed. Within Welsh Liberalism there had been since 1886 a rising tide of nationalistic feeling embodied in the half-cultural half-political movement of *Cymru Fydd* (Young Wales), and the young David Lloyd George, elected MP for Caernarfon Boroughs in 1890, saw his chance as leader within Liberalism of the Young Wales movement. From 1894 to 1896 branches were set up throughout Wales. The movement however broke up over disagreements over such matters as the disendowment of the Church, and the large numbers of highly anglicised Liberals, for example in south east Wales, were suspicious of Lloyd George and his nationalistic schemes.

The last quarter of the nineteenth century had thus seen a most extraordinary period of intensely Welsh politics, Liberals and Radicals looked with some satisfaction at the downfall of the age-old domination of the gentry class, Lloyd-George believing it had happened in 1868, others saw it in the rise of a new class in the county and parish councils or indeed in the new kind of MPs. But all around this new race of politicians a raw and uncomfortable world was fast taking shape, asking questions on social and industrial problems they had not discussed, a world of trade unionists and strikers, or English incomers and settlers, a world of secularists and atheists who cared little for Church or chapels. Just as Wales had become the engine of the British Empire during the nineteenth century, and a country of great consequence, so too it had made a stir for the first time in centuries in the world of politics.

FROM ANGLICANISM TO NONCONFORMISM

In 1750 and for the rest of the eighteenth century the Welsh people were, in the main, traditional Anglican Protestants. But there were signs by 1750 among small minorities of dissatisfaction with the Church: in south Wales there was a scattering of Baptists, Independents and Presbyterians, and since 1735 a small but vigorous Methodist movement had grown up inside the Church, gathering about 8,000 evangelical enthusiasts. The critics of the Church said that it was badly run, no Welshman for example being appointed a bishop in Wales between 1715 and 1870, that unsuitable clerics were appointed, some of them drunken and immoral, its buildings dilapidated, its services badly conducted, sometimes in English in front of monoglot Welsh congregations, and that its poverty meant one cleric serving many parishes, leading to a general neglect of spiritual life. It was said that things became so bad by the 1730s, that it was not surprising that Wales responded warmly to the personal conversion of Howell Harris in Talgarth parish church at Whitsun 1735, and flocked to the preaching meetings he held, and no surprise that other great evangelists such as Daniel Rowland of Llangeitho, was converted at the same time, and that a whole movement within the Church should have begun to ferment between 1735 and 1740.

The conversion of John Wesley to a similar warm personal religion did not occur until 1738, but the word Methodism was used for the separate movements in England and Wales. The revival in Wales first occurred in various parts of the very large diocese of Saint David's, where there had been signs of dissatisfaction with the Church for a generation. Whatever the roots of the movement, Methodism greatly appealed to thoughtful young men and women, who found little place for the individual personality in the orthodox and communal services of the Anglican parishes.

In 1750 when our period begins, Methodism was in trouble because of the quarrel of Howell Harris and the rest of the Methodist leaders, partly because of theological disagreements, partly because of Harris's friendship with Madam Griffith, the estranged wife of a Caernarfonshire squire, but chiefly because of Harris's overbearing character, and by 1752, Harris withdrew to his family home of Trefeca Fach near Talgarth, where he set up a religious 'family' or collective farm for his followers, with the help of Selina, Countess of Huntingdon. The quarrel was made up by 1762, Methodism then launching a second revival, fired by Harris's preaching on indefatigable tours, and partly by William Williams of Pantycelyn's lyrical hymns set to versions of popular folk tunes or to the latest hits from London concerts. In south Wales during the previous ten years the older dissenting sects took advantage of the discomfiture of Methodists and, using some Methodist techniques, they enticed Methodists into their meeting houses, so that from 1762 onwards the great advances of Methodism were generally to be found in virgin territory in mid-Wales and the north. The Methodists attacked what they saw as Welsh religious indifference through their extremely lively preaching sessions, at which people were excited to sing, shout and jump in holy ecstasy, but also through carefully organised private society meetings, called *seiadau,* where the small groups of the converted were counselled and helped with all sorts of problems, and they linked these *seiadau* together in a *sasiwn* (association), or broadly based conference, to deal with administration and policy. They also set up their own printing presses, and produced a large body of literature in Welsh, hymns, sermons, and books of advice, so that their influence was far wider than their numbers. Harris died in 1773 and Williams of Pantycelyn in 1791, and by then the chief centres of the movement were to be found in north Wales. Thomas Charles, an Anglican curate, was from Carmarthenshire, but married and worked in Bala, Merioneth, and one of his most notable contributions to religious developments was to develop the Sunday school. As with many of the features of Methodism, other Welsh dissenting groups soon copied the schools, so that by the nineteenth century they became one of the simplest and cheapest ways for Welsh people to be educated. especially in the Welsh language.

The Church was slow to react to the advance of the Methodist societies, which began to proliferate rapidly at the end of the eighteenth century, but the older dissenters, by copying the fiery sermons and emotional hymns, also proliferated, and as raw new industrial settlements appeared in the hills of Flintshire or Glamorgan and elsewhere, it became clear that workers moving in from rural areas rapidly established 'causes', sometimes in primitive alehouses, or in private houses. The sects late in the century were riven by disputes over the Methodist influence on the older dissenters, and more generally by theological debates over the nature of Christ. By the 1790s the sects were in danger of being blown apart by debates over the rationality of religion, many dissenters becoming anti-trinitarians, and then Unitarians. This tendency often combined with the appearance of political reform and criticism, and the founders of the first Unitarian Association in Wales, that of south Wales in 1802, were political radicals.

The first half of the nineteenth century was perhaps the most remarkable period of change in Wales, as large numbers left the Church to join either dissenting sects, or Methodism, despite the fact that they were all riven with internal debates over theology. From 1800 to 1814 because of the redoubtable missionary zeal of Dr Thomas Coke, a native of Brecon, the most rapidly expanding sect was that of the Wesleyan Methodists. This rapid but short lived outburst forced the Welsh Methodists to define themselves as distinctly Calvinistic and to oppose the

108. Engraving from *Illustrated London News* of Caernarfon Eisteddfod 1862.
109. Hugh Hughes, engraving of Methodist Sasiwn at Bala 1816.
110. R. Bowyer, Daniel Rowland, miniature 1775-90.

more liberal Calvinism of the Wesleyans, which they branded as Arminianism. All the sects gained huge numbers of converts, the most successful of all being the Calvinistic Methodists. These had long been in an anomalous position, officially Anglicans, yet meeting in unlicensed meeting houses. During the French Wars from 1793 to 1815 they were particularly vulnerable to prosecution, and strove bravely to protest loyalty to King and Constitution. In politics they were generally Tory and it was laughable that their enemies should brand the great Methodist preacher John Elias as a Jacobin. The older Dissenters also protested their loyalty, for example when Pembrokeshire was unsuccessfully invaded by a French revolutionary army in 1797. The Methodists for a long time retained a few Anglican priests in their ranks such as David Jones of Llangan in Glamorgan, but once this generation passed away, it then became necessary to confirm a non-Anglican form of ordination of preachers. Eventually in 1811 the decision was taken by the two Methodist Association meetings in north and south Wales to secede from the Church and to become a separate religious body.

The expansion of Methodists and dissenters such as Baptists and Independents was phenomenal, with chapels opening at the rate of one every fortnight and sometimes at times of revivals, at a rate of one every eight days, throughout Wales, not only in the new industrial districts, but even in areas such as Anglesey, where ancient parish churches were legion and often only a few miles apart. In 1810 Wales had 829 Anglican churches and 430 dissenting chapels with 525 Methodist meeting houses; by 1832 there were 1,420 chapels and meeting houses and by 1845 probably about 1,700, and in 1851 when the first religious census was held, Wales had 2,813. The ecclesiastical reforms of the 1830s had made it possible for the Church to begin to put its house in order and to create new parishes and start to build churches, but even so, it could be seen that in 1851 that only nine per cent of the worshippers went to churches while 87% of them frequented what were by then beginning to be called 'nonconformist places of worship'.

The expansion of what came to be called 'nonconformity' came in the form of a series of revivals, usually a frenzy of singing and enthusiastic preaching, as at Beddgelert in 1817, or that spreading through industrial areas in 1828 and 1829 at a time of cholera epidemic and sudden unemployment. In Monmouthshire the colliers withdrew their labour in 1829, the workers at the extraordinary Bute Iron Works in Rhymney (built in 1828 in the style of the temples of Dendera in Upper Egypt) going on strike to throw out all English workers. Many saw revivalism as a way of reaffirming a loyalty to the older and more Welsh religious enthusiasm of their youth in rural areas before the great emigration to the works. The revival of 1849 was one of several associated with the public terror over the inexplicable attacks of cholera. But the far greater revival of 1859, the last of its kind in the century, started in frontier settlements in the USA in 1857, spread to Welsh chapels there, of which there were dozens, and then back to Wales, coming at a time of widespread industrial strife and slump. It has been claimed that the nonconformist leaders had an ulterior motive in encouraging enthusiastic revivalism since it was felt that it might distract workers from trade unionism. It is perhaps rather clearer that one way in which nonconformist leaders dealt with social problems was to use revivalism to encourage self-control, temperance and teetotalism. Starting as a movement among Welsh communities in Manchester and Liverpool, temperance societies were formed in Swansea in 1833 and total abstinence societies in Cardiff and other towns in 1836, these societies coalesced into a truly powerful movement in the 1850s and later using such means as choral singing festivals to occupy idle hands and voices, in a successful attempt to make puritanism fun.

How did the Church react to the 'chapel revolution'? Even before the great ecclesiastical reforms of the 1830s the Incorporated Church Building Society helped many parishes in Wales to repair and rebuild churches, while the reforms made it possible to cut down clerical abuses, and redistribute church wealth and resources. It was symbolic that Bishop Alfred Ollivant came to reside at Llandaff (1843-82), the first to do so for centuries, and that the ruined cathedral should have been rebuilt, and more important, that Ollivant should create new parishes in the industrial districts and consecrate dozens of makeshift churches. Connop Thirlwall at St David's (1840-75) learned to preach in Welsh, and devoted himself also to restoring and rebuilding churches and vicarages, and the same is true of Vowler Short, Bishop of St Asaph (1846-70). The reforms were somewhat different in Bangor, starting with Christopher Bethell, bishop from 1830 to 1859, the new life in the Church here coming from a group of high church tractarians. There were groups of high churchmen often educated at Jesus College, Oxford who brought a new resilience into Church life, and it should be noted that this was a Welsh-language movement in several areas, led by such figures as John Williams 'Ab Ithel' and Morris Williams 'Nicander'. Although the enemies of the Church throughout our period continued to attack it as the 'alien Church', it rapidly regained confidence and vigour in the latter half of the nineteenth century, establishing a presence in rural and industrial communities where it had been invisible.

Before the 1830s the Welsh dissenters had been timid and uncritical in their political attitudes, the Methodists for the most part Tory and even reactionary. But circumstances changed, as the numbers of nonconformists multiplied, the Test and Corporation Acts were repealed in 1828, thus allowing them many civil rights, and reforms such as government grants for education (from 1833 onwards) and the tithe commutation act (1836), and semi-political moral causes such as Anti-Slavery and Anti-Corn Law agitation, drew chapel leaders into political discussion. Local societies even appeared as early as 1836 to demand the disestablishment of the Church in Wales. John Elias, who dominated Methodism from 1814 to his death in 1841, prevented the Methodists from joining the agitation, though other Methodist leaders such as Roger Edwards of Mold took the opposite view, and once Elias had gone, the Methodists – the largest denomination in Wales – threw their weight behind other dissenters. The advance of tractarianism, and eventually ritualism, in the Church, made the gulf between the Church and Methodists unbridgeable.

The relationship of Church and chapel already resembled an angry vendetta because of the arguments over education. This question will be dealt with in the following section, and suffice it here to say that in addition to the quarrels over popular education in Wales, there was the aggravation of the government report into popular education in Wales in 1847, which pilloried the Welsh nonconformists and even more so, the Welsh language. Nonconformists dubbed this commission 'The Treason of the Blue Books', and helped to create a united front amongst the sectarians, persuading them to involve themselves first in local government (such as the bench of magistrates and Quarter Sessions, or newly established Boards of Health) and then in Parliamentary politics, in order to fight for Welsh nonconformist rights.

The first dissenter to be elected MP in Wales was Walter Coffin, a Unitarian mine-owner, elected for Cardiff in 1852. More significant was the work of nonconformist leaders such as Dr Thomas Price of Aberdare, in the press and public meetings in the 1850s and 60s, to create a public attitude or chapel opinion, and to get nonconformists to register for voting and then vote for favourable candidates. The second parliamentary reform act of 1867 greatly increased the electorate in some parts of Wales, and in the following year, the nonconformists felt that when Merthyr elected Henry Richard (a Nonconformist minister) as MP, a new age was dawning. It was not that many Liberal MPs sympathetic to nonconformity had been elected, but that such a rank outsider as Richard had appeared at the core and hub of the Empire. The new Liberal government of Gladstone succeeded in disestablishing the Church of Ireland in 1869, and it is striking that, although unsuccessful, Welsh MPs of the radical wing of the Liberals, put forward a bill to disestablish the Welsh Church as well. Henry Richard and others managed to persuade Gladstone that the nonconformists were in reality the people of Wales, so that there was a fusion of Welshness, political radicalism and nonconformity in this period. As we can see, the Welsh radicals more and more identified Welsh values with the chapel, and pilloried, often quite unjustifiably, the Church people and Tories as un-Welsh. The radicalism of the Welsh MPs went from strength to strength, and so did Gladstone's government's dependence upon their support. It is characteristic that the first piece of legislation to treat Wales as a separate ethnic unit in the United Kingdom was the 1881 Sunday Closing Act for Wales, the result of huge petitions to Parliament from Welsh chapels, to close public houses on Sundays. As our period draws to an end, it is striking that the energies of the Welsh should be devoted to agitation against the payment of tithes (the 'Tithe War' of the 1880s) and growing demands for the disestablishment and disendowment of the Church in Wales. When Forster's Education Act came into force in 1870, it provided for the setting up of school boards, and for using the existing denominational schools as part of the system of popular education. The boards and indeed the whole educational system became a cockpit where church and chapel fought for power and influence, and so it remained for the rest of the century. How and why had education grown to be a matter of such importance?

EDUCATION FROM CIRCULATING SCHOOLS TO NATIONAL UNIVERSITY

In 1752 John Evans, vicar of Eglwys Gymun and a chaplain in Whitehall, London, and later editor of an edition of the Welsh Bible, wrote a book on the Welsh circulating charity schools run by Griffith Jones, rector of Llanddowror, castigating them as nurseries of Methodism. But William Morris wrote from Holyhead to his brother Richard in London (both of them firm Anglicans) to say that he did not mind whether the new Welsh schools were run by Jews or Turks or even Methodists. The schools were such a blessing to their country, and children could learn Welsh 'the poor old British language' free, and this was in total contrast to the time of their father who had to struggle to learn reading from the sole literate man in the parish. He sensed that he was living through a revolution in popular literacy in Europe. Jones (1683-1761) tended to belittle the efforts of previous educationists, but in fact drew a good deal on them, and Sir Humphrey Mackworth, the Welsh industrialist and one of the founders of the SPCK, had suggested in 1719 the system of itinerant or circulating schoolmasters, which lent Griffith Jones's circulating schools their distinctiveness. He set up a scheme of charity schools in 1734, which by 1737 had thirty-seven schools, and 2,400 scholars. In many of his regular reports on his schools, which he sent to his subscribers, many of them in London and Bath, he was most insistent that they had started before Methodism arrived. By the time of his death in 1761 he had organised 3,495 schools, in which 158,237 pupils were taught, and this probably did not include the part-time pupils, usually adults, for example the coal-miners of Llangyfelach parish near Swansea, so that the numbers he had arranged to be taught totalled about 500,000 over a twenty-year period. He left his money to his great friend Bridget Bevan, wife of Arthur Bevan of Laugharne, and she used her considerable

111. Collecting water from St Winifred's Well, 1890s. Residents in Holywell were still coming to the well for their domestic water in the early 1900s. A familiar sight then, was the blind water seller, Joe Barker, making his rounds with donkey and cart.

112 The famous 'Hotel de Marl', 1882. When the Welsh Sunday Closing Act was passed in 1881 it stopped the working man having a drink on Sundays. So men in Grangetown, Cardiff, opened up their own drinking booths on the Marl. They circumnavigated the law by giving the drink away free but between two burly dockers lay a greasy cap which accepted 'donations' for the drink taken by the customers. The booths had their own names: Hotel de Boilermakers, Hotel de Coalminers and a 'cosmopolitan' one - Hotel de Marl. When the drink ran low, for the booths did a roaring trade much to the disgust of the local chapel folk, a lady was despatched with the empty pram to purchase a new barrel from a local 'shebeen' (an illicit liquor shop). Eventually Conservative, Liberal, non-political and later Labour clubs emerged to slake the people's thirst on Sundays.

funds to take the movement to greater heights up to her death in 1779. It is not surprising that the fame of the system spread far and wide, and in 1764 Catherine the Great sent inspectors to see whether such a cheap and economic educational system could be adapted to educate Russia.

Griffith Jones and Bridget Bevan were of course wonderful organisers, business-like fundgatherers, and their reports entitled *Welch Piety* were almost like company reports on every penny well spent. They paid the schoolmasters a pittance, held the schools in the cheapest accommodation, such as church porches, held them free of any charge and in the off-season in farming, when children were not needed as birdscarers or goosegirls or the like. Usually children were taught to read Welsh Bibles and catechisms, during one single winter season. Adults could generally be taught in the same way at night. After a season, the schoolmaster could move on somewhere else, until the whole of Wales was gradually covered. The chief purpose of the schools was to teach poor people to read Welsh, though English was taught in areas such as Gower. Griffith Jones defended the use of Welsh because it was the true historic language of Wales, and it kept the Welsh uncontaminated by English, a language of bawdy novels and dubious literature and worldly commerce, and fundamentally it was all the Welsh needed to be able to understand their religion and help to save their souls.

There were many examples of course of poor people who learned to read and then went on to teach themselves writing, such as Thomas Edwards, Twm o'r Nant, the best known Welsh playwright of the century, who was writing interludes *(anterliwtiau)* at the age of nine. There were also many obscure dame schools, some dissenter charity schools, and a few old grammar schools such as Cowbridge for the middle classes and lesser gentry. Dafydd Cadwaladr (father of Elizabeth Davis, the Crimea War nurse), a preacher in Bala, learned to read from the letters branded on the backs of sheep. Thomas Jones of Pencerrig, the artist, was educated at Llandrindod near his home by a dissenting tutor sent across from the Presbyterian Academy at Carmarthen, before being sent for a while to Christ College at Brecon, then was sent to the dissenting academy at Llanfyllin, and finally for a little while to Jesus College, Oxford. There were many secular reasons for learning to read and write in eighteenth-century Wales, because the country was quickly covered with a network of small printing shops, and booksellers and packmen, and, in some of the politer towns, book clubs, reading societies and lending libraries.

The problem in Wales throughout our period was the education of the common people and the very poor. The Methodist leader in the north, Thomas Charles of Bala, set up in 1785 his own system of circulating schools. After Bridget Bevan's death in 1779 her will was disputed and the schools languished badly. He heard of the new system of Sunday schools in England, but doubted whether they could ever be effective in a wild and thinly populated province such as north Wales. Charles appears to have experimented with Sunday schools in 1787, and he soon found that they were extremely popular with all ages. The dissenters quickly copied Charles's experiment and by 1790 there were 170 Sunday schools in various parts, teaching about 8,000 pupils the rudiments of reading and religion. Charles and other leaders were not interested in social control or discipline, but simply in religion, and the salvation of the souls of poor people, so again, as with Griffith Jones, Welsh would do as the sole language of instruction. They were very cheap to run, since they could meet in the chapels, or in private houses which might eventually become the nuclei of new 'causes', and the teachers taught for nothing. As was the case with Griffith Jones, Charles was anxious to get financial help from English sympathisers and, as a result of his being deeply moved by the self-sacrifice and efforts of young Mary Jones who walked to Bala in 1800 to buy a Bible,

Charles was instrumental in working with others to found in 1804 the British and Foreign Bible Society, which channelled cheap Bibles into Wales. He himself founded his own press in 1803, and up to his death in 1814 he published and distributed some 320,000 books to his scholars. By 1809 the Methodists decreed that attending a Sunday school was as important a means of grace as hearing a sermon or attending a *seiat* (society). The institution had a phenomenal success and in many ways went on expanding right up to the end of the century.

Even before the end of the eighteenth century a rival to the popular system of Welsh Sunday schools had emerged: it is hard to pinpoint when the change occurred, but somewhere around 1800 there appeared pressures for schools teaching English. From 1799 to 1848 Thomas Lloyd's school at Abergele, and from 1810 to 1840 Thomas Phillips of Neuadd Lwyd near Aberaeron, ran schools teaching English, indeed fines against speaking Welsh kept Dr Phillips in tobacco. From 1814 onwards a few schools run by the British Society were set up on undenominational lines, partly inspired by a local society in Swansea for educating poor children founded in 1806, and in 1812 there appeared at Penley in eastern Flintshire a school run on Anglican lines by the National Society, founded in the previous year. In 1832 Wales was treated as a special region by the National Society, and efforts were made to educate the children of dissenters in the schools. Unlike the great mass of previous schools in Wales, all these were in English, though Welsh was used a bridge to learning English. In 1833 the new reforming government agreed to give grants to school organisations which could provide a good deal of their own funding. The National Society was far richer, and better organised than the British, and so Wales was rapidly covered by a network of National schools. The Welsh Methodists and dissenters were of course deeply alarmed at the advance of what seemed to them enemy schools, but many believed that it was immoral for dissenters to receive any form of state aid.

Another rival to the Sunday school was the works or factory school, often set up by industrialists with the help of deductions from workers' wages. Ironworks schools had appeared as early as 1784, there was one at Blaenafon in 1816, the Guests set up a large and influential school at Dowlais (first opened in 1828) and the Vivians had a copper works school at Hafod, near Swansea. There were also large numbers of colliery schools: at Hirwaun in 1820 a school was set up for fifty boys and girls in a room above a stable, and as often in these schools, the workers greatly resented interference in them by the clergy. There were even a number of works Sunday schools. As in England, in Wales in the 1830s and 40s there was a great debate over popular education, but in Wales everything was coloured by the sectarian quarrel of Church and chapel. In 1843 the Home Secretary Sir James Graham introduced his Factory Bill, which dissenters believed would increase the numbers of works schools and put all such schools into the control of the local priests. The bill failed because of ferocious petitioning, many petitions being from Wales. Dissenters such as Independents wanted a Voluntaryist movement, founding schools without state aid. In 1843 Hugh Owen wrote a pamphlet appealing to the Welsh people to agree to accept government grants and found large numbers of non-denominational schools. By 1845 the four chief denominations agreed jointly to encourage this process and in 1846 the Cambrian Education Society was set up by Hugh Owen in London. It should be added that in the main the education they had in mind was secular and progressive, and in English.

In Wales too the debate over popular education was bedevilled by the general belief that the Welsh had become a riotous and even rebellious people: it is striking that when the Privy Council set up its committee on education in 1839, one of its very first tasks was to examine the educational system of the rebellious areas in south Wales. In the wake of the Newport Rising of 1839 it was said that the great strength of Welsh in Wales impeded the forces of law and order, in 1844 in the wake of the Rebecca Riots, it was again stated that Welsh kept the people back from the progress which they should be sharing with the English, that it lessened people's respect for law and administration, and alienated them from the Established Church, and so English should be encouraged amongst the common people. There was of course a frenzy of opening schools and even training colleges in Wales, but the state did not intervene. In March 1846 however William Williams, a Welshman sitting for Coventry, asked in the House of Commons the government to set up a Royal Commission to examine the lamentable state of education in Wales and the general lack of knowledge of English. In the event a commission of the Privy Council's committee on education was set up, and three commissioners examined Welsh schools, reporting in 1847 in the form of immensely detailed reports on Wales – the famous 'Blue Books'.

The commissioners collected evidence from witnesses (mostly Anglican clergy), collated a vast quantity of detailed statistics, and third, gave their own opinion of the state of Welsh popular society. The dissenters protested vehemently against the unfairness of the witnesses' unflattering picture of Welsh chapel life, but Welsh opinion in general took umbrage against the universally critical picture drawn by the three commissioners, showing how atrocious the system of education was, and how hopeless were the attempts to teach English, and how unhelpful the Welsh gentry, clergy and industrialists were in encouraging education. Welsh society was seen as barbaric and uncivilised, the Welsh dirty and mendacious, Welsh women unchaste slatterns. The conclusion of the report was that the Welsh badly needed a system of free state-funded education in order quickly to master English and all the benefits of English progress.

Nothing immediately came of all this because there was such a furious reaction in Wales (first of all from Anglicans and then from dissenters) that no educational experiment in free education could be tried out there. Sir Thomas Phillips of Newport wrote a long and critical analysis of the reports, published in 1849 and Evan Jones 'Ieuan Gwynedd' wrote several short and devastating pamphlets. The sobriquet 'Treason of the Blue Books' did not appear until 1854 when Robert Jones Derfel wrote a Welsh play of that title satirising the government commissioners and their Welsh witnesses, the title being a pun on the ancient Welsh story of the 'Treason of the Long Knives' by which the original Anglo-Saxons had tricked their way into settling in the Island of Britain. The furore entered into Welsh radical nationalistic and nonconformist folklore, forming an undercurrent in later nineteenth century Welsh culture. But the long term effect of the criticism of the Blue Books was to remind the people that their immediate task as an engine of Empire, and a mainstay of British industrial and economic progress, was to fit into British ways as soon as possible through learning English.

There was a gradual decline of the Voluntaryist – that is to reject state aid – movement by about 1853, and dissenters in general came to accept Hugh Owen's arguments that state aid was the only answer, so a large number of British schools were set up in the 1850s and 60s, and a system of training colleges, notably the Bangor Normal College opened in 1858. There was little objection in 1862 when the 'Revised Code' for schools was introduced, and no encouragement was given to learning or teaching Welsh. A whole generation had passed by 1870 when Forster's Education Act eventually brought in free education, and when it came, the Welsh quarrelled endlessly about Church or chapel control of the school boards, but allowed a totally English system of education to rule the roost. The great success of the Sunday schools made Welsh speakers feel that the language was in effect safe in such a fortress.

One important element missing from the Welsh educational system was a university college. It is true that as far back as 1822 Bishop Burgess, with the help of George IV, had founded St David's University College at Lampeter, opened in 1827. But the nonconformist majority regarded Lampeter as a mere Anglican seminary. William Williams MP, who had started the whole rumpus over the Blue Books, and Hugh Owen and others started a public campaign in 1863 for a non-denominational university. It was due in no small degree to Hugh Owen's persuasiveness and indefatigable journeys around Wales gathering moneys from all quarters, including innumerable tiny contributions from chapel members and levies from workers' wages, that the 'University Movement' managed to buy a very large bankrupt hotel in Aberystwyth for use as a college. Government funds were not forthcoming and in 1872 the precarious instituition opened its doors dependent on public contributions. When the Liberals swept to power in 1880 a commission into educational provision in Wales, headed by H.A. Bruce (now Lord Aberdare), recommended that some public aid should go to two new university colleges in Wales, and Cardiff opened its doors in 1883, and Bangor in 1884. Aberystwyth was left to languish, but such was the feeling that in its short life it typified the Welsh national struggle for self-improvement, that it eventually won its battle to survive, and thus in 1893 all three colleges were welded into a federal 'University of Wales'. Welsh was not originally thought of as a subject at Aberystwyth; but public pressure gradually changed the situation, especially when Oxford established a Chair of Celtic in 1877 with the Welsh scholar Sir John Rhŷs as its first holder, and within a few years Welsh and Celtic studies had found a small toehold in the educational system of Wales.

One of the most remarkable achievements of Welsh Liberal Radicals of the period was to achieve cross party support in 1889 for a bill to provide Wales with an Intermediate Education system. This provided Wales with the beginnings of a system of secondary schools, 'county schools' because they were to be administered by the new county councils envisaged by the 1888 local government act. In 1885 the Welsh Language Society had been set up largely by the energies of Dan Isaac Davies, an inspector of schools, and this began to put pressure on the boards and authorities to introduce Welsh into the schools. Once it was realised that Welsh was a school subject, it was also an examination subject, and in 1896 a Central Welsh Board was established to oversee school examinations, a small but important step towards twentieth century developments in devolution of power. The Welsh themselves in the late nineteenth century saw their educational revolution as perhaps their greatest achievement, and they saw it as a story of progress from the schools of Griffith Jones and Thomas Charles. But as far as Welsh itself was concerned, it had been in many ways a story of decline in status from about 1800 onwards, despite the gradual increase of Welsh speakers to close on a million by the end of the nineteenth century, with a general acceptance by 1850 that secular education must be in English, and in that sense it mirrored the paradox of Welsh culture in the period.

7

WALES SINCE 1900

J. Graham Jones

The twentieth century has witnessed a total transformation in Welsh life – in politics, in economics and industry, in society and culture. While economic changes lay at the root of this dramatic metamorphosis, no less dynamic and sweeping a transition has occurred in the political life of Wales. At the beginning of our period, from the 1880s in fact, Wales had become a formidable fortress for the Liberal Party to such an extent that Welsh Conservatives could justifiably be compared with 'white expatriates in a black world' (Robert Blake). Indeed, in their landslide electoral victory of 1906, the Liberal Party captured no fewer than thirty-three of the thirty-four Welsh constituencies; only the second Merthyr Tydfil seat fell to Keir Hardie of the Labour Representation Committee. The party's performance in the two general elections held in 1910 was equally monolithic. Among the solid phalanx of Liberal MPs from Wales were Samuel T. Evans, Ellis Jones Griffith, William Jones, J. Herbert Lewis, D. A. Thomas and, first and foremost, David Lloyd George, the narrow victor of a spectacular by-election in the Caernarfon Boroughs in 1890. The unfortunate Thomas Edward Ellis, torch-bearer of *Cymru Fydd* in Merionethshire since 1886, who had risen to become his party's chief whip under Rosebery in 1894, had died prematurely just before the turn of the century.

The forcible presence of such representatives had certainly yielded positive dividends for Wales at Westminster from the 1880s   several pieces of legislation designed specifically to address Welsh grievances, the appointment of a Royal Commission on Land in Wales in 1892, the grant of a prestigious royal charter to a federal University of Wales in 1893, and the introduction of a tortuous succession of measures to disestablish and disendow the national church. In the early years of the new century the public imagination was captured by the impassioned campaign against the provisions of the Balfour Education Act of 1902, equality for nonconformists in the wake of the religious revival of 1904-05, and later the interest generated by the People's Budget of 1909 and the ensuing battle with the House of Lords, the Parliament Bill and the introduction of national insurance. The Welsh Church Bill finally received the royal assent in September 1914.

Although there were firm indications by the turn of the century that some Liberal associations in the localities had grown somewhat decadent and moribund, the Liberal Party still gave an impression of local buoyancy, sustained by an array of shopkeepers, farmers, and middle-class, professional men like school-teachers and solicitors, the backing of nonconformist ministers and their denominations, and a wide range of local newspapers and periodicals (only the Cardiff daily the *Western Mail* was staunchly Tory). The passage of the 1888 Local Government Act, which had brought about the county councils, and the creation of the urban and district councils in 1894, had led to a powerful Liberal dominance at local level which paralleled its hegemony in parliamentary representation. Nonconformist, Liberal power also came to control the elected offices of the Boards of Health, Boards of Education, Poor Law Guardians and the Burial

113. A photograph taken in the early twentieth century of farming in rural Wales.

114. Cardiff's famous docklands, known throughout the world as 'Tiger Bay'.

115. Picking coal during the national strike in 1912. The dispute by miners over minimum wage rates took place throughout the Welsh coalfields and lasted the whole of March and early April. Eventually, the men were forced to return to work without achieving any improvement in their wages.

Boards. This over-arching Liberal hegemony was sustained still further by its inextricable links with the staple industries of south and north-east Wales – coal, shipping and tinplate – and by its intrinsic embodiment of the spirit of free trade, individual freedom and social equality, reinforced by the ethos of Welsh nonconformity.

This Liberal hegemony was not seriously undermined by the challenge of the Labour Party before the First World War. The victory of William Abraham ('Mabon') as a 'Lib-Lab' aspirant in the Rhondda as early as 1885 did not really imperil the Liberal ethos, while the initial impact upon Welsh society of the fledgling Independent Labour Party, established in 1893, was but slight. There was, however, constant dissatisfaction in the south Wales coalfield because of the operation of the notorious 'sliding scale' which ever since 1875 had linked wage levels to the selling price of coal, and which thus encouraged over-production to minimise prices, lowered wages and posed threats to safety in the mines. From the turn of the century until 1914 an average of about 1,000 colliers were killed in the south Wales coalfield each year. Mine inspection was at best spasmodic, trades unionism was a generally feeble plant, and the supervision of the 'sliding scale' was haphazard and ineffective. But a more militant spirit arose during the hauliers' strike of 1893 which foreshadowed a six months' stoppage in the coal mines in 1898 explicitly directed against the operation of the 'sliding scale'. The outcome was six months of appalling hardship for the miners, an outright victory for the coalowners and a resultant complete rejection of the philosophy and methods of the arch-conciliator 'Mabon'. Seven existing trades unions came together to form the South Wales Miners' Federation (the all-embracing Fed) which became affiliated to the Miners' Federation of Great Britain.

At this point only a handful of Independent Labour Party branches – Cardiff, Treharris, Merthyr and Wrexham – had been established in Wales, but by 1905 their number had increased to twenty-seven by which time ILP candidates were winning some local government and school board elections. Meanwhile, the Labour Representation Committee had been set up in February 1900, and in the 'khaki' general election in October Keir Hardie won the second Merthyr seat standing as a LRC candidate. Within months the 'Fed' had established its own fighting fund to facilitate Labour candidatures in elections, a move which bore positive fruit in 1906 when the Labour group of six MPs at Westminster included four SWMF men, representing the Rhondda, Gower, South Glamorgan and West Monmouth divisions. Their number included William Brace and Tom Richards, both pioneers of the 'Fed'. In the same year the miners balloted in favour of affiliation to the LRC, and from 1908 the miners' MPs sat at Westminster as fully fledged Labour members.

The spectacular growth of the Independent Labour Party in south Wales – there were 84 branches by 1908 – was reinforced by an increasing number of branches of the Plebs League set up in 1909, and the establishment of popular left-wing newspapers like *The Merthyr Pioneer* and *The Clarion*. Their propaganda value in the south was paralleled by the Welsh language writings of R. Silyn Roberts and David Thomas which were widely read in the north. A whole generation of Welsh Labour leaders received a notably left-wing education, firmly grounded in the Marxist ethos, at the London based Central Labour College which had opened its doors in 1909. As a result London produced radical papers like the *Industrial Syndicalist* and *Justice* began to be widely read in south Wales. The burgeoning ILP was by now able to win over to its ranks an increasing number of professional men, including some prominent academics and ministers of religion like the Revd T.E. Nicholas, Glais, a Congregationalist, and the Revd R. Silyn Roberts, Blaenau Ffestiniog, a Calvinistic Methodist. Such men would have been natural Liberals only a few years earlier.

The close bond between the trades unions and political Labour was strengthened by the Taff Vale judgement of 1902 and the Osborne case of 1908, by the setting up of an array of trades union branches throughout south Wales between 1910 and 1914, many of them linked to the docks and the railways, and by the emergence of the trades councils and the co-operative movement. All these significant institutional developments fostered a new generation of working class community leaders throughout industrial south Wales, individuals who also began to win their spurs in local government which complemented the novel career structure at branch and district level which had emerged within the professional trades unions. Those who served as miners' agents and checkweighers within the SWMF became influential, highly respected individuals in their local communities.

The relationship between the Liberals and the emergent Labour movement came to be fashioned by the industrial conflict of the immediate pre-war years which brought to an abrupt end the traditional 'Lib-Lab' compromise. From about 1908 the structural problems of the south Wales coal industry surfaced as geological weaknesses began to reduce the productivity of the pits, while conflict focused on customary rights and practices, a dispute which led to a stoppage in the Cambrian pits in late 1910. As many as 30,000 men became involved in the strike action, and pressure grew for a general stoppage throughout the coal industry. Eventually, the Cambrian strikers were defeated, but the dispute had lasted for a full twelve months, giving rise to a notably militant spirit among the miners, at a stroke defeating the consensus politics so beloved of moderate miners' leaders like 'Mabon', Tom Richards and William Brace. Their more radical successors like George Barker, C.B. Stanton and Vernon Hartshorn, and the activists of the Unofficial Reform Committee, among them Bill Mainwaring and Noah Rees, typified a definite syndicalist presence in the south Wales coalfield.

The protracted Cambrian stoppage had witnessed numerous acts of sabotage against collieries, blackleg strike breakers and the trains which carried them to work, even sporadic bombing attacks and savage clashes between striking miners and the police. One such brutal altercation at Llwyn-y-Pia in the Rhondda was to culminate in the renowned Tonypandy riots in November when a miner died from a broken skull, and the Liberal home secretary Winston Churchill achieved eternal notoriety for sending in the troops to restore order. Churchill acted in the face of alleged excessive looting by rioters, the plunder of local shops by criminals and 'mob' elements, and an apparent complete breakdown of law and order. In time the corporate memory and myth of Tonypandy became confused with events at Llanelli in August 1911 when a rail strike witnessed the deaths of two in the crowd, killed by soldiers sent to restore communications disrupted by the seizure and sabotage of local rail installations. A succession of ferocious reprisals ensued, triggered by the funerals of those killed at Llanelli. Further relentless insurrections followed with the Cardiff seamen's strike and the anti-Jewish riots later in the same year. The class war at its ugliest had truly captured south Wales. The SWMF now donned a new steel, an Unofficial Reform Committee was formed in 1911, and produced in the next year *The Miners' Next Step,* the work of Noah Ablett, Bill Mainwaring and Will Hay, which, in true syndicalist spirit, advocated the use of militancy, strikes and industrial action to achieve a seven hour working day and a minimum wage of 8 shillings per day – a complete repudiation of the gradualist approach favoured by the older generation of miners' leaders. In 1912 the militants formed the Industrial Democracy League, sales of left-wing papers like the *Rhondda Socialist* (later the *South Wales Worker*) soared, and the south Wales coalfield could indeed be described as 'the leading national centre of anarcho-communist activity' (Philip Jenkins).

116. Letter from Asquith to Lloyd George, 8 April 1908, offering him the position of Chancellor of the Exchequer.
117. Victoria Baptist Chapel in Canton, Cardiff, in December 1913. Emily Pankhurst, who started the Suffragette Movement in 1905, claimed that the best political argument was a broken window-pane, and this photograph suggests that her followers agreed.
118. David Lloyd George at Flint Railway Station on 13 November 1922.

In such striking contrast the early years of the twentieth century in rural Wales were relatively peaceable and tranquil. The social and economic tensions which had culminated in the fierce Tithe Riots of 1886-87, and the resultant appointment of the Royal Commission on Land in Wales, had become much less severe by the turn of the century. The intrinsic difficulties posed by the lack of capital, generally primitive agricultural techniques and acute land hunger had been exacerbated by agricultural depression and a dramatic fall in animal prices. Conditions improved in the early 1900s as prices (especially for dairy products) gradually recovered, and many landlords, conscious of a centuries-old bond with their tenantry, had generously modified their rents in a changing economic and political climate. The first decade of the twentieth century actually saw a slight increase in the numbers employed on the land, and some investment in new machinery followed. The rural social scene was improved, too, by the advent of county and parish councils, and the opening of county schools and university colleges, all of which helped to foster a new self-confidence, optimism and breadth of outlook, somewhat eliminating the traditional class distinctions. The anti-landlord campaign, previously so crucial, diminished in intensity, and demands for a Welsh land court were seriously questioned on grounds of its likely ineffectiveness and inefficiency. Farming techniques improved, fertilisers were used more extensively and productivity generally increased. Rural depopulation, so marked ever since the 'starving forties', actually began to slow down.

The same period in the industrial south witnessed continuous, intense expansion of industrial production, manufacturing and commerce, making Wales 'a vibrant, proud, successful country' (Gareth Elwyn Jones). Central to this buoyancy was the surging growth of the coal industry which dominated south Wales from the anthracite valleys of Carmarthenshire to the Rhymney and Sirhowy valleys of Monmouthshire, with outposts in the Wrexham -Rhos district, Flintshire, and in southern Pembrokeshire. At the time of the 1911 census, 14,500 men earned their living in the north Wales coal industry centred on Denbighshire and Flintshire. In the south expansion had taken place on an unprecedented scale. By the eve of the First World War there were 485 Welsh coal mines, 323 of them within Glamorgan. The 5.5 million tons of coal produced by the Rhondda mines in 1885 had shot up to 9.5 million tons by 1913, by which time 41,000 miners worked in the Rhondda pits, and the total south Wales coal output was 56.8 million tons – one-fifth of the total British coal production. More than 250,000 men earned their living in Welsh coal mines. Just under half of British coal exports went from south Wales to Europe, South America and the Middle East, a situation potentially tragic as this phenomenal output was highly sensitive and vulnerable to foreign competition. Welsh coal was truly of world significance.

Other industries survived on a much smaller scale alongside coal. The north-east Wales coalfield had nurtured a small-scale iron and steel industry and some lead smelting, a development facilitated by its proximity to Liverpool and the north-west of England. The slate quarrying industry, centred on Bethesda and Llanberis in Caernarfonshire and Blaenau Ffestiniog in Merioneth, had benefited from access to ports provided by the arrival of a railway network. Employing a workforce in excess of 16,000 in the 1880s, slate became crucial to the economy of these regions. Thereafter, the ever increasing substitution of tiles, transatlantic competition and decline resulting from long term industrial unrest (the Penrhyn quarry strike lasted from 1900 until 1903) had halved this labour force by the eve of the First World War. But in 1898, when the Welsh slate industry was at its heyday, 70% of the slate produced in the United Kingdom was quarried in north Wales, and the Penrhyn and Dinorwic quarries were the biggest in the world. The subsequent decline in the fortunes of the Welsh slate industry was mirrored in the history of

119. Cambrian Colliery, Clydach Vale, *c.*1910. Two serious explosions occurred at this colliery, one on 10 March 1905 and the other on 17 May 1965. Thirty-one miners were killed in each.
120. Nationalisation of the coal industry, 1947.
121. The miners' strike, 1984-85.

other industries. The copper mines of Anglesey, the lead mines of Cardiganshire, and the woollen industry of Montgomeryshire and Merioneth were in steady, irreversible decline.

But continuing economic buoyancy seemed assured by the ongoing prosperity of the metal industries based in south Wales. Clydach, near Swansea, had become the home of the biggest nickel works in the world, built in 1902 by Sir Alfred Mond. During the war years fully 75% of Britain's zinc came from the Swansea area. On the eve of the war, too, eighty-two tinplate works extending along the rim of the coalfield from Llanelli to Port Talbot were producing 823,000 tons of tinplate, fully 544,000 tons of which were for export. Such striking instances of industrial success served to mask the growing problems of ever increasing foreign competition, sharply deteriorating industrial relations and a marked lack of entrepreneurial foresight and investment. Although demand was slackening somewhat compared with the late nineteenth century, the south Wales coal and metal industries continued to expand right up to the outbreak of war in 1914, and the commercial and business infrastructure associated with these primary industries still prospered.

Such frenzied industrial expansion and economic growth inevitably resulted in an amazing (and alarming) population increase. The populace of the south Wales coalfield grew at a rate which was exceeded only by that of the Unites States. The total population of the Rhondda valleys at the time of the 1891 census – 128,000 – far exceeded that of any Welsh county at the beginning of the nineteenth century. By 1911 the Glamorgan population at almost 1,125,000 was higher than that of the whole of Wales sixty years earlier. The inhabitants of Cardiff numbered more than 100,000, those of Swansea almost as many, and the cluster of coalfield valley towns and villages had witnessed a quite dramatic transformation. Transport and other services had expanded in the wake of these developments, most spectacularly the docks at Cardiff, Swansea, Barry and Newport, and the railway network to carry both passenger and freight traffic. The Bute docks and the Roath basin above all made Cardiff the greatest coal exporting port in the world, rivalled by David Davies's Barry docks from 1889, by which time the Marquess of Bute had already amassed a vast fortune. The city had become a sprawling borough with an impressive display of Baroque buildings ringing Cathays Park at its heart by 1914. Its claims to be the capital of Wales were not officially recognized, however, until 1955.

A distinctive, unique social world emerged in the coalfield valleys of the south, composed of the coalowners, their managers and overseers, a distinctive 'middle class' of shopkeepers, professional men and an 'aristocracy of labour' such as checkweighers and miners' agents, and a large, industrial, cosmopolitan proletariat growing in size at an amazing rate, and acting as an irresistible magnet for rural Welsh, English and Irish people alike. Housing was generally substandard, overcrowding rife, health and hospital services primitive, poverty and ill-health common. Yet valley life possessed a richness and a vibrance, a thriving vitality, enriched by the multiplicity of nonconformist chapels, friendly societies and institutes, singing festivals, theatrical and operatic societies, sporting activities, pubs and clubs. Communities were stable, relationships long-lasting, traditions appreciated, a fundamental identity of interest between the classes taken for granted. This cohesion was, as already noted, seriously undermined by the 1898 coal strike which bequeathed a new legacy of industrial conflict and class bitterness in such striking contrast to the conciliatory harmony of 'Mabonism', the old fabric of industrial peace.

The striking contrasts in the industrial, economic and social structures of the various regions of Wales, and the resultant population imbalance, inevitably rendered difficult the preservation of a sense of Welsh national identity. Deep-rooted clashes of economic interest were compounded by questions of personal style and political tradition. Political nationalism, still less separatism, seemed condemned to oblivion ever since the dramatic collapse of the *Cymru Fydd* movement in 1896. While the population of Glamorgan and Monmouth had surged ahead, that of the six least populous Welsh counties totalled fewer than 300,000 individuals by 1911. Would not the industrial, populous, booming 'south' out-vote the rest of Wales in any kind of Welsh state or legislature? Would not the 'Bolsheviks of the South', hailing from 'a hotbed of extreme Labour views' (Dr Thomas Jones CH), and ever 'prey to Marxist extremists', dominate any kind of 'independent Wales'? Any kind of separatist inclination was thus lethally thwarted by this fundamental dilemma of cultural duality and incompatibility.

Cultural renaissance and renewal, however, flourished. A substantial number of quarterly, monthly and weekly publications continued to encourage Welsh language writing and publishing. The increasing use of the language in the education system had been pressed by *Cymdeithas yr Iaith Gymraeg* of the first creation ever since 1885. The nonconformist chapels prospered, too, fostered by the intense, emotional fervour of the revival led by Evan Roberts in 1904-05. As a result total chapel membership in Wales totalled 549,000, weaned on a rich diet of Bible studies, prayer meetings and, above all, impassioned preaching – indispensable fodder to the disorientated inhabitants of the new, dislocated, rapidly growing industrial communities. National and local *eisteddfodau* also flourished mightily in these communities, and impressively classless football clubs re-established themselves in the towns and villages. On a higher intellectual plane, the national university had helped to stimulate an impressive literary renaissance and the first serious attempts to chronicle the history of Wales, primarily the work of Sir John Edward Lloyd. Both these impressive novel departures were transmitted to the level of popular culture by Owen M. Edwards, an Oxford historian and litterateur, who founded, nurtured and edited a formidable array of Welsh periodicals, notably *Cymru* and *Cymru'r Plant.*

When the Liberals swept back into power in 1906, they created new symbols of Welsh national distinctiveness to complement the University – a National Library and Museum, a Welsh Department of the Board of Education (with O. M. Edwards as its first chief inspector), all founded in 1907, a Welsh Insurance Commission and a National Council for Wales for Agriculture. An autonomous Welsh Church soon followed. A Union of Welsh Societies *(Undeb y Cymdeithasau Cymreig)* came into being in 1913, and on the eve of the war there appeared the first number of the English language journal *The Welsh Outlook,* the self-styled 'monthly journal of social progress', the brain-child of Thomas Jones and David Davies, Llandinam, which provided a cogent platform for patriotic Welshmen for fully two decades. During the same period, too, there arose a 'second home rule campaign' headed by E. T. John, a retired Middlesbrough ironmaster who, supported by Lloyd George, was elected the Liberal MP for Denbighshire East in December 1910, and who eventually introduced a Government of Wales Bill in the Commons in March 1914. This ambitious measure, deprived of both parliamentary support and a popular following, inevitably failed to proceed beyond a nominal first reading, and made its nominator the victim of cruel jibes in political circles. Clearly the Welsh renaissance was, first and foremost, cultural, literary and educational, rather than separatist. The Welsh sought equality and recognition within the British system of government, not exclusion from it.

A 'national question' had at least been raised, its implications partly explored, in late Victorian and Edwardian Wales, but it remained very much on the periphery of Welsh life, dwarfed by the land question and the tithes, the continuing disestablishment debate and the campaign for religious equality, and the continued battle for enhanced educational provision. Was this vibrant period a genuine climacteric in Welsh history? Superficially at least it was marked by political achievement, overwhelming industrial and economic growth, educational progress, impassioned religious fervour, even notable sporting prowess – powerful themes difficult to parallel at any·

other time in the nation's history, standing in such striking contrast to the experience of the inter-war years. In any event, the deep-rooted optimism, faith in progress and exuberant self-confidence of this period were soon to be cruelly belied by the holocaust of 1914-18.

Initial Welsh support for a war allegedly fought in support of 'gallant little Belgium' and Serbia exceeded all expectations. The call to arms was backed by Liberals, miners' leaders, nonconformist ministers and prominent intellectuals. As a result Welsh recruitment figures slightly exceeded those for both England and Scotland, and some 280,000 Welshmen were eventually to serve in the armed forces. Patriotic fervour and war hysteria increased as Lloyd George rose to become, successively, minister for munitions, secretary of state for war, and eventually prime minister, soon appointing many Welshmen to important posts in central government. A new Welsh Division was created in the army in November 1914, and a new brigade of the Welsh Guards in 1915. Prominent nonconformist divines adorned the platforms of recruiting meetings, the local Welsh press rendered stalwart support as did influential, widely read, Welsh language weeklies like *Yr Herald Gymraeg, Y Genedl Gymreig, Y Cymro* and *Baner ac Amserau Cymru*. The Merthyr Tydfil by-election campaign which followed the death of Keir Hardie in 1915 proved a powerful demonstration of the strength of war enthusiasm which totally eclipsed the appeal of international Socialism. Indeed, many of the working classes relished the prospect of improved wages provided by the war.

The pacifist tradition largely fell into abeyance. Elements opposed to the war were few: the members of the Union of Democratic Control, and Welsh intellectuals who founded journals such as *Y Wawr* at Aberystwyth in 1915 and *Y Deyrnas* in 1916. Aberystwyth professor Hermann Ethé was hounded because of his German nationality. Conscientious objectors were generally harshly treated; many, such as George M. Ll. Davies and Morgan Jones (the future Labour MP for Caerphilly) were imprisoned for their beliefs. There was, however, some change of public opinion by 1916. The bungling incompetence of the allied generals, the continuing massive loss of life in the trenches, and the attacks on civil liberties all raised serious doubts, increased still further by the coalition government's introduction of military conscription which many Liberals saw as a blatant assault on the freedom of the individual, and which proved politically contentious and divisive. A new Peace Society had been formed at Bangor early in 1915, and in the south the control of the labour force was increasingly resented. In July 1915 Welsh miners went on strike for a new standard wage rate, and demands grew for improved working conditions in the face of the apparently endless fighting. Anti-war sentiment was reinforced still further by the Bolshevik Revolution in 1917. Some Liberals looked askance at the formation of a coalition government, the undermining of local party structures, the wartime electoral truce, and the necessity for a bipartisan approach to 'total war'. The national mood had indeed changed enormously. At the 1915 national eisteddfod Lloyd George stirred up memories of the erstwhile martial glory of Wales as a fillip to the recruitment campaign. Two short years later the announcement at the Birkenhead Eisteddfod that the winner of the bardic chair – Hedd Wyn of Trawsfynydd – had just been killed in action underlined the lethal reality of war, provoking a national outpouring of mourning and grief.

By the time the armistice came in November 1918, people's lives had changed almost beyond recognition. As the historian A.J.P. Taylor wrote, 'Until 1914 a sensible, law-abiding Englishman [and Welshman] could pass through life and hardly notice the existence of the state, beyond the post office and the policeman'. During the next four years the state had intervened in people's lives on a scale hitherto unknown. The concept of 'total war' meant that government boards had been set up to control industries and agriculture, the mines and railways had been put under

122. Members of 2 Royal Welch Fusiliers lining the route at Delhi during the Durbar in December 1911. 'Durbar' is the Indian word for meeting. King George V and Queen Mary were meeting with the Indian Princes to receive homage to them.

123. Recruits to the 11th (Service) Battalion of the Welch Regiment 'Cardiff Pals' still in civilian dress, march down Crwys Road, Cardiff, to entrain for Lewes, Sussex, in September 1914. The Battalion later saw service in France and Macedonia.

124. The 2nd Monmouths in the trenches at Le Bizet, April 1915.
125. In a communication trench at Givenchy in 1915 are, left to right: Capt. Aldworth,
Lt. Leycester, Lt. Betts and Lt. Jones, officers of the 2nd Battalion of the Welch Regiment.
The Battalion served throughout the war on the Western Front.
126. A view over the top for the 2nd Monmouths in the trenches at Le Bizet, April 1915.

public supervision (of particular significance to Wales), and social provision vastly expanded. Local authorities soon began to embark on a major programme of slum clearance and building subsidised housing, and health and hospital provision saw a marked improvement. Food prices were subject to strict controls, and inevitably some commodities were rationed. Public education was radically reformed by the Fisher Education Act of 1918.

Generally, compared with 1914, wages had improved substantially (notably in the coal mining industry) and living standards were higher in both rural and industrial Wales. The membership of the trades unions had soared, while their rights and status were more highly regarded. As labour had played such a vital part in the war effort, political Labour reaped the benefit, and the working classes enjoyed an enhanced prestige and authority, reflected in a newfound status and militancy in the South Wales Miners' Federation. Demands for nationalisation of the coal industry became a corner stone of the policy of the Miners' Federation of Great Britain. Resentment naturally grew at the massive profits made by some businessmen; Cardiff was justifiably dubbed 'the city of the dreadful knights'. The coalition government's response was to appoint a Commission of Industrial Unrest which painted an unnerving portrait of rapidly deteriorating conditions. A new belligerent attitude had certainly surfaced by the end of the war, fuelled by rocketing rental charges and chronic food shortages. Political Labour reaped the immediate benefit; many divisional parties were set up and a number of full-time agents were appointed in both north and south Wales.

For a short time after the end of the war economic prosperity and success continued as the demand for Welsh steam coal appeared unlimited and insatiable, complemented by continuous demand for Welsh milk, livestock and corn in the rural areas. The operation of the Corn Production Act, 1917, ensured a newfound prosperity for the tenant farmer and the farm labourer, but the landowner, the victim of tumbling rental income at a time of severe inflation in land values, faced formidable difficulties. These problems led to sales of substantial portions of many of the Welsh landed estates, often to their long-term tenantry, during what became a 'green revolution'. The impact of war had indeed been profound. At the very least it had acted as a catalyst or stimulant, accelerating processes of political transformation, economic dislocation and social and cultural change already perhaps at work before 1914. The Wales which emerged five years later had changed almost beyond recognition, but the nature of these changes had been apparent long before 1914.

Swift on the heels of the armistice, the Lloyd George-Conservative coalition went to the country, endorsing its chosen candidates, Liberal and Tory alike, with a letter of approval soon dubbed the 'coupon'. The ensuing poll, a kind of quasi-celebration, a 'ceremony of congratulation' to 'the man who won the war', saw an overwhelming victory (526 seats) for the coalition government which also won twenty-five of the re-distributed Welsh constituencies, including Aberdare, captured by Charles Butt Stanton of the New Democratic Party. Henry Haydn Jones (Merioneth) was the only Asquithian Liberal re-elected in the whole of Wales. Far more significant was the election of ten Labour MPs in industrial divisions in south Wales, and the party's polling of 30.8% of the popular Welsh vote. The Labour Party thus became the official opposition at Westminster, while the Liberals, split (perhaps irretrievably) between the followers of Lloyd George and the disciples of Asquith, had devised no effective social and economic policies to counter the mounting Socialist challenge. The popular mood of patriotic frenzy and wartime patriotism, still prevalent to some extent in 1918, rapidly evaporated as the government's so-called social reform programme foundered as mass unemployment began to grip the coalfield valleys of south Wales. The final achievement of church disestablishment in June 1920

proved an enormous anti-climax in an ever more secular society. The government's foreign
policies saw but little success, and the prime minister himself grew increasingly remote from his
Welsh roots and his family home at Criccieth. The deep-rooted Asquith-Lloyd George fissure
was crystallised above all in the famous Cardiganshire by-election of February 1921 when the
premier's personal nominee and private secretary Captain Ernest Evans only narrowly repelled
the challenge of the Asquithian aspirant W. Llewelyn Williams, a former close associate of Lloyd
George who had parted company with him primarily over the introduction of military
conscription in 1916. Even more alarming for the Liberals was the loss to Labour between 1920
and 1922 of a number of coalfield divisions in a succession of by-elections in the industrial
south: Abertillery, Rhondda West, Caerphilly, Gower and Pontypridd. The subsequent victory
of Conservative Reginald Clarry at Newport in October 1922, with the Liberal at the foot of the
poll, was to herald the final collapse of the coalition government. The morale of Liberal Party
workers in the constituencies was visibly plummeting, the government's belligerent Irish policy
(involving the use of the Black and Tans) was highly unpopular in Wales, and, above all, it
appeared decadent and sterile in the face of the mounting problems of the miner and the
steelworker. Even the close association of Liberalism and nonconformity seemed to crumble as
many chapel elders and ministers began to embrace Socialism.

As the traditional Liberal issues – disestablishment, local home rule, temperance legislation –
appeared increasingly irrelevant to the post-war generation, the Labour movement in south
Wales went from strength to strength, basking in renewed self-confidence, ever more class
conscious and assertive, even embracing extreme syndicalism in the valleys of the Rhondda Fawr
and Rhondda Fach. By now the all-powerful 'Fed' was in much more militant hands, among
them those of A.J. Cook, Frank Hodges and Arthur Horner (all three of whom were eventually
to become general secretary of the MFGB), while its membership exceeded 200,000. The blunt
refusal of the coalition government to implement the majority recommendations of the Sankey
Coal Commission set up in 1919 in favour of nationalising the coal industry created an
enormous sense of betrayal and dismay in the coalfield communities. The pits were returned to
private ownership in 1921, following which a three-month lock-out ensued from March during
which the much proclaimed historic 'Triple Alliance' of miners, railwaymen and transport
workers broke down at a stroke on 'Black Friday', 15 April 1921, the day of absolute perfidy in
the miners' mythology. The subsequent return to work on the owners' humiliating terms
inevitably led to a tendency to embrace Communism on the part of some younger coalminers,
notably in the Rhondda, where the Communist Party established a firm foothold and scored
impressive polls in parliamentary elections in the eastern division. Yet the movement failed to
attract the same level of popular support in south Wales as in parts of Scotland and the East End
of London. Generally in south Wales mainstream trades unionism and Labourite politics
prevailed, championed by stalwarts such as Aneurin Bevan, Ness Edwards, Jim Griffiths and
Morgan Phillips, all products of the highly influential Central Labour College.

The growing force of political Labour and trades unionism had far-reaching social effects. The
lodges of the 'Fed' and the classes organized by the Workers' Education Association (the WEA),
and the ever increasing number of pubs and clubs began to erode the influence of the
nonconformist chapels which suffered, too, as a result in the steady fall in the numbers speaking
the Welsh language. The traditional Welsh Sunday was also undermined by the advent of road
transport and the increasing popularity of radio broadcasting and cinemas. Attitudes towards
Welshness and nationalism also changed as many patriots, alienated from the tepid *Cymru Fydd*
nationalism, were attracted by the appeal of internationalism and the new League of Nations. A

Welsh branch of the League of Nations Union was formed in 1922. As efforts to secure some measure of regional devolution for Wales had resulted in a 'catalogue of failure', often heightening the administrative distinction between north and south Wales, and the deliberations of a succession of national conferences had proved embarrassingly futile, a potent new nationalist spirit led to the formation at Pwllheli in August 1925 of *Plaid Genedlaethol Cymru* (later *Plaid Cymru),* a fiercely autonomous, nationalistic grouping, driven by a determination to defend and strengthen the position of the Welsh language. The new movement soon captured the allegiance of a small hard core of Welsh writers and intellectuals, but failed conspicuously to enlist widespread popular support until after the Second World War. Its primary ideologue the writer and literary critic Liverpool-born J. Saunders Lewis was elected party president in 1926.

One of the reasons for the notably tardy progress of *Plaid Genedlaethol Cymru* was its apparent remoteness from the practical, often harsh, reality of everyday life in the 1920s. As early as the autumn of 1920 the coalmining, steel and shipbuilding industries, upon which the Welsh economy depended to an exceptional degree, began to face a severe slump which persisted until the late 1930s. Extolling the 'amazing confidence', the 'very powerful, confident society' of Merthyr Tydfil at the beginning of the century, its MP Ted Rowlands has written, '1924-1939 was a horrendous period'. Welsh unemployment rose from 13.4% in December 1925 to 23.3% in December 1927 and to 27.2% in July 1930, at which time the proportions for England and Scotland were 15.8 and 17.9% respectively. The over-dependence of the coalfield communities on the extractive industries meant that they were powerless to withstand the agonising stagnation of trade and industry in the 1920s, and were unable to benefit appreciably from the demand for motor cars and consumer durables which grew up in the 1930s. The more diverse occupational structure of Cardiff, Swansea and parts of industrial north Wales shielded them from the worst ravages of the depression, but, taken as a whole, Glamorgan and Monmouthshire had the highest proportion of people in receipt of poor relief in the whole of the United Kingdom with the sole exception of County Durham. Rural Wales, too, fell prey to some of the ravages of the depression; Welsh farmers had been very reluctant to embrace mechanization, their meat products were of generally sub-standard quality, and little was done to market effectively their produce.

Successive governments, bound to orthodox fiscal and banking practices, turned a deaf ear to the dire effects of primary poverty and social deprivation at least until the mid-1930s. Only in 1934 did the national government pass a Special Areas Act and make genuine efforts to bring new industries into the depressed areas. A Reconstruction Association was at long last set up in 1936. The Treforest trading estate near Pontypridd received its first factory in 1938. On the eve of the Second World War a sorely needed new ICI plant was established at Merthyr Tydfil which in 1936 had recorded 60.6% of its insured population out of work. In the face of governmental indifference, and apparent inertia on the part of many nonconformist chapels, relief came mainly from voluntary groups like the Quakers and the Salvation Army.

The social consequences of the depression were far-reaching: a steady decline in shops, public entertainments, sporting clubs and chapel attendance, and large scale migration to towns like Dagenham, Slough and Luton in the south-east and centres in the Midlands. No fewer than 430,000 people left Wales between the wars. 'We are losing our population', lamented D. R. Grenfell, Labour MP for Gower, 'and the resources which would enable us to meet our community responsibilities'. The Revd John Roberts of Cardiff noted rather poignantly in 1936, If prosperity does not return very quickly, it will return to find two kinds of men – old men, too old to work, and thousands of young men who have never in their lives done a day's work....

The best hope for a Welsh collier nowadays is to develop into an hotel worker on the promenade in Brighton'. Individual, communal and national dignity were all nigh on destroyed. The effects went even further. The dramatic drop in the government's taxation income and the rates revenue of the local authorities inevitably reduced public services, thereby imperilling the state of public health and hospital provision, and causing working–class housing to deteriorate still further. The problem was highlighted in 1939 with the publication of the Clement Davies Report on anti–tuberculosis services in Wales which vehemently chastised local authorities for their woefully inadequate public health care, and pointed to the utter inadequacy of much of the housing stock. Yet these depression struck communities survived intact, developing an intensely local ethos, looking ever more inwards to the miners' clubs and the 'Fed' libraries, their welfare halls and institutes, cinema palaces and billiard rooms, and above all the medical aid societies and local co–operative stores. They nurtured an indigenous cohesion and self–reliance, and a sense of isolation and remoteness which lasted for a whole generation.

It was during the depression years that a notable new school of Welsh writers – mainly energetic and resourceful scholars and prose writers – first came to prominence. This embraced the pungent literary criticism of W.J. Gruffydd and Saunders Lewis, the sophisticated, subtlely crafted writings of the historian R.T. Jenkins, the short stories and novels of Kate Roberts and D.J. Williams, and the thoughtful prose essays of T.H. Parry-Williams, the last-named also the author of extensive Welsh verse. All these writers displayed in their writings a critical, more contemporary maturity which contrasted starkly with the Welsh literary output of the period before 1914. High standards of literary and linguistic scholarship were also safeguarded within the University of Wales in the work of John Morris-Jones, G.J. Williams, Henry Lewis and Ifor Williams.

The very severity of the depression also served to consolidate the ascendancy of political Labour in much of Wales. In the general election of November 1922 which followed the collapse of the Lloyd George coalition government, the party polled 40.8% of the popular vote in Wales and captured fully half (eighteen out of thirty-six) of the Welsh divisions. These included a great arc of parliamentary seats in the coalfield which extended from Llanelli in the west to Pontypool in the east, and less promising territories in the north like Wrexham and Caernarfonshire, heartland of the slate quarrying industry. Their parliamentary representatives included Dr J.H. Williams, a medical man, at Llanelli and J. Ramsay MacDonald at Aberavon. The party's inexorable rise appeared to be consolidated by the mass unemployment, social deprivation, intense hardship and industrial battles of the 1920s, and extended to an array of urban district councils and the county councils of Glamorgan and Monmouth. The Labour Party increased its representation to twenty Welsh seats in 1923 and twenty-five in 1929. On both these occasions MacDonald became prime minister at the head of a relatively short-lived minority Labour government. The majority of the new breed of Socialist politicians were former coalminers and miners' agents who had progressed through the 'career structure' provided by the SWMF. Many were local councillors, prominent nonconformists (elders or deacons in their local chapels, sometimes lay preachers), 'Lib-Lab' in outlook, generally Welsh speaking, who saw election to Westminster in middle age as a reward for long service to their local communities. Few of them were destined to achieve political distinction at Westminster.

As the 1920s progressed, and the effects of the depression permeated deep into the fabric of Welsh society, political interest focussed mainly on an attempt at a dramatic comeback by the Liberals, again led by Lloyd George since 1926, who captured the headlines with an array of radical new policy statements embodied in the 'Green Book', *The Land and the Nation* (1925), which advocated quasi-nationalisation of agricultural land, the 'Yellow Book', *Britain's Industrial*

CABLE ADDRESS "CONSPRING" JAMAICA

CONSTANT SPRING HOTEL
KINGSTON, JAMAICA
B. W. I.

Dec. 11, 1936.

My dear Gwilym,

Just one word of Christmas greeting to you, Edna and the children, and I hope it will reach you before the festive season begins.

The Tories seem to have once more triumphed; they have got rid of a King who was making himself obnoxious by calling attention to conditions which it was to their interest to cover up. Baldwin has succeeded by methods which time and again take in the gullible British public. He has taken the high line in order to achieve the lowest of aims. I have never seen such a blend of hypocrisy and humbug. But once again it has triumphed, and a really democratic King has been driven from his Throne by the Tories with the help of the Labour Party. The Labourites have played a contemptible part. They must have known that Edward was disliked by the Government because he was showing up conditions which it was inconvenient for them to have exposed. Attlee and his soft-headed junta have been flattered into playing the Tory game. It is the third time within about a year that these fools have thrown away their chances. Before the Election they played into the hands of the Government by their Margate resolutions over disarmament. They did the same thing

127. General Strike, May 1926.
128. Letter from Lloyd George, 11 December 1936, to his son Gwilym concerning the enforced abdication of King Edward VIII.

Future (1928), with its ambitious policies for economic regeneration, soon to be summarised in the 'Orange Book', *We Can Conquer Unemployment* (1929), the party's blueprint on the eve of the general election. They offered a novel scheme – an array of publicly financed initiatives such as road building and house construction – for counter-cyclical government spending policies to combat the slump. The Liberals won a third of the Welsh vote in 1929, but only ten seats, all in rural areas, leading Lloyd George to claim that his party had been 'tripped up by the triangle' in three-cornered contests. The Labour Party, securing twenty-five seats (including Carmarthen, Brecon and Radnor and the three Cardiff divisions) and 43.9% of the total poll in Wales, formed a minority government at Westminster for the second time. Even in October 1931, when the Labour Party was decimated at the polls in the face of a landslide victory for the so-called 'national' government, it held on to its sixteen coalfield divisions in the 'red belt' of south Wales, and even increased its percentage poll slightly to 44.1. By now more colourful Welsh figures were joining the ranks of the Parliamentary Labour Party – Aneurin Bevan (Ebbw Vale, 1929-60), Ness Edwards (Caerphilly, 1929-68), S.O. Davies (Merthyr Tydfil, 1934-72) and James Griffiths (Llanelli, 1936-70). Bevan, Edwards and Griffiths were all to serve as cabinet ministers in Attlee's post-war Labour governments.

The Labour Party had certainly established itself as the vehicle of working class protest in south Wales. The coalfield valleys had displayed a remarkable solidarity in the industrial troubles of the mid-1920s which had culminated in the general strike of May 1926, as it proved a nine day wonder, and the subsequent long lock-out in the coal industry which bequeathed a huge legacy of despair, bitterness and bewilderment following the return to work and the victimisation which ensued. There was an inevitable decline in the resources and membership of the 'Fed' which was undermined still further by the growth of company unionism, large numbers of blacklegs and the Spencer Unions. In the campaign against the Means Test and mass unemployment, the Labour councillors and aldermen rendered an immensely valuable service as they battled valiantly to remove slum housing and improve the standard of health care and welfare services. They did their utmost to withstand the harshest enactments of the national government and created a network of social activity and resourcefulness which fortified these valley communities in the face of adversity and hopelessness. Whereas the founding fathers of Socialism had led their supporters on a march of social progress, their inter-war successors were reduced to defending them against even greater immiseration.

By the 1930s there was little effective challenge to the role of the Labour Party in much of Wales. In the political and constitutional crisis of the summer of 1931 the Liberal Party had split, like Gaul, into three distinct groups. Lloyd George, now leading only a tiny splinter group of four Liberal MPs, all members of his own family, grew ever more remote from Westminster, the Liberal Party and his native Wales. Based largely at his home at Churt in Surrey, fully preoccupied with the drafting of his mammoth *War Memoirs,* and making regular trips abroad, he visited Wales but rarely, generally on ceremonial occasions. His dramatic 'New Deal' proposals which he unveiled with great gusto to his Bangor constituents in January 1935 were little more than a revival of his 1929 policies, and made conspicuously little impression, their creator having become 'a sarcophagus not a symbol' within Wales (Gwyn Jones). Although the Communist Party won some colourful recruits like the Revd T. E. Nicholas ('Y Glais') and a few 'Fed' stalwarts such as Arthur Horner, its president in 1936, it did not pose a serious threat to mainstream Labour. *Plaid Cymru,* too, remained very much on the periphery of Welsh political life, fighting only Caernarfonshire and the University of Wales constituencies in parliamentary elections, but the movement came to sudden national prominence as a result of the arson attack

129. This photograph records some of the damage caused in Wales by air raids, and shows the scene
in Canton, Cardiff, after a raid on 2 January 1941. Local people retained their sense of humour, even
at the worst times. One man trying to hurry a neighbour into a shelter was told to wait whilst she
found her false teeth: 'Never mind those, Hitler's dropping bombs, not sandwiches', he shouted.
130. 1 Royal Welch Fusiliers under enemy artillery fire while dug-in near the river Dyle, May 1940.

131. Through Pagodaland; men from 6th Battalion of the South Wales Borderers advance through Bahe, Burma 1944.
132. Members of the 4th Battalion the Royal Welch Fusiliers clearing a house at Holst, Holland, February 1945, where seventy-two prisoners were taken.

on an RAF bombing school at Pen-y-Berth in the Llŷn peninsula by three of its leaders who were subsequently imprisoned at Wormwood Scrubbs. The much needed fillip which the nationalist movement then enjoyed as a consequence suffered somewhat at the end of the decade because of the rise of continental Fascism and the neutralism and anti-militarism which *Plaid Cymru* advocated as war approached.

When war broke out in September 1939, *Plaid Cymru* was quick to declare its neutrality, but many party followers soon became involved in the allied war effort, very few resisting conscription on nationalist grounds. Indeed, unanimity of support for a people's or workers' war in 1939 far exceeded that in 1914, and no 'crisis of conscience' for Welshmen surfaced as in the First World War. The Labour movement, vehemently opposed to Fascism from the outset, at once took the lead in organizing the communities of south Wales to face the challenge of 'a just war'. The activities of the various pacifist groups, notably *Heddychwyr Cymru* and the Welsh Council of Peace, were generally peripheral. Only the Communists actively condemned the war as an imperialist crusade against Germany, a line it pressed from 1939 to 1941 when its Welsh membership slumped badly. In all sixty-seven conscientious objectors had been imprisoned in Wales up to 1944, but they were treated much more humanely and sympathetically than during the war of 1914-18.

Generally the war years led to a greater integration of Wales into the British state, an increase in collectivism, much more widespread employment of women (especially in the arms factories such as at Bridgend), a marked increase in working-class living standards, and a steady erosion of class differentials. Heartfelt fears were voiced in 1939-40 that the possession of substantial tracts of rural Wales by the War Office, and plans to move four million mothers and children, mainly from English cities to rural Wales, would lead to an assault on the Welsh identity. Substantial numbers did migrate, mainly from London and Merseyside, but these were absorbed effortlessly into the Welsh communities, and many of them quickly returned to their home areas. Alarm at the potential linguistic threat led to the opening of the first Welsh medium primary school under the aegis of *Urdd Gobaith Cymru* (founded by Ifan ab Owen Edwards in 1922) at Aberystwyth in 1939, and to the formation of a language defence committee which later became *Undeb Cymru Fydd* in 1941. The stark reality of war was brought home to the people of south Wales most sensationally as a result of the activities of the German bombers. Initial hopes that south Wales somehow lay beyond the reach of the German bombers were cruelly dashed as Cardiff, the valley towns and above all Swansea fell prey to a number of devastating attacks. Some 985 civilians were killed in south Wales during 1941 alone, 230 of them during February at Swansea, which was the victim of forty-four separate attacks between 1940 and 1943, and which suffered the destruction of its town centre. Llandaff Cathedral and Cardiff Castle were also both damaged by the bombing attacks.

Although the Second World War did not prove to be such a dramatic turning point in Welsh history as the holocaust of 1914-18 had been, its social effects were far-reaching. By 1944 22% of the insured Welsh workforce were in the armed services, and a further 33% were engaged in civilian work associated with the war. The mass unemployment of the 1930s was nigh on eliminated, aided by the migration of more than 100,000 Welsh people to England, many of them women. Others found employment in the arms factories which sprang up to produce munitions. In the wake of the Essential Work Order of 1941 and the Barlow Report of 1942, collectivism and state intervention in the lives of ordinary people increased sharply. In 1939, only 10% of the Welsh workforce was employed in factories; by 1945, this proportion had more than doubled. There was a sharp increase, too, in the number of national and local civil servants. The shortage of mineworkers led to the adoption in 1944 of the 'Bevin Boy' scheme to conscript young men for the coalmines. In the same year some 100,000 Welsh working miners went on strike in protest against the policy of 'thinning out' the labour force in the coal industry. Although the war years generally were a period of severe inflation, working class wages rose dramatically throughout these years. The sorely needed re-structuring of the lopsided Welsh economy had already begun, aided by a huge upsurge in the number of women in employment in Wales (from 94,000 in 1939 to 219,000 in 1944, an increase of 134% compared with only 30% in Great Britain), which greatly augmented the potential labour force, and by the gradual erosion of deep-rooted prejudices and misconceptions concerning the Welsh labour force and industrial practices. The publication of the Beveridge Report on social insurance in 1943 stimulated an awareness of governmental policies and attitudes, as did the appearance of Aneurin Bevan's broadsheet *Why Not Trust the Tories?* (1944). The discussions of the Welsh advisory panel of the Ministry of Reconstruction from 1942 aroused renewed interest in a comprehensive social security system, housing and the development of a national health service.

The Attlee government elected by a landslide majority (including twenty-five Welsh divisions) in 1945, was determined that the unemployment levels of the 1930s should never be repeated, and, in full acceptance of Keynesian economics, passed the Distribution of Industry Act, 1945, sanctioned the utilisation of existing factory space in Wales (made available by the sudden cessation in the output of munitions and weapons), and made provision for new industrial estates, among them Hirwaun, Bridgend and Fforestfach, and for grants, special tax relief and low-interest loans to incoming industries. Two development areas were designated in Wales: the south Wales coalfield, Vale of Glamorgan and Gower, and the north-east industrial belt. Central planning and direct investment were the order of the day, with nationalisation seen as the crucial first step. The coal industry was nationalised in 1947, and steel between 1951 and 1953. So, too, was the Bank of England, the railways, the docks, electricity, gas and road transport, each to be run by a central board. The creation of the Wales Gas Board was, alas, the only concession to Welsh national sentiment by a Socialist government committed to centralized control. When the coal industry was nationalised on 1 January 1947, it still employed 115,000 Welsh workers which represented the largest single body in Wales. The government's predilection for corporate consolidation led to the merger of Richard Thomas and Baldwins, tinplate manufacturers, in 1945, and the formation of the Steel Company of Wales in 1947, soon to open its showcase Abbey Works at Port Talbot. Steel production came to be concentrated at four enormous plants – Port Talbot, Llanwern, Ebbw Vale and Shotton – with cold reduction plants at Margam, Velindre and Trostre. By the time of the 1951 census such was the predominance of the nationalised industries in the Welsh economy and the ever spiralling numbers employed by the public services that more than 40% of the Welsh workforce was in the direct employ of the government.

To some extent the same kind of policies were maintained by the Conservative governments of 1951-64, exciting initiatives which compensated for the inexorable decline of coal. The new departures included a huge oil port at Milford Haven and a new refinery at Llandarcy, the Baglan Bay petrochemical complex, and three major factories at Merthyr Tydfil. By the mid-1960s general manufacturing accounted for 30% of the Welsh workforce (compared with only 11% in 1939). Economic expansion embraced new roads and motorways and the construction of new towns like Cwmbran in Gwent and Newtown in Montgomeryshire. Small-scale light manufacturing industries were established in the market towns of mid and west Wales. Even so, Wales retained its social and economic problems: unemployment remained nigh on double the national average, female employment still lagged far behind England, and the capital assets and average expenditure of the average Welsh individual were still relatively low. Successive governments adopted ambitious regional policies: the Royal Mint came to Llantrisant, Companies House to Cardiff, and the Driver Vehicle Licensing Centre to Swansea, while the Welsh Development Agency was also set up. There was a considerable increase in the numbers employed in service or white-collar occupations in Wales, notably in Cardiff and Newport, while the number of official Welsh agencies proliferated. More women thus entered the Welsh workforce, their proportion increasing from 33% in the late 1960s to 42% in the early 1980s.

Problems mounted from the mid-1970s. Steel followed the path of coal. A contraction of domestic markets led to a decline in the British car industry, while world demand also fell in the face of intense competition from modern plants in Germany, the USA and above all Japan. The Ebbw Vale steel works closed in 1975-76, and East Moors, Cardiff, in 1978, by which time even Llanwern and Port Talbot were operating under threat of closure. Some 9,000 jobs were lost at Shotton. To some extent the flood of new industries ever since the war (and substantial redundancy payments) cushioned the Welsh workforce, but the recession which ensued in the late 1970s demonstrated that the Welsh industrial economy was still more vulnerable than that of most of England. Weaknesses were further highlighted by the sharp decrease in public expenditure which followed the election of the first Thatcher government in 1979, by intrinsic economic deficiencies shared by most of western Europe, and by a contraction on the part of multi-national and English companies which had set up factories in Wales.

Some of the same problems surfaced in rural Wales. Although the operation of the Attlee government's 1947 Agriculture Act had helped to increase production, steady prices and expand markets, encouraging co-operative schemes for storing, grading and marketing produce, rural depopulation continued apace in the face of ever accelerating mechanisation and the amalgamation of holdings. Between the censuses of 1931 and 1951 the numbers engaged in agriculture fell from 91,000 to 77,000, and the total number of agricultural holdings from 60,410 to 52,816. Some marginal farm land was abandoned or surrendered to alternative uses. Grassland and livestock remained all-important in the Welsh agricultural economy, but the relatively small size of most holdings and the poor quality of the land made the average Welsh farmer a comparatively poor man; his average income in 1951 was no more than £346 compared with £1,233 for the UK as a whole. Although the support of the Milk Marketing Board in collecting milk daily from individual farmsteads proved crucial, and receipt of the monthly milk cheque was a great boon to a community on the verge of destitution, a general sense of vulnerability and insecurity persisted, reflected in the formation of the Farmers' Union of Wales (the FUW) in 1955, and in eager participation in agricultural co-operative societies which had a total Welsh membership of more than 54,000 in the same year.

Rural depopulation continued unabated. The fall in the number of farm labourers was compounded by a decline in the demand for the services of rural craftsmen like blacksmiths and saddlers. Rural industries, like the woollen industry and cloth manufacturing, too, were gradually contracting, as was the once vibrant Gwynedd slate quarries which had declined severely so that by the early 1970s only five quarries remained operational, employing no more than a few hundred men. The subsequent growth in demand for products like slate ornaments and clocks from a buoyant rural tourist trade only partly helped to reverse this trend. A few new initiatives helped to arrest the general pattern of decline. During the 1950s the Forestry Commission acquired land at the rate of 10,000 acres a year, providing welcome employment opportunities for displaced farm workers, while new job opportunities surfaced in the wake of capital projects such as the reservoirs at Clywedog, Montgomeryshire and Tryweryn, Merioneth, and the power stations at Trawsfynydd, Merioneth and Wylfa Head in Anglesey. Some posts arose, too, in Anglesey as a result of defence expenditure at RAF Valley, the Rio Tinto Zinc Corporation's aluminium reduction plant near Holyhead, opened in 1970, and the various hydro-electric schemes. But generally rural decay prevailed, accelerated by governmental policy towards transport in these areas, notably the infamous 'Beeching axe' of 1963 which terminated dozens of local lines in Wales, reducing Welsh railway mileage at a stroke from 637 to 363. Only thriving tourism and an influx of elderly residents, seeking a peaceful retirement, provided some stimulus. But English immigrants brought their own problems to rural Wales, posing a menacing threat to the well-being of the Welsh language.

Difficulties increased in the 1980s as depopulation accelerated, and the introduction of harsh quotas on milk production from 1984 and substantial cuts in agricultural subsidies eventually resulted in a cumulative loss of 24,000 jobs in the Welsh farming industry by 1998. By this time agricultural incomes had plummeted to a record post-war low, successive governments appeared indifferent to desperate appeals for help, and many Welsh farmers hovered on the brink of destitution, bankruptcy and ruin.

Generally, however, in rural, urban and city areas alike, Welsh society grew much more affluent and prosperous than during the depressed 1920s and 1930s. The population of Wales grew steadily from 2.5 million in 1945 to 2.75 million by the 1970s. Materially, the Welsh became richer, both as individuals and as a corporate society, than ever before in their history. Even when the severe inflation of the period is taken into account, the average Welsh male wage-earner was twice as wealthy in 1978 as in 1946. The ever increasing employment of women gave rise to even greater prosperity. There was much new house building and sorely needed improvements to the existing housing stock built in late Victorian and Edwardian times. As late as 1966 almost a quarter of Welsh houses had no fixed bath and 4% had no indoor toilet. As slum clearance continued apace, new, rootless housing estates sprang up with no sense of community values. Private home ownership surged ahead, the leasehold problem was tackled, and council owned housing sprang up in urban and rural areas alike. In the early 1960s electricity became universally available, television ownership rapidly increased and the number of motor vehicles and telephones surged ahead. The sale of consumer durables flourished. Diets became much more varied, the range and quality of clothing increased, and even foreign holidays became much more popular. These far-reaching social changes in turn led to the emergence of a distinct middle class in Wales, employed mainly in government and service sectors of the economy, and educated at the rapidly expanding universities, polytechnics and colleges of education.

Much of this social transformation was underpinned by a massive increase from 1945 onwards in the functions of the state and in public expenditure, notably on health, education and the social services, and on environmental matters such as housing, roads and transport. Following the path of the Beveridge Report, the Attlee government hugely increased the role of government. The jewel in its crown was undoubtedly the creation of the National Health Service, the brain child of Aneurin Bevan, which brought all hospitals under the wing of the welfare state and provided universal free medical treatment. Many hospitals had to be re-built, demand surged for medical treatment and new drugs, infant mortality plummeted and the scourge of tuberculosis was nigh on eliminated. The introduction of charges into the 'sacred cow' of the NHS soon became inevitable. A dramatic fall in the number of pit accidents was an inevitable result of the contraction of the coal industry. Even so, illness remained more prevalent in Wales than in the United Kingdom as a whole, housing standards were still lower, and problems could still emerge, most notably the Aberfan disaster of October 1966 which killed 116 children and twenty-eight adults.

When the first Thatcher government was elected in May 1979, 43% of the Welsh working population was employed in the public sector. The determination of the new administration sharply to reduce public expenditure had a disproportionate effect upon Wales. Between 1979 and 1983 employment in the steel industry fell by a massive 70%, in manufacturing by 17% and in construction by 21%. There was no compensatory growth in the service sector so that Welsh unemployment, which ran at 8.5% in 1979, had increased to 16.7% by 1983. During these years no fewer than 130,000 jobs were lost in Wales. By the end of 1981 the total number of unemployed in Wales ran at 170,000, and a further 44,000 were employed in rather tenuous job creation programmes. Wales was clearly in the 'have not' part of the British Isles. Statistics relating to individual areas make alarming reading. Port Talbot, once on the frontier of innovation and prosperity, rapidly fell victim to unemployment (which ran at over 20%), industrial obsolescence and uncompetitiveness, employing no more than 5,000 steel workers by 1985. The social effects were far-reaching: the growth of alcoholism and suicide, social disruption and family breakdown. At some towns like Pembroke Dock and Tenby an unemployment rate in excess of 30% was recorded in 1983, and more than 21% in Anglesey, the victim of the closure of the Holyhead dry dock and reductions elsewhere on the island.

The traditional industries seemed to suffer most severely, above all coal, whose output fell from 28 million tons in 1947 to 18 million in 1968, and 11 million in 1978. At this point the industry still employed 36,000 men, a total which fell to only 20,000 in the early 1980s. Soon not a single coal mine remained operational in the Rhondda valleys, the industry's former heartland. By the end of the decade there were only five 'deep' pits in south Wales and one in the north still producing coal with a total workforce of little more than 4,000 men. The era of mass labour politics came to a painfully symbolic end as a result of the 1984–85 miners' strike. The loyalty of the mining communities during the national strikes of 1972 and 1974 still prevailed in 1984–85 when Welsh fidelity to Arthur Scargill and the NUM leadership was exemplary. But such had been the decline of the Welsh coal industry during the intervening years that events in Wales were at best peripheral to the main battleground in Yorkshire and the north Midlands. The south Wales miners displayed a remarkable solidarity and dignity at a time when the erstwhile communal identity of the south Wales valleys had long come to an end. The traditional loyalty of the mining communities was buttressed by the unstinting support of the womenfolk and an array of community and church leaders.

Although some economic regeneration had taken place and a sense of optimism had grown during the mid-1980s, reflected in the boom of high technology industries, the expansion of multi-national companies, a buoyant demand for consumer durables and luxury goods, and access to European Community funding to promote agriculture and fishing and aid the depressed areas, formidable economic problems still persisted. Foreign investment was unevenly distributed, Japanese employers insisted on rationalised working practices and single-union contracts, redundancies followed still further contraction in the coal, steel and tinplate industries, small industries such as the Brymbo steelworks near Wrexham collapsed, and once prosperous concerns like the renowned Laura Ashley Company contracted severely. The reduction of agricultural subsidies posed further problems in rural areas. By the end of 1991 Welsh unemployment still ran at 9.4%. During the same year no fewer than 2,000 Welsh industries went to the wall. In 1992 the Penallta colliery in Ystrad Mynach was closed, only 1,000 coal miners employed in three pits remained in south Wales, and it was resolved to cease working at the Tower colliery in the Cynon Valley. A White Paper published in 1993 envisaged the complete demise of the coal industry in south Wales. The communities created by coal disintegrated, shattered by depopulation and the necessity to commute to secure new avenues of employment. Problems were compounded as the level of government grants plunged from £197 million in 1981 to £134 million ten years later, and David Hunt's high profile 'Rural Initiative' proved of little avail. Generally, Welsh incomes lagged behind most parts of the UK, living standards at least levelled off, and the incidence of homelessness increased. The housing market was certainly less buoyant than in many other areas, and it was widely felt that the rural areas and industrial valleys were not receiving their full share of EC grants and payments. Although government statistics indicated that Welsh unemployment had fallen from 10% in 1993 to 7.5% by the end of 1996, there was widespread concern that these figures had been manipulated to mask the true level, and that a hard core of long-term and youth unemployed still remained.

Politically Wales remained an apparently impregnable Labour stronghold. The general election of July 1945 proved a veritable Labour landslide, Attlee capturing 393 seats including 25 in Wales, 7 of them gains, and 58.8% of the Welsh popular vote, a full 10% higher than in Britain as a whole. Huge majorities were chalked up in most of the industrial valleys. The demoralized Tories won only four Welsh seats, and the Liberals held on to seven (out of a total of twelve Liberal MPs at Westminster), their number including Major Gwilym Lloyd-George at Pembrokeshire, his sister Lady Megan in Anglesey, and Sir Rhys Hopkin Morris who narrowly re-captured highly marginal Carmarthenshire, the only Labour loss in the whole of Britain. Almost all the eight *Plaid Cymru* candidates forfeited their deposits.

Some Welsh politicians rose to prominence at Westminster, among them Aneurin Bevan, James Griffiths, Ness Edwards and Morgan Phillips, and fervent Welsh approval followed the creation of the welfare state, the achievement of almost full employment, and the nationalisation of major industries and utilities, notably of the coal industry in January 1947 – 'Today the mines belong to the people'. In 1950 the total of Labour seats in Wales increased to twenty-seven, a number repeated in 1951, and the party's share of the poll remained constant at about 60%, an ascendancy which extended to the local authorities of south Wales. Although periodic threats were posed in local elections by *Plaid Cymru* and the 'Ratepayer' candidates, they did not seriously undermine the Labour hegemony which led to 'one-party politics', a near monolithic control of many town councils in the industrial valleys. Party politics meant little, too, in most rural areas where many members, although bred in the traditional Liberal ethos, sat as nominal Independents. Gradually, the tally of Liberal seats in Wales fell in each post-war election until in 1966 Montgomeryshire alone remained true to its traditional faith. Wales remained almost immune from the spasmodic Liberal revivals which touched parts of England and Scotland in the 1950s and 1960s. Labour reached the zenith of its Welsh conquest in 1966 when it captured no fewer than thirty-two constituencies in Wales, among them Cardiganshire, won by Elystan Morgan, a victory which seemed to set the ultimate seal of approval on the Socialist capture of its lands in Wales, so potently reminiscent of the Liberal ascendancy at the end of the previous century. Three successive leaders of the Labour Party – James Callaghan (Cardiff South), Michael Foot (Ebbw Vale) and Neil Kinnock (Islwyn) – represented Welsh constituencies, while George Thomas (Cardiff West) was elected Speaker of the House of Commons. Figures like Callaghan and Foot were really English incomers who contrasted starkly with authentic Welsh speakers such as Cledwyn Hughes, John Morris and Goronwy Roberts, whose ranks were augmented in 1957 by the election of Lady Megan Lloyd George, defeated in Anglesey in 1951, to the Commons as the Labour MP for Carmarthenshire. It was very much apparent by the 1950s, however, that the traditional 'old guard' of trades union activists, the former miners' agents and checkweighers, had been succeeded by middle class, generally university educated, professionals such as lawyers, teachers, university lecturers and journalists. By 1970 only two Labour MPs from Wales – S. O. Davies (Merthyr Tydfil) and Gwilym Davies (Rhondda East) – were the direct nominees of the National Union of Mineworkers. The socialist zeal of the founding fathers had been replaced by the middle class values and centralist tendencies of the new generation.

As Labour apparently reigned supreme in Wales, the only effective challenge came from a resurgent *Plaid Cymru* and demands for measures of devolution and concessions to Welsh national identity. The post-war Labour governments were intransigently hostile to devolutionary demands, advocating strong centralized planning, contemptuously brushing aside appeals for a Welsh secretary of state, and refusing any sop to Welshness when the electricity supply industry was nationalised. There was certainly no unity among the Welsh Labour MPs; prominent figures like Aneurin Bevan and Ness Edwards were implacably opposed to any kind of devolution, while patriots like Jim Griffiths, Goronwy Roberts and Cledwyn Hughes were far more sympathetic and supportive. Concessions were few: the 'Welsh Day' debate first held in the Commons in 1944 became an annual event, and in 1948 Attlee's government grudgingly conceded the setting up of a Council for Wales and Monmouthshire, a nominated body with little authority, which the influential north Wales trades union leader Huw T. Edwards served as chairman until 1957. It was to prove largely 'ineffective from the outset and trudged along for eighteen inglorious years'. When the Conservatives returned to power in 1951, Churchill appointed the Home Secretary Sir David Maxwell-Fyfe to be the 'minister for Welsh affairs', a largely nominal position, and he in turn was succeeded by Gwilym Lloyd-George, Henry Brooke and Sir Keith Joseph. Gradually and hesitantly, the Labour attitude softened. In 1950 the non-party Parliament for Wales Campaign was launched, then limped along for six years and presented a monster petition bearing more than 250,000 signatures to parliament in 1956. Five Labour MPs had become actively involved in the campaign and were duly reprimanded by the party hierarchy. One of their number the colourful Merthyr Marxist S. O. Davies had actually introduced a private member's bill in support of home role in the Commons in 1955, but inevitably the measure made little headway. In 1957 there was uproar in Wales as a result of the government 's decision to allow the flooding of the beautiful Tryweryn valley in Merioneth to provide a profitable water supply for the city of Liverpool. In the debate in the Commons all thirty-six Welsh MPs voted against the Tryweryn Bill.

In its manifesto for the 1959 general election the Labour Party (now facing twenty *Plaid Cymru* candidates, a substantial increase), much influenced by its deputy leader Jim Griffiths, advocated the appointment of a secretary of state for Wales, holding a Cabinet seat. Even Aneurin Bevan, it appears, was won around. The promise was made good in 1964, and fittingly it was the veteran Griffiths, MP for Llanelli since 1936, who became the first 'Charter' secretary of state for Wales, responsible for the Welsh Office based at Cardiff (at long last officially the Welsh capital city since 1955) which gradually built up a wide range of responsibilities and controlled a growing budget. The popular mood was changing in Wales, partly as a result of Saunders Lewis's famous radio lecture in 1962 *Tynged yr Iaith* ('The Fate of the Language), intended by its author as a reprimand to the membership *of Plaid Cymru*, but which was to result in the formation of the much more militant *Cymdeithas yr Iaith Gymraeg* (the Welsh Language Society). Soon the change in the standing of *Plaid Cymru*, widely viewed as a somewhat quixotic movement on the fringes of Welsh political life, was dramatic. In July 1966, Gwynfor Evans, the party's president since 1945, sensationally captured highly individualistic Carmarthenshire in a by-election held on the death of Lady Megan Lloyd George, thereby defeating Labour's Gwilym Prys Davies, himself a tireless advocate of Welsh interests. Soon afterwards the party won more than 40% of the poll at by-elections at Rhondda West in 1967 and Caerphilly in 1968, both in Labour's heartland. Jim Griffiths was soon warned by an unduly apprehensive local mining official, 'You had better realize that all your seats are marginal now'. In the Merthyr Tydfil by-election of April 1972, occasioned by the death of S.O. Davies, *Plaid Cymru* came second with 37% of the poll, and Labour was once again 'humbled in the very heartland of British Socialism', while the Merthyr Tydfil town council briefly came under *Plaid Cymru* control. The party also scored some sensational victories in local and council elections across the towns of 'Welsh Wales'. These stunning victories were paralleled by a similar nationalist upsurge in Scotland.

Small wonder, therefore, that the inner councils of the Labour Party began to consider a more far-reaching scheme of devolution. The growth of nationalist sentiment in Wales and Scotland had compelled Harold Wilson in 1968 to set up the Crowther Royal Commission on the Constitution. Advocates of devolution argued that an elected council for Wales would complement admirably the proposed local government re-organisation and possible British membership of the European Community. When the re-named Kilbrandon Commission duly reported in October 1973, eleven of the thirteen commissioners came down in favour of an elected Welsh assembly with limited powers and six advocated a full legislative assembly. The devolution debate was stimulated still further during 1974 when *Plaid Cymru* won Caernarfonshire and Merioneth in the February general election, and re-captured Carmarthen in October, and, in the wake of an economic crisis, trades union troubles and industrial unrest, the long-standing debate on devolution was firmly on the political agenda. In the spring of 1976 James Callaghan succeeded Harold Wilson as prime minister and, as his tiny majority in the Commons grew ever smaller, the political clout of the nationalist MPs grew to such an extent that in December the prime minister personally introduced a joint Devolution Bill for Wales and Scotland. Its tempestuous voyage through the Commons was sustained somewhat by the 'Lib-Lab' pact, and eventually the highly contentious measure reached the Statute Book in July 1978. In the subsequent referendum campaign five rebel Labour MPs from Wales, led by Neil Kinnock and Leo Abse, defied the party line, campaigning relentlessly to secure a 'No' vote in the crucial poll which was to take place on 1 March 1979. The enthusiasm for the projected assembly seemed largely to evaporate during the run-up to the poll, and in the event only 11.8% of the Welsh electorate (a total of 243,048 votes) polled in favour, and 46.5% (956,330) against. Huge 'No' majorities were recorded in most south Wales divisions, and even in the counties of north-west Wales, the very heartland of the recent nationalist resurgence, the majority against was almost two to one. Interest in devolution fell into abeyance for a whole decade as, within weeks of the devolution vote, a right-wing Conservative government was elected at Westminster, destined to remain in power for eighteen long years. Indeed, the devolution fiasco had played some part in undermining the beleaguered Callaghan administration as it limped towards the end of its constitutional quinquennium, severely undermined by trades union militancy during the 'winter of discontent' of 1978-79.

In May 1979 the Labour Party won only twenty-one Welsh seats and 45% of the popular vote in Wales, while the revitalized Conservatives, under the inspirational leadership of Margaret Thatcher, profited from a right-wing swing of 4.8% to capture Brecon and Radnor and Anglesey from Labour, and the Liberal citadel of Montgomeryshire from party veteran Emlyn Hooson. A junior minister at the Welsh Office boasted justifiably that he could drive all the way from the Severn Bridge to Ynys Môn without leaving Conservative held territory. The Conservatives thus became the second party in Wales, in spite of their emphasis on monetarism and privatisation, while Labour was weakened still further during 1982 by the defection of three of its Welsh MPs to the Social and Liberal Democrats, reducing its Welsh total to 18, a return to the position of 1922. When the first Thatcher government, buoyed up by its success in the Falklands campaign, went to the country in June 1983, in the wake of a re-distribution of constituencies which tended to favour the Conservatives, it won 14 Welsh seats, a twentieth century record for the party, and 31% of the poll, while Labour, now driven back largely into its industrial bastions, retained only 20 seats and 37.5% of the poll, its lowest proportion since 1918. The term of office of the second Thatcher administration was marked by considerable inward investment in south Wales from Japan and the Continent to replace the old staple industries, the miners' strike of 1984-85, and a more interventionist role from the Welsh Office under Nicholas Edwards which was now responsible for just about all aspects of governmental activity in Wales. Economic activity was stimulated somewhat by the loudly trumpeted 'Valleys Initiative' of Peter Walker, Edwards's successor as Welsh secretary from 1987, and the activities of the Welsh Development Agency. To some extent the interventionist style adopted by the Welsh Office under Edwards, Walker and David Hunt stood at striking variance with the anti-statist philosophy which was the main thrust of Thatcherism.

From 1983 the Labour Party was led by a Welshman, Neil Kinnock, MP for Islwyn, who spearheaded the principal voice of protest against the enactments of the Conservative government, assisting his party to re-capture 4 Welsh seats in 1987, striking by-election wins at Pontypridd and the Vale of Glamorgan in 1989 and Neath and Monmouth in 1991, a recovery reflected, too, in an impressive performance in the elections to the European Parliament. In the general election of April 1992 Labour won 27 of the 38 Welsh constituencies and 49.5% of the popular vote in Wales. The Liberal Democrats captured only 12.4% of the poll, forfeiting even Ceredigion and Pembroke North where long-serving MP Geraint Howells lost to Cynog Dafis who stood on the novel joint platform of *Plaid Cymru* and the Green Party. It did indeed seem as if 'Labour was re-emerging phoenix-like to take its rightful place as the radical voice of anti-Tory protest' (D. Gareth Evans). By now there seemed to be little specifically Welsh dimension to politics in Wales; political life revolved around discussion of the ongoing recession, economic crisis and the plight of the NHS. Tory fortunes within the principality seemed to plummet still further as a result of the appointment in May 1993 of John Redwood as secretary of state for Wales, a politician who was somewhat abrasive in his personal relations, and who adopted a rather combative style at the Welsh office. Two years later his decision to stand against John Major for the Conservative Party leadership foreshadowed his departure from the Welsh Office, and the appointment as his successor of William Hague, the MP for Richmond in Yorkshire, who immediately proved more generally popular and acceptable in Wales, especially following his marriage to Welsh-speaking Ffion Jenkins in December 1997 by which time he had succeeded Major as Conservative Party leader.

Indeed 1997 proved to be something of an *annus mirabilis* in British (and Welsh) political life when Tony Blair's 'New Labour' Party swept into power with a sensational 418 seats, including twenty-four (out of forty) in Wales, and fully 54.7% of the Welsh popular vote. The Conservatives were completely driven out of both Wales and Scotland in a memorable left-wing swing. The election of a 'Socialist' government ensured that the question of devolution would at long last receive its due attention. *Plaid Cymru* now held a block of four constituencies on the western seaboard of Wales. Ever since the beginning of the decade the Labour Party was again formally pledged to an elected assembly for Wales, but groups of idealists and journalists alone were vocally proclaiming the cause of devolution. Predictably both the Welsh Office and the Tory government at Westminster were frosty in their response, arguing that the granting of elected assemblies to Wales and Scotland would inevitably lead to the break-up of the United Kingdom. But popular opinion within Wales in favour of an assembly grew partly as a result of the increasing unpopularity of the ever growing number of quangos on which the Conservative government was making use of party 'placemen' to advance its own policies. The much criticized Welsh Development Agency was a particular bone of contention. The Labour Party's devolution proposals had been announced in May 1995, although something of a rift had clearly occurred between party leader Tony Blair and Ron Davies, the ambitious Labour MP for Caerphilly, who had been chosen the Shadow Secretary of State for Wales. In June it was announced by Blair (apparently on his own initiative) that a Labour government would hold referenda on the establishment of national assemblies for Wales and Scotland. The referendum was to be pre-legislative, to be held between the publication of a white paper embodying the government's proposals, and the drafting of a bill. The referendum was held on 18 September 1997; only the total number of votes cast was to be of importance. Two all-party umbrella groups – the 'Yes for Wales' campaigners, and the 'Just say No' advocates – conducted vibrant campaigns during the run-up to the ballot. 50.3% of the Welsh electorate voted. Of these 50.3% voted in favour, and the outcome lay very much in the balance until the very last result from Carmarthenshire clinched the victory for the 'Yes' camp. Perhaps the most striking feature was the solid support which came from the industrial heartland of south Wales to complement the substantial majorities polled in 'Welsh Wales'. The divisive nature of the poll, the split within the Welsh unitary councils (eleven were in favour of an assembly and eleven against), doubts over the conduct of the ballot, and prolonged wrangling over the precise venue of the new assembly which persisted for months, all undermined the sense of elation widely experienced when the results were announced. Intense bickering preceded the decision that Cardiff would be the embryonic assembly's home.

The resultant Government of Wales Act embodied the principle that forty members of the assembly would be elected directly by each constituency on a 'first past the post' system, together with a further twenty regional members elected from pre-established party lists in the five former European parliamentary constituencies. The first elections, held on 6 May 1999, proved memorable. The Labour Party won only twenty-eight of the sixty Assembly seats, and was thus compelled to operate a minority administration. Sensationally, *Plaid Cymru* secured no fewer than seventeen seats, emerging from its rural fortresses in the north and west to capture such Labour strongholds as the Rhondda, Islwyn and Llanelli. Although the Conservatives eventually received nine assembly members, only one of these – David Davies (Monmouth) – was directly elected by a constituency. Much bickering at once ensued over the poor turnout of 46% in the first assembly elections (compared with a much more respectable 58% in Scotland), and adverse publicity was at once attracted by two bruising leadership contests between Ron Davies and Rhodri Morgan and Alun Michael and Rhodri Morgan. Although Morgan was narrowly defeated on both occasions, Michael's resignation as First Secretary of the Assembly early in 2000 enabled his rival eventually to achieve the top post. As the new Welsh Assembly began its deliberations and tasks, a distinct new chapter in Welsh life had opened. Following its remarkable successes in the Assembly elections, *Plaid Cymru* had established itself as the alternative choice, the 'voice of protest' in Welsh politics, the heir to the Welsh radical tradition poised to launch an effective challenge to 'New Labour'. The Government of Wales Act (1998) listed eighteen policy fields which were to fall within the remit of the new assembly. Its success will hang largely on the establishment of a harmonious working relationship between its first secretary, its 'Cabinet' (executive committee) of eight members and the various policy subject committees. Much depends, too, on the role of the assembly vis-à-vis the government departments at Westminster and the secretary of state for Wales.

One of the considerations borne in mind in the context of devolutionary change was the Welsh local government structure. A sweeping re-organisation of boundaries had taken place on 1 April 1974 when eight new counties had been created, together with thirty-seven districts, twenty-three of which were granted borough status. These replaced the shire structure created by the Union legislation in the sixteenth century. In 1991 the Welsh Office made contentious proposals for further reform, suggesting the implementation of a single-tier system of local government, a principle which was generally welcomed. Sharp disagreement, however, ensued on the numbers and areas of jurisdiction of the proposed new authorities. Eventually, on 1 April 1996, in keeping with the terms of an announcement three years earlier, twenty-two unitary authorities were set up. The manifold deficiencies of the new authorities were one of the reasons for the support rendered to devolutionary solutions.

The Welsh society at the end of the twentieth century which saw the creation of the new unitary authorities in 1996 and the election of a Welsh Assembly in 1999 had changed out of all recognition from the Welsh people of the early years of the same century. The workforce had become much more mobile, accepting the necessity to commute sometimes long distances, far less attached to the concept of community, accepting the new style, rather anonymous estates of semi-detached houses rather than the close rows of terraced houses, with their folksy, neighbourly, busybody residents, on the sides and bottoms of the valleys. For those fortunate enough to enjoy permanent employment, wages had improved considerably even in real terms, and society in Wales (as in other parts of the UK) had attained a stability based on ever wider home ownership (exceeding 75%), car and telephone ownership, and consumer-led market prosperity, savouring novelties such as home durables and foreign holidays. Slum clearance had eradicated almost all the unfit dwelling houses which still remained in the 1960s, and very few homes now lacked the basic modern amenities. Private sector house building spiralled from the 1950s to the end of the 1970s. Notable, too, has been the Welsh aptitude for sport, films and cinemas, musical life, radio and television. Broadcasting in particular has developed a distinct Welsh dimension through the twentieth century. A Cardiff radio station was opened on 13 February 1923, swiftly followed by a further station at Swansea in 1924 and one at Bangor in 1934. After a great deal of agitation, a Welsh home service finally came into existence during July 1937. During the 1960s separate BBC Wales and TWW television channels were established. A long, intense campaign resulted in the setting up of S4C, the fourth, Welsh-language, television channel, in the autumn of 1982.

These trends have been counterbalanced by a striking decline in organized religion. The long familiar practice of Sunday attendance and worship was broken decisively during the depression and the Second World War. Social and religious attitudes were transformed by the close association of socialism and secularism, by the dominance of materialism, and the emphasis on a rampant individualism during the 1980s. The traditional Welsh 'Sabbath' was ever more undermined as people worked, shopped, relaxed and holidayed during the weekend. The large chapels of south Wales emptied, combined, closed; those in rural, Welsh-speaking areas still served to some extent as the focal point of their local communities. In many ways the Wales of the year 2000 was less distinctive or unique than it had been in earlier generations. Although the creation of the Welsh Assembly may have countered this trend, ever increasing personal mobility and the dominating influence of the mass media have caused Wales to resemble an English region. Welsh people emulate their English neighbours ever more, even exhibiting behavioural tendencies potently reminiscent of North America.

Perhaps the one feature which remains uniquely distinctive to Wales in the year 2000 is its own language, diverse cultural and literary life (both Welsh and Anglo-Welsh), and its somewhat personal educational ethos. The indigenous Welsh respect for educational opportunity and success has remained constant throughout the century. The provisions of the Butler Education Act of 1944 which created universal secondary education and raised the school leaving age to fifteen were generally welcomed in Wales. But the costs of providing a two-tier system of secondary education (grammar schools and secondary modern) proved prohibitive for many local authorities, and the comprehensive principle, fully implemented in the 1960s and 1970s, had been practised in some areas long before, heralding the demise of the cherished grammar schools. The revered University of Wales expanded, too, benefiting from the award of mandatory grants to undergraduate students, and an expansion in the number of subjects offered at each constituent college. The Welsh College of Advanced Technology was incorporated in 1967, and St David's College, Lampeter, in 1971, as a sense of optimism surged in the wake of rapid growth, reflected in ambitious new building projects on each university campus. At the end of the Second World War the national university had 4,000 students, a total which increased to 11,000 in 1965-66, 14,641 in 1976-77 and 30,625 when the University celebrated its centenary in 1992-93. Even further frenzied expansion ensued in subsequent years to the turn of the century. New challenges came to dominate life in secondary education: the implementation of the national curriculum, with its core and foundation subject areas, an emphasis on vocational training as the key to a successful economy, and the development of increasing Welsh-language education. These trends seemed virtually light years removed from the world of the WEA, the miners' libraries and the welfare halls, and the Sunday schools which for many had constituted the staple diet of the education of the Welsh people before the evolution of a government sponsored education system.

Linked to educational provision to some extent has been the distinctive Welsh literary tradition. Welsh-language literary output has remained impressively buoyant throughout our period. The older generation of bardic prowess – represented primarily by W. J. Gruffydd, T. Gwynn Jones, T.H. Parry-Williams and R. Williams Parry – was duly succeeded by some impressive poets, among them D. Gwenallt Jones, Waldo Williams and Euros Bowen. During the 1960s and 1970s a new generation of poets came to prominence, including Dic Jones, Bobi Jones, Gwyn Thomas and Bryan Martin Davies, and later still Menna Elfyn, Alan Llwyd and Gerallt Lloyd Owen. Many of these remain productive into the new millennium, and have been joined by others such as Gwyneth Lewis and Myrddin ap Dafydd. The Welsh short story was given a potent new lease of life right through from the 1920s to the 1980s by Kate Roberts, whose sensitive, imaginative portrayals of the quarrying communities of her native Gwynedd still command widespread respect and admiration. She also penned a number of powerful novels, as did T. Rowland Hughes in the 1940s and Islwyn Ffowc Elis in the 1950s and 1960s. The nostalgic autobiographical accounts of prominent nationalist D.J. Williams of Fishguard have established themselves as highly acclaimed classics, and Saunders Lewis's dramas and other literary works have proved seminal to the development of the Welsh literary scene. The drama has also flourished in the works of John Gwilym Jones and Gwenlyn Parry, and the advent in

1982 of S4C (the Welsh-language television channel) has led to much greater productivity in this literary genre. The 1960s and 1970s saw the emergence of a new generation of novelists such as Jane Edwards, Eigra Lewis Roberts and John Rowlands. More recent years have witnessed the appearance of a spate of exciting new novels written by Aled Islwyn, Robin Llywelyn, Mihangel Morgan, William Owen Roberts and Angharad Tomos.

This prodigious literary output in the Welsh language was paralleled by the emergence of a new school of Anglo-Welsh writers, writing in the English language but with their roots firmly grounded within Wales. Caradoc Evans, author *of My People* (1915), widely regarded as the first Anglo-Welsh novel, is considered the father of this literary genre. By the 1930s Evans had been succeeded by writers such as Jack Jones, born in the Rhondda, Idris Davies, a native of Rhymney, Alun Lewis of Aberdare, Vernon Watkins of Swansea and, above all, Dylan Thomas. A later generation included Glyn Jones, Roland Mathias, Raymond Garlick and the late lamented R.S. Thomas, all of whom developed the vigour of the Anglo-Welsh tradition in an array of dynamic new journals, among them the *Anglo-Welsh Review,* launched in 1958, *Poetry Wales* (1965) and *Planet* (1970). The 1960s and 1970s witnessed a quite dramatic Anglo-Welsh literary renaissance with the rise to national prominence of a new school of Anglo-Welsh writers, among them novelists Emyr Humphreys and Raymond Williams, and poets Dannie Abse, Harri Webb, John Tripp and Gillian Clarke. The younger generation which has achieved distinction during the last twenty years has demonstrated an ability to take traditional themes into dramatic new directions. Their works include the striking novels of Christopher Meredith and Duncan Bush, the forceful theatre of Ed Thomas, and the poetry of Robert Minhinnick and Tony Curtis.

Above all there remains the Welsh language. 'How long can it last?' has been a constant enquiry throughout the century. The 1951 census recorded that 714,686 (28.9%) of the population of Wales could speak the language, but it was already primarily confined to the rural areas, and the proportion has dropped slightly in each successive census to reach 18.6% (508,098) in 1991. Gwynedd is the only part of Wales which still has a majority of Welsh speakers among its population. The Welsh language has constantly been threatened by steady immigration from English cities, notably of retired people to the rural areas where a significant number of holiday or 'second' homes have been established. During the 1980s more than 40,000 people moved into the three Welsh counties of Dyfed, Gwynedd and Powys. Ceredigion alone saw a net increase of 9,000 people between 1981 and 1991, while there has been a steady drift away from the depressed industrial valleys of the south. These trends contributed to the unemployment problem of rural Wales and caused intense bickering over the teaching of Welsh in rural areas.

But there are many positive grounds for optimism. A striking emphasis on the value and significance of minority languages throughout western Europe has had repercussions in Wales. From the 1960s onwards Welsh has achieved an official status as a result of several intensive campaigns, and the principle of equal validity for the language was enshrined in the 1967 Welsh Language Act. A further act, passed in 1992, made further attempts (although perhaps inadequate) to strengthen the position of the Welsh language. These changes have been buttressed by strenuous efforts within the education system. By 1974 there were sixty-one designated Welsh-medium primary schools attended by 8,500 pupils. In 1956 the first bilingual secondary school – Ysgol Glan Clwyd in Flintshire – opened its doors. Thirty years later there were fifteen such schools, teaching at least the humanities through the medium of Welsh, and an array of other schools which offer some Welsh medium teaching. There has also been an expansion in Welsh medium teaching in the university marked by the appointment of about twenty-four lecturers to teach primarily in Welsh. The fruit of these developments became apparent when the 1991 census revealed a slight increase in the numbers of children and young people with a command of the Welsh language.

Increased government grants and subsidies have helped to sustain a number of Welsh language journals, the Welsh book trade and indeed the National Eisteddfod. The locally based community based newspapers *papurau bro,* the product of the strenuous efforts of volunteers, have enjoyed an enormous and increasing success from the 1970s. On 1 November 1982 the fourth television channel S4C began broadcasting Welsh language programmes at peak viewing times, while in 1993 the Welsh Language Board was set up with Lord Elis-Thomas as its first chairman. All these factors have led to a quite striking transformation in the status of the Welsh language, and a conviction that, in the words of the 1972 manifesto of *Cymdeithas yr Iaith Gymraeg,* 'If the Welsh language were to die... humanity would be impoverished in the sense that one thread among the thousands which make up the cultural pattern of mankind – whose glory is its variety – would be lost'.

FURTHER READING

WALES' HIDDEN HISTORY

Hunter-gatherer communities

Aldhouse-Green, S.H.R., Palaeolithic and Mesolithic Wales. In Lynch, F., Aldhouse-Green, S.H.R. and Davies, J.L., *Prehistoric Wales* (Stroud: Alan Sutton 2000), 1-41.

Aldhouse-Green, S. (ed.), *Paviland Cave and the 'Red Lady': a definitive report* (Bristol: Western Academic & Specialist Press Ltd., 2000).

Aldhouse-Green, S.H.R., Whittle A.W.R., Allen, J.R.L., Caseldine A.E., Culver S.J., Day M.H., Lundquist J. & Upton D., 'Prehistoric human footprints from the Severn Estuary at Uskmouth and Magor Pill, Gwent, Wales', *Archaeologia Cambrensis* 141, (1992), 14-55.

Aldhouse-Green, S.H.R., Scott, K., Schwarcz, H., Grün, R., Housley, R., Rae, A., Bevins, R. & Redknap, R., 'Coygan Cave, Laugharne, South Wales: A Mousterian site and hyaena den: a report on the University of Cambridge excavations', *Proceedings of the Prehistoric Society* 61, (1995), 37-79.

Barton, R.N.E., Berridge, P.J., Walker, M.J.C. & Bevins, R.E., 'Persistent places in the Welsh Mesolithic: an example from the Black Mountain upland of South Wales', *Proceedings of the Prehistoric Society* 61, (1995), 81-116.

Bell, M., Caseldine, A. and Neumann H., *Prehistoric Intertidal Archaeology in the Welsh Severn Estuary* (York: Council for British Archaeology research report 120, 2000).

Green, H.S., *Pontnewydd Cave* (Cardiff: National Museum of Wales, 1984).

Green, S. & Walker, E., *Ice Age Hunters: Neanderthals and Early Modern Hunters in Wales* (Cardiff National Museum of Wales, 1991).

Neolithic

Barker, C.T., *The Chambered Tombs of South-West Wales* (Oxford: Oxbow Books, 1992).

Caseldine, A., *Environmental Archaeology in Wales* (Lampeter: Department of Archaeology, Saint David's University College, 1990).

Darvill, T., 'The circulation of Neolithic stone and flint axes: a case study from Wales and the mid-west of England', *Proceedings of the Prehistoric Society* 55, (1989), 27-43.

Gibson, A., *The Walton Basin Project: Excavation and Survey in a Prehistoric Landscape 1993-97* (London: Council for British Archaeology, Research Report 118, 1999).

Lynch, F., Aldhouse-Green, S. & Davies, J.L., *Prehistoric Wales* (Stroud: Sutton Publishing, 2000).

Thomas, J., *Understanding the Neolithic* (London: Routledge, 1999).

Wysocki, M. & Whittle, A., 'Diversity, lifestyles and rites: new biological and archaeological evidence from British Earlier Neolithic mortuary assemblages', *Antiquity* 74, (2000), 591-601.

Bronze Age

Bell, M., Caseldine, A. & Neumann H., *Prehistoric Intertidal Archaeology in the Welsh Severn Estuary* (York: Council for British Archaeology research report 120, 2000).

Benson, D.G., Evans, J.G., Williams, G.H., Darvill, T., & David, A., 'Excavations at Stackpole Warren, Dyfed', *Proceedings of the Prehistoric Society* 56, (1990), 179-245.

Gibson, A.M., 'Excavations at the Sarn-y-Bryn-Caled cursus complex, Welshpool, Powys, and the timber circles of Great Britain and Ireland', *Proceedings of the Prehistoric Society* 60, (1994), 143-223.

Lynch, F.M., *Prehistoric Anglesey* (2nd edn. Llangefni: Anglesey Antiquarian Society, 1991).

Lynch, F., 'The Later Neolithic and Earlier Bronze Age', in Lynch, F., Aldhouse-Green, S.H.R. and Davies, J.L., *Prehistoric Wales* (Stroud: Sutton 2000), 79-138.

Savory, N.H., *Guide Catalogue of the Bronze Age Collections* (Cardiff: National Museum of Wales, 1980).

Iron Age

Davies, J.L., 'The Early Celts in Wales', in Green, M.J. (ed.), *The Celtic World* (London: Routledge, 1995), 671-700.

Davies, J.L. & Lynch, F., 'The Late Bronze and Iron Age', in Lynch, F., Aldhouse-Green, S. & Davies, J.L., *Prehistoric Wales* (Stroud: Sutton, 2000), 139-219.

Fox, C., *A Find of the Early Iron Age from Llyn Cerrig Bach, Anglesey* (Cardiff: National Museum of Wales, 1946).

Green, M.J., *Celtic Art. Reading the Messages* (London: Weidenfeld & Nicolson, 1996).

Green, M.J., *Exploring the World of the Druids* (London: Thames & Hudson, 1997).

Green, M.J. & Howell, R., *Celtic Wales* (Cardiff: University of Wales Press, 2000).

Manley, J., Grenter, S. & Gales, F., *The Archaeology of Clwyd* (Mold: Clwyd County Council, 1991).

Manning, W.H., 'Ironworking in the Celtic World', in Green, M.J. (ed.), *The Celtic World* (London: Routledge, 1995), 310-320.

Savory, H.N., *Guide Catalogue of the Early Iron Age Collections (in the National Museum of Wales)* (Cardiff: National Museum of Wales, 1976).

Roman

Brewer, R., *Caerleon-Isca* (Cardiff: National Museum of Wales, 1987).

Burnham, B. and Davies, J. (eds.), *Conquest, Co-Existence and Change: Recent Work in Roman Wales* (Lampeter: Trivium no. 25, 1991).

Casey, P.J. (ed.), *The End of Roman Britain* (Oxford: Oxford University Press, 1979).

Dark, K.R., *Civitas to Kingdom: British Political Continuity 300-800* (Leicester: Leicester University Press, 1994).

Green, M. & Howell, R., *Celtic Wales* (Cardiff: University of Wales Press, 2000).

Nash-Williams, V.E., (2nd edition, Jarrett, M.G. (ed.)) *The Roman Frontier in Wales* (Cardiff: University of Wales Press, 2nd ed., 1969).

Potter, T. & Johns, C., *Roman Britain* (London: British Museum Press, 1992).

Salway, P., *Roman Britain* (Oxford: Oxford University Press, 1985).

Thomas, C., *Christianity in Roman Britain to AD 500* (London: Batsford, 1993).

Wacher, J., *The Towns of Roman Britain* (London: Routledge, 1995).

'Dark Age' Wales

Dark, K.R., *Civitas to Kingdom: British Political Continuity 300-800* (Leicester: Leicester University Press, 1994). An important and innovative survey of the sub-and post-Roman period and its consequences.

Charles-Edwards, T.M., *Early Irish and Welsh Kinship* (Oxford: Oxford University Press, 1993). A major study of medieval society.

Davies, W., *Wales in the Early Middle Ages* (Leicester: Leicester University Press, 1981). The major modern study.

Davies, W., *Patterns of Power in Early Wales* (Oxford: Oxford University Press, 1990). An analysis of Welsh political structures in the early medieval period.

Edwards, N. & Lane, *Early Medieval Settlements in Wales AD 400-1100* (Bangor, Cardiff, 1988). A survey of the archaeological record.

Lloyd, J.E., *A History of Wales from the Earliest Times to the Edwardian Conquest* 2 vols., 3rd edition (London: Longmans, 1939). A ground-breaking work which has shaped much of what has been written subsequently.

Loyn, H.R., *The Vikings in Wales* (London, Dorothia Coke Lecture, 1977). A useful survey of the place-name and written evidence.

Maund, K.L., *Ireland, Wales and England in the eleventh century* (Woodbridge: Brewers, 1991). A re-analysis of the period c.980-1100.

Maund, K.L., *The Welsh Kings: the medieval rulers of Wales* (Stroud, Tempus, 2000). A survey of medieval Welsh political life.

Redknapp, M., 'Glyn, Llanbedrgoch, Anglesey', *Archaeology in Wales* 34 (1994), 58-60; 35 (1995), 58-9; 36 (1996), 81-2.

Frontier Wales

Davies, R.R., *Conquest, Coexistence, and Change: Wales 1063-1415* (Oxford: Oxford University Press, 1987); paperback edition under the title *The Age of Conquest: Wales 1063-1415* (Oxford University Press: Oxford, 1991; revised edition, 2000). The best single book on the history of Wales in this period, covering social, economic, ecclesiastical and cultural developments as well as political history, with an extensive bibliography (updated in the revised edition).

Carr, A.D., *Medieval Wales* (Houndmills and London: MacMillan Press, 1995). A useful concise introduction, including a valuable chapter on historiography.

Davies, R.R., *The First English Empire: Power and Identities in the British Isles, 1093-1343* (Oxford: Oxford University Press, 2000). The latest of several recent books which offer fresh perspectives on Wales in this period through adopting an integrative and comparative approach to the history of medieval Britain and Ireland.

Smith, J.B., *Llywelyn ap Gruffudd, Prince of Wales* (Cardiff: University of Wales Press, 1998). A magisterial biography which sets the prince's life and achievements against the wider background of developments in thirteenth-century Wales.

Charles-Edwards, T.M., Owen, M.E., & Russell, P., (eds.), *The Welsh King and his Court* (Cardiff: University of Wales Press, 2000). Focusing on the Welsh lawbooks' section on the royal court, this substantial collection of essays and edited and translated law-texts illuminates many aspects of native Welsh rulership and society in the twelfth and thirteenth centuries.

Gerald of Wales, *The Journey through Wales and the Description of Wales*, translated by Thorpe, L.(Harmondsworth: Penguin Books, 1978). These, the first books written specifically about Wales, provide a vivid, though in some respects misleading, depiction of the country and its people at the end of the twelfth century.

Bartlett, R., *Gerald of Wales 1146-1223* (Oxford: Oxford University Press, 1982). A biographical study which is particularly strong on Gerald's intellectual context and includes valuable discussions of both ecclesiastical reform and the characterisation of the Welsh as barbarians.

Griffiths, R.A. (ed.), *The Boroughs of Mediaeval Wales* (Cardiff: University of Wales Press, 1978). An important collection of papers which illuminates the development of urbanization from the late eleventh century onwards.

Edwards, N. (ed.), *Landscape and Settlement in Medieval Wales* (Oxford: Oxbow Monograph 81; Oxbow Books, 1997). This volume gathers together the fruits of recent research on both rural and urban settlement, mainly between the eleventh and thirteenth centuries.

Cowley, F.G., *The Monastic Order in South Wales, 1066-1349* (Cardiff: University of Wales Press, 1977). A fine study of the impact of Benedictine monasticism, including the Cistercians, on Wales.

Jones, P.H. & Rees, E. (eds.), *A Nation and its Books: A History of the Book in Wales* (Aberystwyth: National Library of Wales, 1998). Between them, Chapter 1, 'The Origins and the Medieval Period', and Chapter 2, 'The Medieval Manuscript', provide an overview of literacy and written culture in medieval Wales.

WALES FROM CONQUEST TO UNION

Carr, A.D., *Medieval Anglesey* (Llangefni: Anglesey Antiquarian Society, 1982). A study of society and government in the island, especially in the later Middle Ages.

Carr, A.D., *Owen of Wales: The End of the House of Gwynedd* (Cardiff: University of Wales Press, 1991). A succinct study of the mysterious Owain Lawgoch.

Davies, R.R., *Lordship and Society in the March of Wales, 1282-1400* (Oxford: Oxford University Press, 1978). A classic, penetrating study.

Davies, R.R., *Conquest, Coexistence and Change: Wales, 1063-1415* (Oxford: Oxford University Press, and Cardiff: University of Wales Press 1987). An admirable survey to the end of Owain Glyn Dŵr's revolt.

Davies, R.R., *The Revolt of Owain Glyn Dŵr* (Oxford: Oxford University Press, 1995). A comprehensive, analytical study.

Evans, H.T., *Wales and the Wars of the Roses* (Cambridge: Cambridge University Press, 1915; new edn, Stroud: Alan Sutton Publishing, 1995). A study which retains its narrative value.

Griffiths, R.A., *The Principality of Wales in the Later Middle Ages, vol. 2: South Wales, 1277-1536* (Cardiff: University of Wales Press, 1971). An analysis of government and administration in the southern part of the principality of Wales.

Griffiths, R.A. (ed.), *The Boroughs of Medieval Wales* (Cardiff: University of Wales Press, 1978). A series of essays on twelve Welsh towns.

Griffiths, R.A., *King and Country: England and Wales in the Fifteenth Century* (London: Hambledon Press, 1991). A series of essays that place Wales's history in a wider perspective.

Griffiths, R.A., *Sir Rhys ap Thomas and his Family: A Study in the Wars of the Roses and Early Tudor Politics* (Cardiff: University of Wales Press, 1993). A study of one of Wales's most prominent families.

Griffiths, R.A., *Conquerors and Conquered in Medieval Wales* (Stroud: Alan Sutton Publishing, 1994). A series of essays especially on revolts and towns.

Griffiths, R.A. & Thomas, R.S., *The Making of the Tudor Dynasty* (Stroud: Alan Sutton Publishing, 1985). Charts the rise of the Tudors in the context of fifteenth-century politics.

Jarman, A.O.H. & Hughes, G.R. (eds.), *A Guide to Welsh Literature*, vol. 2, revised by D.Johnston (Cardiff, University of Wales Press, 1997). A series of expert essays especially on the poetic tradition.

Pugh, T.B. (ed.), *The Glamorgan County History, vol.3: Medieval Glamorgan* (Cardiff, University of Wales Press,1971). A series of expert essays on a major marcher lordship.

Smith, J.B. (ed.), *The Merioneth County History, vol.2: The Middle Ages* (forthcoming, 2002). A series of expert essays on a county of the principality of Wales.

Walker, R.F. (ed.), *The Pembrokeshire County History, vol. 2: The Middle Ages* (forthcoming, 2002). A series of expert essays on an Anglicised county of several marcher lordships.

Williams, G., *The Welsh Church from Conquest to Reformation* (revised edn, Cardiff, University of Wales Press,1976). A ground-breaking study.

Williams, G., *Owain Glyndŵr* (2nd edn, Cardiff. University of Wales Press, 1993). A brief and up-to-date narrative.

Williams, G., *Recovery, Reorientation and Reformation: Wales, c.1415-1642* (Oxford, Oxford University Press, and Cardiff: University of Wales Press,1987). Includes a clear survey of the period up to the act of union.

FROM REFORMATION TO METHODISM

Dodd, A.H., *Studies in Stuart Wales* (Cardiff: University of Wales Press, 2nd ed. 1971). A series of lively essays by a master craftsman.

Jenkins, G.H., *Hanes Cymru yn y Cyfnod Modern Cynnar 1530-1760* (Caerdydd, Gwasg Prifysgol Cymru, p/b ed. 1988). The only textbook which covers the whole of early modern Wales.

Jenkins, G.H., *The Foundations of Modern Wales: Wales 1642-1780* (Oxford, Oxford University Press, p/b ed. 1993). An authoritative synthesis of the period between the civil wars and the industrial revolution.

Jenkins, G.H. (ed.), *The Welsh Language before the Industrial Revolution* (Cardiff, University of Wales Press, 1997). A wide-ranging collection of essays on the role of the Welsh language in early modern Wales.

Jenkins, P., *The Making of a Ruling Class: The Glamorgan Gentry 1640-1790* (Cambridge, Cambridge University Press, 1983). A pioneering work on the emergence and lifestyle of some of the most affluent gentry in Britain.

Jones, J.G., *Early Modern Wales, c.1525-1640* (London: Macmillan, 1994). A discussion of the effects of the Tudor political settlement between the Union and the civil wars.

Morgan, P., *The Eighteenth Century Renaissance* (Llandybïe: Christopher Davies, 1981). An innovative study of the new sense of Welshness in the eighteenth century.

Thomas, W.S.K., *Tudor Wales* (Llandysul, Gomer Press, 1983). A valuable guide to the Tudor age in Wales.

Thomas, W.S.K., *Stuart Wales* (Llandysul, Gomer Press, 1988). A convenient introduction to a neglected period.

Williams, G. *Renewal and Reformation in Wales c.1415-1642* (Oxford, Oxford University Press, p/b ed. 1993). A stimulating overview by Wales's most distinguished historian.

Williams, G., *Wales and the Reformation* (Cardiff, University of Wales Press, 1997). The first full-length study of the Reformation in sixteenth-century Wales.

ENGINE OF EMPIRE

Edwards, H.T. (ed.), *A Guide to Welsh Literature, 1700-1800* (Cardiff: University of Wales Press, 2000). Covers many aspects of culture in this period.

Evans, C., *'The Labyrinth of Flames': Work and Social Conflict in early industrial Merthyr* (Cardiff: University of Wales Press, 1993). One of many recent scholarly volumes in the 'Studies in Welsh History' series which highlight important aspects of this period.

Evans, D.G., *A History of Wales, 1815-1906* (Cardiff: University of Wales Press, 1989). A most helpful general study of the age.

Herbert, T. & Jones, G.E. (eds.) *The Remaking of Wales in the Eighteenth Century* (Cardiff, University of Wales Press, 1988). Contains good source material, as do two other volumes by the same editors, in the same series 'Welsh History and its Sources', published in 1988, *People and Protest: Wales, 1815-1880, and Wales, 1880-1914*.

Howell, D.W., *The Rural Poor in Eighteenth-century Wales* (Cardiff: University of Wales Press, 2000). A counterpart to the author's earlier *Patriarchs and Parasites,* dealing with the eighteenth-century Welsh gentry.

Jarvis, B. (ed.), *A Guide to Welsh Literature, 1700-1800* (Cardiff: University of Wales Press, 2000). Deals with Welsh culture in its broadest sense.

Jenkins, G.H. (ed.), *Language and Community in Nineteenth-Century Wales* (Cardiff: University of Wales Press, 1998)

Jenkins, G.H. (ed.), *The Welsh Language and its Social Domains, 1801-1911* (Cardiff: University of Wales Press, 2000). Part of the series 'The Social History of the Welsh Language', many of which cover part or all of this period.

Jones, D.J.V., *Before Rebecca: popular protest in Wales, 1793-1835* (London, Allen Lane, 1973). The earliest of several of his notable studies of riot and protest, such as the Rebecca Riots and the Newport Rising.

Jones, I.G., *Mid-Victorian Wales: the Observers and the Observed* (Cardiff: University of Wales Press, 1992). The most recent of his three books dealing with mid-nineteenth-century Welsh society.

Morgan, K.O., *Wales in British Politics, 1868-1922* (Cardiff: University of Wales Press, 1970). A classic study, frequently reprinted, of the politicisation of the Welsh.

Parry, G. & Williams, M.A. (eds.), *The Welsh Language and the 1891 Census* (Cardiff: University of Wales Press, 1999). A study of the linguistic situation in each part of Wales.

Williams, G.A., *When was Wales? A History of the Welsh* (Harmondsworth, Penguin, 1985). Contains a great deal of lively comment on the author's own period of specialisation, the eighteenth and nineteenth centuries.

WALES SINCE 1900

Davies, J.A., *History of Wales* (London: Penguin, 1993). A translation of his much-acclaimed *Hanes Cymru* (Penguin, 1990), containing a great deal on the twentieth century.

Evans, D.G., *A History of Wales, 1815-1906* (Cardiff: University of Wales Press, 2000). Contains a mass of factual material, a worthy successor to the same author's *A History of Wales, 1815-1906* (Cardiff: University of Wales Press, 1989).

Herbert, T. & Jones, G.E. (eds.), *Wales 1880-1914* (Cardiff: University of Wales Press, 1988). One of three books from the series 'Welsh History and its Sources' which cover this period, the others being *Wales between the Wars* (also published in 1988) and *Post-War Wales* (Published in 1995).

Jenkins, P., *A History of Modern Wales, 1536-1990* (London: Longmans, 1992). A good general guide to this period.

Jones, G.E., *Modern Wales: a concise history* (Cambridge: Cambridge University Press, 1994). Another helpful pathfinder.

Jones, R.M., *Cymru 2000: Hanes Cymru yn yr Ugeinfed Ganrif* (Cardiff: University of Wales Press, 2000). A rich quarry for those who read Welsh.

Morgan, K.O., *The Rebirth of a Nation: Wales 1880-1980* (Oxford: Oxford University Press, 1981). Probably the best starting point for this period, and contains a very full bibliography.

Smith, D., *Wales! Wales?* (London: George Allen & Unwin, 1989). A stimulating and provocative read of this period.

Williams, D., *A History of Modern Wales* (2nd ed., London: John Murray, 1977). Though dated, this remains a lucid introductory text.

LIST OF ILLUSTRATIONS

COLOUR SECTION

INDEX